D1045556

American Evangelicals and the 1960s

STUDIES IN AMERICAN THOUGHT
AND CULTURE

Series Editor

Paul S. Boyer

Advisory Board

Charles M. Capper
Mary Kupiec Cayton
Lizabeth Cohen
Nan Enstad
James B. Gilbert
Karen Halttunen
Michael Kammen
James T. Kloppenberg
Colleen McDannell
Joan S. Rubin
P. Sterling Stuckey
Robert B. Westbrook

American Evangelicals
and the 1960s

Edited by

Axel R. Schäfer

TABOR COLLEGE LIBRARY
HILLSBORO, KANSAS 67063

The University of Wisconsin Press

The University of Wisconsin Press
1930 Monroe Street, 3rd Floor
Madison, Wisconsin 53711-2059
uwpress.wisc.edu

3 Henrietta Street
London WC2E8LU, England
eurospanbookstore.com

Copyright © 2013
The Board of Regents of the University of Wisconsin System
All rights reserved. No part of this publication may be reproduced, stored in a retrieval system, or transmitted, in any format or by any means, digital, electronic, mechanical, photocopying, recording, or otherwise, or conveyed via the Internet or a website without written permission of the University of Wisconsin Press, except in the case of brief quotations embedded in critical articles and reviews.

Printed in the United States of America

Library of Congress Cataloging-in-Publication Data

American evangelicals and the 1960s / edited by Axel R. Schäfer.
        p.   cm. —(Studies in American thought and culture)
        Includes bibliographical references and index.
        ISBN 978-0-299-29364-2 (pbk.: alk. paper)
        ISBN 978-0-299-29363-5 (e-book)
    1. Evangelicalism—United States—History—20th century.
   2. Christianity and politics—United States—History—20th century.
                        3. Nineteen sixties.
    I. Schäfer, Axel R.   II. Series: Studies in American thought and culture.
                    BR1642.U5A44 2013
                    277.3′0826—dc23
                    2012037153

DEDICATED TO THE MEMORY OF

Paul S. Boyer

Contents

Acknowledgments

The majority of essays in this volume were first presented at a colloquium on "New Perspectives on American Evangelicalism and the 1960s: Revisiting the 'Backlash,'" organized by the David Bruce Center for American Studies at Keele University, United Kingdom, in April 2011. In the sylvan environs of North Staffordshire, close to the "potteries" famous for ceramics brands such as Wedgwood, Minton, Spode, and Royal Doulton, the colloquium brought together a group of primarily younger European and North American scholars who in recent years have pioneered the reinterpretation of the New Christian Right in the United States. As behooves a meeting of this kind, the four-day event also included a trip to the nearby Englesea Brook Chapel and to Mow Cop, the sight of the first camp meeting that led to the emergence of Primitive Methodism in Britain in 1807.

The scholars featured in this volume have been at the cutting edge of questioning and revising one of the most entrenched assumptions about resurgent evangelicalism, namely, that it was grounded in the so-called backlash against the broader sociocultural and political transformations that emanated from the 1960s. By revisiting the fraught relationship between this iconoclastic decade and conservative Protestantism, the participants offered new insights into the origins and meaning of the New Christian Right. They argued that the movement's cultural attractiveness, organizational strength, and political efficacy, rather than being based on its vocal opposition to the iniquities of the sixties, derived from its ability to appropriate, co-opt, and subvert the decade's transformative impulses. They explored how *changes* in evangelical attitudes to, for example, sexuality, the welfare state, and foreign policy that began in the 1960s opened up the necessary space for forging new coalitions between former adversaries. Finally, they showed that the cultural, political, and socio-economic depth-charges dropped by the 1960s did not so much explode the liberal capitalist order as expose its inherent contradictions, opening up opportunities for the New Christian Right and its particular combination of anti-establishmentarianism and relegitimization of core myths of American society.

When it comes to the study of American evangelicalism, one of the scholars whose name even casual observers encounter early on is Paul S. Boyer, the eminent historian, prolific scholar, and leading authority in the field of American cultural, intellectual, and religious history. We all felt very privileged when he agreed to join us as the keynote speaker. What we didn't know at the time was that this was to be one of his last international commitments. While preparing the essays for publication in the Spring of 2012, we heard the sad news that Paul had died. He was an inspiration for our group and touched us all with his wit and wisdom, kindness and generosity, fierce intellect and academic brilliance. Being generous to a fault with advice and insights, Paul even managed to rescue our entirely hopeless cluster of academics from utter ignominy during a very British pub quiz in Keele village's Sneyd Arms pub. It is with a deep sense of gratitude to Paul for being a friend and mentor that we dedicate this volume to a wonderful man and a great scholar.

American Evangelicals and the 1960s

Introduction

Evangelicals and the Sixties: Revisiting the "Backlash"

AXEL R. SCHÄFER

The 1960s constituted a seminal period of fragmentation and realignment for white evangelicalism in the United States, a time when the movement had emancipated itself from prewar fundamentalist militancy but had not yet coalesced into the New Christian Right. Nonetheless, the decade has received remarkably little attention from scholars of the evangelical resurgence. Instead, many academic observers have used "the sixties" primarily as a symbol and a signifier. Those who see resurgent conservative Protestantism as part of a "backlash" speak of the decade primarily in terms of the excesses of the counterculture, the militancy of the civil rights movement, the iniquities of the liberal welfare state, the immorality of growing secularism, and the betrayal of God and country by the anti–Vietnam War protesters. Those who view the revival as part of the adaptation of religion to modernity refer to the sixties as encapsulating large-scale secular transformations in morals and manners, race and gender relations, and socioeconomic patterns.

Each of the twelve chapters introduces a different perspective that contrasts both with viewing the sixties as the polar opposite of resurgent evangelicalism and with seeing it as the modernist yardstick against which conservative Protestantism needs to be measured. The chapters' authors argue that evangelicals not only reacted against or appropriated the 1960s but also shaped the content and meaning of the decade's political insurgencies, liberalizing cultural tendencies, economic transformations, and public policy trajectories in ways that revise established understandings of "liberal" and "conservative." Bringing together younger North American and European scholars who in recent years have pioneered the reinterpretation of the New Christian Right in the United States, the volume collectively suggests an understanding of the evangelical resurgence as both defined by and constitutive of larger social, economic, political, and cultural processes of the 1960s. The authors take religious belief seriously but also maintain that patterns of religious thought, organization, and expression cannot be divorced from distinct cultural and institutional contexts and political exigencies, which, in turn, shape the efficacy of religious beliefs.

The chapters presented here offer alternative readings of both modern white evangelicalism and the 1960s on three levels. First, they recover the diversity of evangelicalism by highlighting the fluidity and contingency of its politics. They view the period from the mid-1950s to the mid-1970s, i.e., the "long" 1960s when evangelical social action and political ideology took shape, not simply as a prelude to the New Christian Right but as a time when opportunities for rather different political alignments and sociocultural identities offered themselves. As Christopher Lasch has noted, we should never forget evangelicalism's potential to find "moral inspiration in the popular radicalism of the past."[1] Though the New Christian Right is most prominent in U.S. politics as a result of a tremendous organizational effort and skillful lobbying, radical and liberal evangelicals continue to vie with the conservatives for political influence, and many in the fold are suspicious of economic conservatism and political liberalism alike.[2]

Second, the authors present an understanding of white evangelical Christianity as part of, rather than as external to, the historical trajectory of the sixties. Instead of offering a set-piece arrangement of two sides vilifying each other, the chapters show that conservative Protestants not only rejected but also shaped and transported sixties impulses in unexpected ways. Evangelicalism was intimately connected to key transformations in this polarized period, including the areas of race and gender relations, youth culture, consumerism, and corporate America. The sixties were a formative period during which the burgeoning religious movement negotiated its relationship with, among other things, desegregation, feminism, deindustrialization, and the expanding welfare state. The decade was thus pivotal not solely because it provided a convenient enemy image but because evangelicals participated in and were shaped by the very movements and developments they professed to oppose.

Finally, the chapters show that the image of the sixties as a catalyst for backlash mobilization was an invention of later years when a fully formed Christian Right sought to construct a unifying historical narrative that ignored the internal battles, ideological compromises, political divisions, and sociocultural adaptations that preceded effective right-wing political mobilization. Seen from this angle, the backlash discourse was part and parcel of an effort to proscribe the internal evangelical debate by an ascendant Right. The culture war was primarily an effective linguistic strategy to define "us" and "the other," the political scientist Rhys Williams has maintained, "Political conflict *is* often between the orthodox and the progressive, but these are not as much descriptions of attitude clusters as they are symbolic markers of identity and difference."[3] In the same vein, the volume challenges the popular view, embraced by many scholars and conservative activists alike, that resurgent evangelicalism was part of a fundamental political transformation in which moral and cultural issues replaced socioeconomic concerns as the basis for electoral mobilization and partisan allegiance.

Taken together, the chapters seek to address what the historian Jon Butler has identified as the "religion problem" in modern American historiography, namely, that scholars treat religion as a "jack-in-the-box" that pops up occasionally to provide a colorful, if disturbing, religious sideshow in the largely secular drama of American society.[4] Of course, in their attempt to fine-tune our understanding of modern evangelicalism, the authors featured in this volume are not the first ones to pay attention to the 1960s. Particularly in the past decade or so, a new generation of researchers has probed more deeply than ever the origins of the evangelical resurgence and has provided us with a more balanced reading of the movement. Noting that the surge started "long before external provocations like the death-of-God theology or the Vietnam debacle had started to rattle evangelical nerves" (Grant Wacker), these observers moved away from a simplistic culture-war approach that depicted the Christian Right as having leapt onto the political stage with a drum roll and a musical score from behind the curtain of subcultural isolation and the fog of obscure morality politics, ready to upset the cozy arrangements of postwar consensus politics. Instead, they uncovered a diverse movement whose ideologies and institutions were molded in the process of interacting with postwar economic changes, sociocultural transformations, political shifts, protest movements, and state-building; whose political identities remained contingent and contested in a complex and uncertain process of internal purges, grassroots organizing, and political coalition-building; and whose cultural resonance combined insurgent impulses with the affirmation of the fundamental trajectories of liberal capitalism and consumerist society. In short, they showed that American evangelicals were engaged with the very culture that purportedly repelled them.[5]

Despite criticizing the reductionist backlash scenario, however, this second-wave scholarship to some extent retained the basic countermovement narrative. The difference was that instead of maintaining that the strength and resonance of the New Christian Right was based on its vocal opposition to the sixties, many observers now argued that it was based on the movement's ability to copy, appropriate, co-opt, and pervert the decade's transformative impulses. The Christian Right, they maintained, effectively utilized for its own ends the language, insignia, symbols, expressive styles, and organizational techniques of the insurgent movements. "The style of extremity, millennialism, intolerance of ambiguity is an operating principle . . . of both the '6os and the backlash," Todd Gitlin noted, "Today's Christian Coalition deplores the decline of civilization as fervently as the most apocalyptic environmentalist or hippie antimaterialist of the late sixties."[6] In the same vein, a number of studies have shown that evangelical organizations in the 1960s and 1970s, such as Campus Crusade for Christ, InterVarsity Christian Fellowship, and the Christian World Liberation Front, explicitly aped the rhetoric of the insurgent movements.[7] As Clarence Lo has concluded, "often, especially if the challenging movement is strong, a countermovement's defense of the established order will adopt parts of the challenging movement's program."[8]

Hence, on a deeper conceptual level, Butler's "jack-in-the-box" continues to haunt the debate about the evangelical revival: While this significant new body of scholarship has provided modern students of religion and politics in the United States with a plethora of new insights into the clientele, motivations, techniques, and politics of resurgent conservative Protestantism, it often continued to view evangelicalism mainly in terms of "episodes of revival" and "political insurgency." Indeed, it tended to align itself with two opposing parties in the historiography of modern religious movements. On one side are those for whom religion is a pre-existing interpretive matrix, which shapes our knowledge and perception of the world. They argue that religious narratives define social experience and political discourses.[9] Challenging this interpretation are those who see religion as a function of something else—be that social adjustment, economic pressures, or cultural assimilation. They interpret religious attitudes as reactions to status anxiety, cultural fears, and socioeconomic dislocation in response to impersonal processes of modernization, secularization, and globalization.[10]

It is by building upon and refining this renewed scholarly engagement with resurgent evangelicalism that the present volume casts a new light on the 1960s. In so doing, it aims to transcend both a "reified" view of white evangelicalism as a spontaneous countermovement opposing the waywardness of American society on the basis of fixed moral beliefs, and an "adaptationist" view of a movement whose content is defined by its efforts to wrap itself in a modernist cloak. Of course, in the process the volume has to confront the often mind-boggling diversity of evangelicalism. Theologically, the term describes an array of groups and liturgical styles shaped by a plethora of historical events and movements, ranging from seventeenth-century Puritanism via the Great Awakenings in the eighteenth and nineteenth centuries to the fundamentalist-modernist debates in the early twentieth century. Both the theologically liberal Evangelical Lutheran Church of America and the theologically orthodox National Association of Evangelicals identify with the term. Even within the orthodox fold, at least a dozen distinct and frequently antagonistic traditions are typically grouped under this umbrella term, ranging from Baptists and Methodists to Pentecostals and the Holiness movement. As a result, Donald Dayton called evangelicalism an "essentially contested concept" and suggested doing away with the term completely.[11]

In contrast, however, the chapters in this volume, while recognizing the significant differences between, for example, neo-evangelicals and Southern Baptists, in the main agree with Mark Noll that the term "evangelical" retains its usefulness in designating a particular strand of Protestantism located somewhere between fundamentalists and mainline moderates.[12] Collectively they introduce a perspective that recognizes the highly diverse and complex nature of evangelicalism, but they also suggest that the styles and content of evangelical activism forged in the foundry of the 1960s constituted a particular way of uniting the evangelical constituency around a combination of both rejecting and embracing the dominant trajectories of American society.

The volume begins with an introductory essay by Paul Boyer that places the fluid setting of 1960s and 1970s white evangelicalism within the movement's broader historical context from the mid-nineteenth to the late-twentieth centuries. Critically reviewing the backlash thesis, Boyer traces its origins back to both the myopia of secularization theorists and the self-constructed image of religious conservatives. Although he doesn't discard the argument in its entirety, he highlights its analytical limitations that obscure the wide range of political positions evangelicals have traditionally embraced and the complex interaction of evangelical religion and modern culture. Politically, evangelicalism's influence has never been exclusively channeled toward the conservative end of the ideological spectrum. Instead, it has also included support for, for example, New Deal welfare programs and social justice campaigns, as well as the radical activism of left and liberal evangelicals such as Ron Sider, Jim Wallis, and John Stott. Culturally, its identity is not based on the backlash but on a symbiotic relationship with the modern world. From contemporary music and mass publishing to Hollywood and fast food, Boyer shows that evangelicalism has deeply penetrated mass-consumer culture, while being shaped by modernity. In providing a comprehensive overview of the diversity of evangelicalism's political and cultural manifestations, the chapter challenges scholars to engage in a more sustained analysis of the movement's intricacies, cross-currents, and historical legacies.

The remainder of the book is divided into three parts. Part 1 features four chapters that show how the movement's engagement with economics, social movements, race issues, and sexuality infused religious content into 1960s culture and shaped the future political positions of resurgent evangelicalism. In conjunction, each chapter in this section shows that evangelicalism's involvement *with*, rather than its reaction *against* the period's main socioeconomic and cultural transformations were key factors in the movement's political resurgence in the 1970s and 1980s. By the same token, the authors indicate that evangelicalism thrived because it was ideologically and institutionally connected with the main developments in American society and politics.

Emphasizing the "uniquely strong bond" between evangelicals and the oil industry, Darren Dochuk presents the 1960s as a crucial decade during which the organizational ties between evangelicals and corporate America were cemented and the religious language that legitimized and spiritualized corporate (petro-)capitalism emerged. Focusing on J. Howard Pew, avid funder of evangelical enterprises and the head of Sun Oil, he shows that evangelicalism's alignment with oil laid the foundation for the organizational infrastructure and political agenda of the New Christian Right. In places where the "Petroleum Belt" and the "Bible Belt" met, evangelicals used monies accrued through oil to build churches, schools, and missionary agencies. Meanwhile, experience in boardrooms, manufacturing plants, and drill sites enabled them to shape America's engagement with the "secular" world of business and global trade. Viewing petroleum as their special providence to be used for the advancement of God's Kingdom, evangelicals fused theologies of personal salvation, individual initiative, and stewardship with the politics of entrepreneurialism, free markets, and easy access to resources. Placing evangelicals at the center of the emergence of modern practices and ideologies of corporate power and politics in the oil industry thus illustrates that the evangelical resurgence was a broader political phenomenon than just a morality-focused culture war.

Eileen Luhr explores evangelical efforts to fill iconic 1960s terms such as "revolution," "direct action," "liberation," and "self-determination" with religious content and thus define their meanings within the period's insurgent movements. Luhr contends that the evangelical framework was well within the range of existing meanings of the terms, since the narratives about the civil rights movement, urban riots, the Vietnam War, and student protests vacillated between an emphasis on structural change and the embrace of personal freedom. In this fluid setting, evangelical youth culture and publications, such as *Campus Life* and the *Hollywood Free Paper*, seized upon the iconic language of the era to combine the challenge to the "status quo" with the promise of individual spiritual change. These negotiations suggest that evangelicals, far from condemning the sixties, sought to engage with and to contain revolutionary sentiment. Recasting the sixties more broadly shows that young evangelicals made religious concepts in revolution terminology explicit, and filled sixties terms and tempers with evangelical content. At the same time, their simultaneous admiration and critique of progressive activism laid the foundation for a new evangelical language of "spiritual revolution" and activism as a cohesive narrative for modern religious conservatism.

Steven P. Miller interrogates the notion that evangelicals in the 1960s remained on the sidelines of or actively opposed the civil rights movement, and only "learned" from its faith-based activism in later years. Instead, he shows that evangelical elites during the sixties, while critical of the civil rights movement, frequently supported basic racial equality. He locates the origins of this ambivalent attitude in the religious pietism and custodialism that underlay evangelical opposition to the liberal state. While this religiously informed anti-liberalism rejected the notion that the federal state can and should play a positive role in reforming American society, however, it was not synonymous with political conservatism. Indeed, from the 1950s to the early 1970s, evangelical celebrities, such as Billy Graham and Carl F. H. Henry, and moderate evangelical publications, such as *Eternity* and *Christian Herald*, outlined ways for evangelicals to support basic racial equality. They pioneered "modes of reconciliation and invocation" for the mainstreaming of civil rights rituals and memory, and helped make tacit support for federal civil rights protections a consensus position. However, evangelical skepticism about the state's role in redressing racial injustice both embedded the popular notion that evangelicals were opposed to the civil rights movement and hindered the advance of racial justice for African Americans during the 1960s.

In the final chapter in part 1, Daniel K. Williams shows that the evangelical mobilization against pornography, feminism, and gay rights was not simply a reaction against the women's movement and the sexual revolution of the 1960s.

Instead, it derived from conservative Protestantism experiencing its own internal sexual revolution that was nearly as profound as the one that had affected secular society. While nearly all of the preaching on sex prior to the 1950s had been focused on helping unmarried people avoid sexual temptation, evangelicals in the 1960s and 1970s began celebrating marital sex, holding seminars on marriage, and writing explicit sex manuals, which included detailed instructions on how to produce a female orgasm. While conservative evangelical women condemned feminism, evangelical theologies of sex offered a way to promote an egalitarian model of women's sexual desire while simultaneously highlighting women's distinct role as "helpmeets" of their husbands. Similar changes were taking place in the area of birth control. While fundamentalists had traditionally preached against birth control, most of the leading evangelical magazines of the 1960s endorsed the practice. They frequently linked their arguments to a call for women's rights, encouraging women to be less focused on marriage. Crucially, however, Williams argues that the new evangelical theology of sex in the 1960s helped shape a particular brand of socially conservative sexual politics, which led to evangelical campaigns against abortion and gay rights in the following decade. As evangelicals began to accept masturbation as a way to prevent premarital sex, for example, they strengthened their opposition to homosexuality. Likewise, while evangelicals had traditionally accepted abortion in cases where pregnancy threatened a woman's health, or in cases of rape, incest, or fetal deformity, their new sexual ethics paradoxically generated their outspoken opposition to the practice in later years.

Part 2 features four chapters that outline new ways of understanding evangelicals in relationship to law and order issues, church-state separation, the welfare state, and foreign policy in the 1960s. Revisiting the fluid setting of the period, they shed new light on the lively debates within the evangelical fold about burgeoning rates of imprisonment, the Supreme Court's school prayer and Bible reading decisions, the War on Poverty, and the escalating war in Vietnam. In so doing, they track the complex processes by which evangelicals gradually revised their traditional attitudes toward the state and public policy in the wake of their growing political activism and involvement.

Kendrick Oliver's study of the origins of evangelical prison ministries challenges the common assumption that evangelicals in the 1960s and 1970s identified primarily with the punitive politics of "law and order" that have become a hallmark of New Right policies in response to growing crime waves, social disorder, and perceived moral decay. Oliver contends that many evangelicals were critical of a system of deterrence and harsh punishment, calling instead for a renewed emphasis on rehabilitative conversionism. Detailing the repercussions of the violent suppression of the 1971 Attica prison rebellion, often seen as a key stimulus to the punitive mood of backlash politics, he shows that many evangelical church leaders and commentators attributed the rebellion to the failure of the prison authorities to respond to legitimate inmate grievances and criticized the violence with which order was restored. In turn, the post-Attica period ushered in the rediscovery of correctional institutions as a mission field among evangelicals. In particular, the chapter highlights the role of Watergate villain and Prison Fellowship Ministries founder Charles Colson, whose commitment to evangelism went hand-in-hand with a radical critique of the criminal justice system. Nonetheless, evangelical ministries like Prison Fellowship eventually became complicit in the structures and values of the "carceral state" through their faith-based rehabilitation programs. However, this more recent history has obscured the origins of prison ministry in the evangelical social action revival of the 1960s that neither conformed to the politics of the backlash nor welcomed retributive mass incarceration.

Emma Long revisits the evolution of evangelical attitudes toward church-state separation in general, and to the public funding for religious schools in particular. While evangelicals in the 1940s and 1950s had been avid separation-ists, they had rejected this position by the early 1980s as promoting a liberal and secular culture. Instead, they embraced an "accommodationist" legal position, which included advocacy for allowing tax dollars to be directed to religious schools. Long, however, challenges the view that the backlash against land-mark Supreme Court decisions in 1962 and 1963 that banned school-sponsored prayer and Bible reading in the nation's public schools was at the core of the evangelical shift in attitude. Instead, she links the evolution of the accommoda-tionist position to more complex legal, political, and economic dynamics of the 1960s and 1970s. Evangelicals realized that *Engel* and *Schempp* were part of a legal climate that considered public aid perfectly constitutional under certain circumstances and opened up new opportunities for asserting religious content. Hence, many of them supported the rulings and actively sought to encourage the teaching of the role of religion in American history within the public school system. As the growing financial crisis in education paved the way for the prag-matic inclusion of religious schools within aid programs, the new evangelical position emerged gradually from the engagement with the new legal and eco-nomic realities, rather than from the rejection of the allegedly secularizing Court decisions.

Axel R. Schäfer re-examines the relationship between evangelicals and liberal social policy in the 1960s and 1970s. He suggests that evangelicals thrived as much on the basis of their engagement with as on the basis of their opposition to the Great Society. Although evangelicals frequently pilloried the policies of the Johnson administration as symbols of moral decline and government intrusiveness, they also benefited from the Great Society's increase in public aid for religious hospitals, educational institutions, and welfare agencies. Likewise, the government practice of tolerating faith-based approaches despite antisectarian clauses in many public funding laws allowed evangelical charities to operate free from severe limitations on their religious freedom. As a result, the War on Poverty engendered the large-scale revision of evangelical church-state attitudes and enabled evangelical groups to gain political and institutional influence within the structures of the welfare state. Seen from this perspective, the political mobilization of evangelicals emanated less from the movement's hostility to liberal social policies than from its ability to combine an antistatist ideology with taking advantage of the opportunities offered by the devolved welfare state. This laid the foundation for the subsequent evangelical embrace of a range of aid-to-religion programs, including the Bush administration's Faith-Based Initiative.

In the final chapter Andrew Preston shifts the focus to the foreign policy arena. He shows that, although evangelical opinion on the Vietnam War was divided, the vast majority of conservative Protestants remained ardent supporters of the Johnson and Nixon administrations. Indeed, many conservative Protestants favored escalation and all-out warfare to defeat the threat of a communist takeover. While this position was gaining ground as part of a broader backlash against the anti-Vietnam protest movement, it was also grounded in an older identification of many evangelicals with America as a redeemer nation, which led them to reject both Christian pacifism and liberal accommodationism. At the same time, this older paradigm of evangelical support, Preston shows, enabled evangelicals to distance themselves from American foreign policy in the wake of the disastrous end of the war. Moving away from simply supporting the crusade against communism, evangelicals combined faith in American exceptionalism with more nuanced notions of global relations that included concerns with "liberal" causes, such as international development and human rights. In this reorientation away from unquestioned support for the American war effort, evangelicals were able to build on two "success stories" of their unwavering pro-war stance and active involvement in Vietnam: their growing influence within the military, and their expanding missionary enterprises in Southeast Asia.

Part 3's cluster of chapters revisit the origins of evangelical political consciousness formation and movement organizing during the 1960s. They explore evangelical linkages with the period's leftwing insurgencies, debunk the notion of conservative Protestantism's pervasive ecumenism, and highlight the domestic significance of its revived foreign missionary activism. In the process, they recover the role of largely neglected impulses as crucial factors in conservative Protestantism's postwar move from cultural isolation, social withdrawal, and political marginality toward a significant political and cultural force in American society.

David R. Swartz's chapter shows that evangelical political mobilization grew out of the evangelical Left's support of key elements of liberal politics. The encounter of the Post-American community in Chicago, the Christian World Liberation Front in Berkeley, and faculty and students at evangelical liberal arts colleges with the civil rights movement added a structural component to evangelicalism's social theory. Likewise, the Vietnam War provoked a substantial structural critique of the nation's complicity in systemic injustice among many evangelicals. Extending their vision beyond soul-winning individualism toward social responsibility paved the way for increased participation in electoral politics. This political impulse took shape in Evangelicals for McGovern, the first explicitly evangelical organization in postwar American politics to support a presidential candidate. Evangelicals for McGovern helped accelerate a new era in which politics was a viable option for evangelicals. In Swartz's analysis, this articulation of social and political engagement pioneered by the evangelical Left was carried even farther by a rising religious Right, complicating the assumption that the backlash against the 1960s alone provoked evangelical political mobilization.

Hans Krabbendam finds clues to American evangelicalism's social and political turn at home in the movement's increasing foreign activities and global connections in the 1960s and 1970s. Highlighting the rapidly expanding evangelical missionary activities in Europe, he connects foreign missions and domestic mobilization on two levels. First, he maintains that the expansion of missionary activities helped evangelicals negotiate the main tensions in their own theological identity as a "third force" between mainline Protestantism and fundamentalism. Forging a distinctive evangelical missionary infrastructure enabled them to theologically justify social action as a legitimate cause, while at the same time confirming the primacy of evangelism. Second, he shows that the changing image of Europe in American evangelicalism functioned as a catalyst for the formulation of the global goals of resurgent evangelicalism. On the one hand, engagement in Europe, such as Billy Graham's crusades in Eastern Europe in the 1970s, tied the evangelical cause to America's national interest in the battle against a godless communist world. On the other hand, the reality of a Europe that had given birth to the Reformation being increasingly pagan and de-Christianized reinforced in the minds of many evangelicals the urgency of expanding the custodial commission at home.

Finally, Neil J. Young critically reviews the notion that ecumenical and transdenominational impulses, spawned by shared backlash sentiments, were at the core of conservative Protestant political mobilization. In contrast, he shows that anti-Catholicism and anti-ecumenism provided important motivations for the political awakening. Analyzing evangelical reactions to the Second Vatican Council, which engineered the modernization of Catholicism between 1962 and 1965, he illustrates that evangelicals worried that the Catholic Church's new ecumenical talk was primarily designed to increase its global dominance and strengthen its position in the United States. Following on the heels of the 1960 Kennedy election, Vatican II revived evangelical concerns that a Catholic president would take direct orders from Rome and threaten the nation's political tradition. Long before any backlash responses to the cultural and political transformations of late-1960s liberalism, American evangelicals thus used anti-Catholic sentiment to advocate their increased participation in the political process as self-declared custodians of the nation's Protestant values. Even as Vatican II revived traditional anti-Catholic sentiment among conservative Protestants, however, evangelicals also hoped that the reforms might facilitate new relationships with Catholic laypersons. Believing that the Bible could change individual lives, evangelicals took comfort in the heightened emphasis placed on scripture during Vatican II. It was on the basis of Catholics' new engagement with the biblical text, rather than with the Roman Catholic Church itself, that evangelicals envisioned new grassroots associations. This distinction between believers and the church would shape relations between evangelicals and Catholics in the years ahead as they forged alliances to oppose abortion and other perceived political and social ills. Despite the ever closer ties between the two faith groups, evangelical attitudes that trace directly to Vatican II thus account for the lingering distrust evangelicals feel about the Roman Catholic Church itself.

In summation, in shifting the analytical focus from the New Christian Right toward the broader postwar evangelical resurgence the volume depicts a multifaceted religious movement thoroughly engaged with, rather than simply opposed to, many of the key developments associated with the 1960s. There are, of course, significant analytical differences in the way individual chapters view and assess this interaction. Some authors, for example, see evangelicals accepting the liberal state, while others argue that they fundamentally rejected it. Likewise, some chapters show how patterns established well before the 1960s defined evangelical public life, while others speak of the 1960s as crucial for

shaping resurgent evangelicalism. Though not offering a fully developed conceptual alternative to the "backlash" paradigm, however, the volume's authors
agree that it is not a particularly helpful analytical tool for understanding the
resurgence. Although evangelicals did engage in a furious backlash against the
perceived excesses and failures of the 1960s, the chapters show that the countermovement scenario obscures at least as much as it illuminates.

A single volume can hardly do justice to the manifold and multifaceted
interactions that characterize the relationship between conservative Protestantism and the "long sixties." Indeed, significant areas of social and cultural
change are largely ignored in this book. These include the rise of television and
new media as well as the growing role of women in the movement during the
1960s. Instead of aspiring to comprehensiveness, the contributors decided to
revisit a wide range of iconic developments, which exemplify the way in which
evangelicals both responded to and were shaped by the seminal events of the
decade. They include the sexual revolution, the civil rights movement, the
Kennedy election, the Great Society, the Vietnam War, landmark Supreme
Court decisions, Vatican II, and the consolidation of corporate America. In
turn, a more complex picture of the modern evangelical movement emerges:
morality politics, doctrinaire biblicism, antistatism and the like, rather than
constituting the bedrock of the New Christian Right, arise as symbolic markers
and rhetorical tools necessary for social movement mobilization. They are
expressions of efforts to juggle an insurgent identity with the integration into
the trajectories of American society in the 1960s and 1970s, and of attempts to
negotiate between competing factions within the evangelical fold.

NOTES

1. Christopher Lasch, *The True and Only Heaven: Progress and Its Critics* (New York:
W. W. Norton, 1991), 532.

2. See, for example, Craig Gay, *With Liberty and Justice for Whom? The Recent Evangelical Debate over Capitalism* (Grand Rapids, MI: Eerdmans, 1991).

3. Rhys H. Williams, "Culture Wars, Social Movements, and Institutional Politics,"
in *Cultural Wars in American Politics: Critical Reviews of a Popular Myth*, ed. Rhys H. Williams
(New York: de Gruyter, 1997), 290, 293.

4. Jon Butler, "Jack-in-the-Box Faith: The Religion Problem in Modern American
History," *Journal of American History* 90 (2004): 1357–1378.

5. Grant Wacker, "Uneasy in Zion: Evangelicals in Postmodern Society," in
*Reckoning with the Past: Historical Essays on American Evangelicalism from the Institute for the Study
of American Evangelicals*, ed. D. G. Hart (Grand Rapids, MI: Baker Books, 1995), 378. For
recent books on evangelical movement organizing prior to the 1970s see, for example,

Darren T. Dochuk, *From Bible Belt to Sun Belt: Plain Folk Religion, Grassroots Politics, and the Rise of Evangelical Conservatism* (New York: W. W. Norton & Company, 2011); Daniel K. Williams, *God's Own Party: The Making of the Christian Right* (New York: Oxford University Press, 2010); Steven P. Miller, *Billy Graham and the Rise of the Republican South* (Philadelphia: University of Pennsylvania Press, 2009); John G. Turner, *Bill Bright and Campus Crusade for Christ: The Renewal of Evangelicalism in Postwar America* (Chapel Hill: University of North Carolina Press, 2008); Larry Eskridge and Mark A. Noll, eds., *More Money, More Ministry: Money and Evangelicals in Recent North American History* (Grand Rapids, MI: Eerdmans, 2000).

6. Todd Gitlin, "Straight from the Sixties: What Conservatives Owe to the Decade They Hate," *American Prospect* 26 (May-June 1996): 56.

7. David R. Swartz, *Moral Minority: The Evangelical Left in an Age of Conservatism* (Philadelphia: University of Pennsylvania Press, 2012). See also Turner, *Bill Bright and Campus Crusade.*

8. Clarence Y. H. Lo, "Countermovements and Conservative Movements in the Contemporary U.S.," *Annual Review of Sociology* 8 (1982): 119.

9. See, for example, George M. Marsden, *Understanding Fundamentalism and Evangelicalism* (Grand Rapids, MI: Eerdmans, 1991), 1–6, 62–82; Joel A. Carpenter, *Revive Us Again: The Reawakening of American Fundamentalism* (New York: Oxford University Press, 1997), 153; William McLoughlin, *Revivals, Awakenings, and Reform: An Essay on Religion and Social Change in America, 1607–1977* (Chicago: University of Chicago Press, 1978), 213–214.

10. See, for example, Jon R. Stone, *On the Boundaries of American Evangelicalism: The Postwar Evangelical Coalition* (New York: St. Martin's Press, 1997), 43–48; Williams, "Culture Wars, Social Movements," 286–293; Geoffrey Layman, *The Great Divide: Religious and Cultural Conflict in American Party Politics* (New York: Columbia University Press, 2001), 53–54; Robert Wuthnow, *The Restructuring of American Religion: Society and Faith Since World War II* (Princeton: Princeton University Press, 1988), 142–143.

11. Donald W. Dayton, "Some Doubts about the Usefulness of the Category 'Evangelical,'" in *The Variety of American Evangelicalism*, ed. Donald W. Dayton and Robert K. Johnston (Knoxville: University of Tennessee Press, 1991), 245. On the problem defining evangelicalism and fundamentalism, see, for example, Marsden, *Understanding Fundamentalism*, 66–68, 100–101.

12. Mark A. Noll, *The Old Religion in a New World: The History of North American Christianity* (Grand Rapids, MI: Eerdmans, 2002), 155.

I

Back to the Future

Contemporary American Evangelicalism in Cultural and Historical Perspective

PAUL S. BOYER

On October 25, 1976, shortly before the election of Jimmy Carter, a self-proclaimed "born again" Christian, as president, *Newsweek* magazine proclaimed 1976 "The Year of the Evangelical." The magazine's gesture underscored a profound transformation underway in American religious life, summed up in the phrase "evangelical revival" or, in a more politically loaded term that would soon gain currency, "the rise of the religious Right."

This transformation was expressed in dramatic membership growth in the nation's evangelical and Pentecostal churches, and a corresponding decline, sometimes precipitous, in the membership of the "mainstream" liberal denominations.[1] In 1976, 34 percent of the respondents to a Gallup poll answered yes to the question, "Would you describe yourself as a 'born again' or evangelical Christian?" By 1998, the percentage stood at 47 percent. A 2005 study set the membership in America's "conservative, evangelical" denominations at some 90 million, almost twice that of the "mainstream" Protestant bodies.[2] *Newsweek*'s designation of 1976 as "The Year of the Evangelical" acknowledged not only membership statistics but also evangelicalism's heightened political and cultural visibility, from Washington, Hollywood, and Nashville to state capitals across America. The Moral Majority, a political lobby started in 1979 by the televangelist Jerry Falwell, would soon underscore the movement's political clout.

Historians are only now coming to terms with this development's complexities, political impact, historical context, and broader culture implications. Historians of American Protestantism, producing denominational histories or broad overviews with little critical introspection, have typically paid scant attention to the nation's evangelical and Pentecostal subcultures, focusing on the mainstream denominations with their national visibility, liberal theology, and activist social agendas.[3] *Protestant, Catholic, Jew,* the influential 1955 sociological study of American religion by the journalist Will Herberg, devoted only the briefest attention to Protestantism's evangelical branches. The sociologist William H. Whyte in *The Organization Man* (1956) treated postwar American religion as shaped by suburbanization and a bureaucratic corporate culture, with church membership providing social rootedness and status confirmation to geographically and economically mobile middle managers. In *The Secular City* (1965), the Harvard Divinity School professor Harvey Cox, a liberal Baptist minister and supporter of the civil rights movement and other 1960s reforms, implicitly dismissed evangelicalism as a dead end. God was more present in the "secular city" than in the churches, he suggested, urging the pious to abandon their "intrinsic conservatism" and support "God's permanent revolution in history."[4] For all their merits, such works shed little light on the evangelical resurgence already glaringly evident in Billy Graham's revival crusades. On the anecdotal level, I recall an American historian in the 1980s who described to me his recent lecture on the early nineteenth-century frontier revivals, with their shouting and other dramatic physical manifestations, and his shock when a student reported that such things still went on in contemporary America!

The historian David Hollinger has recently noted scholars' tendency to avoid rigorous critical scrutiny of religious beliefs or their adherents, out of fear of giving offense or appearing insensitive.[5] Another reason for the neglect of religion by some U.S. historians and other intellectuals has been the strand of European social thought, identified with such heavy hitters as Karl Marx, Max Weber, and Émile Durkheim, which assumed that modernization, scientific rationality, and secularization would go hand in hand, and that religion, certainly evangelical religion, would gradually fade away. William James, while skeptical of secularization theory, acknowledged its pervasiveness in his 1902 work *The Varieties of Religious Experience*: "There is a notion in the air about us that religion is probably only an anachronism, a case of "survival," an atavistic relapse into a mode of thought which humanity in its more enlightened examples has outgrown; and this notion our religious anthropologists at present do little to counteract. This view is so widespread at the present day that I must consider it with some explicitness before I pass to my own conclusions."[6]

The secularization hypothesis has complicated American historians' efforts to understand not only the persistence of evangelical religious belief but also its periodic upsurges, including the most recent one. But historians are becoming more aware of the timeliness of Alexis de Tocqueville's observation from his 1830s tour: "There is no country in the world where the Christian religion retains a greater influence over the souls of men than in America." In fact, G. K. Chesterton, visiting America ninety years later, seconded Tocqueville's judgment: America, he wrote, was "a nation with the soul of a church."[7]

More recently, however, the field of American religious history has attracted more attention, and its practitioners have displayed impressive analytic acuity and sensitivity to the rich diversity of American religious life. The profession as a whole increasingly recognizes the centrality of religion to American history in every time period, including our own. As scholars probe the post-1960 evangelical revival, and attempt an interpretive synthesis, they have confronted its intricate nuances, cross-currents, and historical continuities and discontinuities.

The evangelical resurgence unfolded within the context of profound changes in American society—demographic, political, cultural, and intellectual. The relationship between the era's religious trends and these larger changes is complex and reciprocal, involving more than a simple backlash. Up to a point, of course, the backlash interpretation is plausible and useful. The sexual and cultural provocations of the late sixties/early seventies counterculture and the more explicit treatment of sex in Hollywood films and Broadway plays certainly offended many evangelicals. The gay rights movement, kicked off by the 1969 Stonewall riots in New York City, in which the patrons of a gay bar battled a police raid; the Supreme Court's 1962 ban on public-school prayers; and the 1973 *Roe v. Wade* decision, protecting women's constitutional right to an abortion in the early months of pregnancy, further unsettled religious conservatives.

So did a series of judicial rulings extending First Amendment protection to sexually explicit books, periodicals, and films. The 1970 report of a federal commission on pornography appointed by President Lyndon Johnson argued that in most cases the dangers of pornography were much exaggerated. This report, released after Johnson left office, was repudiated by President Nixon as "morally bankrupt" (and who better to judge moral bankruptcy?) and rejected by the Senate on a 60–5 vote.[8]

These and other developments were read by many American evangelicals (and by conservatives of other faiths) as evidence of an alarming moral collapse. Francis Schaeffer, a conservative American Presbyterian who had founded a retreat center in Switzerland, reinforced this alarm by placing these changes within a broader cultural context in *How Shall We Then Live: The Rise and Decline of Western Thought and Culture* (1976), an intellectually pretentious work ranging from ancient Greece and Rome down through Picasso and James Joyce to the present. Schaeffer spread his message through speaking tours and a ten-part film series for study groups.[9] Re-enforced by Schaeffer and others, the evangelical response to these developments, misleadingly summed up as a repudiation of "the sixties," does give historical plausibility to the view that the evangelical upsurge was simply a massive backlash against unsettling cultural and political developments, arising spontaneously, with little historical context.

Evangelicalism: The Prequel

The backlash hypothesis can be misleading as well as illuminating. For one thing, it presents a simplistic and ahistorical picture of American evangelicalism, taking little account of the period before the late twentieth-century upsurge. In the 1920s and beyond, many observers concluded that "fundamentalism" had received a death blow at the 1925 Scopes Trial, and would gradually disappear. In fact, conservative Protestantism remained strong in the post-Scopes era. A network of colleges, Bible schools, and seminaries, including the Bible Institute of Los Angeles, Wheaton College in Illinois (Billy Graham's alma mater), Chicago's Moody Bible Institute, and William Bell Riley's Northwestern Bible and Missionary Training School in Minneapolis produced thousands of evangelical ministers, missionaries, Sunday school teachers, and lay supporters of the cause. The popularity of Aimee Semple McPherson's Angeles Temple in Los Angeles and the spread of Pentecostalism in these years; Billy Sunday's revivals; the large audiences attracted by Paul Rader's Chicago-based "National Radio Chapel" in the 1920s; and Charles E. Fuller's "Old Fashioned Revival Hour" on the Mutual Broadcasting System beginning in 1937 all suggest evangelicalism's continuing vitality. The 1940s offered further evidence: the InterVarsity Christian Fellowship (1941), a British import targeting college students; the National Association of Evangelicals (1942); Youth for Christ (1945), with its popular Saturday night rallies; and, of course, Billy Graham, beginning with his 1949 Los Angeles tent revival, to which the Russians' first atomic-bomb test gave added urgency.[10]

Apart from the flamboyant Sunday and McPherson and the charismatic Graham, evangelicals remained mostly under the cultural radar in these years. Their modest places of worship paled in comparison to the imposing churches of the mainstream denominations, conveying a visual impression of dominance even as their pews emptied out. Pre-1970 evangelical churches remained mostly apolitical, concentrating on their core agenda of winning souls, supporting missionaries, and nurturing members' spiritual lives. Such activities, while crucial in building the movement, attracted little attention from historians or the media.

The backlash hypothesis can mislead, too, in suggesting a causal link between the evangelical resurgence and the conservative political turn typified by the presidencies of Richard Nixon, Gerald Ford, Ronald Reagan, and the two George Bushes, and by the more cautious, middle-of-the-road Democratic presidencies of Jimmy Carter and Bill Clinton, in contrast to Franklin D. Roosevelt's New Deal, Harry Truman's Fair Deal, and Lyndon Johnson's Great Society and War on Poverty. To be sure, considerable evidence supports such a link. Politicized evangelicalism was, and remains, real and powerful. Falwell's Moral Majority, founded in consultation with Republican party operatives, mobilized evangelicals politically by stressing "pro-life, pro-family, pro-moral, and pro-American" themes they found particularly resonant. Pat Robertson's Christian Coalition, emerging from his unsuccessful bid for the 1998 Republican presidential nomination, led by the political operative Ralph Reed, explicitly highlighted the organization's "Christian" base, in contrast to the more capacious gathering of "moral" forces suggested by Falwell's title. Reed underscored the link years later, calling his time with the Christian Coalition and specifically the 1991 battle to confirm the evangelical Clarence Thomas to the Supreme Court: "That showed me . . . God is still on the throne. . . . There is a genuine struggle between good and evil. . . . Godly men and women can get involved in the political process and . . . build his kingdom."[11]

Many other evangelical lobbies joined Falwell and Robertson in the political arena, including Donald Wildmon's American Family Association (1977); Beverly LaHaye's Concerned Women for America (1979); Louis Sheldon's Traditional Values Coalition (1980); James Dobson's Family Research Council (1983); Rick Scarborough's Texas-based Vision America, which claimed the allegiance of five thousand evangelical pastors prepared to persuade their members to vote; and the Ethics & Religious Liberty Commission of the Southern Baptist Convention, America's largest Protestant denomination, a bastion of hard-edged evangelicalism and hard-ball political lobbying. Richard Land, the Southern Baptists' Washington lobbyist was a frequent media commentator and hosted a regular call-in show on more than five hundred Christian radio stations.[12]

All this paid off at the polls. In 1980, 67 percent of white evangelical voters backed Ronald Reagan; in 1984, 76 per cent. In 2000, 68 percent of this voting group cast their ballots for born-again Christian George W. Bush; a crushing 78 percent in 2004—an election into which James Dobson poured money and effort. Evangelical voters also have exerted clout at the state level, particularly in such key states as Iowa, Kansas, South Carolina, and Texas.[13]

But while these lobbying efforts and voting statistics merit attention, the relationship of evangelicalism and conservative politics is complex, and has varied over time, both in earlier eras and more recently. Historically, theologically conservative Protestants have embraced a range of positions on the social and political issues of their day. In the antebellum era, many evangelicals were among the most committed abolitionists. Harriet Beecher Stowe, daughter of the evangelical leader Lyman Beecher and herself deeply religious, wrote *Uncle Tom's Cabin* (1852), the novel that solidified northern abolitionist sentiment. Theodore Dwight Weld, converted in a Charles G. Finney revival, became an antislavery leader. His 1837 work *The Bible against Slavery* was specifically designed to win evangelicals to the abolitionist cause.[14]

In the later nineteenth century, industrialization, urbanization, and heavy Catholic and Jewish immigration challenged evangelicals in ways that, to them, seemed as formidable as those faced by their late twentieth-century spiritual descendants. How could Protestant churches again "regulate society" as in earlier days, wondered Harriet Beecher Stowe in her 1873 novel *We and Our Neighbors,* as she surveyed the dance halls, brothels, saloons, and other evidences of big-city "paganism."[15]

Evangelicals responded with organizational initiatives broadly encompassing what today would be categorized as "progressive" and "conservative." The U.S. Evangelical Alliance (1867), founded in New York by William E. Dodge in emulation of an earlier British initiative, promoted temperance, urban evangelism among Catholic immigrants, and other reforms. In fact, Dodge (1805–93) offers an interesting prototype of the blend of evangelical piety, Republican politics, and moral reform sometimes assumed to be unique to the late twentieth century. A merchant, railroad investor, timber baron, and founder of the Phelps Dodge mining company, he became one of the era's richest capitalists, leaving an estate (after massive philanthropies in his lifetime) estimated at $6 million, around $140 million in current buying power. The banker J. P. Morgan spoke at his memorial service. A lifelong political conservative, Dodge was a delegate to the 1860 Republican convention that nominated Abraham Lincoln.

A devout Presbyterian and city missionary in his youth, Dodge supported and helped found many moral and religious organizations in addition to the Evangelical Alliance, including Bible and tract societies, the National Temperance Society, and Anthony Comstock's New York Society for the Suppression of Vice. The Sabbatarian cause won his special support. As his *New York Times* obituary noted: "He was one of the most active workers to secure the enforcement of the Sunday provisions of the new Penal Code, and held that all business of a secular nature should be suspended on the Lord's Day. He himself lived up to his belief consistently, and he believed that others should be made to do so."[16] The issues would change, from temperance and Sunday-closing laws to school prayer and gay marriage, but William E. Dodge's amalgamation of evangelical piety, Republican politics, and coercive social activism neatly fits the stereotype of contemporary evangelicalism.

Yet, Dodge also helped found what became the American University of Beirut; supported African American education through benefactions to Pennsylvania's Ashmun Institute (1854, later Lincoln University); served on several boards and commissions to protect Indians rights; and spearheaded efforts to prosecute a U.S. Cavalry officer responsible for an 1870 Indian massacre in Montana—not the kinds of issues typically associated with prevailing stereotypes of evangelicalism.

In the twentieth century's opening decades, evangelicals similarly embraced a range of political and social positions, from far-right and even anti-Semitic views to progressive and radical reforms. At Angeles Temple, Aimee Semple McPherson at least intermittently supported racially integrated services; instituted programs to help unwed mothers and domestic-abuse victims; and sponsored social-assistance efforts during the Great Depression. Other California evangelicals supported New Deal welfare programs and even backed more radical wealth-redistribution schemes. These leftist and progressive tendencies withered in the super-patriotic and anticommunist fevers of the 1940s and 1950s, but they remain part of the story of evangelicalism and politics.[17] This brief historical excursus, from antebellum evangelical abolitionists to 1930s economic radicals, suggests that sweeping generalizations about "evangelicals" in any time period may be risky. Indeed, common sense cautions us that *any* generalizations encompassing millions of Americans over extended time periods should be viewed with skepticism.

If blanket assumptions about earlier evangelicals' political and social views prove unreliable, this remains true for the most recent evangelical resurgence, as Axel R. Schäfer convincingly shows in *Countercultural Conservatives: American Evangelicalism from the Postwar Revival to the New Christian Right* (2011).[18] African American evangelicals, a significant subgroup, generally retained their

Democratic loyalties dating to the New Deal. As for Hispanic evangelicals (a substantial minority of U.S. Hispanics), social class, income, education, and region of origin, as well as differences between the Democratic and Republican parties on economic and immigration issues of concern to Hispanics, all produced quite diverse political allegiances.[19]

Among non-Hispanic white evangelicals, significant numbers have embraced liberal positions on such issues as peace, civil rights, social justice, economic inequity, world hunger, and environmental protection. In *The Great Reversal: Evangelicalism versus Social Concern* (1972), Marquette University sociologist David O. Moberg urged evangelicals to rediscover their nineteenth-century predecessors' commitment to antislavery and social justice.[20] That same year, Messiah College professor Ronald Sider organized evangelicals to support the presidential candidacy of Democrat George McGovern, a Vietnam War opponent. From that effort emerged Evangelicals for Social Action, whose "Declaration of Evangelical Social Concern" (1973) addressed numerous social causes typically identified with liberal Protestantism. Sider went on to publish *Rich Christians in an Age of Hunger* (1977); *Evangelicals and Development: Toward a Theology of Social Change* (1981); and the co-edited *Nuclear Holocaust and Christian Hope: A Book for Christian Peacemakers* (1982), among other works.

In the same vein, Jim Wallis, a product of a Plymouth Brethren upbringing, having joined civil-rights and antiwar protests at Michigan State University and Trinity Evangelical Divinity School, founded a commune committed to social activism that evolved into the Washington, D.C.–based Sojourners movement. Through *Sojourners* magazine and such books as *Agenda for Biblical People* (1976) and *Waging Peace: A Handbook for the Struggle to Abolish Nuclear Weapons* (1982) Wallis, too, became an influential evangelical voice highlighting issues of peace and social justice.

These liberal U.S. evangelicals found a kindred spirit in the Anglican priest and British evangelical leader John Stott, principal author of the Lausanne Covenant (1974). With a flourish of biblical citations, this document called on evangelicals to work for "justice and reconciliation throughout human society, and for the liberation of men and women from every kind of oppression." "Evangelism and socio-political involvement are both a part of our Christian duty," it went on; "The message of salvation implies also a message of judgment upon every form of alienation, oppression and discrimination, and we should not be afraid to denounce evil and injustice wherever they exist."[21]

While liberal social activism among evangelicals peaked in the volatile 1970s, it remained a force thereafter. Books by Sider, Wallis, and others drew respectful attention in evangelical circles. The religious Right leaders often featured in the media, like Robertson, Dobson, Falwell (until his death in 2007), and Land, did not represent all evangelicals. In 1987, sociologist James Davison Hunter reported that younger evangelicals were abandoning such polarizing figures on many cultural and political issues. Ideological divisions surfaced within the National Association of Evangelicals (NAE), whose chief lobbyist, Richard Cizik, resigned in 2008 when Dobson and other ideological enforcers blasted his statements on global warming and gay civil unions. The grassroots response, reported the NAE's president, "overwhelmingly" supported Cizik. He went on to found a new organization, the New Evangelical Partnership for the Common Good. At the polls, while many white evangelicals embraced Reagan and George W. Bush, significant minorities consistently did not. In 2008, 26 percent voted for Barack Obama.[22]

That evangelicalism cannot be conflated with the so-called New Religious Right was underscored by sociologist Alan Wolfe in *One Nation After All* (1998), a report on the "Middle Class Morality Project" in which Wolfe and colleagues conducted in-depth interviews with a representative sampling of two hundred middle-class Americans, including many evangelicals. On cultural and religious matters, they found far higher levels of nonjudgmental tolerance, including among evangelicals, than the pronouncements of religious Right leaders would suggest. Writes Wolfe: "Very few of the . . . people to whom we talked . . . used words like 'sin,' 'moral rot,' 'decay,' or 'Satan,' terms that, whether fairly or unfairly, are usually identified with revivalist preachers, talk show hosts, and conservative Christians." One Oklahoma retiree, while unhappy about America's moral condition, added: "The fanatics took over. They drove away people like us. . . . The God I believe in is a God of love."[23]

My Enemy, My Friend: Evangelicals and Modernity

Implicit in the backlash explanation of evangelicalism's late-twentieth-century vitality is the assumption that it represented a broad repudiation of secular America's values and norms. Certainly some events and trends did dismay evangelicals, as we have seen, but the opposition was selective, not a sweeping rejection. Indeed, evangelicals have long experience at adapting to social change, appropriating new technologies, and shaping their "timeless" message to shifting cultural currents. The Youth for Christ slogan, "Geared to the Times, Anchored to the Rock," sums up the evangelical view of modernity.

The antebellum Bible and tract societies used high-speed steam printing presses and elaborate distribution networks to bring their wares to the frontier

and the burgeoning cities. The evangelical founders of the Chautauqua movement offered the urban middle-class spiritual renewal and restorative retreats
in bucolic settings. Nineteenth-century evangelical novelists, poets, song writers,
and artists adapted the gospel to the aesthetic conventions of a sentimental age.
In the Roaring Twenties, by contrast, evangelist Billy Sunday preached a
hard-hitting faith and a tough, manly Christ. Evangelicals quickly embraced
the new medium of radio, through national programs like Charles E. Fuller's
"Old Fashioned Revival Hour" and M. R. DeHaan's "Radio Bible Class";
Moody Bible Institute's powerful WMBI in Chicago (1927); and countless
sermons and church services on local stations.[24]

   This selective appropriation continues. Indeed, in many respects post-1960s
evangelicalism mirrored the larger culture, adapting themes, technologies, and
institutional forms for its own purposes. Instances abound. Pat Robertson's
Christian Broadcasting Network (CBN) adopted contemporary formats, such
as Robertson's flagship "700 Club," an Oprah-like talk show featuring evangelical writers, politicians, and celebrities. When the evangelist Oral Roberts began
a TV program in 1969, one observer enthused: "It . . . had everything that
would guarantee success for any series—bright contemporary music, attractive
young people, a fast pace, superb technical quality, and a well-known personality
at the center." In due course, evangelicals embraced the Internet, forming virtual
belief communities, discussing doctrinal points and political issues, and sharing
gossip about events and personalities in the evangelical subculture.[25]

   The early 1970s "Jesus Movement" cloned the 1960s counterculture. Explo
'72, a Jesus Movement rally in Dallas sponsored by Campus Crusade for Christ,
was widely seen as an evangelical Woodstock (minus the sex, drugs, and nudity),
with its shoals of laid-back kids and parade of pop musicians. The final night
drew some 150,000 to the Cotton Bowl to hear Billy Graham and Johnny Cash,
plus performances by Larry Norman, Rita Coolidge, and other Jesus Movement
favorites. Just as earlier evangelical gospel songs had echoed their era's jaunty
tunes and sentimental ballads, so modern evangelicalism's Contemporary
Christian Music (as it was called) echoed the secular music trends of the day.[26]

   The organizational forms of the post-1960s evangelical movement similarly
replicated trends in the larger culture. While the evangelical resurgence ener-
gized conservative denominations such as the giant Southern Baptist Convention, the rapidly growing Assemblies of God Church, and smaller bodies such
as the Church of the Nazarene, the Wesleyan Church, and the Free Methodist
Church, much of the growth occurred outside Protestantism's denominational
structure. In the process, the mass revivalism of the Billy Graham crusades
faded, as did the emphasis on an emotional, wrenching conversion experience.

Becoming an "evangelical" in contemporary America represents a consumer choice, like opting for Honda rather than Toyota, or a latte rather than double espresso.

Chuck Smith, a minister of Aimee Semple McPherson's International Church of the Foursquare Gospel, came to the struggling Calvary Chapel in Costa Mesa, California, in 1965, and quickly won a following among local surfers and hippies with his blend of doctrinal rigor and easy-going style. Soon satellite Calvary Chapels sprang up. In 1982, John Wimber, a Calvary Chapel pastor (and former rock musician), broke with Smith to lead another new evangelical/charismatic movement, the Vineyard Christian Fellowship. Like McDonalds, Starbucks, and Burger King, both movements expanded rapidly. By 2010, the Calvary Chapel and Vineyard Christian Fellowship organizations each boasted more than fifteen hundred churches worldwide. In common with other franchise operations, the local churches were independently managed but gained brand recognition from their affiliation with the parent organization.[27]

The evangelical movement's symbiotic relationship with the larger culture is evident, too, in the rise of independent megachurches (defined as churches with two thousand or more members), replicating the rise of Wal-Mart and other big-box outlets. Joel Osteen's Lakewood Church in Houston, with thirty-thousand members, meets in a renovated stadium that formerly housed the Houston Rockets basketball team. The complex includes an Internet café and a fitness room for an aerobics class called "Firm Believers." Services are broadcast on satellite TV and several cable networks.[28]

Adopting the management prescriptions of Peter Drucker and other business gurus, megachurches typically channel their members into smaller groups.[29] Rick Warren's Saddleback Church of Anaheim, California, with twenty thousand members, its mall-like campus sprawling over 120 acres, led the way in adopting Drucker's organizational strategies. Quoting Jesus's words "For where two or three are gathered together in my name, I am there in their midst," Saddleback's website declares: "When it comes to fellowship, size matters—smaller is better." The website includes a questionnaire that new members can complete and submit with a few clicks, to find a nearby group to join, based on their gender, age, education, marital status, particular interests, and the like.[30]

In short, to understand contemporary evangelicalism, one must look not only at beliefs and voting patterns but at the social function of actual churches, whether small fellowships or megachurches, with their intricate webs of interest groups that offer personal ties and emotional support. Dean C. Kelley of the National Council of Churches made this point as early as 1972 in his prescient work *Why Conservative Churches are Growing*. As the novelist Walter Kirn, whose family joined the Mormon Church when he was a teenager in the 1970s, told National Public Radio in 2005: "What people are really looking for are nodes of community amid the sea of suburban sprawl. Politicians who are into excoriating the Christian right without asking what needs they are serving are way off base."[31]

The interpenetration of the evangelical world and the larger culture is evident, too, in the movement's literature. Many of the books marketed to evangelicals by religious publishers mirror the therapeutic literature popular with general readers, dealing with such issues as depression, marital relationships, parenting, aging, diet, money management, etc., supplemented with appropriate biblical quotations. Another popular genre focuses on Bible prophecy interpretation, which looms large for conservative Protestants who revere the Bible as inerrant and divinely inspired. But here, again, larger cultural influences become evident. In earlier times, prophecy interpretation was discussed in weighty tomes explicating specific biblical passages, and at prophecy conferences where specialists discussed their interpretive theories. In this milieu, the premillennial dispensationalist system of the nineteenth-century British churchman John Darby, including the doctrine of the Rapture of the saints, promoted by Cyrus Scofield's 1909 Reference Bible, with Darby's system woven through the interpretive notes, gained a wide following among evangelicals.

Premillennial dispensationalism remains influential in evangelical circles, but the means of promulgating it have changed radically.[32] Hal Lindsey's bestselling *The Late Great Planet Earth* (1970), a popularization of Darby's system, reflected its origins in informal sermons that Lindsey, with Campus Crusade for Christ, gave at UCLA in the late 1960s, at the height of the counterculture and the beginnings of the Jesus Movement. It is written in breezy contemporary slang (the Rapture is "the Ultimate Trip"), and it ingeniously links specific prophecies to current events, from fears of Russia and nuclear war to the rise of Israel and the UN to campus disorders and immorality, as proof that the "End" is near. Prophecy popularizers also exploited environmental fears, citing passages in Revelation foretelling chaos in the natural order as the final crisis approaches. In Pat Robertson's apocalyptic novel *The End of the Age* (1995), a meteor strike in the Pacific triggers tsunamis and earthquakes that inundate the entire West Coast. Hal Lindsey in *Planet Earth—2000 A.D.* (1996) cited rising environmental dangers as the major prophetic fulfillments of the preceding quarter century. The bestseller *Left Behind* series of prophecy novels by Tim LaHaye and Jerry Jenkins, launched in 1995, followed this strategy, incorporating current events and mass-culture allusions to give the ancient message an up-to-the-minute aura.[33]

The publishers of the inspirational works, self-help books, and prophecy popularizations targeting evangelicals emulated the general publishing industry's marketing strategies, promoting their paperbacks through such outlets as Borders, Barnes and Noble, Wal-Mart, and Amazon.com. The *Left Behind* series, marketed globally with multiple translations, generated a dizzying array of spin-off products, from a junior version, *Left Behind for Kids*, to "Ask Me How to Avoid Being Left Behind" coffee mugs. (It also spawned parody products, including "No Beer Left Behind" and "Left Behind and Loving It" T-shirts.)

The Christian bookstore industry, with stores in shopping malls across America, similarly adopted contemporary marketing techniques, with attractive, well-stocked stores offering glossy paperbacks, CDs, videos, greeting cards, jewelry, T-shirts, and religiously themed home-décor items barely distinguishable from what one might find in any gift shop. One company markets Christian candy, with Bible verses on the wrapper, under the slogan, "Reaching the World One Piece at a Time."[34] The evangelical Christian Booksellers Association (CBA), founded in 1950, provides marketing tips and product information to members through its publications and annual convention attracting thousands. The department-store pioneer J. C. Penney addressed the CBA's 1951 convention. By 2007, CBA's member stores reported sales of $4.3 billion. And these were not only modest businesses of the kind my father operated in Dayton, Ohio, from small beginnings in 1927 selling Bibles, greeting cards, and religious mottos door to door to his retirement in 1974. In 2011, the Family Christian Stores chain, launched in 1931 by Zondervan Publishing Company of Grand Rapids, Michigan, comprised 340 stores nationwide. The Baptist Bookstore chain, renamed LifeWay Christian Stores, had 162 stores in 2011. In 2000, Family Christian Stores launched "IBelieve," its e-media component, with a $20 million promotional budget. In 2005, reflecting its members' marketing scope, CBA renamed its annual convention the International Christian Retail Show.[35]

The Contemporary Christian Music (CCM) industry represents another multibillion-dollar component of the evangelical marketing empire, with its own superstars, scandals, trade periodicals, Hall of Fame, and annual awards ceremony, when "the Dove" is bestowed on that year's winner. Larry Norman's albums *Upon This Rock* (1969) and *Only Visiting This Planet* (1972) propelled him to CCM stardom. Amy Grant, the "Queen of Christian Pop," sold over thirty million albums worldwide, beginning with her breakthrough albums *My Father's Eyes* (1979) and *Age to Age* (1982).[36]

Just as the larger culture has shaped contemporary evangelicalism, so the evangelical resurgence seeped into the larger culture. Chick-fil-A, a fast-food chain founded by evangelicals, posted sales of $1.7 billion in 2004 (even while remaining closed on Sunday). The company's "first priority," said founder S. Truett Cathy, "has never been just to serve chicken. It is to serve a higher calling."[37] Elvis Presley's album of evangelical favorites, *How Great Thou Art* (RCA Victor, 1967), featured Presley posing in front of a church. Hollywood films like *The Omen* (1976), *The Rapture* (1991), and *Megiddo* (2001) reflected the widespread evangelical interest in Bible prophecy, as did such songs as Barry McGuire's "Eve of Destruction" (1965); David Bowie's "[We've Got] Five Years" (1972); Bob Dylan's "When He Returns" (1979), a product of his evangelical phase; Alison Krauss's "I'll Fly Away" (from the soundtrack of the 2000 film *O Brother, Where Art Thou?*); and Johnny Cash's haunting "The Man Comes Around" (2002).

Spotting the profit potential of the evangelical market, multinational publishers and record companies acted accordingly. Scott Foresman acquired Fleming H. Revell (founded by Dwight L. Moody's brother-in-law) in 1978. Zondervan (Hal Lindsey's original publisher), with $106 million in annual sales, was acquired by HarperCollins (a part of Rupert Murdoch's media empire) in 1988. Random House, a division of the German publishing conglomerate Bertelsmann, acquired the evangelical publisher Multnomah in 2006. Hallmark Cards bought DaySpring, a Christian greeting card company, in 1999. And religious publishers tapped into the secular market. Thomas Nelson, a venerable house with such titles as *Forty Days with Jesus, Billy Graham Quotes,* and the 2011 bestseller *Heaven is for Real* (an account of a three-year-old's vision of Jesus and heaven while having his appendix out) currently on its list, also publishes Donald Trump's *The Best Real Estate Advice I Ever Received*.[38]

Music-industry giants Capitol Records and MGM released Larry Norman's first two albums. Other CCM musicians moved into the mainstream market (sometimes after scandals involving divorce, extramarital affairs, out-of-wedlock babies, or coming out as gay or lesbian). Amy Grant courted the pop market in 1985 with her *Unguarded* album and then returned to her evangelical roots with *Rock of Ages . . . Hymns & Faith* (1995). Moving back and forth across an increasingly hazy line, Grant symbolizes the blurring of the evangelical world and the larger American culture.

In the realm of ideas, too, the evangelical worldview both influenced and was influenced by broader trends. A number of best-selling books published during the peak years of the evangelical resurgence, including Paul Ehrlich's *The Population Bomb* (1968), Alvin Toffler's *Future Shock* (1970), Barry Commoner's *The Closing Circle: Nature, Man, and Technology* (1971), Jonathan Schell's *The Fate of the Earth* (1982), and Bill McKibben's *The End of Nature* (1990), offered scenarios of approaching catastrophe that echoed the Bible-prophecy popularizations of Hal Lindsey and others. *The Fourth Turning* (1997), by William Strauss and Neil Howe, subtitled "An American Prophecy," saw American history as unfolding in four great cycles, reminiscent of John Darby's "dispensations," with the final two still to come—"Unravelings" and "Turnings," sounding much like the Great Tribulation and the Battle of Armageddon. The title of a 1997 book about the dangers of lethal micro-organisms in the nation's water supply, *And the Waters Turned to Blood*, echoed biblical apocalyptic themes. The ads for the book, warning of "a terrifying new plague" and fishermen afflicted with "lesions that would not heal," evoked Revelation's prophecy of horrible sores breaking out on people's bodies in the last days.[39]

Stephen King's 1978 novel *The Stand*, the basis of a 1991 ABC-TV miniseries, was constructed around an apocalyptic end-of-the-world scenario surely influenced by the prophecy popularizations of Lindsey and others. In King's version, most of the human race dies when a deadly virus is accidently released as a U.S. biological warfare experiment goes awry. As in the classic apocalyptic genre, the survivors align into two camps, one led by a Christlike black woman, Mother Abigail, the other by a charismatic Antichrist figure, Randall Flagg. In the end, righteousness triumphs over the forces of evil. Is *The Stand* an artifact of America's secular mass culture, or an expression of an apocalyptic sensibility rooted in the evangelical religious revival that swept America as the twentieth century ended? Clearly it is both, again underscoring the complex interaction of evangelical religious belief and modern American mass culture.

American history is incomprehensible without close attention to evangelicalism. From the early nineteenth century on, the beliefs and actions of Bible-believing Protestants have influenced American culture and politics, and this remained true in the post-1960s evangelical upsurge. But evangelicalism's relationship to American culture and politics is complex. Culturally, evangelicalism has crucially influenced the secular world, while at the same time modernity in its varied manifestations has impinged on the evangelical realm, sometimes in ways that make this subculture seem almost a mirror image of the larger world beyond. Politically, in both the distant and more recent past, evangelicalism's influence has never been exclusively channeled toward one party or one agenda but spread across the full ideological spectrum. Awareness of this complexity is crucial as historians continue to assess evangelicalism's

protean nature and influence. *Newsweek's* "Year of the Evangelical," it sometimes seems, could well be expanded to encompass the whole of American
history.

NOTES

1. John Corrigan and Winthrop S. Hudson, *Religion in America*, 6th ed. (Upper
Saddle River, NJ: Prentice Hall, 1999), 385; Dean R. Hoge, Benton Johnson, and Donald
Luidens, *Vanishing Boundaries: The Religion of Mainline Protestant Baby Boomers* (Louisville:
Westminster/John Knox Press, 1994); David A. Hollinger, "After Cloven Tongues of
Fire: Ecumenical Protestantism and the Modern American Encounter with Diversity,"
Journal of American History 98 (June 2011): 37; "Christianity Reborn," *Economist*, December
23, 2006, 48–50 (on Pentecostalism).

2. C. Kirk Hadaway and Penny Long Marler, "How Many Americans Attend
Worship Each Week?" *Journal for the Scientific Study of Religion* 44 (September 2005):
307–322. The authors report research suggesting that only about 22 percent of
Americans attend church regularly, rather than the widely reported 40 percent. Larry
Eskridge, "How Many Evangelicals Are There?" http://isae.wheaton.edu/defining-
evangelicalism/how-many-evangelicals-are-there? (Gallup Poll data). Eskridge is associate
director of Wheaton College's Institute for the Study of American Evangelicals. All the
websites cited in this chapter were accessed in June 2011.

3. William Warren Sweet, *Methodism in American History* (Nashville: Abingdon Press,
1954); Henry P. Van Dusen, *World Christianity: Yesterday, Today, Tomorrow* (New York:
Abingdon Cokesbury Press, 1947), recently singled out by David Hollinger for its
"complacent, triumphalist perspective." See Hollinger, "After Cloven Tongues of Fire,"
29, fn. 18.

4. Will Herberg, *Protestant, Catholic, Jew: An Essay in American Religious Sociology*
(Garden City, NY: Doubleday, 1955); William H. Whyte, *The Organization Man* (New
York: Simon & Schuster, 1956); Harvey Cox, *The Secular City: Secularization and Urbanization
in Theological Perspective* (New York: Macmillan, 1965), 206. Cox offered a more positive
view of the evangelical revival in *Fire From Heaven: The Rise of Pentecostal Spirituality and the
Reshaping of Religion in the Twenty-first Century* (Reading, MA: Addison-Wesley, 1995).

5. David A. Hollinger, "Among the Believers: The Politics of Sin and Secularism,"
Harpers Magazine, November 2004, 91–98.

6. William James, *The Varieties of Religious Experience: A Study in Human Nature* (New
York: Modern Library ed., [1936]), 480.

7. Alexis de Tocqueville, *Democracy in America*, ed. Phillips Bradley (New York:
Alfred A. Knopf, 1945), I:314; G. K. Chesterton, *What I Saw in America* (New York: Dodd,
Mead & Co., 1922), 11–12. For a critique of secularization theory, see Rodney Stark and
William Sims Bainbridge, *The Future of Religion: Secularization, Revival, and Cult Formation*
(Berkeley: University of California Press, 1986). By contrast, the British sociologist Steve

Bruce, in *God Is Dead: Secularization in the West* (New York: Wiley-Blackwell, 2002), argues that secularization is a reality in the West, including the United States, despite apparent evidence to the contrary. In *American Grace: How Religion Divides and Unites Us* (New York: Simon & Schuster, 2010), Robert D. Putnam and David E. Campbell conclude that Americans, especially the younger generation, even those who view themselves as very religious, are becoming more accepting of diversity, and thus "functionally secular." In *Holy Ignorance: When Religion and Culture Part Ways* (New York: Columbia University Press, 2010), the French sociologist Olivier Roy contends that the contemporary fundamentalist upsurge is actually a response to long-term secularization trends.

8. Paul S. Boyer, *Purity in Print: Book Censorship in America from the Gilded Age to the Computer Age*, 2nd ed. (Madison: University of Wisconsin Press, 2002), chap. 10, esp. 306–310, on the Obscenity and Pornography Commission.

9. Frances Schaeffer, *How Shall We Then Live? The Rise and Decline of Western Thought and Culture* (Old Tappen, NJ: Fleming H. Revell, 1976); Walter H. Capps, *The New Religious Right: Piety, Patriotism, and Politics* (Columbia: University of South Carolina Press, 1990) discusses Schaeffer's influence in chap. 3, 58–88.

10. William Vance Trollinger Jr., *God's Empire: William Bell Riley and Midwestern Fundamentalism* (Madison: University of Wisconsin Press, 1990); Randall J. Stevens, *The Fire Spreads: Holiness and Pentecostalism in the American South* (Cambridge, MA: Harvard University Press, 2008); Paul S. Boyer, "The Evangelical Resurgence in 1970s American Protestantism," in *Rightward Bound: Making America Conservative in the 1970s*, ed. Bruce J. Schulman and Julian E. Zelizer (Cambridge, MA: Harvard University Press, 2008), 32.

11. "Together Again: Ralph Reed and Pat Robertson Reminiscence," People for the American Way Right Wing Watch, October 21, 2010, http://www.rightwingwatch .org/content/together-again-ralph-reed-and-pat-robertson-reminisce.

12. Ethics and Religious Liberty website, Richard Land biography, http://erlc .com/erlc/richard_land/; "For a Trusty Voting Bloc, a Faith Shaken," *New York Times*, October 7, 2007, 1 (Vision America); Boyer, "The Evangelical Resurgence in 1970s American Protestantism," 44–47.

13. Corwin Smidt and Paul Kellstedt, "Evangelicals in the Post-Reagan Era: An Analysis of Evangelical Voters in the 1988 Presidential Election," *Journal for the Scientific Study of Religion* 31 (September 1992), table 3, 336 (1980 and 1984 votes); Scott Keeler, "Will White Evangelicals Desert the GOP?" Pew Research Center, May 2, 2006, http://pewresearch.org/pubs/22/will-white-evangelicals-desert-the-gop (2000, 2004 elections); Jeremy Leaming, "James Dobson, The Religious Right's 800-Pound Gorilla," Americans United for Separation of Church and State, February 2005, http://www .au.org/media/church-and-state/archives/2005/02/james-dobson.html. For the state-level influence of evangelical voters and lobbyists, see John C. Green, Mark J. Rozell, and Clyde Wilcox, eds., *The Christian Right in American Politics: Marching to the Millennium* (Washington, DC: Georgetown University Press, 2003), and, by the same editors and publisher, *The Values Campaign? The Christian Right and the 2004 Election* (2006).

14. David S. Reynolds, *Mightier than the Sword: "Uncle Tom's Cabin" and the Battle for America* (New York: W. W. Norton Co., 2011); Robert H. Abzug, *Passionate Liberator: Theodore Dwight Weld and the Dilemma of Reform* (New York: Oxford University Press, 1980). For a broader perspective see Abzug, *Cosmos Crumbling: American Reform and the Religious Imagination* (New York: Oxford University Press, 1994). One should note that in the early nineteenth century, before the challenges of Darwinism and critical biblical scholarship, the term "evangelical" encompassed a broad range of Protestants.

15. Harriet Beecher Stowe, *We and Our Neighbors* (New York, 1873), 386, 439–440.

16. "A Good Life-Work Ended," *New York Times,* February 10, 1883, http://query.ny times.com/gst/abstract.html?res=F20E10FEC5511738DDDA90994DA405B8384F0D3.

17. Leo P. Ribuffo, *The Old Christian Right: The Protestant Far Right from the Great Depression to the Cold War* (Philadelphia: Temple University Press, 1988); Darren Dochuk, *From Bible Belt to Sun Belt: Plain-Folk Religion, Grassroots Politics, and the Rise of Evangelical Conservatism* (New York: Norton, 2011); Matthew Avery Sutton, *Aimee Semple McPherson and the Resurrection of Christian America* (Cambridge, MA: Harvard University Press, 2007); Chris Lehman, "Little Churches Everywhere," *Nation,* June 17, 2011, 27–33 (review essay of Dochuk and Sutton).

18. Axel R. Schäfer, *Countercultural Conservatives: American Evangelicalism from the Postwar Revival to the New Christian Right* (Madison: University of Wisconsin Press, 2011).

19. In 2004, 23 percent of Hispanics in the United States self-identified as Protestants or "other [non-Catholic] Christians," including Jehovah's Witnesses and Mormons. In another formulation, 37 percent identified themselves as "born again" or "evangelical." (The larger figure includes Catholic charismatics). Gaston Espinosa, Virgilio Elizonda, Jesse Miranda, eds., *Latino Religions and Civic Activism in the United States* (New York: Oxford University Press, 2005), reported in Bruce Murray, "Latino Religion in the U.S.: Demographic Shifts and Trends," National Hispanic Christian Leadership Conference News, http://www.nhclc.org/news/latino-religion-us-demographic-shifts-and-trend. See also Paul Hughes, "Continental Divide: Hispanic Evangelicals Move Toward the Democrats—and Away from White Evangelicals," *Christianity Today,* February 2008, 13–14.

20. David O. Moberg, *The Great Reversal: Evangelicalism versus Social Concern* (Philadelphia: Lippincott, 1977).

21. "The Lausanne Covenant,"part 5, "Christian Social Responsibility," http://www.lausanne.org/covenant; Timothy Dudley-Smith, *John Stott: A Biography,* 2 vols. (Downers Grove, IL: InterVarsity Press, 1999, 2001).

22. James Davison Hunter, *Evangelicalism: The Coming Generation* (Chicago: University of Chicago Press, 1987); Lisa Miller, "Redemption," *Newsweek,* January 28, 2010, http://www.newsweek.com/2010/01/27/redemption.html (on Richard Cizik); Pew Research Center Publications, "Voting Religiously," November 5, 2008, http://pewresearch .org/pubs/1022/exit-poll-analysis-religion.

23. Alan Wolfe, *One Nation After All: What Middle-Class Americans Really Think About God, Country, Family, Racism, Welfare, Immigration, Homosexuality, Work, The Right, the Left, and Each Other* (New York: Viking, 1998), esp. 39–87, quotes 49, 58.

24. R. Laurence Moore, *Selling God: American Religion in the Market Place of Culture* (New York: Oxford University Press, 1994); Colleen McDannell, *Material Christianity: Religion and Popular Culture in America* (New Haven: Yale University Press, 1995), 67–102; Andrew Chamberlin Rieser, *The Chautauqua Moment: Protestants, Progressives, and the Culture of Modern Liberalism, 1874–1920* (New York: Columbia University Press, 2003); Stephen J. Nichols, *Jesus Made in America: A Cultural History from the Puritans to "The Passion of the Christ"* (Downers Grove, IL: InterVarsity, 2008), 74–98; Stephen R. Prothero, *American Jesus: How the Son of God Became a National Icon* (New York: Farrar, Strauss, and Giroux, 2003), 43–86, 87–123.

25. Quoted in Moore, *Selling God*, 248. For a perceptive interpretive overview, see Christian Smith, *American Evangelicalism: Embattled and Thriving* (Chicago: University of Chicago Press, 1998).

26. "The Great Jesus Rally in Dallas," *Life*, June 30, 1972; Schäfer, *Countercultural Conservatives*; Ronald M. Enroth, Edward E. Ericson Jr., and C. Breckinridge Peters, *The Jesus People: Old-Time Religion in the Age of Aquarius* (Grand Rapids, MI: Eerdmans, 1972); Robert S. Ellwood, *The Sixties Spiritual Awakening: American Religion Moving from Modern to Post-Modern* (New Brunswick, NJ: Rutgers University Press, 1994); Steve Rabey et al., "Age to Age," *CCM magazine*, July 1998, online at www.CCM.com; Nichols, *Jesus Made in America*, 122–145; Robert Glenn Howard, *Digital Jesus: The Making of a New Christian Fundamentalist Community on the Internet* (New York: New York University Press, 2011).

27. Randall Balmer, *Mine Eyes Have Seen the Glory: A Journey into the Evangelical Subculture in America* (New York: Oxford University Press, 1989), 12–30; Calvary Chapel website, "Our History," http://www.calvarychapel.com/index.php?option=com_content &view=article&id=49&Itemid=66; "Vineyard History," http://www.vineyardusa.org /site/about/vineyard-history.

28. "A Church that Packs Them In, 16,000 at a Time," *New York Times*, July 18, 2005, 1. Osteen's "prosperity gospel" places him on the fringe of the evangelical movement.

29. William C. Symonds, "Earthly Empires: How Evangelical Churches are Borrowing from the Business Playbook," *Business Week Online*, May 23, 2005, http:// www.businessweek.com/magazine/content/05_21/b3934001_mz001.htm.

30. Saddleback Church, Small Group website, http://www.saddleback.com /groupfinder/groupsearch.aspx; Malcolm Gladwell, "Letter from Saddleback: The Cellular Church, How Rick Warren's Congregation Grew," *New Yorker*, September 12, 2005, 60–67, on Warren's appropriation of Drucker's management theories. Paul Boyer, "Evangelical Resurgence in 1970s," 41–43.

31. Dean C. Kelley, *Why Conservative Churches are Growing* (New York: Harper and Row, 1972); Paul Boyer, "God's Country: The Conservative Resurgence in Contemporary American Protestantism," in *Europe and America: Cultures in Translation*, ed. Britta Waldschmidt-Nelson, Markus Hünemörder, and Meike Zwingenberger (Heidelberg: Universitätsverlag Winter, 2006), 51–68, esp. 56–57; Kirn quote p. 57.

32. According to a 2011 survey, 62 percent of evangelical leaders embrace premillennialism. "Evangelical Leaders Survey," *NAE Insight*, Spring 2011, 3.

33. Pat Robertson, *The End of the Age: A Novel* (Dallas: Word, 1995), 96; Hal Lindsey, *Planet Earth—2000 A.D.* (Palos Verdes, CA: Western Front, 1996), 81–100, quote p. 90. For further discussion of contemporary Bible prophecy interpretations, see Paul Boyer, *When Time Shall Be No More: Prophecy Belief in Modern American Culture* (Cambridge, MA: Harvard University Press, 1992); Boyer, "The Apocalyptic in the Twentieth Century," in *Fearful Hope: Approaching the New Millennium*, ed. Christopher Kleinhenz and Fannie J. LeMoice (Madison: University of Wisconsin Press, 1999), 149–169; and Boyer, "Bible Prophecy and Foreign Policy," in *Quoting God: How Media Shape Ideas about Religion and Culture*, ed. Claire H. Badaracco (Waco, TX: Baylor University Press, 2005), 107–122.

34. "Religious Retailers Gather to Show off Wares," *USA Today*, July 15, 2005, 11A. Patrick Allitt, *Religion in America Since 1945* (New York: Columbia University Press, 2003) describes the marketing savvy of contemporary evangelical bookstores.

35. Family Christian Stores, Inc., Company History, http://www.fundinguniverse .com/company-histories/Family-Christian-Stores-Inc-Company-History.html; Life-Way, About Us, http://www.lifeway.com/Article/About-Us; CBA Historical Time-line, http://www.cbaonline.org/nm/timeline.htm.

36. Amy Grant, *Mosaic: Pieces of My Life So Far* (Colorado Springs: WaterBrook Press, 2008); John J. Thompson, "Larry Norman, A Tribute," *CCM* magazine, April 2008, http://www.youthworker.com/youth-ministry-resources-ideas/youth-culture-news/11571167/; Enroth, Ericson, Peters, *The Jesus People*, 82.

37. S. Truett Cathy, *Eat Mor Chikin: Inspire More People* (La Grande, OR: Looking Glass Books, 2002), quoted in "Onward, Christian Shoppers," *Economist*, December 1, 2005.

38. "Onward, Christian Shoppers"; "The Media Business: Harper & Row to Acquire Religious Book Publisher," *New York Times*, July 14, 1988; "Random House Acquires Multnomah Publishers," *Los Angeles Times*, August 5, 2006, http://articles .latimes.com/2006/aug/05/entertainment/et-quick5.3.

39. Rodney Barker, *And the Waters Turned to Blood: The Ultimate Biological Threat* (New York: Simon & Schuster, 1997); *New York Times Book Review* ad, April 6, 1997; Michael Barkun, "Divided Apocalyptic Thinking about the End in Contemporary America," *Soundings* 66 (1983): 257–280.

TALKIN 'BOUT A REVOLUTION?
EVANGELICALS IN 1960S SOCIETY
AND CULTURE

TABOR COLLEGE LIBRARY
HILLSBORO, KANSAS 67063

2

Prairie Fire

The New Evangelicalism and the Politics of Oil, Money, and Moral Geography

DARREN DOCHUK

Canadians were in a festive mood in 1967 because of their country's centennial, but locals celebrated in Fort McMurray, Alberta, for reasons all of their own. This year they heralded the opening of the Great Canadian Oil Sands (GCOS) plant. For three years, three thousand workers had labored round-the-clock, turning a $235 million investment into the "world's first commercial venture" to produce synthetic crude out of bitumen. Created to change the world, the GCOS was also a world's creation: over the course of thirty-six months, a multitude of engineers, equipment operators, welders, and riggers had shaped a mass of supplies from around the globe into an enormous complex able to extract one of "the world's largest single energy resources." Spread out over 30,000 square miles from Fort McMurray, with deposits up to 150 feet thick, the oil sands, officials boasted, represented more than six hundred billion barrels of oil. Waiting to be harnessed, this frontier beckoned development on an epic scale, yet even in its humble beginnings, they emphasized, the GCOS stood as a "tribute to man's inventiveness and determination [to overcome] the obstacles of nature" and a signal that the "dawn of a new age" had arrived.[1]

For all of the boilerplate executives used to promote their product on an international scale, GCOS's opening ceremonies pulsated to a provincial beat. In this moment of extraordinary advancement for Canadian petroleum, prairie folksiness was combined with Protestant religiosity to encourage a down-home feel. GCOS's commemorative literature stressed that the project was completed by hundreds of ordinary people who had banded together in a vibrant community that would become a model of multiculturalism. These employees "come from comfortable cities, modest farms, rustic villages," GCOS pamphlets underscored, before noting the presence of former backwoodsmen and Mounties on the company payroll.[2] GCOS also produced a forty-five-minute film called *Athabasca*, which assessed the tar sands project through the lives of two employees. One was Dimitry Silin, a fur trapper who had emigrated to the Canadian North from Siberia. Filmmakers followed him as he trudged through the Athabasca River valley looking for beaver pelts. Through stunning visuals, the movie drove home the message that Silin enjoyed oneness with his environment, that he represented a link to a simpler past now being overtaken by GCOS's industrial might. Instead of steering into some critique of industrialization, though, *Athabasca*'s creators manipulated Silin's testimony so that it testified to their desired truths: that GCOS was every bit as concerned with the environment (and every bit as "one" with it) as Silin, and that its desire to develop Alberta's North was benevolent. Yes, Silin's idyllic realm was about to be civilized, but civilization of the kind GCOS promised embodied the same organic ideals this outdoorsman held dear. The trapper, in other words, need not worry.[3]

The second character on whom moviemakers cast light was the industrialist in charge of the civilizing: J. Howard Pew. If Silin's place in the film illustrated prairie folksiness in the tar sands project, Pew's presence was meant to remind employees that Protestant ethics shaped the entire affair. As the former president of Sun Oil, now chairman of its board of directors (GCOS was Sun Oil's subsidiary), Pew exuded all the refined characteristics of an East Coast elite, and *Athabasca*'s producers made sure to highlight them in stark contrast to Silin's rough edges. Through two years of filming they monitored Pew as he guided Sun Oil in the company's posh Philadelphia headquarters. A devout evangelical Presbyterian, Pew made it known that his company's successes grew out of his commitment to Christ.[4] This conviction was on clear display each time Pew visited Fort McMurray, including on the occasions of GCOS's sod turning in 1964 and dedication in 1967. At the former, Pew stood with Alberta's premier Ernest Manning as the evangelical politician waxed eloquently on GCOS's manifest destiny, before giving way to a Baptist pastor for prayer.[5]

At the latter, more invocations were offered in the same theological discourse Pew used to christen company functions of this sort: "Almighty God, we ask Thy Divine blessing. . . . Protect the efforts of sober and honest industry. . . . Incline the hearts of employers and those whom they employ to mutual forbearance, fairness, and goodwill. May we remember the service and sacrifice of those who have helped build our industry. May Thy guiding spirit continue to be with the officers and employees of our Company that their mutual understanding may be for the betterment of us all."[6] Extracting truths from Pew's life thus proved easy for *Athabasca*'s producers: here was a man whose entrustment of nature's bounties gave meaning to his life; here was a man whose faith in God made the search for black gold something existential, something sacred, something good.

For Pew, of course, such anointing was to be realized on a global stage, and he was hardly alone in his worldview. Indeed, what we see illustrated in the circumstances surrounding the GCOS project speaks to a larger historical truth about evangelical politics in the 1960s as well as about evangelicalism's political place in the modern era: that the business of petroleum and New Evangelicalism share a uniquely strong bond. Like the Pews, countless evangelicals across time and place have seen petroleum as their special providence to be used industriously for the advancement of "His Kingdom" both on American soil and abroad. This sense of custodial care has produced as much angst as hope; in the boom-bust cycles of oil, where crises beget catastrophe, Christian citizens are often reminded that crude can also be a curse. Yet evangelicals, who by virtue of their preponderance in America's oil patches speak as a confident majority, have always understood this trade-off as the price of one's chosen-ness in a fallen world. Whether praying for oil's bounty or for deliverance from its excesses — whether working on their rigs and in their corporate headquarters to maximize oil's proliferation, or in politics to rein it in — they have viewed their place in this sector as special, never doubting the virtues of their quest. All the while they have brought their theology to bear on temporal issues of energy, environment, and governance, and used monies accrued through oil to build sacred empires — churches, schools, and missionary agencies. In deliberate fashion, they have shaped their own "Petrolia" that at once honors God and black gold, a Petrolia over which men like Pew preside.[7]

This is not to say that evangelicals have dictated the course of oil's development, nor is it to suggest that the New Evangelicalism owed its vitality solely to oil. As countless historians have shown, oil is multifaceted. While as an energy source it sets the destinies of cities, suburbs, and indigenous populations, as a commodity it determines market trends on Wall Street, Main Street, and beyond; while as a domestic concern it elicits strong protectionist sentiments—both for and against oil interests—as an international concern it draws some nations together and forces others apart; at once the domain of princes and presidents, oil—"the Prize," as Daniel Yergin deems it—is also a democratic dream for average Americans seeking the good life.[8] Oil, moreover, is highly stratified, with the seven majors nurturing corporate outlooks different from their mid-major and independent competitors, and even within any one company there exist unmeltable divisions between roustabouts and retailers, executives and engineers, meaning religion has no simple purchase on this sector. And as religious historians are apt to point out, "evangelicalism" itself encompasses many persuasions sustained by a host of socioeconomic factors, so to place too much emphasis on one would be misguided. Besides, liberal Protestantism has had much to say about petroleum, too (for every Pew there has been a Rockefeller ready to marshal petro-funds for liberal philanthropic causes), and Catholics and Jews have never been silent either. The marriage of evangelicalism to oil, in short, is neither straightforward nor singular in the unfolding saga of modern industry and religion.[9]

Still, this union *is* uniquely robust and consequential politically. It was so at oil's beginning in the mid-nineteenth century, and it became more so by the 1960s. When writing about the surge of New Evangelical politics in the sixties, in fact, many journalists drew attention to its accord with oil. Especially where the "Petroleum Belt" and "Bible Belt" meet in the "Sunbelt," critics charged, petro-capitalism seemed sanctioned by radical fundamentalists as a conduit for Christ's return, and blessed by God-fearing politicians as the GOP's gift to the nation and America's mission to the world.[10] Whether talking about Barry Goldwater's "conservative conscience" or Ronald Reagan's "creative conservatism," it mattered not: the "Prairie Fire" conservatives sought to unleash on national politics, liberal detractors insisted, was obviously fueled by oil.

As exercises in punditry, most of these appraisals traded in the hyperbole of the backlash interpretation of New Right politics. Rather than see a long history of engagement about matters deeply rooted—literally—in the modern American environment, journalists chose instead to use the marriage of God and black gold as colorful evidence of a parochial, reactionary, and momentary force. Scholars have done very little to correct this tendency, choosing either to ignore the ways in which the New Evangelical Right involved itself in petro-politics, or to focus simply on the more conspicuous dimensions of the "culture wars" that began animating the New Evangelical Right in this decade. Yet, evangelicalism's alignment with oil illustrates a broader political phenomenon that did not start in the 1960s (as backlash interpretations emphasize) but rather began cresting due to decades of steady work in boardrooms, manufacturing plants, and drill sites across the North American West, in the Global South, and around the world.

Indeed, if we look deeper into the lives of four "architects" of the GCOS, we see that the twin forces of oil and evangelicalism have engaged in a much longer and more entwined relationship than any pundit or scholar has imagined. J. Howard Pew stands out for his hands-on role in the project, but three other evangelicals deserve equal mention: Billy Graham, who helped Pew forge friendships with other oil-patch Protestants; Ernest Manning, Alberta's premier who welcomed Graham and Pew's overtures; and R. G. LeTourneau, a manufacturer of large earth-moving equipment who served as a linchpin in the transnational business networks to which all four men belonged. Each represents a distinctive way in which evangelicalism's enchantment with oil produced political effects on an international level. Together they illustrate how evangelicalism's association with this resource has always been a vertically integrated, multinational endeavor that has grown stronger with time.

❖

No one was more instrumental in GCOS's genesis than J. Howard Pew. Granted, the GCOS had been contemplated for decades before Pew entered discussions with checkbook in hand. Karl Clark, a metallurgist at the University of Alberta, began researching the oil sands in the 1920s.[11] After perfecting a hot-water process that facilitated commercial development of this tarlike soil, Clark announced in 1953 that the time had come for a move "by big oil companies."[12] Clark did not have to wait long for a corporate gesture; in fact, Sun Oil was already making its move, acquiring patents and leases and sending geologists into the Athabasca area. Under the guidance of Sun Oil vice president and future GCOS president Clarence Thayer, Sun's interest in Alberta grew steadily. Besides demonstrating a command of oil frontiers, Thayer had helped commercialize the Houdry catalytic cracking process, which placed Sun at the forefront of oil manufacturing in the 1930s, so his opinions were respected at headquarters. At his urging, Pew decided to take the biggest gamble in company history by committing a quarter of a billion dollars to Clark's technology and the creation of GCOS in 1952. Besides breaking company records, this payout represented the "largest single private investment" ever made in Canada.[13] As one Sun insider noted, this "was a daring venture into an un-known field," one that "jolted Wall Street's appraisal of Sun Oil as a conservative company."[14]

Pew's willingness to take such a heavy risk was not so out of character, though, especially considering his family's long ties to wildcatting. Pew was born to Joseph Newton (J.N.) Pew, a "farm boy from Pennsylvania" who grew up in a Presbyterian family that taught him to "pray unashamedly" and weigh his "behavior against the Ten Commandments."[15] At the age of eleven, J.N. grew fascinated with oil speculation in Titusville, just forty miles away, and at the age of twenty he moved to the boomtown to start a gas business. For the next three decades, J.N. and his company floundered in the "oligopolistic environment" ruled by Standard Oil, but in 1901 Sun Oil achieved its breakthrough.[16] Within days of Lucas 1's geyser at Spindletop in Beaumont, Texas, which thrust U.S. oil onto an international stage, J. Edgar Pew, J.N.'s nephew, joined the human deluge of the Gulf of Mexico town, and through the acquisition of numerous drill sites, guaranteed Sun a foothold in this southwestern hub.[17] Over the next few years, Edgar continued to expand Sun's holdings throughout the region, making it competitive even against corporate heavyweights like Texaco and Gulf. By doing so he ensured that his company would always base its operations at the place where the "Bible Belt" met the "Petroleum Belt."

J. Howard was the man responsible for Sun's competitive edge. The young, Cornell-trained engineer assumed chief executive responsibilities in 1912. Joining Howard in the head office was his younger brother, Joseph Pew Jr., who would serve as his right hand for the next fifty years.[18] For most of Howard's presidency, Sun remained a family-run operation, something his father decreed. And his father also set Sun on a conservative fiscal path by resisting debt financing and high-risk ventures. While keeping the company solidly in the black, this strategy prevented it from expanding.[19] Under Howard, Sun became more daring in its outlook, if not in its family-heavy leadership. Between the 1910s and late 1940s, he shaped his domain into a competitive, mid-major oil company whose combination of fiscal responsibility, savvy marketing, and creative manufacturing strategies made it a vital player in the industry. Sun's most dramatic growth came during World War II when it used its new catalytic refining process to make synthetic rubber and aviation gasoline, which proved crucial to the American war effort. Sun Oil's net crude production increased 143 percent during the war years, and by 1947 Sun boasted it had grown by "40 times" since Howard became CEO thirty-five years earlier.[20]

Although resigning as president in 1947, ceding control to Robert Dunlop, the first nonfamily member to hold the post, Howard maintained his authority as director of the board. In many ways, his power increased with the flexibility of his new post, and he used it to broaden his company's reach. Pew worried about an American oil shortage so he instructed Sun to investigate foreign fields.[21] The strategy drove Sun into a sphere of international influence. By the 1960s, it was refining in Canada and Venezuela, marketing its Sunoco products well beyond the U.S. border, carrying a payroll of 20,000 persons worldwide, and operating in every area of the industry, "from drilling and producing through transportation and manufacturing to distribution," making it one of the most successful mid-majors in the "Free World."[22]

Pew also extended his company's reach into politics. Because of his family's deep antipathy toward Standard Oil and its ingrained frontier suspicions of centralized government, a young Howard had internalized the politics of the wildcatter, and they never left him. In the 1930s and 1940s, in a tone that matched his father's in the 1880s and 1890s, he railed against the oil industry's majors that wanted to increase regulations in order to temper fluctuations in pricing, which came with overproduction. Fearful that smaller companies like his would succumb to larger ones that enjoyed economy of scale and price-setting abilities, Pew set out to "democratize" petroleum by helping a number of independent oil associations lobby for deregulated markets and local control. In this same vein, he, along with his brother Joseph, a powerbroker in the Republican Party, played active roles in opposing the New Deal state. Willing, in this instance, to join hands with monopolistic types they opposed in the oil sector, the Pews helped populate the American Liberty League and stir up anti–New Deal sentiment.[23]

Meanwhile, thanks to Sun's inestimable role in national defense during World War II, Pew gained an official voice in Washington, which he used to champion independent oil's political interests abroad. Between 1943 and 1952, as U.S. oil companies looked to the Middle East for new supplies, the federal government and U.S. oil's majors tried to iron out an Anglo-American Petroleum Agreement, which would minimize the ability of British oil companies "to exclude American interests" from their territories and bring an "end to the restrictive provisions of the Red Line Agreement of 1928."[24] Through international cooperation, American and British leaders and oil officials hoped to stabilize the process of exploration, extraction, and production in petroleum's hot zones. For smaller companies, the agreement smacked of collusion, something Pew stressed. He let Senate Foreign Relations Committee members know that the Anglo-American agreement was a "first step in . . . [a] plan for a super-state control covering the petroleum industry in all parts of the world."[25] Pew played no small part in killing this agreement—it would flounder in the late 1940s and die in 1952—nor in ensuring that an aggressively nationalist foreign policy—which, in his mind, best protected the interests of all oil companies— would become ensconced in the American Cold War outlook.[26]

In all of these political endeavors, Pew welcomed the role of watchdog on behalf of the bootstrap, laissez-faire wildcatter, whom he believed embodied

American values' "purest" form. "Nature has been bountiful in the supply of this resource, and we have barely scratched the surface," he charged when speaking out against stricter regulation of petroleum at home and abroad. Why quell individual drive in the present by "preserving supplies of petroleum for the use of generations yet unborn[?]"[27] Echoing independents' nonconformist pleas, he announced that he "didn't want a nurse for his business, nor did he want anyone else to have one."[28] Pew did not want a "nurse" for his church either. Even as he joined forces with independent oilmen to fight centralizing forces in business and government, Pew also joined fundamentalist Protestants in fighting the "monopolizing" tendencies of their liberal counterparts. He saw these fights in parallel terms: in his eyes, preserving the purity of the Protestant church and the purity of oil's founding spirit were the same, since both sought preservation of the uncompromising, pioneering individualism that centered American Christianity and capitalism.[29]

Here too he followed his father's generation. The senior Pew had linked Sun to fundamentalist Protestantism by sending company profits to Dwight L. Moody, the face of orthodoxy in his day, and his employees via company train to Billy Sunday's revivals.[30] Though impressive, J.N.'s assault on modernist trends paled next to those of his contemporary, Lyman Stewart.[31] Like J.N., Stewart caught oil fever in Titusville and joined the rush to drill, though by the mid-1870s he was "dead broke."[32] Imbued with the persistence of the good missionary he dreamed of becoming, Stewart headed to California where his dedication paid off in the form of the Union Oil Company. By 1920 Union owned 800,000 acres of land, produced eighteen million barrels of oil per year, and oversaw a vast network of wells, pipelines, refineries, and service stations.[33] Almost a "major," Union never acquired Standard's status, and Union's president liked it that way, for he saw Standard's founder as the blight on his business and church. As the Rockefellers increased funding for "liberal" Protestant cathedrals, colleges, and pastors, Stewart engaged his competitor in the religious realm. In 1909 he commissioned a treatise defending Protestant orthodoxy, a multivolume collection of articles called *The Fundamentals*, which found a way into millions of homes, seminaries, pulpits, and missionary bases where the battle between fundamentalism and modernism raged. Besides bankrolling this publication, whose precepts would define twentieth-century evangelical conservatism, Stewart funded his own cathedral, college, and pastors.[34] His was a crusade against liberalism that drew no boundary between church, state, and commerce.[35]

In the post–World War II years, J. Howard Pew became the Lyman Stewart of his generation, the petro-capitalist who would finance conservative evangelicalism's defense at home and advance abroad. Internally, he continued his father's pattern of imposing Christian orthodoxy on Sun's corporate culture. When addressing company gatherings, Pew practiced his exegesis: sermons on the origins of the King James Bible or modernist theological trends were staples in his repertoire. His hand in drafting a company creed that championed Christ, capitalism, and patriotism in the context of Cold War petroleum was obvious, as was his influence on corporate literature, which linked Sun's prosperity to providence.[36] Thanks to Howard, such providential assurances colored Sun's global vision as well. Although shaped by an increasingly sophisticated science of oil exploration, Sun's globalization in the mid-twentieth century—like that of American oil generally—never shunned the religious sensibilities of an earlier age. In places like the Middle East, where companies like Aramco vied for the loyalty of Muslim sheiks, God always remained present in the negotiations.[37] Still, few could bring the Bible into foreign dealings like Sun. Calling on their geologists to be "present-day Jeremiahs," prophets willing to sacrifice much to guarantee oil's global advance, the Pews blended the biblical requisites of evangelism with the requirements of the multinational corporation.[38] They sent their "Jeremiahs" into earth's farthest reaches and told them to spread Christian democracy and free-market capitalism even as they searched for the next untapped pool.[39]

Amid this flurry of Christian outreach, Pew found a key ally of singular stature, the "D. L. Moody" of his day: Billy Graham. With fewer company responsibilities holding him back, Howard determined to funnel his energy into conservative causes through the Pew family's new charitable trust. Wanting to match the Rockefeller Foundation's every move, he answered countless requests for aid from church colleges across the South, a region he saw primed for corporate growth, and nurtured economic ties with the nation's leading conservative seminaries, parachurch ministries, businessman associations, and ecumenical organizations such as the National Association of Evangelicals (NAE), the "New Evangelical" clearing house founded in 1943 to offset the Federal Council of Churches.[40] Pew also provided substantial start-up funds for *Christianity Today*, a magazine that New Evangelicals hoped would, like Stewart's *Fundamentals,* offer a strong defense of conservative theological values but in a culturally appealing manner. A cog in these New Evangelical machines, Graham saw Pew as vital to the success of a re-engaged orthodoxy. His courting of the petro-capitalist was in keeping with his own enchantment with black gold. At the moment of his breakthrough during the early Cold War, Graham counted on numerous oilmen for help. While in his ecumenism he networked with Herbert Taylor, a former executive with Sinclair Oil who helped guide the NAE, in his home church (First Baptist in Dallas, Texas) he worshiped with members of the Hunt family and mingled with the Murchisons.[41] Meanwhile, he conversed frequently with Sid Richardson, whose clout gave him inside access to halls of power.[42] In April 1957, the *Ladies Home Journal* profiled the ten richest men in America, which included seven oilmen: Richardson, H. L. Hunt, Clint Murchison, Joseph Pew, John D. Rockefeller III, Paul Mellon, and Howard Hughes.[43] Graham was friend to at least four.

Graham gave as much as he received in this reciprocity. His access to the hearts and minds of Americans helped oil as it sought to redeem itself in the court of public opinion. Since the 1920s at least, average Americans had questioned the "Hobbesian" excesses of the oil industry, pointing to corporate scandals and oil titans' lavish lifestyles as proof.[44] Graham's ability to accentuate the positives in this industry—its throwback values of individual initiative and capitalist drive—proved invaluable. In this formative moment, he counseled titans like Sid Richardson into conversion experiences, then produced movies that told these individuals' salvation stories, one called *Mr. Texas* (1951) and the other *Oiltown, U.S.A* (1953). Thanks to Graham's deft use of popular media, New Evangelicals were thus able to recast petroleum's life story as a redemptive narrative of Christian American exceptionalism. Amid an intensifying Cold War, as conservative Protestants and petro-capitalists latched on to this heartening narrative as justification for a global war against godless communism, the relationship between God and black gold flourished again.[45]

Graham changed more than American hearts and minds, however; his efforts affected oil diplomacy as well, and Sun Oil reaped the rewards. In the early 1960s, as Sun looked more intently at the Athabasca region, Graham and Pew found more reason for friendship. In the fall of 1963 and spring of 1964, Sun officials pressed the Alberta government for permission to mine the oil sands. By now, Canada was central to American oil's foreign outlook.[46] Even as the Middle East captured ever-increasing media attention, U.S. imports from Canadian oil sources rose dramatically, from 4.9 percent of total U.S. oil imports in 1958 to 11.7 percent in 1962. By 1967, U.S. imports from Canada would be 18.7 percent, compared to 8.3 percent from the Middle East.[47] Within this unfolding reality, Alberta's oil sands became evermore appealing. The region's "potential to match Saudi Arabia in volume, if not cost of recovery," and the added benefit "of being more secure politically and strategically" were widely appreciated.[48] Pew knew it was time to act. On several occasions in 1963, Pew and Sun officials visited Fort McMurray to forge a plan whereby the GCOS could become fully operational in the region; the anticipation that had been building since GCOS's creation in 1952 now had its outlet.[49] In November

1963, Sun executives testified before the Alberta Oil and Gas Conservation Board to secure necessary permissions. After promising that the oil sands would not hinder the province's conventional oil production, thriving since the late 1940s, Robert Dunlop highlighted the scale of corporate funds already committed to the project and outlined the terms of purchasing: while Sun would purchase 75 percent of the oil sands' production, Shell Canada Limited would purchase the other 25 percent.[50]

Sun received the desired approval, then moved on to the next round of negotiations with Premier Manning. Throughout the first months of 1964, Manning's office wrestled with Sun over the terms of the GCOS venture. Though enthusiastic, Manning was nervous about how an American company would be received by the rank-and-file Albertan. In one of several letters written from the office of the premier, Manning insisted that Sun's "commercial development of the Athabasca Oil Sands" had to come with concessions: at the very least, a commitment to build a pipeline that suited Alberta's economic and environmental interests, a pledge to hire "local labor . . . as far as it is reasonable and practicable to do so," and most importantly, an agreement that Alberta residents "be accorded an opportunity to purchase up to 15 percent of the initial equity stock of the Company at the same price and on the same terms as those applying to the purchase of such stock by the Sun Oil Company."[51] Albertans, Manning asserted, were not going to give American business a free pass. Sun, in response, hedged, expressing worry that government enjoyed the upper hand. Besides imposing the extra burden of public investors, which added additional risk to an already risky enterprise, the Manning plan also seemed to reduce "Sun's ownership position" and "introduced dangers" by "compromising principles of free enterprise."[52] In summarizing Manning's demands, one Sun official echoed what his colleagues were feeling: "Government is . . . involving themselves in affairs of private enterprise to a peculiar degree in suggesting rearrangement of issued equity that a corporation might consider fits its corporate circumstances. GCOS has authorized 9 million shares, the public knows this, and present shareholders approve. To subscribe to this particular Government observation might imply that GCOS directors would need to check with the Province of Alberta on future issues of shares even now authorized by shareholders."[53] The commentator hoped that his allies could still "impress the free enterprise atmosphere . . . as the project proceeds," but he did not question that the Pews' way clashed with the Province's way.[54]

Between 1964 and early 1965, Sun and Alberta officials continued to negotiate, even as the project moved forward, but relations remained a bit tense: enter Graham and Pew.[55] As developments in the corporate world evolved, exchanges in the church world intensified. With Graham serving as mediator, Pew and Manning began exchanging letters, and soon the correspondence assumed a tone of familiarity that was strengthened by talk about the Bible. In his missives, Pew told of upcoming conferences for Presbyterians and evangelicals, forwarded books for the premier's edification (*Calvin*, by Francois Wendel, and *The Man God Mastered*, by Jean Cadier), and asked if he could use Manning's sermons (no doubt in company settings).[56] Manning responded by sending the sermons, along with thanks for the books, which his son (Preston) was "now perusing with great interest."[57] In another letter the politician encouraged the oilman to continue fighting for the fundamentals. "The need for aroused Christian laymen to take an uncompromising stand for the faith once delivered was never greater than at the present time, particularly in view of the fact that so many pulpits have become mouth-pieces for liberalism and even the outright denial of the divine authorship of Scripture."[58]

Manning's admonitions were in keeping with his spiritual vocation, which was nurtured through years of tireless work in Alberta's Social Credit Party. During the 1920s and 1930s, Manning had come under the mentorship of William "Bible Bill" Aberhart, the charismatic preacher-politician whose populist politics won him the premiership of Alberta. Aberhart was an indomitable force. A fierce proponent of conservative exegetical and prophetic teachings that firmly positioned him on the orthodox side in the raging fundamentalist-modernist controversy of his day, Aberhart did all he could do for the cause by founding a Bible school in Calgary (the Calgary Prophetic Bible Institute), speaking regularly in local churches, and, most importantly, preaching on his radio program, *Back to the Bible Hour*, heard weekly throughout western Canada. Aberhart pursued politics with the same zest, through his Social Credit party, which championed a platform of radical monetary reforms and economic redistribution, anticentralization, local autonomy, and community values, all initiatives that spoke to Alberta's small-town folk during the Great Depression. Aberhart's agenda earned him Alberta's head office, where he served for a decade. Having been educated by Aberhart—both as a regular radio listener and at the Calgary Prophetic Bible Institute—Manning easily slid into leadership positions within the premier's camp. Even prior to Aberhart's 1935 election, Manning could be seen traveling the countryside with the barnstorming politician, junkets that the press referenced when deeming them a father-son team.[59]

After the election, Manning became Alberta's provincial secretary, which placed him at the forefront of Social Credit's proposed economic reforms, and prepared him well for the premiership, which he ascended to in 1943, following

Aberhart's death. For the next two decades, Manning carried Aberhart's tradition on, if in slightly tempered form. As an itinerant preacher he delivered a gospel of evangelical revival in western Canada's pulpits and over its radio waves, and as a politician successfully crusaded on behalf of an ideology that was right-wing in its promotion of local, Christian, family values, but left-leaning in its anticorporate stand. By the early 1960s, when he began corresponding with Pew, Manning had succeeded at trimming the edges off of Social Credit's populism and acclimatizing the party's members to a rising transcontinental conservative mainstream that was more corporate friendly and less caustic in its radicalism. At the same time, he helped steer Alberta evangelicalism out of the cultural margins of the 1920s and 1930s toward the moderate middle, where social responsibility and greater appreciation of government action remained hallmarks of the Canadian way. Indeed, by the 1960s, Manning's brand of western evangelicalism could no longer be labeled by outsiders (those living in eastern Canada especially) as aberrant or merely a troubling American export. By couching orthodox beliefs in a more irenic tone, Manning had helped thrust conservative evangelicalism into the Canadian consciousness as a respected if still minority voice that deserved a fair hearing in the dominant, liberal Protestant discourse of the day.[60]

This shift prepared the way for Manning's dealings, both of the corporate and interdenominational kind, with his American evangelical brethren, including fiscally conservative ones like Pew. Finding that their theology was similar, even if their politics still varied slightly, with Manning maintaining trust in an active government, the two men grew close. In 1964 they shook hands on the shores of the Athabasca River linked not just by business interests but also by "common commitment to Jesus Christ."[61] These two diplomats met again just a few months later, in the more leisurely setting of Jasper, Alberta, a resort town tucked away in the mountains. This time Graham, who kept track of the Pew–Manning accord, joined them, and all three seemed eager to refresh their friendship. Manning had first met Graham while the latter worked with Youth for Christ in the early 1940s, and throughout the 1950s the preacher-turned-politician remained loyal to the star evangelist and the New Evangelicalism he represented. When congregating in Jasper, Manning and Graham surely reminisced even as they schemed a near future when, following Manning's lead, the American would hold revivals in each major Canadian city.[62] It is safe to say that in between golf rounds (Pew scored his age—82—a highlight of his trip), meanwhile, Manning and Pew talked through theology and tar sands, and by all accounts the talks went well.[63] Whatever differences they held politically (which Pew soon found to be minimal), Pew and Manning's soft diplomacy seemed to work—GCOS's dealings with Alberta's government over Athabasca's boggy soil warmed at the very moment these three statesmen met amid the splendors of the Rockies.

There was yet a fourth evangelical statesman who had something vital to add to Alberta's quest for oil—equipment. Besides the fact he had few challengers in the earth-moving business, Robert (R. G.) LeTourneau was perfectly suited to the task. A staunch evangelical businessman who endorsed Graham's New Evangelicalism and Pew's Christian economics, he was from a Canadian family who shared Manning's Prairie Populist sensibilities. LeTourneau's role in the GCOS came late in his life. Born in the 1880s, he was Pew's equal in age, yet it was business politics that drew the two together. During the 1930s he built LeTourneau Incorporated into a leading manufacturer of heavy machinery. Emboldened by his success, LeTourneau also built up a charitable organization through which he distributed profits into evangelistic ministries, and also became active in businessmen's associations supported by Pew. While outside his factory he spoke widely on behalf of the National Association of Manufacturers and free enterprise (and against the New Deal); on behalf of the Christian Business Men's Committee International he championed individual initiative. Inside his factory, meanwhile, he trained his workers in a Christian technical institute. There they learned how Scripture stayed true to laws of mechanics, and how technology explained the human condition; how the laws of traction and torque applied to evangelism, and grades of steel represented stages of Christian growth.[64]

Like the Pews, LeTourneau achieved international influence in the 1940s, preparing him for a key role in New Evangelicalism's ascent. During World War II, LeTourneau's factories (he now had new ones in Georgia and Mississippi) buzzed with activity. Between 1942 and 1945 they turned out seventy-eight new inventions, machinery that carried men ashore at Normandy, carved roads out of jungles in the South Pacific and deserts in North Africa, and dug ditches out of frozen tundra in Alaska. At war's end 70 percent of all heavy earth-moving equipment used by the allies had been built in his plants.[65] In the late 1940s, LeTourneau augmented this success by relocating his base operation to the Sunbelt, centered at a new plant and evangelical technical institute in Longview, Texas. The Longview plant allowed him an international market. In his 88,000 square-foot steel mill, workers produced twenty-five tons of molten steel every three hours, then transported it to the machinery plant where behemoth machines were built for use in the world's largest mines, oil rigs, and dams. Before being shipped to South America and the Middle East, each piece of equipment was tested on the 12,000 acres of proving grounds.[66]

The operation was impressive but not strictly business related; for LeTourneau the massive scale of production promised a massive payoff in religious terms as well. Indeed, as he articulated it while speaking to the 1951 World Trade Conference, the testing he performed on Longview's rusty soil and the machines he exported promised a new order. "God gave us the raw materials to work with for nothing, and there is plenty to be had if we go to work and produce the things we want."[67] By building machines that moved the earth, LeTourneau acted on a theology that told him extracting raw materials from the soil was like extracting truth from the Bible.[68]

LeTourneau fulfilled this maxim in several contexts, all of which made him a vital link between Protestantism and petroleum. In his emerging Sunbelt business community, he helped nurture a culture that celebrated innovative engineering and expanding markets, an internationally focused evangelicalism fueled by the fight with communism and the need for revival before Christ's return, and a fierce political conservatism that encouraged these endeavors. He also expanded LeTourneau Technical Institute, which strove to meet young evangelicals' "spiritual requirements of the modern age; educational demands of a scholastic age; [and] practical needs of a technical age."[69] By 1960, LeTourneau was sending hundreds of graduates to all four corners of the globe. While some stayed to help LeTourneau Inc. design offshore oil rigs for use in the Gulf of Mexico, others began their careers on mission fields LeTourneau himself established. His most successful was in Peru. There, in the late 1950s, LeTourneau reached agreement with the Peruvian president Manuel Odria and Peruvian oilmen, whereby he would complete thirty-one miles of the Trans-Andean Highway, linking the Amazonian hinterland with the Pacific, in exchange for a million acres of uncultivated land. For Odria, the plan promised to open up the hinterland for Mobil and Gulf's Peruvian subsidiaries.[70] Land secured, the engineer-evangelist began leveling forests for Tournavista, a community of natives and missionaries that implemented LeTourneau's plan for a "free," self-sustaining, Christian economy that might be used as a model for "third-world" societies.[71]

Even as he looked to the Global South for opportunities, LeTourneau turned north to his native land. The manufacturer had always been active in Canada, using ties with fellow evangelicals in government to generate large contracts, but GCOS was a project that demanded his special attention, and he eagerly gave it.[72] The industrialist had first visited Edmonton in the late 1940s to address the city's evangelical businessmen; at that time, LeTourneau was already a sensation within evangelical circles as an inspirational speaker who was willing to fly anywhere to sell the gospel of individual salvation, free markets, and a limited state. Still, Ernest Manning helped guarantee a warm, friendly welcome for him on this and subsequent occasions, and through continued co-activism with Billy Graham's ministry and the NAE, Manning and LeTourneau fed a relationship that would last for the rest of their lives.[73] It seemed natural, then, that LeTourneau's equipment made the trip to Alberta in the mid-1960s. By 1965 his scrapers, road tampers, electric shovels, and oversized dump trucks, able to carry eighty-five tons, were carving out seven hundred acres of "muskeg and scrub timber" lining the Athabasca River and GCOS's plant site. By 1966 these same machines, along with hulking bucket-wheel excavators specially designed for the project, were beginning to burrow even deeper, into one hundred feet below the muskeg, glacial boulders, and clay to reach the oil sands.[74] By the point of GCOS's opening in 1967, LeTourneau had quite literally stamped his presence on Alberta's bleakest but richest terrain.

So had LeTourneau's three evangelical allies. Through their executive leadership, evangelical ecumenism, and political power, J. Howard Pew, Billy Graham, and Ernest Manning had shaped a world enterprise from beginning to end. Is it any wonder that the GCOS's opening ceremonies in 1967 pulsated to a Protestant beat? And is it any surprise that this Protestantism reverberated with the confident claims of manifest destiny? When assessing the GCOS for its stockholders, Sun Oil proclaimed, "This venture combines drama (man against nature), daring (the risk of large financial resources), and science (the technology of the operation is itself a fascinating story). It is a pioneering undertaking . . . in more than one respect."[75] LeTourneau could not have said it any better to his students in Longview, nor Pew to his employees in Philadelphia, Manning to his voters in Calgary, and Graham to his parishioners worldwide.

To be sure, the GCOS's sense of evangelical assurance would eventually falter. By the time it entered its third year, GCOS was slumping under the weight of heavy costs due to production difficulties, company financial strains (magnified by Shell second-guessing its own involvement in the GCOS), and Albertans who still demanded their share of the profits. Sun's relations with Alberta's government would remain steady through the 1970s, thanks in part to their continued claims to shared religion. After Manning's retirement in 1968, Sun found a unique rapport with Harry Strom, Manning's successor. A Prairie Populist in Manning's mold, Strom was also a New Evangelical who endorsed Graham's ministry and the Pew worldview. One of his first trips after accepting the premiership was to Washington, D.C., where he attended Richard Nixon's Presidential Prayer Breakfast, an event helped along by Graham and Pew. Strom returned home determined to make his religion count in the political realm. Alberta evangelicals hailed his devotion: "In its new leader the province of Alberta has a man for whom the word 'honor' caries a deeper meaning. The Honorable Harry Edwin Strom, Premier of Alberta, seeks also to honor Jesus Christ."[76] Strom proved loyal to Sun and, in 1970, reduced the level of royalties it was required to pay, thus easing the company's burdens but stirring the wrath of political opponents, who said the act was an "outrageous concession to a subsidiary of a giant multi-national corporation."[77] For their part, Sun officials monitored the backlash, which they attributed to labor unions, and, behind the scenes, negotiated with Strom. In one of the last meetings of his life, Pew convened with Strom in May 1970 at which time Strom stressed he would help GCOS.[78] Even with Strom's aid, GCOS limped forward, suffering from its inability to counter rising production costs and charges from environmentalists that the tar sands project caused ecological disaster. By the 1980s, GCOS would give way to government ownership, and with the added stability would come added success; today the project is more viable than ever, promising a daily output of 2.8 million barrels.[79] But worries over environment persist, so much so that Barack Obama has recently cited the "destructive" Canadian oil sands as reason for withholding approval of a major intercontinental pipeline.[80] Evidently, neither Sun Oil nor its successors has been able to achieve the environmental peace promised Dimitry Silin in 1967.

Despite GCOS's downward trajectory after 1970, its striking ascent prior to this point should remind historians that the relationship between God and black gold has been (and remains) a vital force in modern America's global encounter. Offered abundant power in places where the Petroleum Belt and Bible Belt meet, evangelicals have used it to synchronize their theologies of personal salvation, individual initiative, and stewardship, with the politics of entrepreneurialism, free markets, and easy access to land and its resources. With clear intent they have shaped America's engagement with the world in the "secular" age by finding creases of authority in the "cascade of social, technological, economic, cultural, and political revolutions" that now shape "every dimension of life."[81] By tapping corporate funds and diplomatic channels, they have manipulated machinations of the modern state to further their notions of Christian "traditional values." Yet, contrary to common renderings of modern evangelical politics, these traditional values have always encompassed much more than diktats about home and hearth. For Pew, Graham, Manning, and LeTourneau, the political quest was always about something bigger: the right to extract all of the "bountiful gifts of the great Creator" in ways that affirm their dominion over the earth.[82]

NOTES

1. "GCOS: The Way It Works," *Our Sun* (Autumn 1967), 30, Box 34, Sun Oil Company Collection, Hagley Museum and Library, Wilmington, Delaware (hereafter cited as SOC).

2. "GCOS Is People at Work, *Our Sun* (Autumn 1967), 9, Box 34, SOC.

3. "Film Tells Athabasca Story Through Lives of Two Men," newspaper clipping in Folder 18, Box 641, SOC.

4. Ibid.

5. "Alberta Premier Lauds Athabasca Oil Project," *Sunoco News*, August 1964, Folder 18, Box 641, SOC.

6. These words are illustrative of prayers and sermons Pew offered at company functions throughout his career. This prayer was offered at a company celebration years before GCOS opened its plant, but its same sentiments were heard during Pew's addresses to the company in the months surrounding GCOS's opening. See Sun Oil—Anniversaries—1951—Marcus Hook, Folder 5, Box 639, SOC.

7. These assertions are drawn directly from Darren Dochuk, "Blessed by Oil, Cursed with Crude: God and Black Gold in the Modern Southwest," *Journal of American History* 99 (June 2012): 51–61.

8. Daniel Yergin, *The Prize: The Epic Quest for Oil, Money, and Power* (New York: Simon & Schuster, 1992), 12–16.

9. For further treatment and use of these claims, see Dochuk, "Blessed by Oil, Cursed with Crude," 52–53.

10. Kevin Phillips, *American Theocracy: The Peril and Politics of Radical Religion, Oil, and Borrowed Money in the 21st Century* (New York: Penguin Books, 2006), 42, xiv–xv.

11. "Profiles in Pioneering," *Our Sun* (Autumn 1967), 2, Box 34, SOC; "North American Oil Sands: History of Development, Prospects for the Future," *CRS Report for Congress*, January 17, 2008, 8–9. See also Paul Chastko, *Developing Alberta's Oil Sands, From Karl Clark to Kyoto* (Calgary: University of Calgary Press, 2004).

12. Quoted in "Profiles in Pioneering," 2.

13. Ibid.; "North American Oil Sands: History of Development, Prospects for the Future," 8.

14. Quoted in "Profiles in Pioneering," 2.

15. "J. N. Pew: A Biographical Sketch," *Our Sun: 75th Anniversary Issue* (1961), 11, Sun Oil—75th Anniversary, 1961 Folder, Box 55, SOC.

16. August W. Giebelhaus, *Business and Government in the Oil Industry: A Case Study of Sun Oil, 1876–1945* (Greenwich, CT: JAI Press, 1980), 6–8.

17. "1901–1912: Spindletop and the Rise of Sun," *Our Sun: 75th Anniversary Issue* (1961), 20.

18. Giebelhaus, *Business and Government in the Oil Industry*, 59.

19. Ibid., 60–61.

20. "The Story of Sun," *Our Sun, 75th Anniversary Issue* (1961), 30–33.

21. "Suncor, Inc.: An Account of the First Seventy Years," 7–8, in "Subsidiaries, 1987" Folder, Box 605, SOC [I6810; 6911].

22. Ibid., 32–33.

23. See Kim Phillips-Fein, *Invisible Hands: The Making of the Conservative Movement from the New Deal to Reagan* (New York: Norton, 2009), chaps. 1–4.

24. Stephen J. Randall, *United States Foreign Oil Policy Since World War II: For Profits and Security* (Montreal: McGill-Queen's University Press, 2005), 172–173.

25. Quoted in Randall, *United States Foreign Oil Policy*, 197.

26. Ibid., 173.

27. Quoted in Giebelhaus, *Business and Government in the Oil Industry*, 218; "The Creed We Work By: A Statement of Principles," *Our Sun: 75th Anniversary Issue* (1961), 20; J. Howard Pew, "Management and the Free Market," May 17, 1950, in binder marked "Speeches & Remarks by J. Howard Pew," #54-89, SOC.

28. Roger M. Olien and Diana Davids Olien, *Oil and Ideology: The Cultural Creation of the American Petroleum Industry* (Chapel Hill: University of North Carolina Press, 2000), 204.

29. Dochuk, "Blessed by Oil, Cursed with Crude," 56.

30. Receipt for Pew donation in Box 1, Pew Family Collection, Hagley Museum and Library; "An Album of Sun Memories," *Our Sun, 75th Anniversary Issue* (1961), 34.

31. Robert Martin Krivoshey, "Going Through the Eye of the Needle: The Life of Oil Man Fundamentalist Lyman Stewart, 1840–1923" (PhD diss., University of Chicago, 1973), 16.

32. Lyman Stewart to his children, September 4, 1914, Lyman Stewart Papers, Biola University Library, Biola University, LaMirada, California (hereafter cited as LSP).

33. "Western Securities," *Los Angeles Times*, January 25, 1925, 17; Joseph Ezekiel Pogue, *The Economics of Petroleum* (New York: John Wiley and Sons, 1921), 73; Brendan Pietsch, "Lyman Stewart and the Funding of Fundamentalism," paper delivered at the American Historical Association Annual Meeting, New York, January 2009 (in Dochuk's possession), 1.

34. Jim Killion, "The Script of Fifty-Eight Years on Hope Street: A Pictorial History of the Church of the Open Door," Historical Ephemera, Church of the Open Door Archives, Sierra Madre, California; James O. Henry, "Black Oil & Souls to Win," *The King's Business*, February 1958, 11–41.

35. Lyman Stewart's two-pronged attack on Rockefeller's liberal Protestantism and business practices is detailed in his correspondence with brother Milton Stewart and various allies while they conceived of *The Fundamentals*, in uncatalogued materials, 1909, LSP.

36. "The Creed We Work By: A Statement of Principles," *Our Sun, 75th Anniversary Issue* (1961), 51.

37. See, for instance, Anthony Cave Brown, *Oil, God, and Gold: The Story of Aramco and the Saudi Kings* (New York: Houghton Mifflin, 1999), 12–15.

38. J. Edgar Pew, "The Fifth Dimension in the Oil Industry," Speech to A.A.P.G. Annual Meeting, Houston, Texas, 3 April 1941, J. Edgar Pew's Speeches, A.P.I. Folder, Box 18, SOC.

39. See Dochuk, "Blessed by Oil, Cursed with Crude," 58.

40. Darren Dochuk, *From Bible Belt to Sunbelt: Plain-folk Religion, Grassroots Politics, and the Rise of Evangelical Conservatism* (New York: Norton, 2011), ch. 5.

41. Sarah Hammond, "'God's Business Men': Entrepreneurial Evangelicals in Depression and War" (PhD diss., Yale University, 2010), 207–208.

42. Steven P. Miller, *Billy Graham and the Rise of the Republican South* (Philadelphia: University of Pennsylvania Press, 2009), 70.

43. Margaret Parton, "Who Are America's 10 Richest Men?" *Ladies Home Journal*, April 1957, 72–73, 173–179.

44. Ibid., 23, 36, 171.

45. For fuller treatment of this point, see Darren Dochuk, "Moving Mountains: The Business of Evangelicalism and Extraction in a Liberal Age," in *What's Good for Business: Business and Politics since World War II*, ed. Kim Phillips-Fein and Julian E. Zelizer (New York: Oxford University Press, 2012), 72–90.

46. For a succinct and insightful summary of Canadian-American cooperative ventures in oil, see Paul Chastko, "Anonymity and Ambivalence: The Canadian and American Oil Industries and the Emergence of Continental Oil," *Journal of American History* 99 (June 2012): 166–176.

47. Randall, *United States Foreign Oil Policy*, 282.

48. Ibid., 320.

49. See logbook for "Sunoco Trip #2, Sept. 18–19, 1963," Loose File, Box 35, Series 6, SOC.

50. "New Oil Sands Project May Have Fast Start," *Albertan*, November 26, 1963.

51. Premier Ernest Manning to Mr. D.J. Wilkins, March 9, 1964, Athabasca Tar Sands Project, Great Canadian Oil Sands Correspondence, 1963–1964 Folder, Box 35, Series 6, SOC [5956]. On Manning's view of Alberta oil see http://archives.cbc.ca/science_technology/energy_production/clips/2145/.

52. W. H. Rea to Robert G. Dunlop, September 2, 1964, and Sun memo titled "Investment in GCOS By Albertans," March 30, 1964, Athabasca Tar Sands Project, SOC [6114; 5931].

53. "Memorandum," March 1964, Athabasca Tar Sands Project, SOC [5921].

54. Ibid.

55. "Notes Re Meeting in Sun Aircraft—Quebec City on April 2, 1964—Athabasca Project," Athabasca Tar Sands Project, SOC [5918].

56. J. Howard Pew to Ernest C. Manning, January 4, 1965; J. Howard Pew to Ernest C. Manning, February 23, 1965; and J. Howard Pew to Ernest Manning, March 15, 1965, C-P 1965 Folder, Box 231, J. Howard Pew Papers, Hagley Museum and Library (hereafter cited as JHP).

57. Ernest Manning to J. Howard Pew (via Miss Pauline M. Baker), March 29, 1965, C-P 1965 Folder, Box 231, JHP.

58. Ernest Manning to J. Howard Pew, April 2, 1965, C-P 1965 Folder, Box 231, JHP.

59. Lloyd Mackey, *Ernest Manning: Like Father, Like Son* (Toronto, Ontario: ECW Press, 1997), 17–28.

60. Ibid., 29–35. For an insightful sampling and summary of historical, political, and temperamental differences between Canadian and American evangelicalism see, for instance, David Bebbington, Mark A. Noll, and George A. Rawlyk, eds., *Evangelicalism: Comparative Studies of Popular Protestantism in North America, The British Isles, and Beyond, 1700–1990* (New York: Oxford University Press, 1994).

61. Mackey, *Ernest Manning*, 126.

62. Ibid., 130–131; "Memorandum," Premier of Alberta—Honorable Ernest C. Manning," December 21, 1964, C-P 1965 Folder, Box 231, JHP.

63. Ernest Manning to J. Howard Pew, April 2, 1965, C-P 1965 Folder, Box 231 and June 11, 1965, G 1965 Folder, Box 231, JHP.

64. "Shifting of Load From Traction," *NOW*, February 1, 1962, 2; "Steel to Illustrate A Spiritual Truth," reprinted in *NOW*, September 1971, 1.

65. "Invasion," *NOW*, December 8, 1944, 1.

66. R. G. LeTourneau, *Mover of Men and Mountains: The Autobiography of R. G. LeTourneau* (Upper Saddle River, NJ: Prentice Hall, 1960), 242; "Building the Alcan Highway," *NOW*, January 14, 1944, 1–3.

67. LeTourneau, *Mover of Men and Mountains*, 245.

68. This brief analysis of LeTourneau's business ventures in midcentury draws directly from Dochuk, "Moving Mountains," 75–85.

69. See "LeTourneau College," *NOW*, May 1, 1962, 1.

70. James C. LeTourneau to Mr. M. C. Gleter, August 24, 1961, Mobile Oil Company Del Peru, 1961 Folder, Box JFE; Roy LeTourneau to Mr. R. G. LeTourneau, December 21, 1959, Letters from Roy LeTourneau—1959 Folder, Box BG; Roy LeTourneau to Sterling Stephens, July 1, 1960, Letters from Peru—1960 Folder, Box BG, in R. G. LeTourneau Collection, LeTourneau University Archives, Longview, Texas (hereafter cited as RGLC).

71. "Peru," *NOW*, February 1, 1962, 3; "Feeding the Billions," *NOW*, September 15, 1961, 1.

72. See, for instance, 1950s and 1960s correspondence between R. G. LeTourneau and P. A. Gaglardi, British Columbia's minister of highways, in Mr. P. A. Gaglardi Folder, Box FIT, RGLC.

73. Ernest Manning to R. G. LeTourneau, April 18, 1945, Premier Correspondence, premier Ernest Manning Papers, Alberta Museum and Archives, Edmonton, Alberta.

74. "Athabasca: One Year to Completion," *Canadian Petroleum*, September 1966, 43–45.

75. "Athabasca Press Conference Proposal," Athabasca Tar Sands Project, SOC.

76. "Meet Alberta's New Premier," *Power for Living*, May 3, 1970, 7, attached to correspondence between W. S. Woods Jr. and Robert Dunlop, July 21, 1970, Great Canadian Oil Sands, Ltd., 1970 Folder, Box 36, Series 6, SOC.

77. See Robert Dunop to Honorable Harry Strom, June 12, 1960, and "Notley Raps Royalty Reduction," July 2, 1970, untitled clipping, in Great Canadian Oil Sands, Ltd., SOC [16559].

78. F. O'Sullivan to Robert Dunlop, July 9, 1970, Great Canadian Oil Sands, Ltd., SOC [16547; 6550]; Memorandum of Meeting, April 28, 1970, labeled "Confidential," Great Canadian Oil Sands, Ltd., 1971 Folder, Box 36, Series 6, SOC [16667].

79. Mark Humphries, CRS Report for Congress: "North American Oil Sands: History of Development, Prospects for the Future," January 17, 2008.

80. See Sheldon Alberts, "U.S. President Obama Cites 'Destructive' Canadian Oilsands, Hints at Withholding Approval of Keystone Pipeline," *Vancouver Sun*, April 7, 2011, 1.

81. Walter Russell Mead, *God and Gold: Britain, America, and the Making of the Modern World* (New York: Alfred A. Knopf, 2007), 274.

82. Dochuk, "Moving Mountains," 81.

3

A Revolutionary Mission

Young Evangelicals and
the Language of the Sixties

EILEEN LUHR

Historical accounts of the 1960s frequently place young people at the center of reform and opposition movements. Yet college-age evangelicals seldom occupy the central role in narratives about the civil rights movement, urban riots, the Vietnam War, student protests, and liberation movements. So it is surprising that in October 1967, Biola College purchased an ad in *Campus Life*, the magazine for Youth for Christ. Biola's advertisement, titled "REVOLUTION," featured an illustration of a small mob, including a main figure carrying a lit torch, standing before what appeared to be a city block engulfed in flames. The subtitle asked, "Are you ready for it?" The copy alluded to recent uprisings in the United States and around the world: "In Chicago, Detroit, Berkeley, across the nation and around the world, it's happening—the social revolution," which was attacking the "status quo" in "city slums, universities, even in churches."

At this point, the message turned against the "revolution," stating "some causes may be noble, but the methods are doubtful, the outcome frightful." Biola—that is, the Bible Institute of Los Angeles, a school established amid the fundamentalist controversy and located just fifteen miles from the site of the

Figure 1. An image from a 1967 Biola advertisement invoked the language of revolution. (*Campus Life*, October 1967, p. 27)

Watts riots—was aware that its prospective students might be excited by the notion of change, yet it sought to limit the methods. Whereas the first half of the ad spoke excitedly about upheaval, the second half promised to channel energies toward individual transformation. Rather than encouraging its students to engage in unpredictable—and potentially "frightful"—revolution, Biola instead vowed to mold students into "a dynamic force that can help change the world."[1]

The term "revolution" was among the most contested terms of a decade dominated by struggles over rights, meanings, values, and symbols. The Biola ad demonstrates that evangelicals found inspiration in this atmosphere of change and sought to insert their definition of "revolution" into the cultural discussion. While acknowledging young people's efforts to challenge the "status quo," the Biola advertisement ultimately struggled to reconcile structural assaults on existing powers with the promise of personal transformation through spiritual growth. Biola's advertisement thus captures the ambivalence of conservative evangelicals toward national and global events during the late sixties.

This chapter compares the language deployed in two youth-oriented publications—*Campus Life* and the *Hollywood Free Paper*—as a means for exploring the central tension between structural change and personal conversion among young believers during the 1960s. The magazines occupied different positions within evangelicalism, yet they each delimited a range of acceptable change. Rather than creating a new vocabulary, each youth-targeted magazine seized upon the iconic language of the era to describe the promise of personal transformation through spiritual growth and overseas mission work. In these publications, "revolution" and "liberation" could exist only as internal events of the soul, never as structural changes to society. Nevertheless, these negotiations suggest that evangelicals, far from condemning the sixties, sought to engage with—but also strictly limit—the social, political, and cultural transformations of the era.

The term "revolution" connoted a diverse range of international and domestic meanings during the '60s. In its clearest sense, revolution meant a political overthrow of an existing government, as when nationalist groups invoked the term as they sought to throw off the yoke of colonial powers. Yet an ideological understanding of the term requires us to understand it in cultural as well as political terms. Beth Bailey explains, "revolution" served as a metaphor that allowed a "diverse set of changes" to be described under a single term, with the result being that "Americans conflated changes that had different origins, intentions, and outcomes."[2]

Factions within the domestic student movement contested the meaning of "revolution" and similar terms throughout the decade. The vocabulary of change permeated the speeches, slogans, newspapers, and songs that inspired its members. Since activists disagreed whether change should begin with political and economic change or with personal freedom, factions defined the term differently. The Port Huron Statement, for example, promised students "participatory democracy," a term, as James Miller notes, with limited value as "an analytical tool" but one that possessed rhetorical "resonance," "elasticity," and, ultimately, "instability."[3] New Left historians, such as Todd Gitlin, note that activists initially sought liberal goals of "self-definition" and "self-determination" against "forces of management" before language shifted from "protest" to "resistance" and, finally—as frustrations mounted and militancy prevailed—to radicalized "revolution."[4] The yippies Jerry Rubin and Abbie Hoffman sought change via cultural means by publishing books with "revolution" in the title.[5] Young African Americans also used the term, as when H. Rap Brown of the Student Non-Violent Coordinating Committee declared in 1967 that America was on "the eve of a black revolution," and the Black Panthers considered themselves to be a revolutionary party seeking domestic black liberation amid a broader series of Third World revolutions.[6] Still later, the term acquired additional cultural meaning as it became associated with sexual liberation movements.

Recent research has expanded the scope of those enthusiastic about dramatic change beyond those who embraced the cause of structural reform. In *The Conquest of Cool*, Thomas Frank argues that American capitalism—in the form of Madison Avenue marketers—was "as dynamic a force in its own way as the revolutionary youth movements of the period" as it sought to transform its operations and self-imagination.[7] When the sixties are recast more broadly, young evangelicals' enthusiasm for transformation becomes a critical piece of the decade. The contested meaning of terms like "revolution" offers further evidence that student movements were primarily an existentialist search for self-meaning and only secondarily a leftist attempt at structural change.[8] Concepts of transformation—not just "revolution" but also "direct action," "liberation," "self-definition," and "self-determination"—appealed to young evangelicals who sought to articulate their beliefs in ways that differentiated themselves from their elders. Many of these ideas eventually crystallized into an evangelical New Left movement (described by David Swartz later in chapter 10, this volume). Nevertheless, the early and frequent engagement with "radical" terms among established evangelical publications like *Campus Life* as well as upstart broadsides such as the *Hollywood Free Paper* shows that political progressives did not hold a monopoly over youth, reform, or rebellion.[9]

The evangelicals under examination in this chapter admired and echoed the language of liberation and revolution, but they seldom sought to align themselves with the era's progressive political or cultural movements. Yet they shared a sense of idealism, moral clarity, and individualism, as well as a sense of youth agency. Additionally, the rhetoric of transformation had the power to mobilize and revitalize believers. Moreover, young evangelicals argued that they, as emissaries of God, were the agents of true, positive, and—in the words of the Biola ad—"dynamic" change in the world.

The language of revolution and liberation resonated with young evangelicals' understanding of the rate, cause, direction, and consequences of personal and historical improvement. Terms like "revolution" indicated a new direction and quickened rate of change in history. Revolution—like religious conviction—could be advanced through exhortation, it often occurred suddenly, and it denoted a dramatic reorientation and creation of an entirely new world-view. In keeping with evangelical rhetorical tradition, "revolution" denoted a marginalized outsider's distance from (and eventual restoration to) the seat of power. And yet there remained a critical difference: a political or social revolution might result, in a Marxist sense, from a heightened set of historic contradictions, or it might result from an imposed political or social change. In the publications under examination, however, revolution resulted from internal conviction. Among existing believers, the term suggested a call for a renewal of evangelical mission and the possibility of a radical re-evaluation of the meaning of living a religious life.

The Pedagogy of Young America

During the early Cold War, Billy Graham, the first full-time evangelist for the interdenominational group Youth for Christ International, became closely identified with youth ministry. This group reached out to young evangelicals through domestic and international crusades, high school and campus activism, annual meetings, and youth-targeted magazines like *Campus Life*. Like Graham, the magazine sought to shape a new generation that might exert great influence around the globe through youthful optimism paired with Christian devotion. The key personnel for the magazine during this period, in fact, became influential leaders in the larger evangelical world when their teen audience had become adults. Harold Myra, the magazine's editor during the 1960s, later became the publisher of *Christianity Today*, and Philip Yancey, who edited the magazine during the 1970s, subsequently became an influential evangelical author. Their assumed audience grew up in conservative Christian faiths in middle-class, white households. The magazine believed it needed to interpret national and world events for this audience, whom the magazine often addressed as "Young Americans." Its message conveyed a sense of engagement but also included a sense of responsibility—at one point coined "teenitiative"—for world and social conditions.[10]

The magazine proceeded from the assumption that all social change derived from individual conversion. In 1971 the magazine explained its vision of reform in a special forum: "*Campus Life* asserts that we can reach for genuine heroism in a vast drama of good vs. evil which we are all (whether we know it or not) participating in. We assert that we must go beyond protesting bigotry and hypocrisy, that there is a radical Christian life-style upon which we can build—changing individuals, and therefore society itself."[11] This understanding of world events gave Christians agency even if the ultimate outcome of those events remained uncertain.

Articles presumed that the magazine was shaping the minds of a new generation of Christian leadership who needed to take an interest in American and world affairs. As early as 1958, the magazine added a feature called "Global Countdown" that drew youths' attention to transformations of the day. A few years later, the magazine included a regular feature titled "Wake Up to Your World," which sought to bring a "Christian" perspective of the world to young evangelicals who were, as the title suggests, becoming aware of their expected place in the world. And that place involved a role in epic global and eternal dramas that aligned evangelicals with Cold War notions of "benevolent supremacy."[12] In a 1971 article about the Middle East, the editors explained to readers, "We are infiltrators in a fallen world working for the true Leader of the planet against the Evil Usurper. Each of us has the potential to contribute toward God or the Enemy. And even though we don't always have the General's battle plans, as individuals we must wrestle in God's power against evil forces."[13] Here the magazine set individual Christian action within a teleological divine drama, thus recalling the pervasive sense of obligation for world mission among earlier evangelicals.[14]

In keeping with the evangelical belief in the power of one-on-one witnessing, the magazine often introduced its readers to foreign cultures through individual stories of salvation. The language was less about embracing revolution so much as it was about quelling global chaos through personal witness. The articles reflected a growing concern for understanding other cultures and the transformational possibilities resulting from conversion.[15] At the same time, the idea of transformation aligned evangelism with American Cold War foreign policy objectives that, according to the historian Christina Klein, imagined international cooperation (i.e., "integration") through economic and political as well as sentimental and cultural means.[16] Readers learned about the other parts of the world through individual first-person parables that taught the fruitlessness of social rebellion: readers learned about India through the testimony of a South Asian student (and former rock musician) who had become an active participant in Youth for Christ meetings and about "Red China"—the United States' "No. 1 enemy," according to the article—through a Wheaton College junior who arrived in the United States in 1957.[17]

Some first-person narratives sought to show students the impact of effective witness. In 1968, the magazine published a first-person narrative titled "The Desperate Will Take Arms." The Peruvian author, raised in poverty, claimed to have been radicalized by Marxist professors before working in a laboratory with an American Christian chemistry student. After months of individual witness, the student went from advocating "a change of structure and power" for Peruvian peasants to having a born-again experience, which brought him a sense of "tranquility" and "peace."[18] The author's desire for social justice, meanwhile, faded into the background. In the story, the combination of the Bible and religious mentoring by a college-age student from North America served as an antidote to Third World revolution. The message thus aligned with the magazine's goal of inspiring individual Christian activism through Christian witness. The social conditions of a particular location mattered insofar as they offered proselytizers an empathetic entry point into individual minds; the goal of mission work, however, was to achieve spiritual, not economic, amelioration.

In addition to presenting accounts of simmering communist threats, articles repeatedly presented readers with examples of American cultural hegemony. These features emphasized the need for readers to take an active interest in other cultures and demonstrated the magazine's proclivity for blending teleology and youth agency. *Campus Life* also co-sponsored "Wake Up to Your World"–tours of Europe and the Holy Land for students aged fifteen to twenty who were "anxious to relate their faith to an exploding world"; the tours promised participants that they would "see the people as they live and work."[19] Things did not always go as planned. The first tour of the Middle East—scheduled to tour Rome, Beirut, Damascus, Cairo, Jerusalem, Hebron, Bethlehem, Jericho, Tel Aviv, and Athens during June 1967—began days after the Six-Day War; students were re-routed to what the magazine described as "New Testament cities of Greece and Turkey" followed by "Reformation highlights" of a few European nations.[20] Undeterred, the following year a tour of Israel promised tourists they would see the "scene of recent warfare" while also traveling through "the dark and winding corridors of Christian history, lit only by the Bible." The tour promised to help participants deepen their understanding of "the prophetic significance of recent events" and the "new political boundaries in the Middle East."[21]

Consistent with evangelical traditions of voluntarism, *Campus Life* believed that evangelical activists had to choose to become activists. Yet despite calls for individual action abroad, the magazine's belief in self-transformation complicated reflexive anticommunism. Two types of articles about the war in Vietnam exemplify this outlook. In the first type of story, the editors challenged young evangelicals' views of the war in Vietnam. One article, written by the magazine's editor in 1966, featured a picture of a young Vietnamese boy with a headline that read, "Hate this Boy!" Despite the title, the article sought to

Figure 2. *Campus Life*'s "Wake Up to Your World" tours sought to generate youths' interest in the world around them. (*Campus Life*, November 1967, p. 5)

humanize the student by describing the boy's age and his possible life experiences. The real point of the article, however, was to ruminate on evil, choice, and patriotism. The article asked readers, "How do we reconcile our patriotism and desire for America's victory in its fight for freedom with the command of Christ to *love* our enemies?" This question captured the editorial board's basic belief in the nation's intrinsic "goodness" on the one hand and its discomfort with a completely externalized "Evil" on the other hand.[22] As a result of this outlook on evil and sin, the editorial board of the magazine became skeptical of the war at about the same time as their counterparts in the New Left.

The second type of story demonstrates that evangelicals were open to cultural and religious interventions abroad that were in line with efforts to put "faith into action." The need for individual conversion required intensive mission work, an endeavor that suggested American cultural and religious leadership; mission work also sought to proselytize based on the liberal ethic of "choice." Moreover, young Americans were assured of the righteousness of their endeavor. One 1966 article urging more intensive mission work abroad noted, "The U.S. may have its faults, and you know that some bad is mixed in with the good, but in Christ, you are sure the war you are waging is righteous, and you're sure of victory over the enemy."[23] In July 1966 the magazine published a story about a young American missionary in Vietnam. At the end of the interview, the missionary lamented the "lack of personnel in this battle against Evil"—citing examples of individual vice such as sin, vice, and prostitution rather than murder—and, using a military metaphor, noted that it would take "personnel" to "[win] the battle for Jesus Christ."[24] Another article, "Tourists on the Edge," offered a man's reflections about a trip with his wife to Vietnam and his lament that Americans arriving in Southeast Asia were military, not missionary, recruits. As in other pieces, the article concluded with a call to action; the author vowed never to be an "onlooker, a spiritual 'tourist' enjoying his ease while others die in battle. I must be a participant, tangibly involved in these days of responsibility and opportunity for the cause of freedom and the cause of Christ!"[25]

Just as the magazine saw opportunity in changes that occurred abroad, it also viewed domestic movements as a chance for activism. In line with secular activists who believed direct action might change political and economic institutions, *Campus Life* created a usable past of Christians as authentic world revolutionaries. For example, an October 1970 forum began by stating that "Christians, of all people, shouldn't be afraid of revolution," since the first Christians led a "spiritual revolution." Nevertheless, the article suggested, the modern Christian "finds himself in a world of many revolutions which he did not make."[26] A major piece of the reinvention of revolution involved reimagining Jesus as a revolutionary figure while excising rebellion from his actions. In a 1966 article titled "The Tallest Placard," Gordon Maclean described a masculine Jesus who supported an activist faith. Maclean complained of contemporary portraits of Jesus that made him appear to be a "weak, mild, emaciated individual desperately in need of some vitamins, if not Geritol!" In contrast, Maclean envisioned a Jesus who was "a real man" who became the "greatest Revolutionary history has ever known." Maclean never defined "revolutionary," choosing instead to explain with examples that suggested the wrongheadedness of contemporary reform movements. Jesus, according to Maclean, "declared that man's basic problems do not stem from his color, environment, or educational inadequacies" but rather their "corrupt innate nature," a problem that could not be solved by "psychotherapy, a better standard of living or a higher culture."[27] Maclean's "revolutionary" Jesus, like the young Christian men he sought to inspire, exhibited masculine and individualistic traits while maintaining a high level of individual piety.

At other times, the magazine drew inspiration from radical groups in lamenting their own inaction. In November 1968, the magazine opened its election preview edition with an article titled "Change the System," which expressed disgust with the political and social options presented to the nation. Addressing its readers, the opening editorial stated, "Sure, you want to affect [the] world . . . maybe even change [its] systems. But you have to have something to offer."[28] While using student activists' language of "system," the board remained focused on positive individual action rather than protest. In another section, the magazine conducted interviews with Christian students from eight states regarding their desire to be involved in reform efforts. A question about the yippies—who by then had helped stage student protests at the 1968 Democratic National Convention in Chicago—prompted one student to acknowledge an activism gap: after criticizing Christian complacency, he noted that the yippies were activists "the way we should be activists for Christ. The hippies haven't changed a thing by sitting around, and Christians aren't going to change a thing by sitting around either." Even with reservations, these comments suggest admiration for activism that sought to bring about change.[29]

Revolutionizing Jesus: The *Hollywood Free Paper*

By the time *Campus Life* asked young Christians about yippies and hippies, a new cohort of young Christians had already started to fuse evangelicalism and countercultural ideas. Beginning in 1967, areas such as the Haight-Ashbury district and the Sunset Strip witnessed an explosion of youth religiosity that became known as the Jesus Movement. This religiosity manifested itself in Jesus music as well as the proliferation of coffee shops and, eventually, print culture like the *Hollywood Free Paper* (*HFP*). The spiritual turn, which also included explorations of Eastern religions, allowed disillusioned youths to focus on transformation of the self rather than social structures.[30] The Jesus Movement, moreover, drew many converts from members of the counterculture who had turned away from politics and to explore the experiential and transformative possibilities of drug use.

Whereas *Campus Life* wrote from a confident mainstream evangelical position, the *HFP* presented religious conservatives as a righteous minority marginalized by established powers. In this respect, although the paper shared some beliefs in common with youth-oriented evangelical publications like *Campus Life*, the paper owed a debt to the free newsweeklies founded as a skeptical, adversarial alternative to mainstream media outlets.[31] Looking for a way to bring youthful outcasts into religious devotion, the evangelical entrepreneur Duane Pederson seized upon the format and published the first issue of the *HFP* in October 1969.

If *Campus Life* sought to pursue specific transformation through individual action in discrete situations, the *HFP* sought to capture the implicit energy in the rhetoric of revolution. It's not that conservatism did not offer a vocabulary of anger: in 1964 Barry Goldwater had defiantly noted, "Extremism in the pursuit of liberty is no vice"; William F. Buckley countered what he considered to be liberal elitism by establishing the Young Americans for Freedom; and legions of "suburban warriors" organized coffee klatches to stop the twin threats of communism and big government.[32] But the language at work in the *HFP* was not the language of anticommunism or white flight. It was the language of revolution—albeit one that required an overthrow of the self rather than society.

Underground Christian papers like the *HFP* offer insight into the continued redefinition of "revolution" in the late 1960s. By that time, the People's Labor Party had seized control of SDS, and activists began to speak about "revolutionizing youth."[33] Todd Gitlin recalled the heightened rhetoric of the decade's days of rage, when revolution emerged as the "supreme talisman" of the movement.[34] The Jesus people, too, found inspiration in the language of revolution: the dramatic universal sweep of historical events, the guaranteed global impact of its effects, the clarity of purpose among its proponents, and—finally—the narrow view of those who doubted the cause, especially those identified with "the Establishment" and the status quo.

Although critical of the actions taken by student radicals, evangelical centrists rarely accused secular activists of willfully oppressing evangelicals. The *HFP*, on the other hand, routinely published accounts suggesting ways that evangelists had been slighted, marginalized, harassed, or repressed by government officials or campus radicals. In adapting this "outsider" rhetoric, they drew upon long-standing Judeo-Christian traditions of apocalyptic prophecy, dissent, and deliverance articulated by a "righteous remnant."[35]

Yippies fulminated against establishment forces, but flamboyantly militant language could also serve the purposes of Christians with fears about persecution from power structures. For example, as the Jesus Movement flourished throughout Southern California, converts began holding Bible studies not just in churches or coffee houses but also at private homes; in fact, the *HFP* classifieds provided a weekly index of nightly Bible studies available to young believers. In early 1970, officials in Glendale closed down one such meeting for violating county zoning ordinances.[36] The paper responded in anger, concluding "You can throw a beer-bust, a pot-party, or a swingin' sex orgy—but you can't have a prayer meeting in your home! . . . Is America the America our founding fathers meant for it to be or have we allowed it to slip from us?"[37] In this instance the paper suggested that they had been wrongfully dispossessed of their rights. In the same issue, the paper published an "open letter" to "the American Establishment and those in high office" that made further claims of persecution. The editors sought an investigation into the "extreme cruelties inflicted on our people by recent court decisions and civilian actions."[38]

Features in *Campus Life* generally sought to explain political and international situations in order to render a "Christian" vantage point. As the events of the 1960s pushed people like Tom Hayden, in the words of the historian James Miller, "beyond the pale of respectable dissent, embracing a defiant, often apocalyptic kind of rhetoric," the *HFP* followed suit. The publishers of the *Hollywood Free Paper*, in fact, thrived on confrontation and accusation, whether with the government or other young activists. In another "open letter" to the "Attorneys and Friends of the Chicago Conspirators," an unnamed author went on a brutal tear against the establishment:

> The CHICAGO CONSPIRACY has blown our minds. Are we going to allow this to continue? Or are we going to become true revolutionaries? Not just "re-acting" to issues forced down our throats by a corrupt establishment. But, by taking "ACTION" And Seize the Time!!!
>
> Have we forgotten what history tells us about the Greatest of all revolutionaries? How HE was conspired against—found guilty of ridiculous crimes dreamed up by the establishment just to have HIM locked-up, shut-up and

finally killed—dying wasn't enough—the soldiers guarding HIS dead body had to plunge their shining swords into HIS belly . . . just to make sure!

But HIS death is VICTORY! WHY? Because three days later HE proved HIMSELF *to be* the revolutionary HE said HE was!

TODAY HIS REVOLUTIONIZING SPIRIT STILL EXISTS!

Become REVOLUTIONIZED! Right now, say "Jesus, come into me and revolutionize me! Talk to my spirit and cause me to take positive ACTION!"

Welcome to God's Forever Family.

ALL POWER THROUGH JESUS![39]

The piece offers a familiar pattern of engagement with leftist political activists: although echoing the anger at a corrupt system and expressing amazement at the action initiated by the New Left, the *Hollywood Free Paper* ultimately failed to align itself with revolutionary, liberationist, or even progressive politics. The paper sought not to engineer a radical reorganization of politics and society but rather to reorient every individual with the "revolutionizing spirit" of Jesus.

The same movement that echoed the language of contemporary youth culture and social reform also offered the broadest condemnations of it. *HFP* writers cared little about placing events in historic or contextual terms of any kind. The paper sought out broad audiences to preach withdrawal, and it followed a range of '60s-style activism, from student marches and speech platforms to countercultural hangouts to claims of government repression, to disseminate its message.

Although the *HFP* repeatedly denounced New Left members, the paper's tactics paralleled those of the decade's savviest media activists, the yippies. The journalist Abe Peck explains that the yippies formulated their media activism by using "symbols—music, clothing, drugs, energy—that spoke directly to the constituency they wanted to reach."[40] Similarly, the *HFP* prided itself on its seeming command of countercultural styles and argot in a triumph of the new style of "relational ministry." In one example, illustrators mimicked an iconic R. Crumb drawing to tell readers to "Keep on Truckin' for Jesus."[41] Despite the paper's suspicion of authority, its full-page illustrations offered hopeful (and universal) sentiments for unity and peace—achievable through Christianity— that still appealed to young people in the latter days of the era. While student activists venerated Third World revolutionaries, members of the Jesus Movement posited Jesus as a parallel revolutionary. In the first issue, the paper published a copy of a "Wanted: Jesus Christ" poster that had become popular among young people.[42] As the language of the era moved from "revolution" to "liberation," so, too, did the paper's description of Jesus morph from "revolutionary" to "liberator."[43]

Figure 3. As the language of the 1960s changed from "revolution" to "liberation," the *Hollywood Free Paper*'s description of Jesus morphed from "revolutionary" to "liberator." (Duane Pederson Collection, Archives, David Allan Hubbard Library, Fuller Theological Seminary, Pasadena, CA)

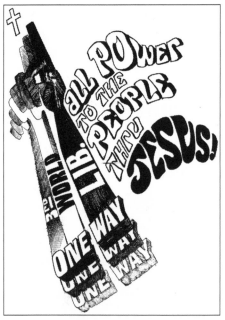

Figure 4. The *Hollywood Free Paper* seized the militancy of black radicals by closing articles with a take off on a phrase "All Power to the People" popularized by the Black Panthers. (Duane Pederson Collection, Archives, David Allan Hubbard Library, Fuller Theological Seminary, Pasadena, CA)

The paper's engagement with the language and imagery of the Black Panthers best illuminates its simultaneous admiration and critique of activism. For example, articles intended to mobilize believers closed with the cry, "JESUS PEOPLE UNITE! ALL POWER THROUGH JESUS!"[44] By closing articles with a take off on the phrase "All Power to the People," popularized by the Black Panthers, the paper seized the militancy of black radicals while limiting the sentiment and solution in significant ways. In January 1971 the paper featured another full-page poster with the slogan, this time with multiple-shaded "One Way" fists that also combined to read "3rd World Liberation."[45] The paper solidified the militant sentiment with black armbands and headbands that proclaimed "Jesus" on sale in the publication's marketplace section.[46]

Whereas the appropriation of Black Panther imagery indicated a degree of admiration, the *HFP* directly confronted peace activists. The disdain may have arisen from confrontations with students; the paper's classifieds regularly noted "Free Speech" times at southern California universities such as Cal State Los Angeles (CSULA) and UCLA, as well as local community colleges.[47] Several cartoons published in 1971 show how the paper viewed these interventions. One cartoon, which appeared just two weeks after the Kent State shootings, showed student radicals who, having tied an administrator to a burning stake, had turned on a Christian witnessing atop a platform labeled "Cal-State Free Speech Platform." The word "freedom" had an asterisk with further explanation: "freedom" meant "freedom to do whatever you want as long as you're not Christian, and you agree with us."[48]

In another drawing, which adorned the paper's cover asking "How Moral is War" in May 1971, two student protesters holding bricks and picket signs—and backed by a faceless crowd with raised fists as well as "Women's Lib" and "Stop the War" signs—confront a smiling Christian and ask whether he had been a peace activist. A building labeled "Blank of America" points to the arson attack in Santa Barbara in 1970. The protesters ask a young man if they recognized him from the protests of 1969. The young man responds, "For Sure!. . . But that was before I found real peace in Jesus!"[49]

Although the *HFP* mimicked the tone of the underground weeklies, the same weeklies—as well as the movements that inspired them—came under sharp criticism from the *HFP* for their inability to solve social and cultural problems. Structural problems were, in fact, unsolvable without human regeneration. In fact, like their more centrist evangelical counterparts at *Campus Life*, the writers for the *Hollywood Free Paper* asserted that human sin was the cause of social ills; unlike *Campus Life*, the *HFP* lacked optimism about youth agency or the desire to work within established powers.

Figure 5. The *Hollywood Free Paper* confronted student activists in cover illustrations that depicted Christians as victims. (Duane Pederson Collection, Archives, David Allan Hubbard Library, Fuller Theological Seminary, Pasadena, CA)

Figure 6. The *Hollywood Free Paper* suggested that only Jesus could bring about peace. (Duane Pederson Collection, Archives, David Allan Hubbard Library, Fuller Theological Seminary, Pasadena, CA)

Conclusion

During the 1960s and early 1970s, the language of revolution permeated American discourse. Young evangelicals, like their counterparts in campus movements, found inspiration in the connotations of change, yet their definition of revolution and change varied. Yet, in line with the theme of "revisiting the backlash," evangelical engagement with "revolution" demonstrates that there was a time when conservative Christians were not so afraid of change. Indeed, the engagement with the language of the sixties *Campus Life* and the *Hollywood Free Paper* demonstrates considerable flexibility and, at times, optimism about the direction of contemporary events. At the same time, convinced of the need for American and Christian leadership in the world, evangelicals also attempted to confine the meaning of change and revolution along spiritual lines. By examining evangelical views about the language of transformation, this chapter complicates the understanding of evangelical Christianity within, rather than outside, the historical trajectory of the sixties.

NOTES

1. "Revolution," *Campus Life*, October 1967, 27.

2. Beth Bailey, *Sex in the Heartland* (Cambridge, MA: Harvard University Press, 1999), 2.

3. James Miller, *Democracy Is in the Streets: From Port Huron to the Siege of Chicago* (New York: Simon & Schuster, 1987), 142, 152.

4. Todd Gitlin, *The Sixties: Years of Hope, Days of Rage* (New York: Bantam Books, 1987), 185, 282.

5. Both Abbie Hoffman and Jerry Rubin were known for their manipulation of the media. Hoffman published *Revolution for the Hell of It* in 1968, and Rubin, in addition to appearing in a Revolutionary War outfit when called before HUAC, published *Do It! Scenarios of the Revolution* the following year.

6. Abe Peck, *Uncovering the Sixties: The Life and Times of the Underground Press* (New York: Pantheon Press, 1985), 65.

7. Thomas Frank, *The Conquest of Cool: Business Culture, Counterculture, and the Rise of Hip Consumerism* (Chicago: University of Chicago Press, 1997), 6.

8. Doug Rossinow, *The Politics of Authenticity: Liberalism, Christianity, and the New Left in America* (New York: Columbia University Press, 1998), 8.

9. For an analysis of the organizational challenges to leftist student groups on college campuses, see John G. Turner, *Bill Bright and Campus Crusade for Life: The Renewal of Evangelicalism in Postwar America* (Chapel Hill: University of North Carolina Press, 2008), chap. 5.

10. Dr. Ted Engstrom, "Resolutions or Revolutions," *Campus Life*, January 1962, 16.

11. "The *Campus Life* Forum," *Campus Life*, January 1971, 11–16.

12. Melani McAlister, *Epic Encounters: Culture, Media, and U.S. Interests in the Middle East since 1945* (Berkeley: University of California Press, 2001), 47–55.

13. "Israel: the Beginning of the End," *Campus Life*, August/September 1971, 62. The letters section mitigated the oversimplifications. An October 1971 letter asked, "Your fundamentalism is showing again. . . . Snatches of Ezekiel, Micah, and Zechariah alongside photos of modern Israel—how romantic. . . . How do you think Israelis and Arabs feel when they meet American Christians with the entire destiny of the Middle East all figured on a chart?"

14. Usama Makdisi, *Artillery of Heaven: American Missionaries and the Failed Conversion of the Middle East* (Ithaca, NY: Cornell University Press, 2008), 4.

15. Richard Quebedeaux, *The Worldly Evangelicals* (New York: Harper and Row, 1978), 98.

16. Christina Klein, *Cold War Orientalism: Asia in the Middlebrow Imagination* (Berkeley: University of California Press, 2003).

17. Ken Gnanakan as told to Murray Lennox, "The Trojan," *Campus Life*, July 1967, 9–12; "Red China: I Wanted to Stay," *Campus Life*, August 1966, 16.

18. "The Desperate Will Take Arms," *Campus Life*, January 1968, 6–10.

19. "Join us this summer on one of these Wake Up to Your World Tours," *Campus Life*, October 1967, 79.

20. "Like Kids at a Carnival," *Campus Life*, December 1967, 58–61.

21. "Join us this summer," 79.

22. Harold Myra, "Hate this Boy!" *Campus Life*, June 1966, 12–13.

23. Jay Kesler, "A Blunt Hard-Nosed Proposal," *Campus Life*, October 1966, 20–21.

24. Sam Wolgemuth, "Saigon Interview: YFCI President interviews a young missionary in Viet Nam," *Campus Life*, July 1966, 22–25.

25. Ken Anderson, "'Tourists' on the Edge," *Campus Life*, August 1966, 30–31.

26. "The *Campus Life* Forum," *Campus Life*, October 1970, 7.

27. Gordon Maclean, "The Tallest Placard," *Campus Life*, July 1966, 44–46.

28. "Change the System," *Campus Life*, November 1968, 62.

29. Jim Whitmer, "We want to DO Something," *Campus Life*, November 1968, 54–59.

30. Stephen A. Kent, *From Slogans to Mantras: Social Protest and Religious Conversion in the Late Vietnam War Era* (Syracuse, NY: Syracuse University Press, 2001), chap. 3.

31. Peck, *Uncovering the Sixties*, 183.

32. Lisa McGirr, *Suburban Warriors: The Origins of the New American Right* (Princeton, NJ: Princeton University Press, 2001).

33. Miller, *Democracy Is in the Streets*, 310.

34. Gitlin, *Sixties*, 345, 347.

35. Norman Cohn, *The Pursuit of the Millennium: Revolutionary Millenarians and Mystical Anarchists of the Middle Ages* (New York: Oxford University Press, 1957), 20–23.

36. This type of closure had been common in Chicago during the Great Migration, when recently transplanted congregations did not have access to larger spaces. See Milton Sernett, *Bound for the Promised Land: African American Religion and the Great Migration* (Durham, NC: Duke University Press, 1997), 157, 160.

37. "Christian You're Next," *Hollywood Free Paper*, February 3, 1970, 1.

38. "Open Letter," Hollywood Free Paper, February 3, 1970, 2.

39. "Open Letter," *Hollywood Free Paper*, February 17, 1970, 3.

40. Peck, *Uncovering the Sixties*, 102.

41. "Keep on Truckin' for Jesus," *Hollywood Free Paper*, May 4, 1971, 10.

42. "Wanted: Jesus Christ," *Hollywood Free Paper*, October 7, 1969, 7.

43. "Jesus is the Liberator," *Hollywood Free Paper*, January 5, 1971, 14.

44. "Christian You're Next," *Hollywood Free Paper*, February 3, 1970, 1.

45. "All Power to the People Thru Jesus," *Hollywood Free Paper*, January 19, 1971, 14.

46. "Christian You're Next," *Hollywood Free Paper*, February 3, 1970, 1.

47. "The Wall," *Hollywood Free Paper*, January 6, 1970, 5. For a description of specific confrontations on Southern California campuses, see Turner, *Bill Bright and Campus Crusade*, 127, 132.

48. Dale Yancy, "The Opressed [*sic*] Minority," *Hollywood Free Paper*, May 19, 1970, 1.

49. Dale Yancy, "How Moral Is War?" *Hollywood Free Paper*, May 4, 1971, 1.

4

The Persistence of Antiliberalism

Evangelicals and the Race Problem

STEVEN P. MILLER

In *Divided by Faith: Evangelical Religion and the Problem of Race in America* (2000), the sociologists Michael Emerson and Christian Smith offered a devastating in-house critique of the relationship between white evangelicalism and racial inequality in the United States. Only a few years earlier, the evangelical men's group Promise Keepers had made racial reconciliation a major point of emphasis, and the *Wall Street Journal* had praised conservative evangelicals as "the most energetic element of society addressing racial divisions." Emerson (the primary author of *Divided by Faith*) did not deny such good intentions, but neither did he flatter them. His conclusion was pointed: the evangelicals in the study (most of whom were white) used a "tool kit" of "accountable freewill individualism," "relationalism," and "antistructuralism" to "actually reproduce and contribute to racial inequality." Regardless of their intentions, white evangelicals were making things worse. *Divided by Faith* made quite a splash in evangelical circles, garnering plaudits from *Christianity Today* and, on its ten-year anniversary, attracting a well-attended retrospective conference at Indiana Wesleyan University.[1]

This chapter explores the history behind *Divided by Faith*. Emerson documented the popularization of trends that had been present among evangelical elites for nearly half a century. His evaluations could have been—and, indeed, were—uttered in the 1960s about numerous pillars of the evangelical establishment, including racial moderates like Billy Graham. By the early 1970s, a vocal evangelical Left—including a rising generation of black evangelical activists—sharply attacked the "benign neglect" of evangelical leaders on race. Moreover, Emerson's critique did not apply only to evangelicals. Scholars have long offered similar indictments of what the title of one recent study terms "the myth of a color-blind society." Emerson's book cited late 1960s survey data suggesting that, then as now, many white Americans appealed to the virtues of race-blindness in opposing affirmative action policies.[2]

The history behind *Divided by Faith* takes on new significance when it is not solely about self-identified evangelicals but also about the phenomenon of evangelical*ism*—specifically, the interplay of evangelicalism and the civil rights movement. Over the last two decades, a scholarly near-consensus has emerged in support of two theses: (1) the civil rights movement was a religious undertaking, and (2) the subsequent Christian Right "learned" something from the earlier faith-based movement. One of the many ways in which Jerry Falwell backed away from his segregationist past was by invoking the earlier ministerial activism of Martin Luther King Jr. to justify his own. "Obviously, I'm doing now what Dr. Martin Luther King did fifteen years ago," Falwell told journalist Robert Scheer in 1981. For this and other reasons, *New Yorker* journalist Frances Fitzgerald speculated in an article published that same year that the civil rights movement "may have benefitted Falwell and other white fundamentalists as much as or more than it benefitted the blacks in the South." A handful of black evangelicals, such as Los Angeles minister E. V. Hill (an early supporter of King), even played roles in the nascent Christian Right.[3]

Yet the civil rights–evangelicalism dynamic also could hold a very different set of implications. The 1976 Democratic National Convention, for example, climaxed with presidential nominee Jimmy Carter and running mate Walter Mondale on stage with civil rights legends Andrew Young, Coretta Scott King, and Martin Luther King Sr. Also present, along with other Democratic power brokers, was the anti–civil rights emblem George Wallace. "Surely the Lord is in this place," said the elder King when giving the benediction. "Surely the Lord has sent Jimmy Carter to come out and bring America back to where it belongs." Afterwards, the convention crowd—journalists included—swayed to the civil rights anthem, "We Shall Overcome." Wallace could not bring himself to sing, but he managed to shake hands with King. Here, evangelical modes of reconciliation and invocation intersected with, and influenced, the politics of civil rights memory, not to mention the old-time gospel of electoral coalition building.[4]

Post-1960s American evangelicalism, then, could mean—and could signify—a host of things politically. It could lend assistance not just to the conservative backlash but also to the mainstreaming of civil rights rituals. The obvious contrast between Jerry Falwell and Jimmy Carter reveals the malleability of public evangelicalism, and the broader influence of those two figures suggests the ways in which, even with their obvious theological peculiarities, evangelicals were not always so different from their fellow Americans. Evangelicalism was, and is, not the sole property of evangelicals. The purpose here is not to propose that evangelicals somehow were not distinctive in beliefs or influence, but rather to argue that scholars miss part of the story when they treat recent American evangelicalism primarily as a subculture.

A more capacious heuristic is necessary in order to fully situate American evangelicalism in the history of recent American political culture. This chapter proposes a theme that can lend some order to the above anecdotes: *religiously informed antiliberalism*, a deep and reflexive skepticism about the post–New Deal use of the federal state for progressive ends (accompanied by skepticism about the ideological assumptions justifying such use of the state). To be sure, any such ordering risks the very reductivism against which this chapter already has warned. As explicated here, however, evangelical antiliberalism was (and is) not the same thing as evangelical political conservatism. Indeed, it arguably assisted Jimmy Carter before it helped Ronald Reagan.[5] More than is usually appreciated, evangelical leaders embraced the language of national "consensus" during the postwar years. Yet as a whole they did not subscribe to the central assumption of modern U.S. liberalism: that the state should (and could) be, as the historian Gary Gerstle has written, "an institutional medium capable of reconstructing society and of educating citizens in the task of intelligent living."[6] That distinction made a good deal of difference during the civil rights era. By the 1960s, the agendas of modern liberalism and the civil rights movement clearly overlapped; one's view of the former invariably shaped one's view of the latter. This fact was evident in the two sets of case studies explored here: first, two oft-cited evangelical elites (Billy Graham and Carl F. H. Henry) and, second, two understudied moderate evangelical publications (*Eternity* and *Christian Herald*). Antiliberal assumptions were present at the start of the late twentieth-century evangelical renaissance, and they have remained a pillar of evangelical political instincts.

Billy Graham and Carl Henry were emblematic of the postwar *neo-evangelical project*: the effort to raise the public profile and influence of born-again Protestantism and, in doing so, to restore evangelicalism to its previous custodial position in American public life. (Neo-evangelicals might just as well be called post-fundamentalists.)[7] If Billy Graham was the public face of the neo-evangelical project, then Carl Henry was its chief theologian. One of the major thrusts of the neo-evangelical project involved attempting to speak to the issues of the times from a particularly evangelical perspective. "Attempting" is the appropriate word, because this goal was more easily announced than accomplished. "For the first protracted period in its history," Henry wrote in his famous 1947 tract, *The Uneasy Conscience of Modern Fundamentalism*, "evangelical Christianity stands divorced from the great social reform movements." Graham, likewise, worried that the secular world was getting ahead of Christians on the issue of race. The "Church is on the tail end—to our shame!—of progress along racial li[n]es in America today," he told the National Association of Evangelicals (NAE) in 1952. (The NAE made tepid endorsements of racial tolerance in 1949 and 1951 before passing a 1955 statement supporting "the creation of that cultus of life which will provide equal rights and opportunities for every individual.") Graham knew that the eyes of the postwar world were on the United States in the area of race. The nation, he wrote, was "in a fish bowl with the whole world looking in." No doubt he hoped that evangelicals could attract as much attention as America's political leaders.[8]

The above anecdotes must be weighed against the essential accuracy of historian Curtis Evans's recent contention that, as he put the matter, "evangelicals were opposed to the civil rights movement and did very little in practical terms to advance racial justice for African Americans during the 1960s." At the same time, the political scientist Robert Booth Fowler was accurate in noting that, by the close of the decade, "the message of white thinkers within the [mainstream evangelical] fold was almost unanimous in affirming the religious truth of racial equality and in faulting the questionable accomplishments in this area by many evangelicals."[9] If prominent postwar evangelicals were not in any real sense activists, then neither were they quietists. Graham, the most prominent American evangelical then or arguably since, spoke out all the time about race. When he did so, however, he usually voiced skepticism about legally driven change (rooted in pietism) and, by the early 1960s, fears about challenges to civil authority (rooted in custodialism). For Graham, antiliberalism was something of a reflex. For Carl Henry, though, it was very much a theology.

Because Henry wrote at the start of the evangelical renaissance, he can be seen as the theological antecedent both of the evangelical Right and of the evangelical Left. Writing from the latter perspective, the theologian Peter Goodwin Heltzel recently hailed Henry as "a prophet before his time" whose "call for racial justice would not be heeded until decades later in the wake of the civil rights movement." If so, Henry was among the more sedentary prophets of the mid-twentieth century. Heltzel acknowledges Henry's "skepticism of the state" but links it with his "prophetic Baptist" tendencies. Time and time again, however, that skepticism translated as opposition to the drift of modern liberal politics. As editor of *Christianity Today* from the mid-1950s until the late 1960s, Henry faced constant push-back from the deeply conservative Nelson Bell (father-in-law of Billy Graham) and J. Howard Pew (*Christianity Today*'s major benefactor). Yet Henry's conservatism resounded beyond the pages of that flagship neo-evangelical publication.[10]

Ultimately, Henry exhibited greater concern with the socio-theological status of evangelicalism than with the particulars of a given policy stance. He worried in *The Uneasy Conscience* about the "suspicion on the part of non-evangelicals that there is something in the very nature of Fundamentalism which makes a world ethical view impossible." Henry included race on a long list of issues (labor, war, etc.) that presented an "opportunity" to end evangelicalism's "embarrassing divorce from a world social program" and "to recapture its rightful leadership in pressing for a new world order." Yet he was unclear about whether specific policies should, or even could, further such an effort. A persistent stumbling block for Henry was the state, which he saw as a rival to the church in the area of custodial authority. He argued that "the state has steadily supplanted the church as the indoctrinating agency" of modern society, even while insisting that fears of statism should not "obscure the evangelical obligation to press the Christian world-life view upon the masses." He struggled to delineate the precise relationship between a "new world order" and a "Christian world-life view." In the end, Henry called "for condemning racial hatred and intolerance, while at the same time protesting the superficial view of man which overlooks the need of individual regeneration."[11]

Henry was clearer about what he did not favor—broadening the reach of the modern liberal state. His perspective goes a long way toward explaining why he sat out the most important social movement of the twentieth century. He minced few words here. In a 1962 piece for *Christian Herald* (not the Pew-funded *Christianity Today*), Henry took pains "to contrast the historic Christian approach to welfare with that of modern collectivism." He argued that the "expansion of welfare statism is, in fact, a part of the main thrust toward totalitarianism." More than three years later, Henry penned an evangelical response to the civil rights movement. He revisited the themes of *The Uneasy Conscience*. "Surely," he wrote, "evangelical Christianity has more to offer mankind than its unique message of salvation, even if that is its highest and holiest mission." Yet reasons abounded in Henry's mind to be cautious—first and foremost, the monopoly that liberal Protestants had on the discourse of Christian social activism. (Here, Henry could not resist pointing out that Alabama's governor George Wallace belonged to the Methodist Church, which was "at the forefront of liberal social action programs.") Still, had Henry possessed any faith in the liberal state itself, he might have found an evangelical justification for civil rights laws. The intellectual pivot of his essay concerned the turn from faith to politics. "Current proposals to detach the Gospel from 'right-wing' social reaction and current pleas for 'political compassion,'" he argued, "are rooted in leftist political ideology more often than in an authentic spiritual view of the role of government." For Henry, then, a critique of liberal theology was necessarily a critique of liberal politics, as proponents of the former failed "to distinguish between the social concerns of *Law* and the social concerns of *Gospel*." Henry saw the state not as an imperfect agent of democratic aims (which could, with input from believers, be Christian aims, too), but as an ordained other, which commanded standoffish acquiescence more than sustained input. "Evangelicals," he pronounced, "do not view government as an instrument of benevolence or compassion, since love is preferential and shows favor or partiality." Hence, in his formulation of evangelical social ethics, "the best alternative to the 'welfare' state is the just state, and the best alternative to political demonstrations is civil obedience." Henry's perspective had rich theological antecedents, of course, but it ultimately reinforced the midcentury political marginalization of evangelicalism. The upshot was ironic in light of Henry's ambitions for evangelical public witness. More than a decade later, when matters of "personal holiness" (a category that Henry elevated over "public holiness") became more salient, this marginalization ceased.[12]

Of course, many contemporaries saw Graham and Henry as occupying the right flank (or perhaps the center-right flank) of the neo-evangelical continuum. Thus, it is instructive to see varieties of evangelical antiliberalism at work in two moderate publications, *Eternity* and *Christian Herald*. They are among the least-studied postwar evangelical periodicals. This is especially true in the case of *Christian Herald*. Its reported circulation in 1961 was 426,739, more than two-and-a-half times that of the much more extensively reviewed *Christianity Today*. *Eternity*'s subscription base in the early 1960s was much smaller—at most one-sixth of *Christianity Today*'s—but was growing precipitously. A likely reason for the oversight is the tendency of scholars studying postwar evangelicalism to focus almost exclusively on postfundamentalists (rather than the broader community of persons who were comfortable calling themselves evangelical Christians). *Christian Herald* reflected the concerns of the many evangelicals who remained within "mainline" Protestant denominations or who belonged to conservative "confessing" denominations, such as the Lutheran Church–Missouri Synod or the Christian Reformed Church. While *Eternity* was a product of postfundamentalism, its founder, Donald Grey Barnhouse, pastored Philadelphia's Tenth Presbyterian Church, which stood as a dissenting voice within the mainline Presbyterian Church, USA.[13]

A survey of *Eternity* and *Christian Herald* during the 1950s and 1960s shows that it is possible to speak of a postwar elite evangelical consensus on race. Admittedly, *Eternity* and *Christian Herald* are somewhat tricky to study, as they often featured countervailing opinions within their pages. Nonetheless, their editorials and the general thrust of their feature articles evince telling similarities with the earlier analysis of Graham and Henry.

From the 1950s through the mid-1960s, *Eternity* modeled a way for evangelicals to support basic racial equality and even basic civil rights without supporting the civil rights movement itself. *Eternity* reflected neo-evangelicalism at its most irenic. Donald Grey Barnhouse had a reputation as a firebrand dispensationalist; the publication was known as *Revelation* until 1950. Yet by the time of the name change, the magazine was less separatist and less reflexively wary of political engagement than was postwar evangelicalism as a whole. (Its urban base might have contributed to this relative openness; then again, the Moody Bible Institute was based in Chicago, Biola College in Los Angeles, and so on.) Editors and contributors quite readily made the theological case for antiracism (and did so in a particularly clear-cut way when the topic was church segregation)—although it is worth noting that the editors felt a need to publish articles criticizing popular segregationist proof texts. A 1953 article cited the already well-circulated line that "11 o'clock Sunday morning is the most segregated hour of American life," while four years later a headline screamed, "The Church Must Be Color-Blind." The international stage also loomed large in *Eternity*'s analysis. Articles cited the Cold War, decolonization, and especially missionary interests to suggest that race issues deserved the attention of evangelicals. Finally, some writers saw the reputation of American evangelical Christianity as at stake, and here African American voices entered the pages of this overwhelmingly white publication in a pronounced but ambiguous way. A 1956 editorial quoted a group of "outstanding Negro leaders" who asked, "Why is it that we Negroes are accepted by the Communists, by the Roman Catholics, and by the Modernists [i.e., liberal Protestants], but that we have our hardest fight among the Evangelicals to win any acceptance?" The implications were ominous. According to the black evangelical B. M. Nottage, "Our colored churches have been largely taken over by the liberals." (Indeed, *Eternity* regularly presented black churches as bastions of theological laxity.) One letter writer went so far as to muse, "As God used Babylon to chasten Israel, is not God using the so-called 'liberal' brothers in Christ as well as outright non-believing groups to somehow chasten and shame" evangelicals for failing to address the sinful legacy of slavery?[14]

While the theological case for antiracism seemed fairly straightforward (missionary work and basic fealty to the Bible demanded it), the theological mandate for social action was much less clear. The Philadelphia neighborhood that housed Barnhouse's church was undergoing demographic transition and witnessing rising crime rates. Barnhouse himself was far from a wholesale integrationist in civil or conjugal matters. He was not above using the word "amalgamation," and his first editorial response to the *Brown* decision was to resort to a premillennialist truism: "These are problems which can be solved, I believe, by nothing less than the Second Coming of Christ and the enforcing of righteousness by Him." Even the somewhat more liberal members of *Eternity*'s staff (whose perspectives became more pronounced after Barnhouse passed away in 1960) shied away from theological discussions of law and rights—the two issues that were, of course, at the center of how educated whites responded to the civil rights movement. *Eternity*'s staff writers did not offer a Henry-style theological critique of statism; quite the contrary, the magazine supported the 1957 Civil Rights Act and most such subsequent legislation. When doing so, though, editorialists tended to skirt outright theological claims. Instead, they leaned on pragmatic appeals to Americanism, averring that "certainly these matters should be decided in accordance with the law of the United States especially the Bill of Rights and Fourteenth Amendment of our Constitution." As the civil rights movement intensified in the early 1960s (and, hence, registered in the minds of more *Eternity* readers), the editors grew increasingly critical of evangelicals for keeping "our heads in the sand" and supporting the segregation-ist "status quo." When endorsing (or effectively endorsing) the Civil Rights Act of 1964, however, their reasoning was quite secular. The editorial in question had an ambiguous title, "Wrongs Do Not Make Civil Rights," and it is worth quoting at length:

> While the Bible clearly commands love for one's neighbor as a basic principle, there are few specific instructions for dealing with evils in the social order. . . . As American citizens we favor the passage of the civil rights bill—even though it is not a perfect instrument and even though it brings the federal government into areas of legislation into which it should not be forced. We feel this is the minimal position that should be taken by Americans whether they are Christians or not.

Only a year later did an editorial explicitly link rights with faith. The editors backed the Voting Rights Act of 1965 because, they wrote, "We are for the rights of minorities. Not only do we think that this is in keeping with the Constitution of the United States, but we also believe that it is in keeping with the Scripture." They likened their support for civil rights to their endorsement of recent Supreme Court decisions restricting prayers and Bible readings in public schools. "The rights of minorities must be safeguarded," the editorial continued. "In the foregoing two causes we realize that we are on the side of the political liberals. So be it."[15] Despite its defensive tone, the editorial was a notable departure, first, from evangelical wariness of challenging the law through activism, and second, from evangelical wariness of using the law to promote positive rights.

As the contents of *Christian Herald* reveal, evangelicals who were not also postfundamentalists exhibited less skepticism about the modern state. The venerable publication dated back to the 1870s and reflected the consensus spirit of the era preceding the bitter fundamentalist-modernist conflicts of the 1910s and 1920s. The longtime *Christian Herald* editor Daniel Poling put forth a vision of non-separatist evangelicalism well before neo-evangelicalism existed as a conscious concept. Poling described himself as "conservative though not reactionary in theological matters" in a 1964 *Time* magazine profile, which labeled him "a gentle fundamentalist." Still, as the highest-circulation evangelical magazine in the postwar decades, the New York City–based *Christian Herald* was more than an ecumenical museum piece. It was very much an "evangelical family magazine," right down to the advertisements for Bob Jones University and the Moody Bible Institute. Like Carl Henry, Poling grouped race with other pressing social concerns for evangelicals. According to its masthead, the *Christian Herald* was "independent and interdenominational . . . dedicated to the promotion of evangelical Christianity, church unity, religious and racial understanding, world peace; the solving of the liquor problem," and so on.[16]

More than was true with *Eternity*, *Christian Herald*'s writers largely assumed (rather than explicated) the sinfulness of racism. Poling had long seen his publication and related ministries as racially progressive, pointing out that they were integrated decades before the civil rights movement began. The publication highlighted examples of racial progress in the years preceding the *Brown v. Board of Education* decision, while noting the changing racial dynamics of the urban and (for an increasing number of readers) suburban North. "Gradually, America is outgrowing racial discrimination," declared monthly columnist "Gabriel Courier" (the editorial pen name of staff writer Kenneth L. Wilson) in 1952.

Courier thus could cast the subsequent *Brown* decision as "inevitable," noting that the most pressing task was to prepare the church to do its part in an era of social and legal change. Contra Henry, Courier found it acceptable for the church to follow the world in this case.[17]

Compared to its postfundamentalist peers, then, *Christian Herald* was less ambivalent about the role of the state in postwar social change. It did not reflect the postfundamentalist impulse to draw lines of distinction and to worry about the theological integrity of public actors. Martin Luther King Jr. received favorable references as early as 1958, and civil rights demonstrations were not reflexively dismissed as out of line. Poling (an active Republican who was more conservative politically than most of his staffers) distinguished between marches (acceptable) and civil disobedience (questionable). Like *Eternity*, *Christian Herald* supported civil rights more than it did the civil rights movement. Still, both Poling and Courier understood that demonstrations, however distasteful in their minds, had paved the way for progress, which the law, in turn, needed to ensure. The church still had to do its part, of course. "Now that the Civil Rights Act has become the law of the land," Fred R. Zapp wrote in late 1964, "what are churches and church people going to do about it?" The question became more pressing after a 1965 readers' poll revealed that many readers did not connect their personal antiracist theologies with support for civil rights. The results, lamented the editors, "showed a greater general willingness to accept persons of other races as churchmembers [*sic*] than as neighbors—a disparity between tolerance as applied to church life and as applied to community life." *Christian Herald* thus renewed its focus on practical integration in churches and community life. "The whole matter of an integrated society has now arrived at it second phase," wrote its editor Ford Stewart in 1967, "—the working level." By then, though, supporting integration also meant holding the line against the Black Power attack on it. The publication featured numerous informational pieces on Black Power, but overall the tone was critical (*Eternity* ran similar pieces, although it was less negative in tone). Article and editorial titles during the late 1960s ranged from "Something Must Be Done" and "Take the Fear Out of Integration" to "Is It Too Late for Integration?" and "There Is No Civil Right to Riot."[18]

Back in 1956, the neo-evangelical theologian Edward Carnell published an article in *Christian Century*, long considered the flagship publication of liberal Protestantism. Carnell, who served as president of Fuller Theological Seminary, wrote in part to defend Billy Graham against Reinhold Niebuhr's high-profile criticisms of the evangelist. The race problem drove Niebuhr's attack, as he argued that Graham's conversion-centered formula for social change lacked a crucial ingredient: an appreciation for collective sin (i.e., social injustice) and, by extension, possible nonpietistic (i.e., legal) remedies for it. Carnell, the author of a book critical of Niebuhr's theology, tried to turn the renowned theologian's trademark emphasis on human pride against him, questioning the feasibility of singling out the sin of racial pride and then blithely pursuing legal solutions. Even so, Carnell had to concede one "stubborn fact—and orthodoxy should come to terms with it." The fact was that "humanists often develop a finer sense of justice and bear a heavier load of charity than those who profess faith in Christ."[19]

A decade later, Carnell's concession largely still stood. A major reason why was the skepticism about liberal statism (in short, the antiliberalism) that profoundly shaped the postwar neo-evangelical project. Evangelical elites, such as Henry, saw the state as a threat to the goal of bolstering the public influence of conservative Protestantism. This skepticism was less pronounced outside of postfundamentalist circles (as seen with *Christian Herald*), and even neo-evangelicals drew the line at different places (as seen with *Eternity*). Still, when it came to the civil rights movement, both publications hedged more than they marched. Their partial exceptionalism serves to reinforce the rule: Three-and-a-half decades removed from the "Year of the Evangelical" (1976), antiliberalism stands as a profound form of continuity within the larger evangelical renaissance.[20]

The spirit of antiliberalism persisted in spite of the great diversity within post-1960s evangelical public witness. It endured even as prominent southern fundamentalists retreated from segregationism, and even as an assertive evangelical Left blasted the old neo-evangelical establishment. It endured even as the civil rights movement came to influence publicly engaged evangelicals in complex and sometimes ironic ways—even as Jimmy Carter and Daddy King sang "We Shall Overcome" at the 1976 Democratic Convention, even as Jerry Falwell cited the younger King's activism, even as antiabortion activist Randall Terry likened his cause to that of civil rights crusaders, and even as the Christian Coalition head Ralph Reed candidly conceded that, unlike his liberal opponents, conservative evangelicals had been "on the wrong side of the most central cause of social justice in this century." The most prominent brand of evangelical activism, the Christian Right, clearly called for greater government regulation of personal morality. Nevertheless, Christian Right leaders cast themselves as opposing liberalism in the form of state support for abortion, feminism, and gay rights.[21]

Finally, evangelical antistatism endured by evolving into the colorblindness of later generations. Skepticism about the state's role in redressing the product of human sinfulness (racism) became criticism of color-conscious state policies that acknowledged the depth of injustice (affirmative action). The "biblical racial reconciliation" embraced by Reed and Promise Keepers in the 1990s, while a notable development, did not challenge this paradigm. Indeed, it overlapped greatly with neoconservative critiques of the civil rights establishment.[22] At the end of the twentieth century, then, the obverse logic of Edward Carnell's concession (i.e., that evangelicals have hindered the cause of racial justice) became the thesis of *Divided by Faith*.

NOTES

1. Michael O. Emerson and Christian Smith, *Divided By Faith: Evangelical Religion and the Problem of Race in America* (New York: Oxford University Press, 2000), 3, 76, 110; Douglas A. Blackmon, "For Heaven's Sake: Racial Reconciliation Becomes a Priority for the Religious Right," *Wall Street Journal*, June 23, 1997 (Proquest); "CT's Annual Book Awards," April 23, 2001, http://www.christianitytoday.com/ct/2001/april23/2.82.html; "*Divided by Faith*: A Decade Retrospective," October 15–16, 2011, http://usreligion.blogspot.com/2010/08/divided-by-faith-conference-schedule.html.

2. On Graham, see Steven P. Miller, *Billy Graham and the Rise of the Republican South* (Philadelphia: University of Pennsylvania Press, 2009), 94–95 passim. See the July–August 1975 special issue of *The Other Side*, especially "Growing Together: A Conversation with Seven Black Evangelicals," 31–46. "Benign neglect" quoted in Robert Booth Fowler, *A New Engagement: Evangelical Political Thought, 1966–1976* (Grand Rapids, MI: Eerdmans, 1982), 171; Michael K. Brown et al., *Whitewashing Race: The Myth of a Color-blind Society* (Berkeley: University of California Press, 2003); Emerson and Smith, *Divided by Faith*, 88–89. Antony W. Alumkal offered a brief, helpful critique of Emerson and Smith for not fully relating their subjects to "other systems of racial ideology." See Alumkal, "American Evangelicalism in the Post–Civil Rights Era: A Racial Formation Theology," *Sociology of Religion* 65 (2004): 209.

3. On the civil rights movement as a religious phenomenon and a model for Christian Right activism, see Mark A. Noll, *God and Race in American Politics: A Short History* (Princeton, NJ: Princeton University Press, 2008), 102–175; Frank Lambert, *Religion in American Politics: A Short History* (Princeton, NJ: Princeton University Press, 2008), 160–183; and David L. Chappell, *A Stone of Hope: Prophetic Religion and the Death of Jim Crow* (Chapel Hill: University of North Carolina Press, 2004), 87–104, 178. On Falwell, see Flo Conway and Jim Siegelman, *Holy Terror: The Fundamentalist War on America's Freedoms in Religion, Politics and Our Private Lives* (New York: Delta, 1984), 91; and Robert Scheer, "The Prophet of 'Worldly Methods,'" *Los Angeles Times*, March 4, 1981, in *The New Right: Readings & Commentary*, vol. 2 (Oakland, CA: The Data Center, 1981), 126. See also

Frances FitzGerald, *Cities on a Hill: A Journey Through Contemporary American Cultures*, rev. ed. (New York: Simon and Schuster, 1986), 170–171, quote p. 171. On Hill, see Darren Dochuk, *From Bible Belt to Sunbelt: Plain-Folk Religion, Grassroots Politics, and the Rise of Evangelical Conservatism* (New York: Norton, 2010), 285–291, 390–391; and Daniel K. Williams, *God's Own Party: The Making of the Christian Right* (New York: Oxford University Press, 2010), 199.

4. On the Democratic convention, see Randall Balmer, *God in the White House: A History: How Faith Shaped the Presidency from John F. Kennedy to George W. Bush* (New York: HarperOne, 2008), 87; Edward E. Plowman, "The Democrats: God in the Garden?" *Christianity Today*, August 6, 1976, 34; and Lloyd Rohler, *George Wallace: Conservative Populist* (Westport, CT: Praeger, 2004), 84. See also Hendrik Hertzberg, "Jimmy Carter: 1977–1981," in *Character Above All: Ten Presidents from FDR to George Bush*, ed. Robert A. Wilson (New York: Simon & Schuster, 1995), 181–182; and R. W. Apple Jr., "A Jubilant Party: Minnesotan Cheered as He Scores Ford on Nixon Pardon," *New York Times*, July 16, 1976 (Proquest).

5. While there is an enduring Western tradition of non-Marxist antiliberalism, the type of antiliberalism considered here was neither as historically rooted as, say, Alexis de Tocqueville's European conservatism, nor as philosophically grounded as, say, Alasdair McIntyre's more recent critique of liberal individualism. See Stephen Holmes, *The Anatomy of Antiliberalism* (Cambridge, MA: Harvard University Press, 1993), xi–xvi, 1–10. My understanding of antiliberalism puts particular stress on the final component of Jason Bivins's valuable treatment of "Christian antiliberalism" as "a broad religio-political impulse" that rejects liberalism's "conception of citizens, its emphasis on negative liberty, and its strict division between public and private—as well as many of the institutional forms that have developed in the United States to pursue these political ends. Christian antiliberals believe specifically that post–World War II liberalism has made it increasingly difficult to practice religions faithfully in the United States." Jason C. Bivins, *The Fracture of Good Order: Christian Antiliberalism and the Challenge to American Politics* (Chapel Hill: University of North Carolina Press, 2003), 6, 3.

6. Wendy L. Wall, *Inventing the "American Way": The Politics of Consensus from the New Deal to the Civil Rights Movement* (New York: Oxford University Press, 2008). Gary Gerstle, "The Protean Character of American Liberalism," *American Historical Review* 99 (October 1994): 1046.

7. Neo-evangelicalism, or postfundamentalism, dated back to the 1940s, when an influential group of moderate fundamentalists (many of whom became involved with the National Association of Evangelicals, founded in 1942) self-consciously embraced the label "evangelical." On neo-evangelicalism, see Darryl G. Hart, *That Old-Time Religion in Modern America: Evangelical Protestantism in the Twentieth Century* (Chicago: Ivan R. Dee, 2002), 115–145; Joel A. Carpenter, *Revive Us Again: The Reawakening of American Fundamentalism* (New York: Oxford University Press, 1997), 141–232; and Mark Silk, "The Rise of the 'New Evangelicalism': Shock and Adjustment," in *Between the Times: The Travail of the Protestant Establishment in America, 1900–1960*, ed. William R. Hutchison (New York:

Cambridge University Press, 1989), 278–299. My understanding of evangelical custodialism owes a debt to Grant Wacker, "Uneasy in Zion: Evangelicals in Postmodern Society,"
in *Reckoning with the Past: Historical Essays on American Evangelicalism from the Institute for the
Study of American Evangelicals*, ed. D. G. Hart (Grand Rapids, MI: Baker, 1995), 376–393;
and "Searching for Norman Rockwell: Popular Evangelicalism in Contemporary
America," in *The Evangelical Tradition in America*, ed. Leonard I. Sweet (Macon, GA: Mercer
University Press, 1984), 289–315.

    8. Carl F. H. Henry, *The Uneasy Conscience of Modern Fundamentalism* (Grand Rapids,
MI: Eerdmans, 2003 [1947], 27. Miller, *Billy Graham*, 24. NAE resolutions in Miles S.
Mullin II, "Postwar Evangelical Social Concern: Evangelical Identity and the Modes
and Limits of Social Engagement, 1945–1960" (PhD diss., Vanderbilt University, 2009),
416–419, 424.

    9. Curtis J. Evans, "White Evangelical Responses to the Civil Rights Movement,"
Harvard Theological Review 102 (2009): 247. Fowler, *A New Engagement*, 172.

    10. Peter Goodwin Heltzel, *Jesus & Justice: Evangelicals, Race, and American Politics*
(New Haven, CT: Yale University Press, 2009), 73, 76, 83–84.

    11. Henry, *Uneasy Conscience*, 11, 3–4, 76, 68–69, 87.

    12. Henry, contribution to "Who is My Brother's Keeper?" *Christian Herald*, January
1962, 15, 58; and "Evangelicals in the Social Struggle," *Christianity Today*, October 8,
1965, 3–11.

    13. Circulation numbers for *Christianity Today* and *Christian Herald* in Phyllis Elaine
Alsdurf, "*Christianity Today* Magazine and Late Twentieth-Century Evangelicalism"
(PhD diss., University of Minnesota, 2004), 136, n427. *Eternity*'s circulation estimated
from subscription statistics mentioned in "Report from the Editors," *Eternity*, August
1961, 5; and "Report from the Editors: A Magazine Moving Up," *Eternity*, December
1963, 6. Curtis Evans briefly covered *Eternity* in "White Evangelical Responses to the
Civil Rights Movement," 270. *Christian Herald* was not consulted in Robert Booth
Fowler's landmark early 1980s study of evangelical political thinking. See Fowler's list
of "Periodicals Systematically Consulted" for *A New Engagement*, 289. Barnhouse in
Carpenter, *Revive Us Again*, 50. Robert Wuthnow, in his famous survey of postwar
American religion, noted the extent to which in the immediate postwar years "evangeli-
calism continued . . . to be a prominent emphasis within the established denominations
themselves." See Wuthnow, *The Restructuring of American Religion: Society and Faith Since
World War II* (Princeton, NJ: Princeton University Press, 1988), 177. Richard G.
Hutcheson Jr. made similar observations in *Mainline Churches and the Evangelicals: A
Challenging Crisis* (Atlanta, GA: John Knox Press, 1981), 19–20, 40, and passim.

    14. James D. Fairbanks, "Politics and the Evangelical Press: 1960–85," in *Religion
and Political Behavior in the United States*, ed. Ted G. Jelen (New York: Praeger, 1989), 249.
Harold Lindsell, "The Bible and Race Relations," *Eternity*, August 1956, 12–13, 43–44.
James O. Buswell III, "Segregation: Is It Biblical?" *Eternity*, October 1962, 14–17, 36, 38.
"The Most Segregated Hour," *Eternity*, July 1953, 8. Martin H. Scharlemann, "The

Church Must Be Color-Blind," *Eternity*, July 1957, 23–24, 45–46. Helen Sigrist, "Prejudice: The Respectable Sin," *Eternity*, October 1953, 14–15, 36–37. C. Stacey Woods, "We Must Change Our Missionary Methods," *Eternity*, September 1954, 8–9, 46–48. "Interracial Conference in South Africa," February 1954, 12. "Race," *Eternity*, August 1956, 10. B. M. Nottage, "You've Neglected My People," *Eternity*, December 1957, 12–13. "The Tragic Results of Racial Separatism," *Eternity*, September 1963, 8. Letter from James H. Goodner (Fort Belvoir, Va.), November 1963, 3.

15. "Amalgamation Has Its Problems," *Eternity*, July 1954, 42. "NAACP," *Eternity*, June 1958, 4–5. "Race," April 1955, 8. "Civil Rights Bill," *Eternity*, November 1957, 24. "Let's Face up to the Race Issue," *Eternity*, August 1963, 5–6. "Wrongs Do Not Make Civil Rights," *Eternity*, June 1964, 4–6, 36. "Yes, We're for Minority Rights," *Eternity*, October 1965, 7.

16. "A Gentle Fundamentalist," *Time*, December 11, 1964 (Academic Search Complete). Fairbanks, "Politics and the Evangelical Press," 248. *Christian Herald*, February 1950, inside cover, 7. *Christian Herald*, March 1950, 2.

17. Daniel Poling, "With All ~~Deliberate~~ Speed," *Christian Herald*, September 1963, 15. Buford Stefflre, "Problems to Him are Color Blind," *Christian Herald*, September 1950, 61–63. Kenneth G. Gehret, "He Took Down the Sign 'For Whites Only,'" *Christian Herald*, April 1959, 26–28, 71. Gabriel Courier, "Sikeston," *Christian Herald*, August 1953, 11; "Problem," *Christian Herald*, September 1952, 12; "Stones," *Christian Herald*, October 1957, 10; and "Court," August 1954, 10. Courier's identity in "Courier and Lives," *Christian Herald*, February 1966, 27.

18. Courier, "St. Louis," *Christian Herald*, February 1958, 12; "Nobelity," *Christian Herald*, February 1965, 7; and "Race," *Christian Herald*, May 1960, 6. See also "A Gentle Fundamentalist." Poling, "Freedom Always Has Been Marching!," *Christian Herald*, November 1963, 42–43; and "With All ~~Deliberate~~ Speed." Courier, "Birmingham," *Christian Herald*, July 1963, 5; "Race," *Christian Herald*, June 1964, 6–7; and "Corroded Conscience," *Christian Herald*, May 1965, 19. Fred R. Zepp, "Integration and You," *Christian Herald*, November 1964, 14. "The Poll Report: Integration and You," *Christian Herald*, February 1965, 22–26. Ford Stewart, "Something Must Be Done," *Christian Herald*, February 1967, 8–9. James L. Johnson, "Take the Fear Out of Integration," *Christian Herald*, August 1967, 16–19, 46. John L. Perry, "Is It Too Late for Integration?" *Christian Herald*, January 1969, 8–9, 24, 54–59. "There Is No Civil Right to Riot," *Christian Herald*, October 1967, 5.

19. "Too much stress on racial injustice," Carnell wrote, "will divert the sinner's attention from the need to repent of his . . . self-centered life. . . . It is not that we are *unwilling* to do the Christian thing by our brother. The problem is that being sinners, we are powerless to approach racial injustice from a perspective higher than a prudential balance of personal interests." See Edward John Carnell, "A Proposal to Reinhold Niebuhr," *Christian Century*, October 17, 1956, 1197–1199, quote p. 1198. The Carnell article is also discussed in Evans, "White Evangelical Responses to the Civil Rights Movement,"

256–257. On Carnell, see Rudolph Nelson, *The Making and Unmaking of an Evangelical Mind: The Case of Edward Carnell* (Cambridge: Cambridge University Press, 1987), 65, 76, 86, 182–183.

20. Pollster George Gallup Jr. declared 1976 "The Year of the Evangelical," and a subsequent *Newsweek* cover story popularized the interpretation. See "Counting Souls," *Time*, October 4, 1976 (Academic Search Complete); and Kenneth L. Woodward, "Born Again! The Year of the Evangelicals," *Newsweek*, October 25, 1976, 68–78.

21. Curtis W. Freeman, "'Never Had I Been So Blind': W. A. Criswell's 'Change' on Racial Segregation," *Journal of Southern Religion* 10 (2007), http://jsr.fsu.edu /Volume10/Freeman.pdf. On the evangelical Left, see David R. Swartz, *Moral Minority: The Evangelical Left in an Age of Conservatism* (Philadelphia: University of Pennsylvania Press, 2012); and Brantley W. Gasaway, "An Alternative Soul of Politics: The Rise of Contemporary Progressive Evangelicalism" (PhD diss., University of North Carolina, 2008). On Terry, see Williams, *God's Own Party*, 223–226. Ralph Reed, *Active Faith: How Christians are Changing the Soul of American Politics* (New York: Free Press, 1996), 68. On the Christian Right's rhetoric of antistatism, see Seth Dowland, "'Family Values' and the Formation of a Christian Right Agenda," *Church History* 78 (September 2009): 628.

22. Blackmon, "For Heaven's Sake." For the neoconservative comparison see Alumkal, "American Evangelicalism in the Post–Civil Rights Era," 201, 203–205. Alumkal noted that the Promise Keepers' brand of "racial reconciliationist theology" represented the popularization of the significantly more radical theologies voiced by black evangelical activists and their allies in the late 1960s and early 1970s (198–203).

5

Sex and the Evangelicals

Gender Issues, the Sexual Revolution, and Abortion in the 1960s

DANIEL K. WILLIAMS

Spirit-filled born-again Christians, Tim LaHaye wrote in 1969, had better sex than anyone else. They "enjoy the sublimities of physical union in marriage far more than people without Christ," he said. Such advice, which the future Moral Majority board member and end-times prophecy writer peddled in *Christian Life* magazine and in a marital advice manual that he published through an evangelical press, might have struck some nonevangelical observers as surprising. After all, LaHaye, a Bob Jones University graduate and a San Diego Baptist pastor, had first broken into the national news for his leading role in an unsuccessful campaign for a statewide antipornography referendum in California in 1965. Anyone who knew LaHaye was aware that he was firmly opposed to the cultural permissiveness of the times. But LaHaye also took a leading role in encouraging evangelicals to celebrate the joys of marital sex. In 1976 he and his wife, Beverly, published a sex manual for evangelical couples, which included detailed advice about how to create a female orgasm.[1] The LaHayes were hardly alone among evangelicals in talking about marital sex. Indeed, during the 1960s, evangelicals experienced their own sexual revolution—a revolution that would shape their politics for the remainder of the twentieth century.

Evangelicals' public reactions against the sexual revolution and the feminist movement have been the focus of several recent studies, but the development of a new evangelical theology of sex and gender that emerged during the 1960s as a response to the nation's changing sexual mores has received little scholarly attention.[2] This chapter examines evangelical writings from the 1960s to explore the transformation in evangelical thinking about sex and gender during that decade, and argues that in the 1960s a new evangelical theological celebration of marital sex emerged as a response to the sexual revolution of the time. Ironically, evangelicals' reaction against the sexual revolution led them to devote more attention to sex than they ever had before, and even to liberalize their sexual ethics in some areas, such as birth control and masturbation. Yet their new emphasis on the joys of marital sex ultimately induced them to take more conservative stances on women's rights, homosexuality, and abortion, a development that would determine the course of the culture wars that would dominate American evangelical politics for much of the late twentieth century.

Prior to the sexual revolution of the mid-1960s, evangelicals had often discussed the importance of the family as a bulwark of society and warned about the dangers of sex outside of marriage, but there had been little sign of a cohesive evangelical theology of sexuality. Indeed, during the 1950s and early 1960s, evangelicals treated the subject of sex almost exclusively as a subject for teens. The only time that evangelical Christian magazines discussed sex at the beginning of the 1960s was in the context of teenage moral behavior, and invariably the question that they addressed was how teenagers could remain chaste until marriage. Evangelicals had also written a few books about sex that were designed for the education of Christian teens. Most of the books featured a brief discussion of anatomical differences between men and women, followed by a lengthy discussion of the biblical verses condemning fornication, and concluding with the author's own warnings about the dangers of masturbation, "petting," and premarital sexual intercourse. Evangelicals cautioned against the excesses of the larger culture, believing that a culture of early dating and early marriage had been disastrous for young people's sexual mores. They encouraged their teen readers to postpone "going steady" with a boyfriend or girlfriend until they were ready for marriage, and they advised against early marriages at a time when it was not uncommon for seventeen-year-olds to head to the altar.[3]

Despite their differences with nonevangelicals on a few issues of sexual behavior, most evangelicals did not view sexual mores as the primary area of difference between themselves and the larger society. On most sexual issues, such as homosexuality, adultery, and even premarital sex, they remained confident that most of their nonfundamentalist neighbors shared their views, at least tacitly.[4] But by the end of the 1960s, they believed that the greatest assault on Christian values was occurring in the area of sexual morals, and they began to define their theology in reaction to that assault. The result would be a sea change in evangelical culture.

By the mid-1960s, rising rates of sexual promiscuity, the rapid proliferation of sexually explicit magazines, and the open discussion of sex in Hollywood films and network television presented an unprecedented challenge for guardians of a conservative standard of sexual morality. Although rates of premarital sexual activity had been on the rise since the early twentieth century, the nation's political, ecclesiastical, and media leaders had, until the 1960s, frowned on such behavior, especially when young, white, middle-class women were involved. But in the mid-1960s, some liberal Protestant ministers, influenced by the new primacy that they accorded to individual rights in their ethical teaching, suggested that perhaps the relaxation of public sexual morals was a positive development. Television executives and movie producers likewise welcomed the relaxation of restrictive codes that had once circumscribed the discussion of sex on screen. After a series of Supreme Court decisions extended First Amendment protections to pornographic literature, politicians seemed powerless to stop the developing sexual revolution.[5]

Reacting to the Sexual Revolution

In the midst of these societal changes, evangelicals faced a new challenge when they argued for a conservative standard of sexual behavior that many people were discarding. They were alarmed at the rapid shifts in societal values. But what especially disturbed them were the changes that they saw in their own families and churches. To their dismay, their own teenage children were adopting the new attitudes and behavior encouraged by the sexual revolution. A youth minister at a suburban evangelical church in the Philadelphia area received the "shock of his life" in early 1966 when he conducted a written survey of the thirty teens at his church and discovered that only six of them had not had "illicit sexual relations."[6]

Evangelicals believed that preserving a conservative societal standard of sexual ethics was of paramount importance, because the stability of the family required that sex be confined to marriage, and the continued existence of the nation—and indeed, of civilization itself—depended on maintaining the cohesiveness of the family. "Sexual promiscuity," the evangelical authors of *Toward Christian Marriage* (1958) wrote, "spells the ruin of all nations and tribes which permit it to go unchallenged among them."[7] They therefore had to do everything possible to deter their young people from losing their virginity before marriage.

By the mid-1960s, many evangelicals were beginning to realize that their traditional approach to teaching sexual ethics to teens was not working. In 1965, a *Moody Monthly* article titled "Can the Church Reach the Teens of '65?" complained about the failures of evangelical Sunday school lessons to give teenage boys practical help in the fight against sexual temptation. The standard evangelical Sunday school lesson for teens on sexual matters consisted mainly of a list of New Testament verses on the subject, invariably including Paul's statement in 1 Corinthians 6:18 (KJV) that a Christian must "flee fornication." By the mid-1960s, many evangelicals believed that they needed to give teens a more comprehensive theology of sex that would go beyond a list of "Thou shalt nots." "Nostalgia and hand-wringing" were not the answers either, John Scanzoni, an evangelical sociology professor at the University of Indiana at Bloomington, proclaimed: "Only the development of a Christian philosophy of sex is a viable alternative."[8]

To teach young people about sex, evangelicals began encouraging churches to adopt a modern, comprehensive sex education curriculum that would go far beyond the traditional Sunday school lessons on the subject. Initially, evangelicals expected parents to take the lead in conveying this message to their children, a strategy that they outlined in articles such as "Sex Education is the Parents' Job" (published in 1965). But they quickly realized that churches could play a role in helping parents in this task. "Some parents don't know how to approach the subject and neglect to provide needed information," a *Christian Life* article titled "Is Sex Education the Church's Responsibility?" stated in 1967. "The church can give the facts and the Christian viewpoints on life and love." The choices for a church sex education curriculum were limited in the mid-1960s. No evangelical publishing house had produced a comprehensive sex education curriculum, so evangelical churches that began offering sex education programs in 1965 often had to resort to Anglican-produced materials, which some of them considered too liberal because they approved of dancing and treated homosexuality as a disease rather than a sin. Evangelicals were delighted in 1967 when Missouri Synod Lutherans, the most conservative wing of the Lutheran Church, produced a six-volume set of books and filmstrips on sex that were designed for use by churches in educating young people about both the biology and morality of sex.[9]

In 1965, the Billy Graham Evangelistic Association signaled a new turn by releasing a film titled *The Restless Ones,* which raised controversy among evangelicals because of its frank discussion of teenage sex. "I would call it pornography," one Texas reader of *Christian Life* wrote in disgust after seeing the magazine's summary of the film. But Graham defended his organization's approach. "The Bible does not adopt a hush-hush, Victorian attitude toward [sex]," Graham said in 1967, "rather, the Bible talks plainly about it. . . . Sex is a creative energy within us. If we give this energy to Christ, it becomes a power, a dynamic, that will drive and carry us to heights undreamed of; but if misused, it will destroy both body and soul." The best way to confront America's sexualized culture, evangelicals believed, was to engage in an open discussion of the practice. As one *Christian Life* reader stated in response to the magazine's positive review of Graham's film, "God did not hesitate to show sex in reality in the Bible," and teenagers therefore had a "right" to "ask questions" about sex and expect honest answers.[10]

The message that evangelicals tried to convey to young people about premarital sex was that sex outside of marriage could destroy their lives. Graham's film depicted the early death of one of its lead characters as a result of her sexual promiscuity. More realistically, perhaps, evangelicals argued that indulging in sexual lust and forbidden sexual behavior would lead to long-term guilt and regret. "Free love is neither free nor love, but bondage," *Christian Life* declared in 1966.[11] Such warnings about premarital sex had long been a staple of evangelical culture, although evangelicals in the mid-1960s were devoting more attention to the subject than they once had and were becoming increasingly frank in their descriptions of sexual sin. Their willingness to privilege practical arguments over biblical quotations in their appeals to young people was also a sign that they felt the need to repackage and update their message if they hoped to be able to convince their sons and daughters to resist the temptations of the sexual revolution.

Celebrating Marital Sex

Perhaps the most surprising feature in evangelicals' updated theology of sex was an open celebration of the joy of sex within marriage. Evangelical books on marriage in the 1950s had made brief references to the "sacred" value of marital sex, but they had given little detail or instruction about sexual intimacy in marriage. Nearly all of the evangelical preaching on sex prior to the 1950s had been focused on helping unmarried people avoid sexual temptation. But in the 1960s, evangelicals began championing marital sex as a divine gift and sacred pleasure. In April 1964, *Christian Life* broke a long-standing taboo among evangelical periodicals by running a cover story on "Sex in the Middle Years," a two-page spread aimed not at young people but at their parents. "The God-given gift of the sex drive is no less sacred or significant in middle age than in youth," the author, a Presbyterian minister, explained. "The spiritual love which two people feel for each other needs tangible expression with frequency. Perhaps the primary purpose for which God has given every normal man and woman the sex drive is to have a miraculous means of expressing the depth of spiritual love by physical means."[12]

The article disturbed many of *Christian Life*'s readers. All of the initial reactions that *Christian Life* published two months after the article appeared were negative. "Why do we have to have sex exploited on a Christian magazine?" one woman from Beckemeyer, Illinois, asked. Some even suggested that the discussion bordered on the pornographic, although the article was far from explicit. But the wave of initial negative reactions prompted other readers to send in positive reviews.[13]

Readers were still debating the April article in October, six months after its publication, but by then *Christian Life* had already published more articles on marital sex, including "Love's Many Dimensions," an article by the chair of Wheaton College's philosophy department. "Love's Many Dimensions" clearly stated that sex belonged only in marriage, and it rejected the "ultra-Freudian notion that the supreme end of man is sex." But the article also celebrated marital sex as a "sacrament of union," and gave practical (though nonexplicit) advice about how men and women could improve their response to each other by recognizing men's propensity to respond to visual erotic stimuli and women's natural response to touch.[14]

Evangelicals had long been uncomfortable with the Roman Catholic idea of marriage as a "sacrament," but in the mid-1960s, they began applying this word to marital sex. Yet in celebrating marital sex as pleasurable, evangelicals distanced themselves from the Catholic view that sex could not be separated from its procreative purpose. For evangelicals, marital sex was sacred because God had ordained it as a means of joining husband and wife, regardless of whether they chose to have children or not. Most of the leading evangelical magazines of the 1960s endorsed birth control.

A generation earlier, fundamentalists had preached against birth control, and as late as 1961 *Eternity* magazine published an article condemning the practice. In the early 1960s, evangelical publications hesitantly began endorsing birth control, saying that it was a matter of Christian liberty that was up to each couple to decide for themselves. Nevertheless, they still suggested that couples who decided not to have any children at all were sinning against God's plan for marriage.[15]

By the mid-1960s, many evangelicals, armed with their new theology of sex as a pleasurable end in itself (so long as it was confined to marriage), were preaching the value of birth control as a positive good. The Bible did not say anything directly against birth control, they argued, and its positive celebration of marital sex seemed to be sufficient reason to encourage married couples to use any means at their disposal to control their fertility so that they could enjoy intimacy without the fear of pregnancy. "More of us have found our way back to the Bible concept that sex is a fact of God's creation, a means of expressing love between husband and wife as well as the means of procreation," an article in *Eternity* magazine titled "The Ring and the Pill" declared in September 1966. "Those who believe that sex in marriage is significant in its own right, not requiring procreation to justify it, can accept birth control."[16]

Many evangelicals had also accepted the idea that the world was becoming overpopulated—a concept that Catholic intellectual leaders resisted—and that every child should be a "wanted" child. The mass starvation that would result from an impending population crisis, a *Christianity Today* article declared in 1967, "may be this century's great moral crisis." Indeed, Merville O. Vincent, an evangelical doctor who frequently contributed articles on sexuality to Christian magazines in the 1960s and 1970s, argued in *Christianity Today* in 1968 that "over-production of children may be as sinful as selfish avoidance of parenthood." "Contraception in Christian marriage," he asserted, "not only is permissible but has a very significant value." That same year, the evangelical Protestant Symposium on the Control of Human Reproduction called for "Christians' involvement in programs of population control at home and abroad."[17] At a time when books such as Paul Ehrlich's *The Population Bomb* (1968) were popularizing concerns about the dire consequences of overpopulation, evangelicals largely embraced the rhetoric of their secular counterparts on the issue.

When Pope Paul VI issued an encyclical in 1968 reiterating the Roman Catholic Church's teaching against artificial birth control, evangelicals were quick to condemn it as the outdated view of a "reigning, absolute monarch" that had "moved the Church back in spirit three centuries."[18] While the pope felt constrained by a centuries-old continuous tradition of Christian teaching against birth control, evangelicals, convinced that the Bible said nothing against the practice, were free to embrace their contemporaries' view of birth control as liberating.

Evangelicals also broke with Catholics on the issue of masturbation. The Roman Catholic Church taught that masturbation was a sin because it separated sexual pleasure from marriage and procreation, and evangelicals had once preached a similar message. The leading evangelical sex advice book of the late 1940s had contained strong warnings against masturbation, placing it in the same category of such sexual sins as homosexuality and prostitution. Even in the early 1960s, some evangelical sexual advice books for teens still contained warnings about masturbation, but by the end of the decade, those warnings had disappeared, because evangelicals who noticed that the Bible said nothing directly about masturbation believed that they had made a mistake to proscribe it.[19]

Evangelicals' shift on masturbation resulted partly from the influence of Christian psychologists who pointed out the prevalence of masturbation and argued that there was no evidence that it resulted in psychological harm. But even more importantly, evangelicals' belief that they were losing the battle against the sexual revolution prompted them to look to masturbation as a way for teens to avoid the temptation to have sex with someone to whom they were not married. Charlie Shedd's *The Stork Is Dead: Straight Answers to Young People's Questions about Sex* (1968), which *Christian Life* described as possibly "one of the top books for 1969 on the subject of sex," went so far as to claim that masturbation could "be a positive factor in your total development," because it could help a teen avoid premarital sex. "Teenage masturbation is preferable to teenage intercourse!" Shedd wrote. "The chances are that you will need some release. . . . Which brings me to what I told my own children. What I taught them is that *masturbation is a gift of God!*"[20]

Homosexuality

While evangelicals began to accept masturbation as a way to prevent premarital sex, they strengthened their opposition to homosexuality and gave increased emphasis to their promise to be able to "cure" homosexuals of their same-sex desire. Evangelicals had never accepted the legitimacy of homosexual sex, but in the 1950s and early 1960s they had generally placed it in the category of other sexual sins without singling it out for special vilification. They said that because it might partially result from psychological causes, those seeking to overcome their homosexual desires and behaviors should probably consult with a psychologist.[21]

The development of a fledgling gay rights movement in the late 1960s and the new proclamations of some liberal Protestant ministers that homosexuality was "morally neutral" forced evangelicals to re-examine the issue of homosexuality.[22] Evangelicals uniformly believed that the Bible's condemnations of "homosexuals" or its command that a man should not "lie with mankind, as with womankind" prevented them from ever condoning homosexual intercourse. Nevertheless, for a brief moment, some evangelicals did suggest that in view of the findings of medical and psychological science, they should not view a homosexual orientation as a choice or promise homosexuals deliverance from their sexual desires.

In October 1967, *Christian Life* dared to publish a lengthy review of evangelical positions on homosexuality that included a three-page article by a twenty-nine-year-old British Christian psychologist who pointed out that few homosexuals were being "cured" through psychological treatment. He argued that instead of expecting homosexuals to become heterosexual after they became Christians, evangelicals should instead expect them only to "control" their desires. "Contrary to popular belief, probably the majority of homosexuals are not so by choice," he said. Evangelicals should therefore treat them with compassion, and should not be surprised to find homosexuals in their churches who would continue to struggle with their homosexual inclinations as long as they lived.[23] *Christian Life* asked four evangelical medical doctors to respond to the psychologist's claims, and three of them concurred, saying that homosexual inclinations, which were not sinful per se, needed to be distinguished from homosexual acts, which were.

Yet even this limited concession to an emerging gay rights consciousness was too much for many evangelicals. Dr. William Standish Reed, *Christian Life*'s medical columnist, insisted that homosexuals could be "delivered" through the Holy Spirit. No type of homosexuality, he said, "whether it be overt and practiced or something held in abeyance," can be "condoned by God." Homosexuality was dangerous, he argued, because it was "productive of extreme social catastrophe, not only on the family level, but also in churches and business and wherever else it occurs."[24]

After the rise of the gay rights movement in the 1970s, Reed's views became dominant among conservative evangelicals. Indeed, even in 1967, most of the readers who responded to *Christian Life*'s articles on homosexuality endorsed Reed's position. The endorsements included one testimonial from a person who claimed to have been "heal[ed]" from same-sex desire and even included a letter from a gay Christian who said that although he had not yet been delivered from homosexual inclinations after a prolonged period of intense prayer, he still had faith that God would someday give him a "miracle" and make him a "new creature" by freeing him from homosexuality. Such lines became evangelical orthodoxy for the rest of the twentieth century. Arguing that Christians must "hate the sin but love the sinner," evangelicals vehemently denounced homosexual practice while claiming that true love for homosexuals meant offering them a chance to be "born again" in Christ, which ultimately included release from their homosexuality. Books such as Tim LaHaye's *The Unhappy Gays* (1978) argued that homosexuality stemmed from environmental, rather than genetic, influences, and that it could be cured. Later, ex-gay ministries such as Exodus International promised "freedom from homosexuality" for those who wanted to change their sexual orientations.[25]

Evangelicals' theology of sexuality made it difficult for them to do otherwise. By celebrating marital sex as a "sacrament" and an exalted pleasure, and by excoriating the Roman Catholic Church for mandating celibacy for priests, which they claimed was unnatural, evangelicals left little room for a mandate of lifelong celibacy for gay people. One evangelical book on sex from 1963 was especially pointed on the subject: "The person who rejects the vocation of marriage, except in response to a call of God for some particular task, deprives himself of immeasurable grace and strength, and exposes himself to manifold temptations." By the late 1960s, evangelical advice on this subject had become more nuanced, because evangelicals were beginning to recognize the needs of singles in their churches and were urging that they be treated with compassion, which meant not commanding them to get married. But they still assumed that marriage would be the goal for most people.[26] As a result of their reaction against the Catholic Church's glorification of celibacy and their concomitant proscription of all sex outside of marriage, they were forced to argue that homosexuals could change their orientation and pursue a fulfilling life as heterosexuals.

Feminism

Homosexuality also challenged evangelicals' increasingly conservative views of gender. At the beginning of the 1960s, most evangelicals had taught that wives should submit to their husbands, but female submission had not been a major emphasis of their preaching. Indeed, in an era in which social pressures steered middle-class white women to marry early and devote their time to raising children, some evangelicals attempted to challenge societal stereotypes and encourage women to be less focused on marriage.[27]

Evangelicals of the 1950s and early 1960s believed that their theology was liberating for women, and missionary reports from abroad frequently stressed the way in which the Christian message freed women in non-Christian countries from traditional oppression. Throughout the 1950s, evangelical publications encouraged their male readers to view women as intellectual and spiritual equals. While they took it for granted that there were distinct differences between the sexes, they sometimes seemed to suggest that society had taken this idea too far in its regimented differentiation between male and female roles. "The truth of the matter is that men do cry sometimes, women do enjoy athletics, and although men usually work away from the home, women frequently do, too," Clyde Narramore, who was probably the most well-known evangelical psychologist of the early postwar era, wrote in 1958. "Since boys and girls are first of all *people*, they are more alike than they are different. There is much overlapping of masculine and feminine activities."[28]

When the second-wave feminist movement developed after the publication of Betty Friedan's best-selling *The Feminine Mystique* (1963), a few evangelical women argued for egalitarian gender roles in marriage and the church. Although theirs was a distinctly minority viewpoint among their evangelical compatriots, evangelical feminists such as Letha Scanzoni began publishing articles in Christian magazines in the mid- to late 1960s that argued that Jesus's egalitarian treatment of women, the apostle Paul's statement in Galatians that in Christ there was "neither male nor female," and the presence of female prophets in the first-century church meant that women could legitimately take a leadership role in ministry and that the traditional hierarchical view of male-female relations was indeed unbiblical. Scanzoni told *Eternity* readers in 1966 that the male leaders at her conservative Baptist church were uneasy when she began teaching mixed-gender adult Sunday school classes, a position from which women had traditionally been barred, but that that had not deterred her from breaking traditional gender barriers. Scanzoni went on to take a leading role in the organization of the Evangelical Women's Caucus in 1973, and she wrote several books and articles in the late 1960s and 1970s arguing for an egalitarian view of gender relations in all facets of life.[29]

Scanzoni believed that her egalitarian view of gender relations was thoroughly biblical and evangelical. She was firmly committed to the evangelical reverence for Scripture and indeed, to evangelical conservative mores in other areas. At the same time that she was promoting egalitarian gender relations, she also published *Sex and the Single Eye*, a defense of chastity that contained strong warnings against premarital sex.[30] Scanzoni did not view herself as a rebel against the evangelical tradition, at least initially. Instead, she hoped that her fellow evangelicals would accept a Christian feminism as a logical outgrowth of their long-standing biblicism. But she was soon disappointed.

Instead of becoming more egalitarian, most evangelicals began giving increased emphasis in their writings to the idea of innate biological differences between men and women. They did this because they viewed the feminist movement as an attack on the traditional family. Evangelical magazines began publishing more articles about the scriptural command for wives to submit to their husbands, and they began to devote more attention to championing "full-time" mothers and criticizing those who chose to work outside the home. "God's feminine mystique places a wife under the authority of her husband," an *Eternity* magazine article stated in January 1968, in a critique aimed squarely at Betty Friedan.[31] Evangelicals frequently bolstered their conservative views of gender by citing verses from the Pauline epistles commanding women to submit to their husbands and to be silent in church. But as with their reaction to the sexual revolution, evangelicals found that merely quoting Bible verses would not be sufficient to stop the feminist movement's influence on their churches. Instead, they needed to develop a comprehensive theology of gender. Paradoxically, they relied on women to develop this theology, thus giving women more power in their churches than they had ever previously enjoyed.

In the early 1960s, articles on women's roles were usually written by men, but by the end of the decade, evangelicals had developed an unspoken expectation that women should be the ones to defend women's place in the home and tell other women to submit to their husbands. Several Christian magazines introduced women's columns—which were invariably edited by women—for the first time in the mid-1960s, and some also gave women oversight of editorial space that had previously been controlled by male pastors. At the beginning of 1968, *Christian Life* gave its column "Tell Me, Pastor," which provided a forum for readers to ask pastors troubling questions about aspects of Christian life, to the beauty queen Vonda Kay Van Dyke and changed the column's name to "Dear Vonda Kay." Van Dyke continued to champion conservative standards of behavior, just as the men who had formerly edited the column had done. Like male editors, she warned against premarital sex. But *Christian Life* apparently thought that the message might be more persuasive if a young, attractive woman presented it instead of an aging male pastor. By the end of the decade, the covers of *Christian Life*, *Eternity*, and other Christian magazines began featuring color photographs of female Christian celebrities, such as Anita Bryant, along with headlines that focused on the needs of mothers, wives, and even single women.[32]

In the late 1960s, many evangelical churches began holding women's retreats—a new idea for some of these congregations—giving their female congregants an opportunity to escape from their household responsibilities for a weekend and gather together with other women to pray and listen to inspirational female speakers. Indeed, women's retreats and women's seminars became the springboard for national speaking careers for many evangelical women, because many churches that frowned on women speaking from the pulpit were perfectly willing to allow female speakers to address other women before audiences that sometimes numbered in the thousands. In the 1970s, Beverly LaHaye, Marabel Morgan, Anita Bryant, and several other evangelical women embarked on national speaking tours that made them household names among conservative evangelicals.[33]

Yet while the women's retreat movement seemed to empower women by giving them a forum within church traditions whose leadership had traditionally been all male, the women who attended the retreats, along with those who organized the sessions, were thoroughly committed to traditional gender roles. Most of the sessions at the retreats focused on women's domestic duties, including the requirement that wives submit to their husbands. Jill Renich, a Michigan evangelical whose "Winning Women" retreats were attracting more than a thousand participants by 1967, described herself as a "Detroit housewife" and wrote articles for *Moody Monthly* insisting on the need for women to submit to their husbands in everything even if the men in their lives demonstrated poor judgment or a lack of godly priorities.[34]

While this message was directly opposed to the emerging feminist consciousness of the era, some conservative evangelical women found it appealing, because it glorified their domestic duties as a divine calling and highlighted women's unique role in God's creation plan. Borrowing heavily from the "separate-spheres" ideology of the Victorian era, the conservative evangelical women who emerged as leaders in their movement in the late 1960s and 1970s outlined a vision for women that placed them at the center of the social moral order. Because evangelicals believed that the home was the foundation for a stable society, a social vision that highlighted women's role as moral guardians of the home appeared to give them a tremendous degree of moral authority. At a time when the feminist movement was beginning to make national headlines, conservative evangelical women posited an alternative model of female empowerment—one which many women outside of conservative evangelical culture viewed as restrictive, but which some women inside the movement embraced as God's plan for their lives.

In a move that coincided with and paralleled the growth of women's retreats, evangelical publishing houses began issuing guides to women's roles that were written by female authors. Evangelical women had been writing inspirational fiction and biographies for decades, but they had rarely had opportunities to write about theology or even Christian living. In the mid-1960s, evangelical publishing houses decided that there was a market for books written by women defending a conservative theology of gender. One of these new titles was Ella May Miller's *I Am a Woman* (1967), which included a defense of full-time home-making. "Woman's primary role and greatest contribution is that of being a mother," Miller wrote, "God purposely made woman a unique person to be helper to man—to be mother of mankind. This is her supreme role!"[35]

Conservative evangelical women sounded very traditional in their condem-nations of feminism, but they were thoroughly modern in their acceptance of the new evangelical theology of sex and their insistence that women's need for sex was just as strong as men's. "God gave them sexual desire as well as men, and it's normal for women to feel this desire," Lou Beardsley and Toni Spry declared in *The Fulfilled Woman* (1975). Most of the books on women's roles devoted several pages to sex, and much of the discussion was unusually frank, at least when compared to evangelical literature published before 1965. Ironi-cally, despite their criticism of feminism and the sexual revolution, evangelical women realized that those movements had produced a welcome attention to women's sexual needs that liberated them from the strictures that their mothers and grandmothers had faced, and they were conscious that they were breaking new ground in bringing attention to women's sexual desires in the context of Christian marriage. "Throughout the Victorian period, a 'good' woman was not supposed to appreciate sexual experience," Anna Mow wrote in *The Secret of Married Love*, an evangelical advice book for married women published in 1970. "The sex cult that has deluged our culture today has had one good effect: a woman can now be honest with her husband, and she can enjoy her relation with him without feeling guilty."[36]

Women's newfound freedom to discuss their sexual desires openly did not result in any compromise of their orthodox evangelical theological views on sexuality. Indeed, it reinforced these views. The evangelical theology of sex that had emerged in the late 1960s made women's sex advice literature possible, because evangelicals could now openly celebrate the pleasures of sex while insisting that those pleasures must be confined to marriage. Marabel Morgan's *The Total Woman*, which sold ten million copies after it was released in 1973, included a chapter on "Super Sex," which encouraged women to make erotic phone calls to their husbands during the workday and to take the lead in ini-tiating sex. "Be the seducer, rather than the seducee," Morgan advised.[37]

Yet if Morgan's sexual advice might have shocked evangelicals only a decade earlier, her advice on wifely submission could hardly be considered progressive. "It is only when a woman surrenders her life to her husband, reveres and worships him, and is willing to serve him, that she becomes really beautiful to him," Morgan wrote, "She becomes a priceless jewel, the glory of femininity, his queen!"[38] Evangelical theologies of sex offered a way to promote an egalitarian model of women's sexual desire—in saying that women wanted sex just as much as men did—while simultaneously highlighting women's distinct role as "helpmeets" of their husbands. It was in the sex act that biological differences between men and women may have been most obvious, so it was hardly surprising that a theology of gender difference would give so much attention to sex.

Abortion

The evangelical theology of sex also shaped evangelicals' views on abortion. Most Protestants, including Southern Baptists, had long accepted the legitimacy of abortion in cases in which a woman's life was in danger, and in the postwar period, they were generally reluctant to challenge the movement for the legalization of abortion for cases in which pregnancy threatened a woman's health, or in cases of rape, incest, or fetal deformity. In the mid-1960s, when liberal Protestant ministers began campaigning for more permissive abortion laws, evangelicals did not join in this campaign, which was identified with the individual rights-based ideology and sexual permissiveness that they opposed. But they also refused to support the Roman Catholic effort to preserve bans on abortion, which they thought lacked biblical support. "The Bible definitely pinpoints a difference in the value of a fetus and an adult," a *Christian Life* article on abortion stated in 1967. For that reason, the author did not object to laws that allowed abortion in cases of rape, incest, and fetal deformity. But he cautioned against abortion laws that were too permissive, because he was concerned that the availability of abortion would make young, unmarried couples less reticent to engage in premarital sex. "Even with birth control pills, fear of pregnancy is an important deterrent to sexual promiscuity," he wrote. "Remove that with an easy out in the safety and security of a hospital, and sexual promiscuity would increase."[39]

Southern Baptists expressed a similar attitude toward abortion. A survey of Southern Baptist pastors conducted in 1970 showed that nearly 80 percent opposed abortion-on-demand and were thus unsympathetic to the abortion-rights campaign that some liberal Protestants had endorsed. Yet they were equally unsympathetic to the Catholic-led pro-life movement. Seventy-one percent had no objection to abortion in cases of rape and incest, situations in which a woman was clearly not using abortion as a means to escape the consequences of promiscuity. Seventy percent favored allowing abortion in cases in which a pregnancy endangered a woman's mental or physical health, and 64 percent said that abortions should be legal in cases of fetal deformity. In 1971, the Southern Baptist Convention passed a resolution in support of abortion legalization in cases of "rape, incest, clear evidence of severe fetal deformity, and carefully ascertained evidence of the likelihood of damage to the emotional, mental, and physical health of the mother."[40] In other words, Southern Baptists and other evangelicals opposed allowing abortion-on-demand, which they thought would encourage sexual promiscuity, but they saw no reason to prohibit abortion for clearly delineated problem pregnancies that had no connection to sexual licentiousness.

Similarly, a conference of twenty-five evangelical scholars who came together to discuss the issue in August 1968 at the Protestant Symposium on the Control of Human Reproduction expressed discomfort with abortion, but acknowledged its permissibility in some circumstances. "The Christian physician will advise induced abortion only to safeguard greater values sanctioned by Scripture," they declared.[41]

By the early 1970s, when the abortion-rights campaign was receiving endorsements from the National Organization for Women and *Playboy* magazine, evangelicals began to see that the campaign for legal abortion was closely connected with their two inveterate enemies—the sexual revolution and the feminist movement—and they distanced themselves from their earlier qualified endorsements of abortion rights. In 1969, *Christianity Today* issued an editorial on abortion that stated that while the "revision" (that is, the liberalization of) existing abortion laws was needed, the revised abortion laws should allow abortion only on "substantial medical and other grounds that are biblically licit." Allowing "abortion merely on demand or for convenience" was wrong. In 1971, *Eternity* magazine published one of the strongest condemnations of abortion that any evangelical magazine issued prior to *Roe v. Wade*. In that piece, one of the most preeminent evangelical theologians of the time, Carl F. H. Henry, argued that abortion constituted the taking of human life. Yet Henry also continued to allow for the possibility of abortion in cases of rape and incest, implying that if a woman had not chosen to have sex and was pregnant through no fault of her own, she should not be forced to carry her pregnancy to term. Even as he framed his opposition to abortion in terms of the sanctity of fetal life, Henry continued to evaluate the legitimate reasons for abortion on the basis of the presence or absence of moral responsibility for the sex act.[42]

Only after *Roe v. Wade* did evangelicals gradually begin to arrive at a consensus that abortion was a moral evil, permissible only if necessary to save a woman's life. By the end of the 1970s, evangelicals, influenced by Roman

Catholic theology on abortion, phrased their opposition to the procedure in terms of their high respect for unborn human life.[43] But in the late 1960s and early 1970s, when most evangelicals were still arguing that unborn human life did not have the same value as the life of an adult mother, their views on abortion often stemmed more from their sexual ethics than their concern for fetal rights.

Taking the Theology of Sex into Politics

Like its secular counterpart, the evangelical sexual revolution—along with evangelical opposition to abortion, gay rights, and the feminist movement—continued long after the tumultuous changes of the 1960s gave way to the anxieties of the 1970s and the conservatism of the 1980s. Evangelicals became far more explicit in their discussions of the joys of marital sex, and by the end of the 1970s, sex manuals for married couples, which included not only the LaHayes' *The Act of Marriage* but also Ed and Gaye Wheat's equally explicit *Intended for Pleasure* (which was later reissued with the subtitle *Sex Technique and Sexual Fulfillment in Christian Marriage*), had become featured titles at Christian bookstores. Evangelical churches began offering marriage seminars, and evangelical Bible studies began mining the Hebrew love poetry of the Song of Solomon for insight into how to restore sexual excitement in modern marriages.[44]

As evangelicals became more rhapsodic in their praise of the sexual dimension of heterosexual marriage, their opposition to perceived threats to such marriages—threats such as feminism, gay rights, and abortion—intensified and became the basis for a new series of grassroots political campaigns. Evangelical condemnations of homosexuality, which had once been confined to churches and the pages of Christian magazines, entered popular politics in 1977, when the Southern Baptist singer Anita Bryant, joined by such evangelical luminaries as Jerry Falwell and the future Southern Baptist Convention president Adrian Rogers, led a successful campaign for the repeal of a gay rights ordinance in Miami, Florida. Evangelical discomfort with abortion translated into political action in the late 1970s, when evangelicals joined Catholic pro-life activists in calling for a constitutional amendment to ban all abortions in America except when the procedure was needed to save a woman's life. Evangelical opposition to feminism led many evangelical women to join Phyllis Schlafly's campaign against the Equal Rights Amendment and then to sign up for Beverly LaHaye's Concerned Women for America, an organization intended to be a political counterforce to the National Organization for Women and the feminist movement.[45]

The national influence that evangelical women had first gained as anti-feminist writers and speakers in the late 1960s and 1970s increased over the next several decades. LaHaye's Concerned Women for America claimed half a million members by the mid-1980s and became a significant lobbying force on Capitol Hill, while LaHaye herself became a widely read author. By the end of the century, evangelical female authors such as Beth Moore and Stormie Omartian were selling millions of copies of their Bible study guides and devotional books, which accepted conservative views of gender roles even as they gave women a new voice in the shaping and proclamation of evangelical theology. Women also held many of the national leadership positions in pro-life organizations. In each of these cases, evangelical women rose to prominence within conservative religious circles by denouncing the principles of feminism, even as they enjoyed new opportunities to pursue careers as nationally influential writers, speakers, and political lobbyists.[46]

Although outside observers often assumed that the religious Right's campaigns of the late twentieth century were reactionary political movements led by people who wanted to turn back the clock to the pre-feminist 1950s, the reality was that the Christian Right's political ideology reflected evangelical views on sex and gender, which were in reality a product of the post-fifties era. While other Americans were experiencing a sexual revolution, the future leaders of the Christian Right were likewise undergoing profound shifts in their own thinking. The competing political visions that resulted from these two very different sexual revolutions led to culture wars that continued for decades. What was often forgotten in the ensuing melee is that the changes of the 1960s shaped the views of people on both sides of the conflict, because both the Right and the Left were fighting for ideologies of sexuality that they had forged in the same turbulent decade.

NOTES

1. Tim LaHaye, "Making the Most of Your Differences," *Moody Monthly*, March 1969, 25; Tim LaHaye, *How To Be Happy Though Married* (Wheaton, IL: Tyndale, 1968); Tim and Beverly LaHaye, *The Act of Marriage: The Beauty of Sexual Love* (Grand Rapids, MI: Zondervan, 1976).

2. The many studies of the emergence of culture war politics among evangelicals include Darren Dochuk, *From Bible Belt to Sunbelt: Plain-Folk Religion, Grassroots Politics, and the Rise of Evangelical Conservatism* (New York: W. W. Norton, 2011); and James Davison Hunter, *Culture Wars: The Struggle to Define America* (New York: Basic Books, 1991). The transformation of evangelicals' own understanding of sex has received comparatively little scholarly attention, but two works that do touch on this issue are Janice M. Irvine,

Talk about Sex: The Battles over Sex Education in the United States (Berkeley: University of California Press, 2002), 81–88; and Amy DeRogatis, "What Would Jesus Do? Sexuality and Salvation in Protestant Evangelical Sex Manuals, 1950s to the Present," *Church History* 74 (2005): 97–137. Both of these works focus primarily on the 1970s in exploring the origins of the transformation in evangelical theologies of marital sex, while largely ignoring the developments of the 1960s that are the focus of this chapter.

3. Mel Larson, "Bride and Gloom," *Moody Monthly*, June 1962, 69–70. For evangelical books on sex published in the 1940s and 1950s, see Frank A. Lawes, *The Sanctity of Sex* (Chicago: Good News, 1948); W. Melville Capper and H. Morgan Williams, *Toward Christian Marriage: The Privileges and Responsibilities of Sex* (Chicago: InterVarsity Press, 1958); and Jack Wyrtzen, *Sex and the Bible* (Grand Rapids, MI: Zondervan, 1958).

4. For an overview of conservative sexual mores in the 1950s and early 1960s, see Beth Bailey, *Sex in the Heartland* (Cambridge, MA: Harvard University Press, 1999), 1–104.

5. For analyses of shifts in societal views of sexual morality, see John D'Emilio and Estelle B. Freedman, *Intimate Matters: A History of Sexuality in America* (New York: Harper & Row, 1988); Bailey, *Sex in the Heartland*; and David Allyn, *Make Love, Not War: The Sexual Revolution: An Unfettered History* (Boston: Little, Brown, 2000). For examples of some liberal Protestant ministers' acceptance of the loosening of public sexual morals, see "The Church and the Sexual Crisis," *Christian Century*, June 29, 1966, 823; and "The Passing Scene," *Christian Century*, January 25, 1967, 102.

6. Leslie H. Stobbe, "Confused Teens Look for Answers," *Christian Life*, June 1966, 22.

7. Capper and Williams, *Toward Christian Marriage*, 83.

8. Bill Eakin, "Can the Church Reach the Teens of '65?" *Moody Monthly*, June 1965, 18; Keith L. Brooks, "Purity," *Moody Monthly*, October 1964, 83–85; John Scanzoni, "Are America's Sexual Codes Changing?" *Eternity*, January 1969, 43.

9. Irene Klingberg, "Sex Education Is the Parents' Job," *Christian Life*, January 1965, 41–42; Alma Gilleo, "Is Sex Education the Church's Responsibility?" *Christian Life*, September 1967, 78; Ralph D. Manning, LTE, *Christian Life*, August 1964, 8; Alma Gilleo, "Standards for Sex Morality," *Christian Life*, February 1965, 51–52; "Sex Education Series," *Moody Monthly*, February 1968, 64.

10. James F. Collier, "The Restless Ones," *Christian Life*, July 1965, 25–27, 41–43; S. James Dempsey, LTE, *Christian Life*, January 1966, 9; "Billy Graham, "Questions Teens are Asking," *Moody Monthly*, June 1967, 70; Carolyn Sherman, LTE, *Christian Life*, March 1966, 15.

11. "Positive Side of Morality," *Christian Life*, May 1966, 25.

12. Robert H. Meneilly, "How Important Is the Sex Drive in the Middle Years?" *Christian Life*, April 1964, 38.

13. "Readers Write," *Christian Life*, June 1964, 8; "Readers Write," *Christian Life*, October 1964, 8.

14. Arthur F. Holmes, "Love's Many Dimensions," *Christian Life*, September 1964, 26, 28.

15. John Roach Straton, *The Menace of Immorality in Church and State* (New York: George H. Doran, 1920), 73, 82, 115; John R. Rice, *The Home: Marriage, Courtship, and Children* (Murfreesboro, TN: Sword of the Lord, 1945, 1974), 164; "Birth Control: Which Methods Are Moral?" *Christianity Today*, 17 February 1967, 43; Stuart Barton Babbage, *Christianity and Sex* (Chicago: InterVarsity Press, 1963), 34–39.

16. Irene Soekren, "The Ring and the Pill," *Eternity*, September 1966, 32.

17. "Birth Control," 43; M. O. Vincent, "A Christian View of Contraception," *Christianity Today*, November 8, 1968, 15; "A Protestant Affirmation on the Control of Human Reproduction," *Christianity Today*, ibid., 19.

18. Ralph L. Keiper, "Birth Control: Still a Catholic Problem," *Eternity*, October 1968, 8–10, 31.

19. For evangelical warnings against masturbation from the late 1940s through the early 1960s, see Lawes, *Sanctity of Sex*, 25–27; Capper and Williams, *Toward Christian Marriage*; Wyrtzen, *Sex and the Bible*, 29; and Donald F. Tweedie Jr., *The Christian and Sex* (Grand Rapids, MI: Baker Book House, 1964), 51.

20. Clyde M. Narramore, *Life and Love: A Christian View of Sex* (Grand Rapids, MI: Zondervan, 1956), 146–153; Review of Charlie W. Shedd's *The Stork Is Dead*, *Christian Life*, April 1969, 16; Charlie W. Shedd, *The Stork Is Dead: Straight Answers to Young People's Questions about Sex* (Waco, TX: Word Books, 1968), 70 (emphasis in original).

21. Wyrtzen, *Sex and the Bible*, 40–41.

22. For liberal Protestants' views on homosexuality in the 1960s, see "Equality for Homosexuals?" *Christian Century*, December 13, 1967, 1587; "The Passing Scene," *Christian Century*, January 25, 1967, 102; and H. Kimball Jones, *Toward a Christian Understanding of the Homosexual* (New York: Association Press, 1966).

23. Brian R. Munday, "The Homosexual: Does He Belong in the Church?" *Moody Monthly*, October 1967, 38, 63–65.

24. William Standish Reed, "No Christian Homosexual," *Moody Monthly*, October 1967, 68; *Christian Life*, May 1967, 16.

25. "Readers Write," *Christian Life*, January 1968, 6; Tim LaHaye, *The Unhappy Gays: What Everyone Should Know about Homosexuality* (Wheaton, IL: Tyndale House, 1978). For evangelical ex-gay ministries, see Tanya Erzen, *Straight to Jesus: Sexual and Christian Conversions in the Ex-Gay Movement* (Berkeley: University of California Press, 2006); and Exodus International, "What Does Exodus International Believe about Sexual Orientation and Change?" December 18, 2009, http://exodusinternational.org/2009/12/sexual-orientation-and-change/.

26. Stuart Barton Babbage, *Christianity and Sex* (Chicago: InterVarsity Press, 1963), 52; Elmer L. Towns, "The Church and the Single Adult," *Eternity*, October 1968, 18–19.

27. See, for example, Jean M. Neely, "I Broke the Engagement," *Christian Life*, July 1961, 26; and Mel Larson, "Bride and Gloom," *Moody Monthly*, June 1962, 69–70.

28. C. Gordon Beacham, "Africa's Hope: Womanhood," *Christian Life*, December 1960, 25–27; Clyde Narramore, *How To Tell Your Children about Sex* (Grand Rapids, MI: Zondervan, 1958), 80.

29. Letha Scanzoni, "Women's Place: Silence or Service," *Eternity*, February 1966, 14–16; Letha Scanzoni, "Elevate Marriage to Partnership," *Eternity*, July 1968, 11–14; Letha Scanzoni and Nancy Hardesty, *All We're Meant to Be: A Biblical Approach to Women's Liberation* (Waco, TX: Word Books, 1974); Pamela D. H. Cochran, *Evangelical Feminism: A History* (New York: New York University Press, 2005), 12–39.

30. Letha Scanzoni, *Sex and the Single Eye* (Grand Rapids, MI: Zondervan, 1968). For studies of evangelical feminism and analyses of why it remained a minority movement within evangelicalism, see Sally K. Gallagher, "The Marginalization of Evangelical Feminism," *Sociology of Religion* 65 (2004): 215–237; and Cochran, *Evangelical Feminism*.

31. C. Peter Wagner, "Those Contemporary 1st Corinthians: Wine and Women," *Eternity*, January 1968, 20.

32. Janice Gosnell Franzen, "All in a Woman's Day," *Christian Life*, February 1965, 21; Vonda Kay Van Dyke, "Dear Vonda Kay," *Christian Life*, May 1968, 22. For an example of the new emphasis on women's issues and female celebrities in evangelical magazines of the late 1960s, see the October 1968 issue of *Christian Life*, which featured a cover photograph of Anita Bryant under the headline, "Entertainer without Tarnish." The issue also included the article "Miss California Discusses Her Faith" (26).

33. "Winning Women," *Moody Monthly*, April 1967, 30–31; Jennifer Heller, "Marriage, Womanhood, and the Search for 'Something More': American Women's Best-selling 'Self-Help' Books, 1972–1979," *Journal of Religion and Popular Culture* 2 (Fall 2002): 1–51.

34. "Winning Women," 30; Jill Renich, "How to Help Your Husband Get Ahead," *Christian Life*, June 1963, 22–24.

35. Ella May Miller, *I Am a Woman* (Chicago: Moody Press, 1967), 14, 16.

36. Anna Mow, *The Secret of Married Love* (Philadelphia: Trumpet Books, 1970), 41.

37. Marabel Morgan, *The Total Woman* (Old Tappan, NJ: Fleming H. Revell, 1973), 127.

38. Ibid., 80.

39. S. I. McMillen, "Abortion: Is It Moral?" *Christian Life*, September 1967, 50, 53.

40. Paul L. Sadler, "The Abortion Issue within the Southern Baptist Convention, 1969–1988" (PhD diss., Baylor University, 1991), 25–26; Southern Baptist Convention, "Resolution on Abortion," June 1971, SBC Resolutions, http://www.sbc.net/resolutions/amResolution.asp?ID=13.

41. "A Protestant Affirmation on the Control of Human Reproduction," *Christianity Today*, November 8, 1968, 18.

42. "Capital Consistency," *Christianity Today*, June 20, 1969, 21; Carl F. H. Henry, "Is Life Ever Cheap?" *Eternity*, February 1971, 20–21; Eric Miller, "Elusive Unity," *Touchstone*, April 2005, http://touchstonemag.com/archives/article.php?id=18-03-012-v.

43. For evangelical opposition to abortion after *Roe v. Wade*, see "Abortion and the Court," *Christianity Today*, February 16, 1973, 32–33; and Francis A. Schaeffer and C. Everett Koop, *Whatever Happened to the Human Race?* (Old Tappan, NJ: Fleming H. Revell, 1979).

44. Ed and Gaye Wheat, *Intended for Pleasure* (Old Tappan, NJ: Fleming H. Revell, 1977); DeRogatis, "What Would Jesus Do?" 97–137.

45. For evangelical grassroots political campaigns of the 1970s, see Daniel K. Williams, *God's Own Party: The Making of the Christian Right* (New York: Oxford University Press, 2010), 105–158.

46. John Rees, "Christian Leader Beverly LaHaye: An Exclusive Interview with the Pro-Family President of the 500,000-Member Concerned Women for America," *Review of the News*, May 8, 1985, 31–38; Sarah Pulliam Bailey, "Why Women Want Moore," *Christianity Today*, August 2010.

RAGING AGAINST LEVIATHAN?

EVANGELICALS AND THE LIBERAL STATE

6

Attica, Watergate, and the Origin of Evangelical Prison Ministry, 1969–1975

KENDRICK OLIVER

In January 1977, Charles Colson was at the annual convention of National Religious Broadcasters in Washington, D.C., watching from the wings as Billy Graham met with the press. Colson's own news conference was due to begin as soon as Graham had finished. Colson listened as a Dutch broadcaster asked America's most prominent evangelical preacher how recent reports of a national religious revival were to be reconciled with evidence that the country was simultaneously in the throes of a moral and social breakdown: "We read all about people in America being born again, that this was the Year of the Evangelical, that thousands—perhaps millions—are coming to Christ. Yet, we also see in America abortion on the increase, deterioration of the family structure, the crime rate increasing. How is it that so many can be born again and your society still be so sick?"[1]

Colson later recalled that he had whispered a prayer of thanks that the question had not been asked of him, as well it might have been. After all, he had made his name during the first Nixon administration as a pioneering

architect of backlash politics, working to construct and then consolidate a new
Republican majority from social groups disillusioned with liberal responses to
the crises of the 1960s—rapidly rising crime rates among them. Then, in 1974,
Colson became a crime statistic himself when he admitted to Watergate prosecutors that three years previously he had leaked information likely to be prejudicial
to the trial defense of Daniel Ellsberg, who had released the Pentagon Papers to
the *New York Times*. Pleading guilty to a charge of obstructing justice, Colson
had received a prison sentence of between one and three years. By this time,
Colson had also joined the ranks of recent converts to evangelical Christianity.
Indeed, his striking public metamorphosis from political henchman into prayer-
ful penitent may have served as a key initial stimulus for the media's subsequent
efforts to compass evangelical culture and measure its significance. Colson was
released from prison in early 1975. The next two years saw him publish a best-
selling memoir, *Born Again,* and establish an organization, Prison Fellowship,
with the objective of selecting and training prison inmates to work as chaplains
in their own correctional institutions, providing moral and spiritual support to
other prisoners and offering a route to rehabilitation through the inculcation of
Christian values. The inmate chaplains, with the help of Prison Fellowship,
would also try to match individual prisoners to Christian mentors outside, who
would offer advice and assistance both during their term and after their release.[2]
In such initiatives, Colson believed, lay a plausible solution to crime—or at
least to high rates of recidivism, which contributed so substantially to overall
crime statistics. He told *Christianity Today,* "If enough people went into the prisons
with the idea of taking a personal interest in one man or one woman you would
quickly, quickly begin to reduce the prison population and the crime rate in the
United States."[3]

Here, then, was Colson's articulation of the relationship of the evangelical
revival to a society ridden with crime and with the fear of crime, a society that
seemed both committed to incarceration as means of social control but unable
to break the fateful cycle whereby many offenders upon their release from
prison came quickly to re-offend. His prayer, he wrote in his second book, *Life
Sentence,* was that the churches would turn "into mighty instruments for God's
transforming work in our society," and in particular that "many thousands of
spiritually renewed people" would "begin to visit the prisons of America,
bringing light and hope into dark and despairing cells."[4]

It was significant, however, that Colson presented this vision of the redemptive role of the modern evangelical as a prayer, not as a description of current
realities, not even as prophetic expectation. He was aware that not all evangelicals were prepared to accept such a commission. In a speech to the National

Association of Evangelicals in February 1977, Colson reflected on the deepening division in the churches throughout the twentieth century, "the social activists moving to the left, the soul winners to the right." The hazard for evangelicals, he observed, was that, absent a commitment to meet the needs of mankind, their own journeys of faith became diminished—an errand that ended with not much more than "cheap grace"—and meanwhile, outside their churches, the world continued "spinning dizzily out of control."[5] In an interview with *Sojourners* magazine in July 1979, Colson went further. He noted that he had encountered hostility to his efforts not just from evangelicals who regarded social issues as irrelevant to their faith but also from evangelicals who rejected social action on ideological grounds. The members of evangelical churches, he said, were predominantly "white, middle- or middle-to-upper class, and they tend to be conservative. They equate conservative theology with conservative politics. They will accept the simplistic notion 'crack down on criminals and you're going to stop crime,' and they believe that the ultimate crackdown is capital punishment."[6]

In the mid-to-late 1970s, therefore, Charles Colson's hopes for an evangelical ministry that might result in the emptying of the nation's prisons were haunted by an apprehension that the actual preferences of most evangelicals, with respect to the problem of crime, pointed in entirely the opposite direction: toward a punitive, retributive model of punishment, which ignored New Testament narratives of reconciliation and redemption, drawing instead upon earlier, sterner Mosaic law. Colson described the "cold silence" in which he was heard when he spoke in evangelical churches of the need to care for the imprisoned; but there was also evidence beyond his own experience to suggest that evangelicals might not rally behind his cause.[7] In a 1971 survey, 66.3 percent of Southern Baptist pastors and 56.2 percent of Sunday school teachers registered their support for capital punishment, figures that were significantly higher than those returned in polls of broader national opinion at the time.[8] The identification of evangelicals in the late sixties and seventies with the politics of "law and order" also seems consistent with the now-standard interpretations of the advance of the New American Right through constituencies worried by social disorder and the signs of moral decay.[9] In addition, as both Philip Jenkins and Anne-Marie Cusac have observed, deepening anxieties about crime and the increased recourse to incarceration as a solution to crime reflected the renewed cultural salience of concepts of intrinsic evil.[10] These were concepts that had never become a stranger to most evangelical minds. Their return to popular discourse at the same historical moment that the American prison population embarked on its endless upwards rise and the death penalty was restored to statute books across the nation spoke not of Colson's antithesis of punitive justice and biblical religion, but instead of their elemental affinity.

Indeed, not all commentaries upon Colson's ministry in the prisons see it as incompatible with the backlash politics of the 1970s. Jeff Sharlet, for example, has questioned whether there was really much difference between Colson's efforts during his time in the Nixon White House to consolidate the conservative hold on power and his attempts through Prison Fellowship to persuade inmates to become obedient to God. Both campaigns—in Sharlet's view—worked to achieve social peace on the terms of those already in charge. "Colson's work," he writes, "is shot through with a cagey regard for Plato's 'noble lie,' by which the elite must govern masses who don't know what's good for them."[11] According to Tanya Erzen, the emphasis placed by Prison Fellowship on personal religious conversion as a solution to criminal behavior amounts to a kind of "testimonial politics." What the testimonies of prisoners spiritually transformed through the work of Prison Fellowship declare, in effect, is the obsolescence of state-run programs focused on structural social problems. These narratives, Erzen asserts, "work in conjunction with a neoliberal vision in which social services are privatized rather than funded by the federal government."[12] Winnifred Fallers Sullivan, meanwhile, has noted the "convergence and mutual dependence" of two markers of American difference compared with other advanced industrial societies: the extent to which Americans "profess attachment to religion" and "the high rate at which they incarcerate their fellows."[13] That religion had become complicit in the regime of mass imprisonment was evidenced by the "faith-based" rehabilitation programs operated by Prison Fellowship, which asked offenders—as part of the transformative process—to acknowledge that their crimes were a sin against God and that they were deserving of the punishment they received at the hands of the state. "Whether one can conclude," Sullivan observes, "that dominant contemporary Christian theologies of punishment actually contributed directly to the increased punitive nature of U.S. society, there is no question that the two are culturally congruent and mutually recognizable."[14]

On the question of whether evangelical religion played a constitutive role in the evolution of a punitive justice system through the seventies and eighties, the criminological literature is actually rather reticent. Most scholarly accounts of the rise of mass incarceration acknowledge the influence of populist "law and order" politics as well as the emergence of conservative theorists like James Q. Wilson who sought to discredit the hitherto dominant rehabilitative goals of American corrections policy and asserted the need to restore deterrence and therefore punishment to the center of the fight against crime.[15] But these accounts also emphasize that the shift toward punitive sanctions and expressive justice occurred because progressive political opinion was also losing confidence in the rehabilitative paradigm around this time. Progressive critics variously argued that the paradigm was constructed upon a very limited base of empirical research; that, where implemented, it was usually chronically under-resourced; and that it was intolerant of cultural difference and coercive in its effects. Sometimes—as with respect to sanctions against domestic violence—they actually asserted that the justice system was not punitive enough. Given the peculiar vulnerability of the American state to populist pressures, the hemorrhaging of progressive support for rehabilitation created opportunities for conservative policy entrepreneurs to make forceful pleas based upon "common sense" conceptions of the necessity of deterrence. In particular, criminological accounts note the irony that progressive assaults upon the discretionary powers of judges, prison administrators, and parole boards to set, review, and alter individual sentences, and the subsequent progressive advocacy of fixed and uniform penalties for particular categories of crime, ultimately opened the door to conservative politicians to claim the fight against crime as their own by bidding up the length of such mandatory penalties—and filling up the prisons.[16]

The criminological literature often identifies the Quakers as significant progressive critics of the American prison system, but it offers little concrete detail about any religious forces that may have been arrayed on the other side.[17] David Garland sees the religious Right, increasing in political significance over the course of the 1970s, as expressing "a strikingly *anti-modern* concern for the themes of tradition, order, hierarchy and authority."[18] But he ascribes the religious Right no particular agency, independent of secular conservatism, in the rise of mass incarceration. James Whitman, meanwhile, comments that the harshness of American justice "has something to do" with the strength of the nation's religious tradition: "Part of what makes us harsher than continental Europeans is the presence of some distinctively fierce American Christian beliefs."[19] Despite that assertion, though, he goes no further, hardly mentioning religion again, let alone evangelical religion, in the rest of his book.

So what can we actually say about American evangelicals and the law and order issue as the sun began to set on the long 1960s? Did the mid-seventies season of the evangelical revival and the emergent politics of mass incarceration share more than just a coincidence of birth? To what extent were they conceived from the same theology? The remainder of this chapter represents an attempt to move the scholarship on from its current presumptive, empirically impoverished answers to those questions. In particular, it assesses the motivations of evangelicals drawn to an increasing involvement with prison ministry and their attitudes toward the values and practices of the American correctional system during the deathwatch of the rehabilitative paradigm.

The American penitentiary was, in large measure, the invention of religious reformers, concerned to rescue criminals from the path of sin by saving their souls. By the late 1960s, however, religious institutions had mostly withdrawn from involvement in the rehabilitation of prisoners, conceding that task to secular educational, training, and therapeutic programs. Prison chaplains, indeed, complained that many mainline churches were far more interested in ministering to the affluent than engaging in the uncertain, challenging work of walking convicted criminals back to God. Comfortable in their own suburban captivity, these congregations were—according to Byron E. Eshelman, a chaplain at San Quentin—"indifferent to the prison ministry which would focus on the deprived and rejected minorities out of the inner city ghettos and the rural slums."[20] The situation was not much different with respect to evangelicals. These were years in which evangelicals, having identified the U.S. armed forces as a key mission field, were enthusiastically seizing the opportunities presented by the military chaplaincy for proselytizing American soldiers.[21] But there was no equivalent evangelical march through the nation's correctional institutions. A 1957 survey conducted by the Christian Life Commission, the agency that functioned as the conscience of the Southern Baptist Convention on social and moral issues, indicated that evangelical ventures in prison ministry were fitful and subject to marked local variations. Some theological seminaries sent their students to conduct services in nearby prisons, others did not.[22] Six years later, in 1963, a committee appointed by the convention's Home Mission Board identified a handful of local Baptist initiatives to aid released convicts, such as halfway houses and mentoring and sponsorship programs, but this hardly amounted to a consistent pattern of engagement. One Baptist field director quoted in the report asserted that the church had "long ignored" its responsibilities "in terms of providing a meaningful ministry" to both juvenile and adult offenders.[23] Ten years on again, in 1973, Baptists were still being accused of a collective failure of concern and compassion with respect to those held in the nation's jails. "Baptists as a whole want vengeance and want the criminal kept in prison," declared Tennessee's Commissioner of Corrections, Mark Luttrell, who was himself a Baptist layman.[24]

Still, there were no hard and fast theological barriers to evangelical participation in prison ministry. Just as there were evangelicals who could point to a biblical justification for their opposition to capital punishment, so too was it possible to find a persuasive scriptural and ethical basis for taking the message of God's love into the prisons.[25] Evangelical advocates of prison ministry commonly cited Matthew 25, when Christ described his Second Coming and the terms on which he would proclaim the Last Judgment.[26] To the righteous, he would say: "Naked, and ye clothed me: I was sick, and ye visited me: I was in prison, and ye came unto me." Moreover: "Inasmuch as ye have done *it* unto one of the least of these my brethren, ye have done *it* unto me." Those condemned into the everlasting fire would be told: "I was a stranger, and ye took me not in: naked, and ye clothed me not: sick, and in prison, and ye visited me not."[27]

Moreover, by the time of Luttrell's comments, there were already signs that more evangelicals were questioning whether the priority traditionally placed by their churches upon the winning of souls for Christ necessarily excluded action to address social injustice and the other problems of the secular world. Behind the scenes at *Christianity Today*, throughout the mid-to-late 1960s, the issue was a source of considerable tension. The editor, Carl Henry, had long believed that evangelicals should speak out against social evils. The magazine's principal benefactor, J. Howard Pew of the Sun Oil Corporation, objected to any church involvement in economic, social, and political affairs. The result was a carefully parsed editorial line, which observed that individual Christians or groups of Christians might reasonably engage in social action, but that this did not fall within "the mission of the Church as Church."[28] But it was not obvious that this distinction could be maintained. Evangelicals did not necessarily want their churches to be indifferent to social evil. For many, spiritual ministry was itself a form of social action. It represented the most secure long-term solution to the troubles of the world.

Indeed, the new forms of evangelical social action that seemed most directly sympathetic to traditional evangelical thinking were not those that sought to address material wants or reduce racial strife in the cities, but rather those where social effects could be connected to individual changes of heart. It may not be surprising, therefore, that evangelicals in the early 1970s started to look to the nation's correctional institutions as an arena for involvement, nor that it was often impossible to discern in such involvement the operations of a social conscience separate from an impulse to convert. In November 1970, *Christianity Today* described the role that could be played by Christian-sponsored halfway houses in counseling and training released prisoners so that they were better able to resist the temptation to re-offend. These houses could do some of the work that state parole agencies, underfunded and overloaded, could not. Moreover, the journal declared, they would "afford an excellent opportunity to proclaim the good news of divine forgiveness for even the worst of crimes."[29] In June 1971, the annual meeting of the Southern Baptist Convention in St. Louis passed a resolution criticizing the country's "over-crowded, unsanitary, and destructive" prison systems and calling for their reform, with the goal of "redemptive rehabilitation" rather than punishment. The resolution also urged Southern Baptists "to follow the teaching of Jesus by caring for those in prison by working to provide funding, education, ministries, and other innovative programs."[30]

If any single event in the long sixties seemed to exemplify the themes of backlash politics—and also its lethal potentialities—it was the violent suppression of the Attica prison rebellion in September 1971. The *New York Times* columnist Tom Wicker observed "the building mood of hatred" around the environs of the prison as the rebellion stretched into its fourth day: inside, over two thousand inmates, almost 80 percent coming from the major urban centers, blacks in the majority, holding forty-two prison officers and civilian employees hostage; outside, a rapidly assembled force of state troopers and prison officers, heavily armed, predominantly drawn from the white working-class communities of rural upstate New York.[31] The assault that restored control of the prison to the state, ordered by New York's governor Nelson Rockefeller, was responsible for the deaths of twenty-nine inmates and ten hostages. Initially, the authorities declared—and the media reported—that the hostages had been killed by their captors, their throats cut with knives. According to Heather Ann Thompson, "any sympathy for the plight of America's incarcerated, any sense that they needed a greater voice in society or needed advocates among the nation's voting population, began to evaporate in that instant."[32] In the White House, Charles Colson later recalled, Nixon declared that Rockefeller had done the right thing: "The public want no more nonsense from criminals. The public will cheer him on. 'Gun 'em down,' they'll say."[33]

It is possible, then, to read the Attica rebellion as a key stimulus to the punitive temper of backlash politics. Making a fateful association between prison inmates and the "dangerous classes," Americans disavowed whatever had remained of their faith in rehabilitation and reduced their expectations of what prisons could and should achieve to the basic function of social control. But actually much of the evidence points the other way. "The Attica uprising," observes Marie Gottschalk, "prompted an outpouring of public and scholarly interest in how to make prisons more humane and in how to reduce the prison population."[34] In one Harris poll, published in February 1972, 58 percent of those surveyed agreed that rebellions like Attica were "the result of prison authorities not understanding the needs of inmates." Only 23 percent judged that they were a consequence of "too easy" a prison regime.[35] Among those who attributed the rebellion to the failure of the prison authorities to respond to legitimate inmate grievances, and who criticized the violence with which order was restored, were church leaders and religious commentators, some of them evangelical.[36] *Christianity Today* emphasized the need to think of offenders as human beings and to treat them with dignity, as Christ himself had done on the cross when he "encouraged one of those criminals hanging with him to talk rather than to rail." It urged Christians to become involved, both by "taking the life-transforming Gospel to men in jails and prisons" and by fulfilling their duty as citizens to ensure that correctional institutions were managed in such a way "as to make as many inmates as possible into more responsible participants in an admittedly imperfect society."[37] Six months later, *Christianity Today* repeated the call to its readers to engage in prison ministry: "It won't be easy, but remember the figurative words of our Lord himself: 'I was in prison and you visited me.'"[38]

One consequence of Attica was indeed a distinct quickening of religious interest in prisons and in prisoners. The social agencies of mainline denominations devoted renewed attention to the subject of prison reform; they also studied existing grassroots church-led projects, such as programs to monitor conditions in local jails and initiatives to assist released offenders—and commended them as models for wider implementation.[39] Many of these activities permitted and involved collaboration with secular charitable and advocacy organizations, for the objectives were not expressly and immediately religious. A number of enduring evangelical prison programs also had their origins in the post-Attica period, though—in contrast to mainline initiatives—they were usually explicitly described as ministries. In 1972, International Prison Ministry was founded by Chaplain Ray Hoekstra, and Christian Prison Ministry by Frank Costantino.[40] In July of that year, Bill Glass—a former gridiron star turned evangelist—organized a three-day prison crusade at the Marion Correctional Institution in Marion, Ohio. The crusade combined religious services with a series of athletic clinics featuring other sporting celebrities.[41] "I saw the Lord overcome unbelievable barriers and obstacles and soften the hearts of hardened criminals," Glass later reported. Well over a hundred inmates, he said, were still involved in Bible study and prayer months after the crusade.[42] In March 1973, following a second prison crusade in Tehachapi, California, Glass declared that "we have hit upon a unique and exciting ministry that will not fail."[43] Six months later, after a crusade at the Waupun Correctional Institution, Wisconsin, which produced decisions for Christ from over a third of the inmates, Glass's organization resolved to place a "strong emphasis" on prison ministry in its future activities.[44]

Still, by this time, the opportunities that prison ministries offered to evangelicals seemed of little consequence compared with the challenges presented by the Watergate affair. Billy Graham in particular found it difficult to reconcile his personal friendship with President Nixon with the expectation of many commentators that his role as "America's pastor" required moral pronouncement upon the abuses of power for which Nixon was responsible. But Graham's response to Watergate was not without significance for evangelical work in the prisons. Graham tended to define Nixon's actions as evidence of a universal, rather than individual, condition of sinfulness: "There's a little bit of Watergate in all of us," he said. The solution to the crisis, therefore, lay in a national change of heart—though, as Steven P. Miller has noted, Graham "ultimately issued this call in individuated terms." The country's redemption would be an aggregate effect of millions of individual acts of repentance, evangelism, and conversion.[45] In the wake of Watergate, therefore, it was harder for evangelicals to think of criminals as a species apart. As *Christianity Today* declared, "we must be careful to include *all* crimes against our fellow men in our purview, not just those practiced by the usually less affluent members of our society." Permeating the Christian attitude to crime, it went on, "should be the awareness that our crimes against God, our disobedience to his commandments, leave none of us righteous, no, not one."[46] There was a logical corollary: if the criminal receiving his punishment at the hands of the state was not much different in kind from the ordinary sinner, then this was true of his soul as well. Like all others, and like that of the nation as a whole, it existed to be won for God.

In the event, it was not Richard Nixon who best dramatized the theme, for—despite Billy Graham's best efforts—he did not convert or even really repent.[47] Gerald Ford intercepted Nixon's fall from grace before he landed up in jail. Instead, evangelicals found the lesson they were looking for in the transformation of Nixon's former aide Charles Colson. Here apparently was an exemplary evangelical tale of spiritual crisis, conversion, repentance, and penance, eventually achieving redemption in the form of a mission to guide other sinners—in Colson's case, prisoners—back to the Lord. In fact, there was much in Colson's passage from epiphany to ministry that had to be elided before it could conform to a conventional conversion narrative. Initially, although he knew he was under threat of criminal indictment, Colson recognized in himself only the sin of pride. What had driven him in his career, he now understood, "was the need to satisfy my own ego, to impress my friends and family and associates with really how good I was and how much I could accomplish."[48] It was this realization that had precipitated Colson's conversion. His arrogance had carried him into his present predicament; seeking release from that predicament, he surrendered himself to God.[49] Even though at first he regarded his conversion as a private matter, Colson believed it had salience for the nation as a whole. He wrote to President Nixon asserting that the best hope for bringing an end to the current political turmoil was to encourage the country toward "a rebirth of faith and a renewed commitment to God." He urged the president to ask Congress to enact a resolution calling upon Americans "to unite in prayer to heal the wounds of Watergate."[50]

By the spring of 1974, however, it was evident to Colson that Nixon had no taste for genuflection. Nor was it likely that a presidential call for national spiritual renewal, even if it had been made, would have satisfied Nixon's critics or persuaded the Watergate prosecutors to close down their investigations. Moreover, Colson's maturing Christian conscience was now reviewing his record in Nixon's service and diagnosing more than the sin of pride: "It weighed heavily on me that while I might not have been guilty of the specific offenses for which I was going to be indicted, I could not regard the sum of my conduct in the White House as guiltless."[51] In particular, he had leaked information that might have prevented Daniel Ellsberg from receiving a fair trial. Colson believed that his conversion would not be completed until he had settled his moral debts. Judging that he "could not be true to Christ and remain in the position of defending my own former conduct," Colson decided—against the advice of his legal representatives—to plead guilty to a charge of attempting to obstruct justice.[52]

Although Colson's plea involved no bargain with respect to sentencing, he allowed himself to hope that he would not be imprisoned.[53] He regarded incarceration with dread, not as an opportunity for prison evangelism.[54] After his conversion, he had been adopted by the Fellowship Foundation, a network of elite Christians headquartered at Fellowship House in northwest Washington, D.C. Over the early summer of 1974, as Colson waited to learn his fate, the Fellowship Foundation had embarked on a ministry at Lorton Reformatory in Virginia.[55] But insofar as Colson and the foundation were making plans for his future, there was no thought of work with prisoners. Douglas Coe, who led the foundation, believed that Colson's talents would be best employed in developing an outreach ministry directed at young people.[56] It was not to be. At a court hearing in late June, Colson was sentenced to between one and three years in prison.

After the hearing, Colson stood outside the courthouse and told the assembled reporters that what had happened was "the Lord's will—I have committed my life to Jesus Christ and I can work as well for Him in prison as well as out."[57] For the first few weeks of his sentence, however, Colson found only limited occasion for such work. He was initially confined at Fort Holabird, a detention facility for government witnesses, some of whom, like Colson, were waiting to give their testimony in other Watergate trials and hearings. Colson renewed his friendship with Herb Kalmbach, Nixon's personal lawyer, and convinced him to accept Christ into his life. This was Colson's first experience of making a convert. "I feel a little bit like a child with a new toy," he wrote his Fellowship "brothers" back in Washington.[58] Otherwise, Colson spent much of his time at Holabird alone, studying the scriptures and drafting a book on Watergate.

After Nixon had resigned and been pardoned by President Ford, Colson became much less useful to the Watergate prosecutors, and so in mid-September he was transferred to a federal prison at Maxwell Air Force Base in Alabama. Here, Colson experienced for the first time the alienation and deprivation that structured the lives of inmates in an ordinary American jail: "The conditions are really worse than I expected," he told his Washington "brothers." Indeed, after only twenty-four hours at Maxwell, he had begun to envisage a future for himself that combined ministry to his fellow inmates for the duration of his stay and then, after his release, a campaign for penal reform. He wrote: "When I leave I hope I can do something about the concept of rehabilitation and punishment. It's time we called it what it is—punishment;—all the high sounding names given to it—deterrence, rehabilitation are so much bull. If it is punishment, so be it but maybe it is more humane to whip a man's body than destroy his soul slowly."[59] Indeed, for much of Colson's time in prison, his commitment to Christian fellowship and evangelism went hand in hand with a strikingly radical critique of the criminal justice system. Ministry was essential because correctional institutions had abandoned their charges to conditions of bitterness and despair. It was "sheer folly" to expect these institutions to succeed at rehabilitation, and where they tried, the effort was inevitably coercive: "The Christian must ask himself whether man has the right to try to reshape another man's soul, to make him something he wasn't and isn't." Only by opening men's hearts to the Holy Spirit could real rehabilitation be achieved. But Colson also judged that ministry alone would not be enough. Imprisonment, he thought, was necessary in some cases to protect the public and also to satisfy the biblical concepts of restitution and retribution. Still, 80 percent of prisoners could be punished in other ways, "ways that can be more beneficial to the individual and society."[60] He wrote to Douglas Coe: "Politicians might be less inclined to seek political profit by feeding the hunger of the masses for revenge, advocating long jail terms and harsh treatment for criminals, if they could experience the deprivations inflicted on those imprisoned."[61] Colson had been reading Dietrich Bonhoeffer's letters from prison, and took from them the need for more than obedient, silent discipleship. He wrote: "We live by God's Plan for us and His justice is perfect. I accept it fully but I also think that God expects us to fight against injustice as we find it here. We can't expect him to do it all for us."[62] At Maxwell, Colson began to use his legal training to help his fellow inmates with their appeals against conviction and their petitions for parole.[63]

Colson's dualism of a commitment to Christian witness and a desire to contest the injustices of the prison system was informed by more than his observations of the deprivations around him among the men he encountered in prison. Colson also felt himself to have been unjustly treated; having presided over Watergate, Nixon had been pardoned, but Colson was left to languish in prison, without any indication of when he would be freed. "It is all capital punishment of the soul," he observed in his diary, "simply a question of degree, whether man's flesh is destroyed in electric chair or one year is taken away—is it humane under *any* circumstances unless man is threat to society?"[64] Like Bonhoeffer, he refused to be reconciled to his fate until he had acted to change it and failed, for only then could he be sure that it was God's will.[65] He continued to petition for his release. And in the meantime, his fellowship with other Christian prisoners and his attendance at a weekly prison service conducted by a local Southern Baptist preacher helped him stave off depression. In late October, he gave his testimony at the service: "Man, these Southern Baptists are something, singing praise to Jesus at the top of their lungs. Coming from the more restrained churches of the Northeast as I do, it is something of a shock but I must say I love it and I love the people."[66]

Colson's prison diaries and letters, therefore, express a conviction that prisoners should be the object of compassionate evangelical concern. Certainly, he believed it important that evangelicals should work to win these prisoners for Christ, but he was also sure that a Christian conception of justice required effort on a wider scale: to address the wrongs of the existing system and to find alternatives to mass incarceration. By the mid-1970s, such arguments were not entirely unfamiliar to the evangelical mind. However, Colson himself bears a measure of responsibility for obscuring the relationship between the imperative of ministry and the imperative of reform. In late January 1975, he was released from prison on compassionate grounds after his son had been arrested for possession of marijuana. For some time thereafter, Colson found it difficult to commit to the future of ministry and advocacy that he had laid out for himself during his time in prison. Only in April did he conceive of the initial inmate chaplaincy program from which Prison Fellowship, the organization, would eventually evolve. In *Life Sentence*, he attributed the program to an epiphany—though around the same time *Christianity Today* had returned to the subject of crime, urging readers to combat its "root cause" by winning hearts for Jesus: "*There* is the place where Christians have a special responsibility beyond that of their fellow citizens."[67] Perhaps understandably, as Colson tried to encourage evangelical involvement in prison ministry and as he negotiated access arrangements with the Federal Bureau of Prisons and state correctional agencies, he spoke only sotto voce about the need for systemic change. Garry Wills noted in August 1976 that "Colson is a bit shuffling and apologetic over his reform efforts, since much of the evangelical movement opposes the social gospel."[68]

By the late 1970s, Prison Fellowship had nearly fifty employees, an income of over $1.8 million, and a network of four thousand community volunteers involved in inmate ministry.[69] At this point it began to engage in more concerted and conspicuous advocacy, with Colson emphasizing restitution as an alternative to imprisonment.[70] In the early 1980s, he founded Justice Fellowship to advise policymakers on how to improve prison conditions and to develop practical models for the application of restorative justice.[71] But Colson was also at work articulating the concept of Christianity as a worldview, as an intellectual system founded upon the authority of God as a creator.[72] According to Colson the system-builder, Western traditions of justice were grounded in the same concepts of divine authority. Although he could find plenty of modern laws that he did not like, the rule of law in itself was an elemental social good, without which there was no hope of achieving God's order on earth.[73] It was partly by means of this conflation of the law of the state and the will of God that Colson could justify Prison Fellowship's recent ventures in running actual prison units on behalf of some state departments of corrections. In 2009, three years before his death, it also persuaded him to withdraw his opposition to capital punishment.[74] Colson's acute apprehension, as he sat in prison, of the difference between the justice of men and the justice of God, seemed to have dissolved. But Prison Fellowship's recent embrace of an authoritarian worldview should not be permitted to obscure the organization's origins. These lay in a season of evangelical concern with prisons and prisoners in which the imperatives of saving souls, alleviating human suffering, and seeking institutional reform were combined, conforming neither to the politics of the backlash nor welcoming the metastasis of the carceral state.

NOTES

1. Charles Colson, "Religion Up, Morality Down," *Christianity Today*, July 21, 1978, 26–28.

2. Colson, "Proposal for Inmate Chaplains in Federal Prisons," May 1, 1975, Box 12, Folder 4, Prison Fellowship Papers, Billy Graham Center Archives, Wheaton College, Wheaton, Illinois. For an account of the early years of Prison Fellowship, see Kendrick

Oliver, "'Hi, Fellas. Come on in': Norman Carlson, the Federal Bureau of Prisons, and the Rise of Prison Fellowship," *Journal of Church and State* (forthcoming).

3. "'Watergate or Something Like It Was Inevitable': An Interview with Charles Colson," *Christianity Today*, March 12, 1976, 4–7.

4. Charles Colson, *Life Sentence* (Old Tappan, NJ: Fleming H. Revell Company, 1979), 10–11.

5. Charles Colson, Speech to National Association of Evangelicals, February 24, 1977, Box 149, Folder 16, Charles Colson Papers, Billy Graham Center Archives, Wheaton College, Wheaton, Illinois (hereafter cited as CCP).

6. "'Society Wants Blood': An Interview with Chuck Colson," *Sojourners*, July 1979, 12–15.

7. Ibid., 14.

8. Kenneth Hayes, "Church Leaders Take 'Hardline' Positions on Death Penalty," *Baptist Press*, January 28, 1971, Southern Baptist Historical Library and Archives, http://www.sbhla.org/bp_archive/index.asp; Stuart Banner, *The Death Penalty: An American History* (Cambridge, MA: Harvard University Press, 2002), 268. Not all Southern Baptists in the 1970s identified themselves as evangelicals. "We are *not* evangelicals," declared Foy Valentine, head of the Southern Baptist Convention's Christian Life Commission. "We don't share their politics or their fussy fundamentalism, and we don't want to get involved in their theological witch-hunts." See Kenneth L. Woodward, "Born Again!" *Newsweek*, October 25, 1976, 76. But it would not be long before such distinctions seemed quaint, even deluded, as fundamentalist Baptists embarked on a determined and successful campaign to shift the convention theologically and politically to the right. See Nancy T. Ammerman, *Baptist Battles: Social Change and Religious Conflict in the Southern Baptist Convention* (New Brunswick, NJ: Rutgers University Press, 1990). See also James Leo Garrett Jr., E. Glenn Hinson, and James E. Tull, *Are Southern Baptists "Evangelicals"?* (Macon, GA: Mercer University Press, 1983).

9. See, in particular, Thomas Byrne Edsall with Mary D. Edsall, *Chain Reaction: The Impact of Race, Rights, and Taxes on American Politics* (New York: Norton, 1992); and Lisa McGirr, *Suburban Warriors: The Origins of the New American Right* (Princeton: Princeton University Press, 2001).

10. Philip Jenkins, *Decade of Nightmares: The End of the Sixties and the Making of Eighties America* (Oxford: Oxford University Press, 2006), 134–151; Anne-Marie Cusac, *Cruel and Unusual: The Culture of Punishment in America* (New Haven: Yale University Press, 2009), 109–133.

11. Jeff Sharlet, *The Family: The Secret Fundamentalism at the Heart of American Power* (New York: Harper Perennial, 2009), 235.

12. Tanya Erzen, "Testimonial Politics: The Christian Right's Faith-Based Approach to Marriage and Imprisonment," *American Quarterly* 59 (September 2007): 992.

13. Winnifred Fallers Sullivan, *Prison Religion: Faith-Based Reform and the Constitution* (Princeton: Princeton University Press, 2009), 2.

14. Ibid., 101.

15. James Q. Wilson, *Thinking About Crime* (New York: Vintage Books, 1977).

16. For key accounts of the rise of mass incarceration, see Katherine Beckett, *Making Crime Pay: Law and Order in Contemporary American Politics* (Oxford: Oxford University Press, 1997); David Garland, *The Culture of Control: Crime and Social Order in Contemporary* Society (Oxford: Oxford University Press, 2001); Marie Gottschalk, *The Prisons and the Gallows: The Politics of Mass Incarceration in America* (Cambridge: Cambridge University Press, 2006); Robert Perkinson, *Texas Tough: The Rise of America's Prison Empire* (New York: Picador, 2010); Michael Tonry, *Thinking About Crime: Sense and Sensibility in American Penal Culture* (Oxford: Oxford University Press, 2004); James Q. Whitman, *Harsh Justice: Criminal Punishment and the Widening Divide between America and Europe* (Oxford: Oxford University Press, 2003).

17. In 1971, the American Friends Service Committee sponsored *Struggle for Justice: A Report on Crime and Punishment in America* (New York: Hill and Wang, 1971).

18. Garland, *The Culture of Control*, 99.

19. Whitman, *Harsh Justice*, 6.

20. Byron E. Eshelman, "The Prison Ministry," *Federal Probation* 32 (September 1968): 37-41.

21. Anne C. Loveland, *American Evangelicals and the U.S. Military 1942–1993* (Baton Rouge: Louisiana State University Press, 1996), 139-180.

22. See, for example, Allison to Miller, January 21, 1957; Hendricks to Miller, January 22, 1957; Manning to Miller, January 24, 1957; all in Box 1, Folder 17, Christian Life Commission Resource Files, Southern Baptist Historical Library and Archives, Nashville (hereafter cited as CLCRF).

23. "Report of Committee to Study 'The Attitude and Role of the Church in Helping the Released Offender,'" n.d., Box 14, Folder 11, Home Mission Board Executive Office Files, Southern Baptist Historical Library and Archives, Nashville (hereafter cited as HMBEOF).

24. Luttrell's remarks were recorded in Lee Porter, "Southern Baptists Working for Criminal Justice," in *Southern Baptists Working for Criminal Justice: Addresses from Conferences at Glorieta Baptist Conference Center, July 1973*, Box 46, Folder 1, CLCRF.

25. See, for example, untitled essays by John Howard Yoder and Charles S. Milligan in "Capital Punishment and the Bible," *Christianity Today*, February 1, 1960, 3-8.

26. See, for example, Lutker to Miller, February 21, 1958, Box 1, Folder 17, CLCRF; "Report of Committee to Study 'The Attitude and Role of the Church in Helping the Released Offender,'" n.d., Box 14, Folder 11, HMBEOF.

27. Matthew 25:31-46 (King James Version).

28. On Henry, Pew, and *Christianity Today*'s editorial stance, see Carl F. H. Henry, *Confessions of a Theologian: An Autobiography* (Waco, TX: Word Books, 1986), 264-271; Richard J. Mouw, "Carl Henry Was Right," *Christianity Today*, January 2010, http://www .christianitytoday.com/ct/2010/january/25.30.html. The magazine's editorial position is stated in "Christian Social Action," *Christianity Today*, March 14, 1969, 24-25; and "U.S. Congress on Evangelism: A Turning Point?" *Christianity Today*, October 10, 1969, 32-33.

29. "Halfway Help," *Christianity Today*, November 6, 1970, 35.

30. "Resolution on Prison Reform," June 1971, Southern Baptist Convention Resolutions, http://www.sbc.net/resolutions/amResolution.asp?ID=673.

31. Tom Wicker, *A Time to Die* (New York: Quadrangle/The New York Times Book Company, 1975), 215. For another detailed account of the rebellion and its suppression, see *Attica: The Official Report of the New York State Special Commission on Attica* (New York: Bantam Books, 1972).

32. Heather Ann Thompson, "The Attica Uprising," *Against the Current*, 126 (January/February 2007), http://www.solidarity-us.org/node/313. For a similar view, see Perkinson, *Texas Tough*, 302.

33. Colson, *Life Sentence*, 14–15.

34. Gottschalk, *The Prisons and the Gallows*, 181.

35. Louis Harris, "Public Rejects Force in Quelling Prison Riots," *Chicago Tribune*, February 7, 1972, 18.

36. "Religious Reaction to Attica," *Christian Century*, October 6, 1971, 1159.

37. "Attica's Eloquence," *Christianity Today*, October 8, 1971, 31–32.

38. "Visiting Prisoners," *Christianity Today*, May 26, 1972, 27–28.

39. See, for example, Robert C. Chapman (Executive Director, Department of Social Justice, National Council of Churches) to Denominational Executives in Social Concerns and to Black Caucus Leaders, December 23, 1971, Box 55, Folder 9, CCRF; a special prison-focused issue of *Engage*, monthly journal of the Board of Christian Social Concerns of the United Methodist Church, February 4, 1972, in Box 55, Folder 8, CLCRF; and a special issue of *JSAC Grapevine* titled "Criminal Justice and Prison Reform," February 4, 1973, in Box 46, Folder 1, CLCRF.

40. "About IPM," http://www.chaplainray.com/index.php; Obituary: Bishop Frank Joseph Costantino, *Orlando Sentinel*, April 4, 2006, http://www.legacy.com/obituaries/orlandosentinel/.

41. "Tentative Schedule for Prison Crusade, Marion, Ohio July 28–30," Box 3, Folder 15, Champions for Life Papers, Billy Graham Center Archives, Wheaton College, Wheaton, Illinois (hereafter cited as CFLP).

42. Bill Glass "Prayer Team" newsletter, November 1972, Box 2, Folder 3, CFLP.

43. Minutes, Executive Committee Meeting, March 30, 1973, Box 3, Folder 15, CFLP.

44. Minutes, Executive Committee Meeting, October 4, 1973, Box 3, Folder 15, CFLP.

45. Steven P. Miller, *Billy Graham and the Rise of the Republican South* (Philadelphia: University of Pennsylvania Press, 2009), 184–194.

46. "Crime: The Broad View," *Christianity Today*, April 27, 1973, 28.

47. Miller, *Billy Graham*, 190–191.

48. Colson to Soden, June 11, 1974, Box 11, Folder 7, CCP. See also Charles W. Colson, *Born Again* (London: Hodder and Stoughton, 1980), 121–125.

49. Colson, *Born Again*, 127–128.

50. Colson to Nixon, November 21, 1973, Box 102, Folder 8, CCP.

51. "Statement by Charles W. Colson Regarding the Offense," June 12, 1974, Box 79, Folder 1, CCP.

52. "Colson Conversion Story: Working Outline," 26, ca. November 24, 1974, Box 92, Folder 13, CCP.

53. Colson, *Born Again*, 260.

54. Ibid., 247–248.

55. Stu Murtoff, "Review of Time Spent at Lorton Reformatory," ca. Summer 1974, Box 1, Folder 10, Fred B. Rhodes Papers, Southern Baptist Historical Library and Archives, Nashville.

56. Coe to Soden, June 12, 1974, Box 79, Folder 1, CCP.

57. Colson, *Born Again*, 273.

58. Colson to "Brothers," August 1, 1974, Box 10, Folder 7, CCP.

59. Colson to "Brothers," September 18, 1974, Box 10, Folder 7, CCP.

60. Colson to Elwood, November 11, 1974, Box 102, Folder 4, CCP.

61. Colson to Coe, ca. early October 1974, Box 10, Folder 7, CCP.

62. Colson to LeSourd, January 16, 1975, Box 102, Folder 3, CCP. See also Colson prison diary, November 14, 1974, Box 10, Folder 6, CCP.

63. Colson, *Born Again*, 326–328.

64. Colson prison diary, November 17, 1974, Box 10, Folder 6, CCP.

65. Colson to LeSourd, January 16, 1975, Box 102, Folder 3, CCP.

66. Colson to "Brothers," October 23, 1974, Box 10, Folder 7, CCP.

67. Colson, *Life Sentence*, 40–41; "Crime: Emphasizing Deterrence," *Christianity Today*, April 25, 1975, 28–29. Around the same time, Colson also received a copy of a letter written by Paul Kramer, a member of his prayer group in Maxwell. The letter, addressed to one of Kramer's friends, expressed the firm conviction that Colson remained committed to helping "the people who are 'trapped' within the Prison System." Kramer to Bowles, April 17, 1975, Box 10, Folder 7, CCP.

68. Garry Wills, "'Born Again' Politics," *New York Times Magazine*, August 1, 1976, 48.

69. Prison Fellowship Annual Report 1979, Norman A. Carlson Subject Files, Federal Bureau of Prisons Records (in author's possession following Freedom of Information Act [FOIA] request).

70. See, for example, Charles W. Colson and Daniel H. Benson, "Restitution as an Alternative to Imprisonment," *Detroit College of Law Review* (Summer 1980), 523–598.

71. Colson's recent thinking on restorative justice can be found in Charles Colson, *Justice that Restores* (Leicester: InterVarsity Press, 2000).

72. See, especially, Charles Colson and Nancy Pearcey, *How Now Shall We Live?* (London: Marshall Pickering, 2000).

73. Colson, *Justice that Restores*, 13–45.

74. Chuck Colson, "Capital Punishment: A Personal Statement," June 29, 2009, https://www.justicefellowship.org.

7

Making Lemonade
from *Lemon*

Evangelicals, the Supreme Court, and the Constitutionality of School Aid

EMMA LONG

In 1983, the National Association of Evangelicals (NAE) issued a policy state-ment on the issue of public funding for religious schools.[1] In it, the NAE argued that the additional financial burden on parents of paying for their children to attend a religious school amounted to double taxation, which, in turn, unfairly penalized those parents for exercising their First Amendment right to freedom of religion. Furthermore, the association implied, failure to provide public funds for secular programs in religious schools, which in secular private and public schools were paid for by public funds, amounted to discrimination on the basis of religion. The NAE's 1983 policy statement brought the organization into line with Roman Catholics who had been advocating public funds for religious schools, so-called "school aid" programs, since before World War II. It also allied them with conservative politicians, legal scholars, and religious groups who had for some time been arguing that the Establishment Clause of the First Amendment ("Congress shall make no law respecting an establishment of religion . . .") should not prevent tax dollars being provided to religious organizations, including schools, which provided a public service.

In legal and constitutional debates about the Establishment Clause, those favoring views similar to the NAE and other conservative Christians are referred to as accommodationists. They argue that government may make accommodations to the beliefs of people of faith and to their needs without violating the Establishment Clause and, in some cases, must do so to avoid violating the Free Exercise Clause of the First Amendment. In the school aid cases of the 1970s and 1980s, the "accommodation" demanded was justified on the grounds of easing the financial burden on parents and relieving struggling state governments of some of the burden of financing education within their states. Opponents of this view are referred to as strict separationists. Their general position is that the Founding Fathers designed the Establishment Clause to maintain a complete separation of the spheres of church and state, the metaphorical "wall of separation" of Thomas Jefferson and Roger Williams, to protect the integrity of both. For separationists, the arguments made about school aid by Roman Catholics, the NAE, and others were little more than a veil for blatant demands for government financing of religion, a clear constitutional violation.

As evangelicals increasingly allied themselves with the political Right through the late 1970s and 1980s, they came to be seen as part of a religious and secular political movement, supported by conservative politicians, judges, and legal scholars, that sought a reinterpretation of the "traditional" view of the Establishment Clause, a breaking down of the wall of separation. The problem with the political shorthand that equates evangelicals, conservatives, and a self-interested grab for public funds is that it oversimplifies to the point of potential misinterpretation. First, no distinction is made between the later period of evangelical-conservative alliance and the era of the 1960s and 1970s when evangelical groups were beginning to engage more directly with the political realm. Second, it overlooks the fact that from the late 1960s the Supreme Court was making decisions in school aid cases that, while termed accommodationist by critics, rested on rather different reasoning. It implies an accepted interpretation of the Establishment Clause, which Court cases and legal scholarship suggest did not exist. And third, it fails to take account of the broader political and economic debate in which religious schools were increasingly considered as viable options for financial and pedagogical, rather than religious, reasons. Any assessment of the views expressed and roles played by evangelicals in school aid debates in the late 1960s and 1970s needs to take into account this broader context.

Evangelicals and School Aid

The traditional interpretation of evangelicals' growing support for school aid legislation in the late 1970s suggests it was a reaction to, or a backlash against, events of the 1960s. In the area of education, two targets are most frequently presented: the Supreme Court and its decisions in *Engel v. Vitale* (1962) and *Abington School District v. Schempp* (1963) and, as a result of those decisions, the nation's public schools. In *Engel* the Supreme Court held that a daily, non-denominational prayer designed to be recited in New York public schools violated the Establishment Clause. At the very least, Justice Hugo Black wrote, the clause meant "it is no part of the business of government to compose official prayers for any group of the American people to recite as part of a religious program carried on by the government."[2] The following year in *Schempp*, the Court continued to uphold the principle that school-day religious activities required by school authorities were unconstitutional by striking down the widespread practice of reading passages from the Bible. Evangelicals, as well as fundamentalists, mainline Protestants, Catholics, and others were so incensed by this apparent secularization of the public schools, the traditional view suggests, that they pilloried the Court, abandoned public schools in favor of their own denominational schools, and then demanded public money to support them.

The reality, however, was far more complex. Initial political and religious reaction to the cases showed many were upset and outraged at the rulings and what they perceived as their potential implications. Francis Cardinal Spellman declared himself "shocked and frightened" by the decision in *Engel*, arguing that "the decision strikes at the very heart of the Godly tradition in which America's children have for so long been raised."[3] Francis James Cardinal McIntyre found the situation "positively shocking and scandalizing . . . it is not a decision according to law but a decision of license." And the Roman Catholic bishop of Dallas–Fort Worth predicted, "American public schools will have to start bootlegging religion into the classroom."[4] The Reverend John Wesley North, Methodist bishop of Washington, stated: "It seems to me in this decision one of the ancient landmarks of our American culture and tradition is being removed." This sentiment was echoed by his Georgia colleague, the Reverend John Owen Smith, who said, "it's like taking a star or stripe off the flag."[5] Meanwhile, Dr. Billy Graham claimed, "this is another step toward the secularization of the United States."[6]

Religious leaders were supported by members of Congress in their expression of such sentiments. Senator Herman Talmadge (D-GA) denounced *Engel* as "unconscionable . . . an outrageous edict," and Representative Frank Cheef

(D-KY) suggested the majority "ought to be ashamed and ought to resign."[7] Representative John Bell Williams (D-MS) insisted the decision constituted "a deliberate and carefully planned conspiracy to substitute materialism for spiritual values"; Senator John Sparkman (D-AL) called it "a tragic mistake"; and Representative Frank Becker (R-NY), who would become the leader of the political opposition to the Court on this issue, suggested *Engel* was "the most tragic decision in the history of the United States."[8] Opposition to *Engel* and *Schempp* crossed party lines and united a broad range of religious groups, a fact reflected not only in the initial reactions but in testimony before congressional committees considering proposals to overturn the rulings by constitutional amendment in 1962 and 1964.[9]

On the meaning and consequences of *Engel* and *Schempp* evangelical opinion divided. Groups such as the NAE, International Council of Christian Churches, National Sunday School Association, and the National Home Missions Fellowship, as well as individuals such as Billy Graham, Dr. Carl McIntire (president of the International Council of Christian Churches), and Dr. Daniel Poling (editor of the *Christian Herald*), saw in the Court's rulings an overarching secularism that threatened the moral foundations of the country generally and of education specifically. "The resulting revolutionary changes in long-established practices," the NAE stated in 1963, "are beginning to create a moral and religious vacuum in our educational system in which secularism, humanism, practical atheism, and amorality are beginning to take root and thrive."[10] Others, however, took a more moderate view. *Christianity Today*, the leading evangelical periodical, editorialized in June 1964: "While we recognize that other evangelicals feel differently, nothing in this present debate has changed our position respecting the unconstitutionality of state-proscribed devotions in public schools."[11] *Christianity Today*'s concern for the danger posed by amending the Bill of Rights and the call for "a renewal of educational commitment" in the home and church echoed arguments being made before Congress opposing school prayer by groups such as the Baptist Joint Committee on Public Affairs, Protestants and Other Americans United for the Separation of Church and State, as well as secular groups such as the American Civil Liberties Union, rather than pro-prayer arguments being made by evangelicals such as Carl McIntire and Daniel Poling. Leading contributors to the magazine continued to express similar sentiments throughout the following decade and evangelical groups remained divided in their support for subsequent prayer amendments in 1966 and 1971.[12]

A further difficulty is posed by evangelicals' continued interaction with the nation's public schools. After failing to overturn *Engel* and *Schempp* by constitutional amendment, evangelicals turned against the increasingly secular public schools and created their own denominational schools as an alternative, much as Roman Catholics had done in the nineteenth century—or so the backlash hypothesis would have us believe. But despite a significant growth in the number of students attending non-Catholic religious schools across the country in the 1960s and 1970s, the statistics do not suggest a mass expansion in the number of evangelical and fundamentalist schools.[13] While the number of such schools clearly increased, the numbers do not reflect a wholesale abandonment of the nation's public schools by evangelicals. Bureaucratic and practical difficulties in establishing new schools, as well as the growing financial problems in the 1970s, undoubtedly account for some of this limited growth. More importantly, however, evangelicals continued to engage with public schools and encouraged others to do so.

In a 1963 policy resolution on church and state, the NAE stated: "This does not mean that we are recommending abandonment of the public school system, but rather the correction of the existing problem within that system." The "problem" identified by the NAE was "an inherently hostile" stance toward a "religiously based view of life" the organization perceived developing in some states' school systems as a result of *Engel* and *Schempp*.[14] The NAE proposed a number of ways in which evangelicals could and should encourage a more congenial atmosphere toward those of faith within the public schools. Beyond the prayer amendment, the NAE encouraged the teaching of the role of religion in American history and the "respectful teaching of the Bible as history and/or literature as an integral part of the public school curriculum."[15] The proposal drew on both an overlooked footnote in Black's opinion for the Court in *Engel* and an explicit comment by Justice Tom Clark for the Court in *Schempp*, which made clear that the Constitution did not prevent teaching *about* religion, only those practices that inclined toward the teaching of, or indoctrination in, religious belief. The same year, *Christianity Today* editorialized: "To those who consider such teaching useless, evangelicals reply that the Word of God is not bound and that no school board or teacher can nullify God's promise that his Word will not return unto Him void."[16] Nearly ten years later, in response to a new prayer amendment, the magazine renewed its call for "use of the Bible as a reference work" and "the study of Scripture for its literary and historic qualities."[17] In cooperation with the National Education Association, which had encouraged such courses in public schools since the 1950s, school boards in Indiana, Florida, Nebraska, and Pennsylvania, among other states, introduced such programs with the aid and advice of evangelicals and other religious groups.[18] Although not universal, and not in some places without controversy, the existence of such courses, and evangelicals' willingness to engage with such programs as advisers, school board members, and parents, suggests the image of wholesale evangelical disassociation with public schools is misleading.

In its 1964 resolution, the NAE also called for Christian teachers to engage with the public schools and "to witness by example and personal life to the effects of Christian commitment."[19] Evangelicals teaching in public schools were not, thus, called to abandon the schools as institutions antithetical to their faith, but to actively participate within them. By doing so, evangelicals could show that public schools were accepting of those of faith and, as committed Christians could "witness to Christ" through their very presence in the school, thus making public schools amenable to students and staff with religious convictions.[20] James Panoch and David Barr of the Religious Instruction Association (RIA) criticized the church for withdrawing from public education and for failing to fully understand "the good that could come from the proper use of the Bible and religion in the schools."[21] At the same time, groups such as the RIA and the National Educators Fellowship (NEF), an organization of Christian professional educators in public schools, sought to encourage greater evangelical engagement with the public schools. The very existence of groups like the RIA and NEF showed continued evangelical interest in public education. Combined with the growth of programs teaching about religion and the relatively limited growth in numbers of Christian schools, the emerging picture is not of evangelical abandonment of public education in favor of Christian schools but of a continued willingness to work within the public school system to address some of the concerns about the treatment of religion and faith that emerged after *Engel* and *Schempp*.

The final element of the traditional interpretation of evangelicals' support for school aid suggests that having withdrawn from the nation's public schools in favor of religious schools as bastions of religious and moral education, evangelicals turned to federal and state governments to demand public funds to support them. The NAE's 1983 advocacy of tuition tax credits or tax relief, combined with vocal support for school aid programs from mainline Protestant and evangelical groups aligned with the religious Right, as well as support from conservative politicians, provide some evidence for this interpretation. But two key difficulties emerge with this view: first, the NAE position represented a clear policy change by the group, and second, evangelicals were once again divided on the issue and had been since the 1960s.

Compared with earlier statements by the NAE on the issue of government funds for religious schools, the association's 1983 support of tax benefits represented a substantial shift of position. In 1963, the NAE "note[d] with concern current attempts to procure government funds for church-related schools through legislation to aid education," and held that "extreme caution is necessary if church institutions are to maintain the freedom which derives from carefully hewing to the line of church-state separation." Although recognizing and supporting the right of Christian schools to exist, the support of such schools remained the sole responsibility of parents and the church. Even if Christian day schools became the only option to avoid hostility to a religious worldview, the NAE insisted in 1964 that such a religious education involved a "personal sacrifice by Christian parents and Christian teachers" implying, in part, the financial sacrifice of paying tuition fees or taking a salary reduction. In 1965, the NAE repeated its opposition to federal aid, "whether it is given directly to the institution in the form of categorical aid to improve its facilities or for the benefit of individuals in the schools for specific educational needs," while in 1964 and again in 1965 it specifically opposed arguably the most innocuous form of aid: the subsidy of bus transportation to take pupils to religious schools.[22] Such statements reveal that any "grab" for public funds for religious schools was neither an immediate nor an automatic response by evangelicals.

A review of evangelical discussion and commentary on school aid issues shows broad differences within and between individuals and denominations that existed as early as the 1960s and continued well into the following decade. In 1964 and again in 1969, *Christianity Today* presented debates between leading evangelical thinkers and academics divided on the issue of accepting school aid. Commentators throughout the 1960s and 1970s presented a variety of views on the issue of school aid but if any overarching evangelical response existed, it echoed the views of former co-editor of *Christianity Today* and headmaster emeritus of Stony Brook School, Frank E. Gaebelein: "To accept or reject federal aid is a matter of conscience that different Christian institutions will determine differently."[23] Heard just as frequently as calls for public funds for Christian schools were appeals to evangelicals to renew their dedication to Christian education in the home and the church. "[The] family, not the school or the church, is the single most effective educational agency," wrote Gaebelein, "it is a shame that many a parent who openly deplores the cessation of devotional observations in the public schools cannot be bothered to say grace at his table or to think about family worship."[24] Parents, some evangelicals argued, must take greater responsibility for their children's awareness of and participation in the faith and life of the church. Equally, the church itself should take more of a role in educating its members in the knowledge of the faith. "The Sunday School is sick," argued one commentator, while another commented, "evangelicals are not yet serious about assuring quality Christian education in the local church."[25] If the church and parents would take on greater responsibility for their children's knowledge of faith, then the lack of prayer in public schools would be less problematic and Christian schools would remain educational options for Christian parents, not substitutes for them. Such calls undermine claims of a widespread, automatic shift to demanding funds for religious schools.

By the 1980s, evangelicals were more strident and rather more united in their calls for school aid as they allied with political conservatives. While broader reasons for this alliance remain outside the scope of this chapter, in the realm of education, two key issues combined to raise evangelical concerns about public and Christian schools. First, the impact of *Roe v. Wade* (1973) was exacerbated by programs of sex education in public schools to heighten evangelical concern about the moral education their children were receiving. Second, action by the Internal Revenue Service to remove the tax-exempt status of religious schools that were deemed to have racially discriminatory policies enraged the founders of such schools. From the perspective of evangelicals, especially those whose schools did not discriminate by race, this was unwarranted government interference in institutions designed to be their refuge from a world in which they no longer felt entirely comfortable.[26] But we must be careful not to read history backwards. The dominant evangelical position on school aid in the 1980s was a product of events of that decade as well as the 1970s, rather than an ingrained, pre-existing attitude. Nor can the views of the NAE and others be easily explained as a reaction against *Engel* and *Schempp*. Not only did some evangelicals support the decisions by the Court, there was no mass abandonment of public schools in the 1960s and early 1970s, and not until conservative Christians of all denominations felt threatened by government action did support for school aid increase. Evangelical support for government funds for Christian schools must thus be explained by factors outside the church-state debate.

The Supreme Court and
the Constitutionality of School Aid

The most common portrayal of the Supreme Court's Establishment Clause jurisprudence dealing with school aid is that, as well as being hopelessly confused and incoherent, it represents a slow move away from heavy restrictions on government funds aiding religious schools or their students to a broad acceptance that all but the most direct forms of funding do not violate the Constitution.

The reality, however, is not quite so simple. The general portrayal of the Court's trajectory in Establishment Clause cases is broadly correct, but it fails to distinguish between different periods in the Court's history. The conservative majority on the Rehnquist Court from 1986 on quite clearly moved the Court toward greater accommodation. Analysis of the preceding Burger Court, however, suggests a different approach to such cases. The separationist-accommodationist axis distracts attention from a less ideological, more pragmatic foundation for decision making by the Burger Court in this field. It also implicitly assumes that the Court began from a position of complete separation of church and state. Given that the Court's first two school aid cases, *Everson v. Board of Education* (1947) and *Board of Education v. Allen* (1968) permitted bus transportation of students to religious schools and the loan of secular textbooks to students attending those schools, such a claim is difficult to defend. Analysis of the Burger Court's school aid jurisprudence in the late 1960s and throughout the 1970s suggests that the changing position of evangelicals, including the NAE, on the issue may have been influenced, in part, by Court decisions holding that not all school aid violated the Constitution.

Even a cursory survey of the Burger Court's decisions from 1968 on reveals that the Court continued to permit some forms of aid to flow to religious schools and their students: if the wall envisioned by the separationists ever existed, the Burger Court never accepted it as a foundation for its jurisprudence.[27] The question thus raised is, on what foundation *did* the Court base its opinions and reasoning? Consideration of the reasoning offered by the justices in their opinions suggests a series of informal concerns, which became an informal framework for deciding Establishment Clause cases. These significant but unstated questions were whether the benefit was received directly by the schools or indirectly through parents or students, whether the aid was financial or non-financial in form, and whether a challenged program took place on or off religious school campuses. This was a fluid, functional set of guidelines that, while rarely stated explicitly by the Justices in opinions, was nevertheless highly influential in deciding cases.

Lemon v. Kurtzman was the foundation for the Court's development of these concerns. The first major school aid case heard by the Burger Court, it was only the third such case in the Court's history. *Lemon* involved a challenge to a Pennsylvania program, which permitted the state superintendant of public instruction to reimburse religious schools for the costs of teachers' salaries, textbooks, and instructional materials where such resources were employed for secular subjects. A companion case concerned a Rhode Island statute, which supplemented the salaries of nonpublic school teachers teaching secular subjects by up to 15 percent. *Lemon* differed from the Court's earlier cases in that it involved direct financial benefits to the schools concerned. After detailed consideration of the operation and intention of both programs, the Court, in an opinion written by Chief Justice Burger, struck down both statutes as violating the Establishment Clause.

Lemon's most enduring significance was in the eponymous three-part test Burger formulated against which Establishment Clause violations could be judged: "First, the statute must have a secular legislative purpose; second, its principal or primary effect must be one that neither advances nor inhibits religion . . . ; finally, the statute must not foster an excessive government entanglement with religion."[28] For the first time the Court had a specific test to employ in school aid cases. However, Burger warned against unqualified adherence to tests and argued that the main aim was to guard against the "three main evils" the Establishment Clause was formulated to prevent: "sponsorship, financial support, and active involvement of the sovereign in religious activity."[29] Significantly, *Lemon* and the test it spawned did not adhere to a strict separationist position: Burger explicitly rejected this approach early in the opinion.[30] However, finding that Pennsylvania's program involved a direct financial subsidy to religious schools and Rhode Island's salary supplement could be easily misused, Burger concluded for the majority: "The cumulative impact of the entire relationship arising under the statutes in each State involves excessive entanglement between government and religion."[31]

The areas of concern identified by Burger and the *Lemon* majority continued to shape the school aid jurisprudence of the Burger Court. The direct-indirect aid distinction was first drawn in *Everson* in 1947 when the Court held that New Jersey could not provide aid to religious schools but that reimbursing parents for the cost of bus transportation provided only an indirect benefit to the schools concerned. This was underscored in *Lemon* when Burger struck down the programs because the aid went directly to the schools. Direct aid related closely to the concerns of the Founding Fathers in that one way to establish a religion was to finance it. In the case of school aid this analysis rested heavily on the perception of church-affiliated schools as "pervasively sectarian" institutions, permeated to such an extent by the doctrines of the church that they could be perceived as nothing other than religious institutions. Such concerns were articulated most clearly by Justice Potter Stewart for the Court in *Meek v. Pittenger* (1975). Having established the nature of the schools in question, Stewart stated: "We agree . . . that the *direct* loan of instructional material and equipment has the unconstitutional primary effect of advancing religion because of the *predominantly religious character of the schools* benefiting from the Act."[32] In one sentence

Stewart cogently summarized the link in the majority's mind between direct aid and the religious nature of the schools in question; the message to legislators and school districts was that in order to pass constitutional muster, programs of aid must not be aimed at the religious schools themselves but at easing the burden of parents or children.

The second of the informal considerations addressed by the Court involved differentiating between programs that provided, or appeared to provide, financial aid and programs that provided materials or equipment. Government programs exhibiting signs of transferring public funds to religious schools incurred far greater scrutiny from the Court. Implicit in Chief Justice Burger's argument for the Court in *Lemon* was the concern that controlling the use of money is far more difficult than controlling the use of a textbook. In *Committee for Public Education and Religious Liberty v. Nyquist* (1973) the Court employed a similar argument to rule unconstitutional maintenance and repair grants to nonpublic schools in low-income areas: not only did the grants directly subsidize the religious function of the school, there were no practical restrictions which could be imposed upon their use. The effect was to impose much greater scrutiny on financial aid programs and to require far stricter limits on them than on alternative forms of aid. The message from the Court was clear: financial benefits were far more likely to be considered a direct aid to the religious function of the school because, simply, the use of such benefits was virtually impossible to regulate and any attempt to do so would have to be so extensive that it would raise entanglement concerns.

The Court's concerns regarding financial aid influenced analysis of non-financial aid programs too: the aid provided must be of a kind that could not be diverted or subverted to religious purposes. The most striking example of this train of thought was *Meek v. Pittenger* (1975). In *Meek*, the Court addressed challenges to Pennsylvania's programs of textbook loans, loans of instructional materials, provision of auxiliary services, and the loan of instructional equipment to religious schools and their students. A fractured Court upheld the textbook loans but struck down the remaining three programs. Textbook loans had already been upheld by the Court in an earlier case, a fact relied on heavily by Stewart for the Court, in addition to noting that the books were lent to the students and not to the schools. In contrast, the instructional materials and equipment were loaned directly to the nonpublic schools that, to the majority, equated to the aiding of the religious function of the school, thereby violating the First Amendment. Two years later in *Wolman v. Walter* the distinction became clearer when the Court addressed Ohio's programs of textbook loans, testing and scoring services, the provision of diagnostic, therapeutic, guidance, and remedial services, loans of instructional materials and equipment, and reimbursement for the cost of field trips. Limited by their medical, health-related nature, diagnostic hearing, speech, and psychological services could take place on religious school campuses because the content was effectively self-regulating. In contrast, therapeutic services, including those provided as a result of the testing services, allowed the therapist to "establish a relationship with the pupil in which there might be opportunities to transmit ideological views" and as such could only be upheld if taking place at "truly religiously neutral locations."[33]

Reading between the lines in these cases it is possible to see the Court's fear that overhead projectors paid for with public funds might be used to show biblical images and texts, that tape recorders would be used to play hymns and sermons, and that maps, globes, and photographs might be employed in theology or religious studies classes. Because there was no way, without unconstitutional entanglement, to limit the use of the aid, the possibility that it might be misused was sufficient to render the loans unconstitutional. The auxiliary services, including remedial instruction, guidance counseling, and speech and hearing services, suffered a similar fate. Unlike books, which, arguably, could be read once and the religious content determined, the teachers, guidance counselors, healthcare professionals, and equipment used by them could not be simply and easily monitored and thus no way existed to ensure that those benefits would not be employed for religious purposes, particularly when the religious environment was so pervasive. Benefits whose use was known were thus acceptable; any uncertainty about that use and the immediate presumption was of unconstitutionality.

The third of the Court's considerations drew a distinction between on-campus benefits and those provided off campus. Despite controversial beginnings the distinction remained an integral part of the Court's analytic framework, and shared many similarities with the direct-indirect distinction as interpreted by the Burger Court: aid provided on campus, such as auxiliary and therapeutic services, was frequently considered closer to direct aid than to indirect aid. The distinction had a significant symbolic element too. The image of teachers or others entering religious schools or setting up mobile classrooms on school grounds implied a relationship between the two, a relationship less obvious when aid was provided to individuals or at alternative locations. Concerned to avoid actual entangling relationships between church and state, the Court was unwilling to allow even the appearance of improper ties.

Vincent Blasi has provided the most convincing explanation for the Court's approach to Establishment Clause cases. Writing in 1983 he identified what he called the "rootless activism" of the Burger Court, the control exercised by the men at the Court's political center.[34] The consequences of this control by the center were narrowly written opinions, closely related to the specific facts of the case. For the Justices of the center the Constitution required pragmatism, not dogma, and their respective approaches to the cases reflected this clearly. For an understanding of evangelicals and the school aid issue, this has significant impact. First, it reveals that the NAE's shift to advocating government funds for religious schools took place against a backdrop of Supreme Court cases, which held that under certain circumstances such aid was perfectly constitutional. Any attempt to portray it as a blatant attempt to undermine the Establishment Clause while gaining state finance for religious purposes requires a closer examination of the background to each particular case. School aid programs under the Burger Court's rulings were not per se unconstitutional. Second, the Court's approach to school aid reveals that there are reasons to support such programs beyond the strictly ideological. Justices Blackmun, Powell, and Stewart would not have classed themselves as accommodationists. Thus, evangelical support for school aid is not, by itself, evidence of a challenge to the Court or of growing evangelical attempts to undermine the provisions of the Establishment Clause.

Politicians and State School Aid Programs

In the 1970s, Americans experienced what President Jimmy Carter famously termed the "crisis of confidence." The result of a combination of factors—the loss of the Vietnam War and the fall of Saigon to the Communists, the effects of the social upheaval of the late 1960s, Watergate, OPEC price rises and the energy crisis, and inflation and unemployment—the impact of the "crisis" was as much financial as emotional. As Americans struggled financially throughout the decade, a debate about how to fund education efficiently and effectively emerged in most states.[35] Inflation affected schools and school budgets severely. Basic education costs soared, consuming allocated funds faster than anticipated. Inflation also reduced state aid: in many states school finance was provided partly on the basis of real estate wealth; as local property values soared districts became "wealthier" and thus eligible for less state aid. The combination of inflation and unemployment made many Americans unwilling and unable to pay increased taxes instituted to cover spiraling costs.[36] States sought new ways to finance education that might offset some of the cost increases. Such initiatives had little impact as costs spiraled and budgets suffered real as well as proportional cuts. In the Gallup annual survey of public attitudes toward education, "lack of proper financial support" rated among the top five "major problems confronting the public schools" for most of the decade.[37]

The financial crisis coincided with a growing disenchantment with the public school system. The experiences of desegregation and busing had disillusioned parents across the country, and the Court's decisions in *Engel* and *Schempp* in the early 1960s led to fears of growing secularism in the public schools. Studies showing high dropout rates, falling standards as measured by standardized tests, increased truancy, poor discipline, and high suspension rates raised questions about the effectiveness of the nation's public schools. The problems were worst in inner-city schools, which more often than not catered to students facing such problems as "poverty, slums, racial discrimination, disorganized families, disease . . . [and] injustice."[38] The financial cuts forced on schools by reductions in state aid only reinforced perceptions of the decline of the public schools as enrichment programs such as music programs, school trips, and team sports were cut as being nonessential to the education function; the number of guidance counselors was reduced; and class sizes increased as teachers were let go.[39]

School aid programs with indirect benefits for religious schools were nothing new by the 1970s. A 1967 study showed that in the areas of subsidized public transportation for pupils attending religious schools and the loan of secular textbooks to those same students, seven states required or permitted both while thirty-six states permitted or required at least one. Only four states expressly forbade either form of benefit.[40] Significantly, such programs ran in states whose constitutions included provisions, so-called Blaine Amendments, which prohibited state funding of religion or religious institutions. Four years later, as the Court heard argument in *Lemon*, a second study revealed that thirty-seven states had at least one program of aid with direct or indirect benefits to religious schools. Of these, Connecticut, Michigan, New York, Ohio, and Rhode Island operated the largest number of programs. Bus transportation, aid for disabled students, health services, dual enrolment, nutrition, and textbook loans were the most common of the broad range of programs operated at state level by the end of the 1960s.[41] As the financial crisis in the country developed throughout the 1970s, politicians at the state level began to realize that for relatively little aid through such programs, religious schools provided education for a sizable number of children, children the state did not have to pay to educate. New Jersey's governor William T. Cahill argued in 1973 that, "we believe that it is in the overall public interest to provide the financial assistance needed to ensure the continued viability of the nonpublic schools. If these schools were forced, one by one, to close their doors, the burden of educating these children would be shifted to the state public school system."[42] Across the country states with large, nonpublic school systems sought to enact legislation that would ease the financial burden of such schools, ensuring their survival and thus easing the potential financial burden on public schools.

Among the leading state politicians actively supporting and advocating school aid was Nelson A. Rockefeller of New York. A longtime supporter of aid to religious schools, Governor Rockefeller oversaw the second largest number of aid programs within any state with an annual cost—$56 million in fiscal year 1969–70—that was significantly higher than in any other state.[43] A survey of Rockefeller's speeches, papers, and responses to press questions reveal that financial problems in New York schools were a pressing problem as early as 1959. "Providing adequate finance for our schools and colleges," he stated, "is undoubtedly the most critical problem facing our educational system in the decade ahead."[44] In 1961, though, Rockefeller remained circumspect on the issue of school aid: "There is no clear line of demarcation as to what kinds of aid are constitutional," he argued, and in an argument similar to that made by the Supreme Court a decade later, he asserted: "A decision must be made on the basis of the particular type of aid which would be given under a particular program."[45] By 1964, however, Rockefeller appeared to have clarified his thinking: "I believe that certain forms of aid which have purely educational objectives as distinct from religious objectives, can be granted to or for our students in nonpublic schools and colleges."[46]

Rockefeller and his administration followed two routes to provide aid to religious schools and their students in New York. The biggest restriction was the state's Blaine Amendment; embedded in the State Constitution since 1894, the amendment explicitly prevented public funds paying for religious institutions. In 1967 and again in 1969, Rockefeller and his supporters, including Democrats, Roman Catholics, the AFL-CIO, and a large number of Lutherans and Episcopalians, sought to repeal the amendment and remove the barrier to aid for the state's religious schools. Both attempts were unsuccessful. By the time of the second failure, the Court had announced the *Lemon* test suggesting that some forms of school aid would be permissible under the federal Constitution, especially if benefitting students and parents rather than the schools directly. The administration began to discuss options for statewide legislation. Although this has sometimes been perceived as an attempt to undermine or circumvent the Court's restrictions, internal discussions show a clear awareness of the limits imposed by *Lemon* and an understanding that any new program must meet the requirements of the *Lemon* test. Tax deductions and credits, building funds, scholarships, tuition vouchers, shared time, facilities, and services, remedial education programs, and a state-run "teachers corps" to provide secular education in religious schools were all considered as potential options. Maintenance and repair grants, tuition reimbursement, and tax deductions were struck down by the Supreme Court in *Committee for Public Education and Religious Liberty v. Nyquist* in 1973; reimbursement for the cost of record-keeping and state-mandated testing was also struck down by the Court four years later in *New York v. Cathedral Academy*. However, the state's program of remedial education services, funded in part by federal funds through Title 1 of the Elementary and Secondary Education Act (1965), remained operational until 1985. As governor, Nelson Rockefeller continued to support school aid programs, looking for alternative options each time existing programs were rejected as unconstitutional. Asked in 1971 why he supported such programs, Rockefeller echoed the views of many other educators and politicians across the country who were engaged with similar issues: "Without help, many of these nonpublic schools face actual collapse. And when they fail, their burden falls directly onto the public schools. In New York City alone there are 448,000 students in nonpublic schools. Far better to give some help to keep these schools afloat than to have their costs descend on already overburdened public schools."[47]

The political debate about the role of religious schools in the American education system that developed in the 1970s, exemplified by the actions of Rockefeller, Cahill, and others, is important for understanding the changing views of evangelicals. Just as the Court's position that not all school aid programs were unconstitutional presents grounds for evangelical support beyond the simply religious or ideological, the growing acceptance that religious schools played a valuable role in educating students and keeping state education costs low at a time of financial difficulty presents pragmatic foundations for evangelical support of school aid. Financial and pedagogical reasons were put forward by politicians and educators for including religious schools of all denominations within the scope of key educational programs. While political affiliation and accommodationist views cannot be entirely disregarded as influences, sufficient numbers of participants in the debate offered alternative arguments to suggest they were not all seeking to cover up less savory motives. Thus, the evangelical shift toward greater support of school aid must be seen in the broader context of greater political and educational support for such programs, offering alternative explanations beyond claims of blatant attempts to undermine the Constitution.

Conclusion

It is clear that any simple conclusions about the position of evangelicals on the issue of school aid are almost impossible. Those who equate evangelicals with the conservative political and legal movements of the late 1970s and early 1980s, which actively sought to reinterpret the Establishment Clause, have grounds for their argument. The problem, however, is with any claim that this explains the evangelical position as a whole. Some evangelicals did react adversely to the Court's rulings in *Engel* and *Schempp*, sought refuge in Christian schools, and then made claims for government funds for those schools. Many, if not most, did not. Large numbers of evangelicals, whether parents, teachers, ministers, lawyers, or politicians, actively sought to work within the public school system, aware that the Court had not banned *all* religion or religious activities, only those endorsed or organized by the school authorities. They supported *Engel* and *Schempp*, and found ways to work within those rulings to try to ensure public schools did not become the religion-free zones critics claimed they were. The establishment of Christian schools and the demands for public funds for them cannot thus be explained, at least in full, as an evangelical backlash against the Court's prayer rulings of the 1960s.

The other problem with the traditional view of evangelicals is that it rests on the assumption that all supporters of school aid programs in the 1970s were part of the conservative movement to return prayers to schools, fund religious organizations, and in the process, undermine the "wall of separation" between church and state. As detailed consideration of the Supreme Court's rulings on school aid show, this was not the only foundation on which school aid could be supported. The Court itself asserted that the Constitution did not invalidate all forms of such aid. Equally, in the context of growing dissatisfaction with the nation's public schools and a financial crisis that saw education budgets reduced, educators and politicians saw clear, practical, economic reasons for including religious schools within school aid programs. Whether legal or economic, both arguments reveal alternative foundations for support of school aid programs, which demands a reassessment of evangelicals' stated positions in the late 1970s and 1980s.

NOTES

1. NAE Policy Statement, "Tuition Tax Credits," 1983, http://www.nae.net /resolutions/323-tuition-tax-credits-1983.

2. *Engel v. Vitale* 370 US 421, 425 (1962).

3. Quoted in *Washington Post,* June 26, 1962, A8.

4. "Court Edict on Prayer is Decried," *Washington Post,* June 27, 1962, A6; *Newsweek,* July 9, 1962, 44.

5. *Washington Post,* June 27, 1962, A6; *Newsweek,* July 9, 1962, 43.

6. Quoted in *Washington Post,* June 26, 1962, A8.

7. *Congressional Record* (hereafter cited as *Cong. Rec.*), 108th Cong., June 26, 1962, 11.675; *Washington Post,* June 29, 1962, A8.

8. *Cong. Rec.*, 108th Cong., June 26, 1962, 11.719, 11.844.

9. See US Senate. Committee on the Judiciary. Hearings on Prayer in Public Schools and Other Matters, 87th Cong., 2nd sess. (1962); US House of Representatives. Committee on the Judiciary. Hearings on Proposed Amendments to the Constitution Relating to Prayers and Bible Reading in the Public Schools, 88th Cong., 2nd sess. (1964).

10. NAE Resolution, "Religion in National Life," approved October 1963, http://www.nae.net/resolutions/112-church-a-state-separation-1964.

11. *Christianity Today,* June 19, 1964, 22.

12. For example, James Panoch, "Is Prayer in Schools an Illegal Maneuver?" *Christianity Today,* September 30, 1966, 3–6; "The Prayer Amendment," *Christianity Today,* October 8, 1971, 32; "Making No Amends for Prayer," *Christianity Today,* December 3, 1971, 31; David Barr, "Religion in Schools: Four Questions Evangelicals Ask," *Christianity Today,* January 21, 1972, 4–6.

13. The exact numbers of students enrolled in Christian schools is difficult to determine since many fundamentalist schools refuse to provide the information to government agencies, and there is no central body governing Christian schools to maintain statistics regarding the number of such schools and the student numbers. The National Center for Education Statistics reported an increase of students in non-Catholic religious schools, including but not exclusive to Christian schools, from just over half a million students in 1970 to 1.3 million in 1980. Other sources suggest between 225 and 1,000 Christian schools opened each year between 1967 and 1980. See Henry Buchanan and Bob Brown, "Will Protestant Church Schools Become a Third Force?" *Christianity Today,* May 12, 1967, 3–5; Arthur Corazzini, "The Non-Catholic Private School," in *Economic Problems of Nonpublic Schools: A Report to the President's Commission on School Finance* (University of Notre Dame, Office of Educational Research, 1971); Paul Parsons, *Inside America's Christian Schools* (Macon, GA: Mercer University Press, 1989), x–xvii.

14. NAE Policy Resolution on "Church and State," adopted 1963, http://www.nae.net/resolutions/421-church-and-state-1963.

15. NAE Resolutions on "Church and State Separation," 1964, http://www.nae.net/resolutions/112-church-a-state-separation-1964.

16. "What About the Becker Amendment?" *Christianity Today,* June 19, 1964, 22.

17. "Making No Amends for Prayer," *Christianity Today,* December 3, 1971, 31.

18. Belden Menkus, "Evangelical Responsibility in Public Education," *Christianity Today,* February 12, 1971, 10–12; Thayer Warshaw, "Teaching English Teachers to

Teach the Bible," *Phi Delta Kappan* 52 (May 1971): 539–540; David Barr, "Religion in Schools," 4–6; Kenneth Briggs, "Bishops Ask Religious Teaching in the Public Schools," *New York Times*, February 20, 1976, A55.

19. NAE Resolutions on "Church and State Separation," 1964.

20. Peter Cousins, "The Christian Teacher," *Christianity Today*, October 9, 1970, 17.

21. James Panoch and David Barr, *Religion Goes to School: A Practical Handbook for Teachers* (New York: Harper & Row, 1968), 5.

22. NAE Policy Statement, "Federal Aid to Education," 1965, http://www.nae .net/resolutions149-federal-aid-to-education-1965; NAE Resolutions on "Church and State Separation," 1964; NAE Resolution, "School Bus Transportation," 1965, http:// www.nae.net/resolutions/301-school-bus-transportation-1965. At least part of this opposition can be explained by long-standing antagonism between evangelicals and Roman Catholics. Even as late as the mid-1960s advocacy of school aid was linked with Catholic demands for state funding of their faith, a demand that had emerged in the 1830s with Catholic opposition to public schools and reemerged in the twentieth century as federal government involvement in education expanded. See, for example, Frederick Binder, *The Age of the Common School, 1830–1865* (New York: John Wiley & Sons, 1974); and Diane Ravitch, *The Great School Wars, New York City, 1805–1973: A History of Public Schools as Battlefields of Social Change* (New York: Basic Books, 1974). On anti-Catholic feeling among evangelicals in the 1960s, see chap. 12 by Neil K. Young in this volume.

23. Frank E. Gaebelein, "Crisis in Christian Education," *Christianity Today*, May 21, 1971, 6. This was echoed by an NAE statement in 1988 on "Public and Private School-ing": "Feelings on what are appropriate for the Christian family run deep and there is no one position that prevails within the evangelical community." http://www.nae.net /resolutions/281-public-and-private-schooling-1988.

24. Frank E. Gaebelein, "Rethinking the Church's Role," *Christianity Today*, February 18, 1966, 6.

25. Ibid., 3; Belden Menkus, "Evangelical Responsibility," 12.

26. Paul Boyer, "The Evangelical Resurgence in 1970s American Protestantism," and Joseph Crespino, "Civil Rights and the Religious Right," in *Rightward Bound: Making America Conservative in the 1970s*, ed. Bruce Schulman and Julian Zelizer (Cambridge, MA: Harvard University Press, 2008), 29–51, 90–105.

27. See, for example, *Meek v. Pittenger* 421 US 349 (1975), upholding the loan of secular textbooks to students attending religious schools, and *Wolman v. Walter* 433 US 229 (1977) upholding the provision of funds for standardized testing and scoring in religious schools and diagnostic hearing and speech services provided on religious school campuses. However, in *Meek* the Court also struck down loans of other instructional materials such as maps, tape recorders, and overhead projectors, while in *Wolman* the Court also struck down reimbursement for the cost of field trips and remedial education and guidance services provided on religious school campuses.

28. *Lemon v. Kurtzman* 403 US 602, 612–613 (1971) (internal references and quotation marks omitted).

29. *Lemon v. Kurtzman* 403 US 602, 612 (1971).

30. *Lemon v. Kurtzman* 403 US 602, 614 (1971). The joint dissent by Justices Black and Douglas was far closer to strict separation. 403 US 602, 625–642.

31. *Lemon v. Kurtzman* 403 US 602, 614 (1971).

32. *Meek v. Pittenger* 421 US 349, 356, 363 (1975) (emphasis added).

33. *Wolman v. Walter* 433 US 229, 247 (1977).

34. See Vincent Blasi, ed., *The Burger Court: The Counter-Revolution That Wasn't* (New Haven: Yale University Press, 1983).

35. See J. Alan Thomas and Robert Wimpelberg, eds., *Dilemmas in School Finance* (Chicago: Midwest Administration Center, University of Chicago, 1978); K. Forbis Jordan and Nelda Cambron-McCabe, eds., *Perspectives in State School Support Programs* (Cambridge, MA: Ballinger Publishing Co., 1981); Stanton Leggett, ed., *Managing Schools in Hard Times* (Chicago: Teach 'em Inc., 1981). For a discussion of the Supreme Court's role in this debate see Caroline Wagstaff, "Race, Class and Federalism: A History and Analysis of *San Antonio Independent School District v. Rodriguez* (1973)" (PhD diss., University of Kent, 2001).

36. Albert Shanker, "Where We Stand," *New York Times*, May 18, 1975, E11. The most extreme reaction was California's Proposition 13 (1978), which limited property tax to 1 percent of market value.

37. The Annual Gallup Poll of Public Attitudes Towards Education is published annually in the *Phi Delta Kappan*.

38. Albert Shanker, "Where We Stand," *New York Times*, February 4, 1973, E9. On the problems of inner-city schools, see Gerry Rosenfeld, *"Shut Those Thick Lips!": A Study of Slum School Failure* (New York: Holt, Rinehart and Winston, 1971); Laurence Iannaccone, "Problems of Financing Inner-City Schools: Political, Social, and Cultural Constraints Upon Financing Improved Urban Education and Proposals to Overcome Them: A Report to the President's Commission on School Finance" (Washington, DC: President's Commission on School Finance, 1972); Sheldon Marcus and Philip Vairo, eds., *Urban Education: Crisis or Opportunity?* (Metuchen, NJ: Scarecrow Press, 1972); Ray Rist, *The Urban School: A Factory for Failure* (Cambridge, MA: MIT Press, 1974).

39. E. Fiske, "New York Crisis Forcing Schools to Stress the 3Rs," *New York Times*, June 22, 1976, A46.

40. Austin Swanson and Joseph Igoe, eds., *Should Public Monies Be Used to Support Non-Public Education? A Review of the Issues and Practices* (Danville, IL: Interstate Printers and Publishers, 1967).

41. Janet Foerster, "Public Aid to Nonpublic Education: A Report to the President's Commission on School Finance" (Washington, DC: October 1971).

42. Quoted in R. Sullivan, "Church Schools Lose Jersey Aid," *New York Times*, April 6, 1973, A45. Thomas Schwartz estimated the cost of such absorption to be between $1,348,655,147 and $3,176,371,885 in 1971, with New York facing the highest cost and New Jersey the fourth highest. See Schwartz, "The Estimated Marginal Costs of Absorbing all Nonpublic Students into the Public School System," in *Economic Problems of Nonpublic Schools*, 301–350.

43. Ohio faced the second largest cost of school aid programs at $19.7 million for the same year. Foerster, "Public Aid to Nonpublic Education."

44. "Better Education for Americans: A Financial Program to Meet This Mounting Challenge," Rockefeller Archive, Record Group III 15, Series 17, Issue Books, Subseries 1, Box 17, Folder 95.

45. Statement reported in *US News and World Report*, September 5, 1963, Rockefeller Archive, Record Group III 15, Series 17.1 Gubernatorial Issue Books, Folder 17.

46. Rockefeller Archive, Record Group III 15, Series 17, Issue Books, Subseries 1, Box 17, Folder 98.

47. Statement on nonpublic schools, Rockefeller Archive, Record Group III 15, Series 10.3 Counsel's Office: Robert R. Douglass, Box 59, Folder 652.

8

The Great Society, Evangelicals, and the Public Funding of Religious Agencies

AXEL R. SCHÄFER

One of the abiding enigmas of U.S. politics is that popular antistatism and ritualistic invocations of the "free market" have historically gone hand-in-hand with persistent calls for government subsidies. In his classic study of the American West, for example, Richard White has shown that, in contrast to many westerners' vociferous denunciation of meddlesome federal bureaucrats and overbearing regulation, westernizing took place under the sponsorship of a growing American state, not a weak central government. The West thus became the "Kindergarten" of the nation-state as direct and indirect subsidies to corporations in transportation, extractive industries, and the military sector pioneered the corporate welfare state; infrastructure investment and tax policies translated into a strong federal presence; and Indian policies and the administration of the public domain laid the foundation for modern regulatory agencies.[1] Likewise, resurgent populist conservatism since the 1970s, while ideologically committed to laissez-faire capitalism, small government, and free enterprise, has not really hampered the growth of the state. Despite decades of "government is the problem"–mantras, the historian Matthew Lassiter recently concluded that "Conservative politicians and interest groups, just like their liberal counterparts, have pushed for 'big government' intervention through state subsidies and regulation when it suited their material interests and ideological agendas, and for 'small government' and deregulation when it did not."[2]

The key to understanding this enigma lies in the difference between the terms "small" and "limited" as applied to government. What characterizes American political culture is not so much the effort to reduce the size of government than the attempt to proscribe the interventionist capacities of a centralized bureaucracy. As the historian Brian Balough has shown, Americans traditionally opposed government intervention when it was direct and overt, but accepted it when it was indirect and hidden. They preferred tax breaks, subsides, tariff policies, and public aid to nongovernmental providers to visible state provision.[3] Modern public policies, ranging from the Pacific Railroad Act of the 1860s to federal support for suburban development after World War II, thus furthered state building in ways that limited federal interference, rather than expenditure. In other words, what clashed in American politics historically were two different statist traditions, rather than calls for an expanded role for the state with an equally persistent tradition of antistatism.

On the basis of applying these findings to the analysis of resurgent evangelicalism and its interaction with the Great Society, this chapter challenges established notions of an antagonistic relationship between the two. On the one hand, it maintains that the Great Society was significant for the political mobilization of conservative Protestants not simply because it was an easy target for charges of "immorality" and "permissiveness," but because it generated a new attachment to indirect state expansion among evangelicals. Liberal social policies of the 1960s—though commonly identified as the epitome of overt governmentalism—relied not so much on direct federal control than on aiding third-sector providers, including evangelical educational, health care, and social-service agencies. In turn, the growing funding ties between the federal government and evangelical agencies during the 1960s and 1970s further diluted the traditional rejection of public aid for religious agencies among evangelicals that had already started during World War II. Building upon this revision of separationist attitudes and practices, the New Christian Right since the late 1970s, despite its vilification of the liberal state, helped perpetuate the established patterns of postwar state building within a post-Vietnam and post-Watergate climate of opinion.

On the other hand, as the programs of the Great Society integrated evangelical agencies into the devolved welfare state, they provided grassroots conservatives with important knowledge and experience for their broader political quest. Heeding the lesson that, as the journalist Russell Baker put it, "All politics is to a great extent about who gets the lion's share of the money at a government's disposal," conservative Protestants obtained access to the corridors of political power and gained influence within the structures of the state.[4] In effectively blending the rhetoric of limited government with the increasingly savvy use of public aid available for religious agencies, they preserved an anti-statist and insurgent identity while building up evangelical charities with tax-payer funds.

The following examination of the link between postwar patterns of evangelical mobilization and liberal social policy starts with a brief review of the postwar history of public funding for religious organizations and the main legislative legacy of the War on Poverty in this area. It then explores in more detail how evangelicals in the 1960s positioned themselves within this particular trajectory of the U.S. welfare state. This is followed by a closer look at how the evangelical engagement with the Great Society benefited the rise of the Right within conservative Protestantism. Finally, the chapter outlines how these findings revise established interpretations of both resurgent evangelicalism and the liberal state.

Religious Agencies and the "Subsidiarist State"

Historians of public policy have suggested an impressive variety of terms to describe the distinctive growth of the American state that relies on the administrative capacities of nongovernmental providers. These include the "allocative state," the "second welfare state," "government by proxy," "third-party government," and "governing out of sight."[5] The term "subsidiarity," however, best captures the large-scale devolution to nongovernmental agencies and the underlying ideology that reduces the federal government from a direct provider to a funding agency. Derived from Catholic social thought, it describes three interrelated components: (1) a policy instrument that devolves policy implementation to lower levels; (2) an emotive concept that views mediating structures as less impersonal than government bodies and thus superior; and (3) an ideology that defines social problems in terms of rehabilitative intervention, rather than large-scale socioeconomic redistribution.[6]

World War II and the Cold War nurtured the public-nonprofit relationship to an unprecedented extent. Combining national security and welfarist components, subsidiarist policies made federal funding available on a large scale to private businesses and nonprofit organizations in order to shore up higher education, defense-related research, hospital building, social services, foreign aid, urban renewal, and community development. Landmark legislation such as the 1944 G.I. Bill and the 1946 Hill–Burton Act provided billions of dollars of federal funds via tax deductions, loans, credit guarantees, purchase-of-service contracts, surplus property donations, and direct cash grants. Although commonly associated with the conservative backlash of the 1990s, the devolution and privatization of social services, as the political scientist Peter Dobkin Hall has noted, "actually describes the fundamental dynamic of American government over the past half-century."[7]

In their eagerness to expand the human service infrastructure through links with intermediaries, postwar policymakers could hardly ignore the administrative capacities of religious charities, which constitute around 40 percent of the organizations in the nonprofit sector, receive as much as two-thirds of all donations, and employ over 60 percent of the volunteer labor force. While church organizations were barely involved in the vast New Deal social programs, the federal government began in the mid-1940s to significantly broaden its use of religious agencies in its pursuit of the expansion of human services.[8] As a result, religiously based nonprofits were among the prime beneficiaries of government aid long before the Bush administration's Faith-Based Initiative. Although religiously based agencies shared fully in the public-nonprofit networks, their role in the subsidiarist state has received little systematic attention in public policy research. As Stephen Monsma has pointed out, while the "two characteristics of nonprofit service organizations—their receipt of large amounts of government funds and the religious nature of many of them—overlap," granting tax dollars to sectarian organizations remains "one of the best kept secrets in the United States."[9]

The programs of the Great Society largely made use of the same subsidiarist principles. They emphasized not so much the expansion of federal control than the devolution of responsibility to third-sector actors. The key difference was that the Johnson administration sought to shake up the bureaucratically complex, financially insecure, politically dubious, and economically wasteful funding arrangements that existed between charities and state and local government by putting the emphasis on direct federal-to-nonprofit allocation. Key legislation, such as the higher education acts of 1963 and 1965, the Community Mental Health Centers Act (1963), the 1964 Economic Opportunity Act (EOA), the 1965 Medicaid and Medicare programs, and the landmark 1967 Social Security amendments (Title IV-A), in part sought to circumvent traditional mediating levels via new direct federal aid.[10]

In the same vein, the Great Society significantly furthered the integration of religiously based organizations into the subsidiarist state by breaking through long-standing restrictions on federal funding of religious and other voluntary social services. In turn, churches emerged as major beneficiaries of government support and became administratively involved in a wide range of federally funded social programs. "Three or four years ago it was impossible for a federal agency to give a direct grant to a religious group," the Office of Economic Opportunity (OEO) director Sargent Shriver remarked in 1966, "today we are giving hundreds of grants without violating the principle of separation of church and state."[11] By the end of the decade, then, critics worried that the Great Society had created a revolving door between church and state, because "literally thousands of Protestant ministers and Roman Catholic priests and nuns have left their positions with the church in order to become administrators of antipoverty programs." As Shriver commented, so many clergy had gone to work for his office that "OEO now means Office of Ecclesiastical Outcasts."[12]

What is more, among the least recognized features of Great Society social policies is one of the most intriguing aspects of the postwar funding networks: They involved not only mainline Protestant, Jewish, and Catholic organizations, but also white evangelicals. Although conservative Protestants had traditionally been the most outspoken opponents of closer funding ties between church and state, the ideological and institutional needs of the Cold War state in conjunction with the postwar political awakening of evangelicalism laid the foundation for new political and financial links between the two. Indeed, the Great Society opened up new opportunities for a previously marginalized religious grouping to assert itself administratively, politically, and discursively in the social policy arena.[13]

Evangelicals, Subsidiarity, and the Great Society

In February 1961 a small group of leading representatives of the National Association of Evangelicals (NAE) met in the Hotel Continental in Washington to discuss church-state relations in light of the apparent permanence and likely expansion of government funding of religious social services. Participants included the NAE's executive directors R. L. Decker and George Ford, *United Evangelical Action*'s editor James DeForest Murch, and the NAE's Office of Public Affairs director Clyde Taylor. The meeting was prompted by a growing sense of unease within the NAE about what the church historian Bernard Coughlin has called the "two streams of influence" in conservative Protestantism: while ·

church leaders often spoke of the danger of relying on tax money, local agency administrators frequently accepted government funds.[14] "The principle of separation of Church and State would dictate that we should oppose subsidies of religious or church organizations by government in any form," the meeting records noted bluntly, but then added an important qualifier: "When laws are passed which would benefit religious or church organizations it may be proper, conscience permitting, for evangelicals to accept their share of the benefits on the basis of equal justice."[15]

The Great Society's vast expansion of public support for religious agencies heightened this policy dilemma. On the one hand, evangelicals remained eager to project a traditional separationist image and to hone their antistatist credentials, driven by their fear that taking public funds would undermine the organizational autonomy of religious social services, lead to their absorption into a government-run system, and marginalize spiritual content. On the other hand, in seeking to build up their institutional infrastructure, conservative Protestant organizations on the ground increasingly partook in public funding streams, notwithstanding church pronouncements that ran counter to such involvement. As these tensions increasingly came to the fore in the movement's heated internal discussions about public aid, they ushered in a crucial transformation in traditional evangelical church-state attitudes.

The NAE in particular exemplifies the often tortuous efforts to wrest a new church-state position from a diversity of evangelical views. As the main organization of the evangelical establishment between the 1940s and the 1980s, the NAE was simultaneously a distinctly northern organization with ties to the Republican party and representative of the broader evangelical fold. Although the jewel in the crown—the membership of the Southern Baptist Convention (SBC) and the Lutheran Church–Missouri Synod (LCMS)—kept eluding the NAE, the organization paved the way for overcoming the North-South divide in American evangelicalism in ways that resonated particularly with future SBC leaders, such as Richard Land and Albert Mohler.[16]

Of course the NAE was never in a strict sense an advocate of the separation of church and state.[17] Nonetheless, it had traditionally resisted any form of public aid to religious educational, health care, and social-service agencies. Since the 1940s, however, five main factors had begun to water down evangelicalism's traditional separatism. First, World War II and evangelical identification with Cold War anticommunism nudged religious conservatives into a new engagement with the state. In particular, it eased the transition for evangelicals from their traditional insistence on limited government toward the embrace of state power in the name of national security and global influence.

Second, growing fears that Roman Catholics were taking the lion's share of new public funds fuelled a new interest in subsidiarity. Despite the NAE's consistent opposition to "parochiaid" and its vociferous campaign against Catholic efforts to obtain public support, denominational competition subtly shifted the evangelical debate from a critique of the dangers of a state-church combine toward demands for equal evangelical access to government programs.

Third, fears that evangelical inaction would open the floodgates for secularism revived evangelical interest in utilizing the instrumentalities of government for the promotion of Christian morality and a new willingness to enter into funding contracts with the state. In particular, the 1962 and 1963 Supreme Court decisions outlawing prayer and Bible reading in public schools engendered concerns that secularists were using separationist arguments to remove religion from the public sphere altogether. Fourth, worries about the lack of church support for religious charities and normative pressure exerted by the availability of funds ushered in a policy rethink. Fears of financial shortfalls proved a powerful incentive for many church administrators to tap into federal aid. Finally, the indirect funding streams and absence of intrusive restrictions on evangelizing that characterized subsidiarist policies gradually alleviated traditional evangelical fears about public aid. Evangelicals increasingly recognized that public funding arrangements provided extensive administrative leeway, safeguarded the organizational independence of religious agencies, and effectively sanctioned the faith-based practices of sectarian providers.

Although the NAE had started out by noisily denouncing public funding of religious agencies, it gradually softened its separationist dogma in favor of fighting constraints on religious providers partaking in aid arrangements. As R. L. Decker warned in 1963, the "complete observance of separation of Church and State often times seem to evangelicals to be encouragements toward the development of a purely secular state."[18] Three key areas where the Great Society expanded aid to religious agencies highlight this transformation: higher education, primary and secondary education, and health care and social services.

Higher Education

Religious higher education was one of the main beneficiaries of postwar federal funding. The G.I. Bill, which granted stipends for tuition and living expenses of veterans, funneled large amounts of federal monies into religious colleges and universities. The 1958 National Defense Education Act provided new funds for college construction, student loans, and science teaching. Loans for the construction of dormitory facilities were often obtained under laws that provided financing for public housing. Moreover, many religious colleges and universities benefited from urban renewal programs by being able to obtain prime inner-urban sites at heavily discounted prices.[19]

Building on this, the Great Society programs were crucial in establishing new church-state funding streams. The higher education acts in particular made an unprecedented amount of federal money available to church colleges via federal student loans, capital financing, research contracts, and subsidized construction loans. Religious colleges and universities, which prior to the Second World War had been entirely supported by revenues from private sources, also benefited from the programs of the OEO, such as Upward Bound, which funded college recruitment of low-income students for summer courses.[20] "All efforts to remove church colleges were defeated," a conservative Protestant lobbyist noted with chagrin, acknowledging that the new laws gave "equal opportunity to church colleges along with public schools in getting aid for their medical and dental colleges and universities."[21]

Throughout the 1950s and 60s, the NAE frequently reiterated its rhetorical opposition to any kind of federal aid to colleges and universities, and denounced alleged abuses of federal funds by Catholics. By the 1960s, however, as various laws expanding federal aid to education were debated in Congress, the NAE found it increasingly difficult to pursue a consistent separationist policy. James DeForest Murch, chairman of the NAE's Evangelical Action Commission (EAC), noted grudgingly that the organization had "been handicapped, especially in the field of higher education, in formulating a position representative of the NAE" because "a large number of evangelical colleges have accepted Federal aid of various kinds."[22] The association even found itself unable to testify in opposition to a federal aid to church colleges bill at the House Subcommittee on Education hearings in 1962. Though it had vigorously rejected aid to parochial schools in previous hearings, Murch had to concede during the presentation of a modified bill granting aid to church colleges that "we felt we could make no consistent or valid protest because of the large number of evangelical colleges which have accepted such aid from the USA."[23]

At its seminal church-state conference in 1963, the NAE sought to clarify the evangelical position and to draft new resolutions on federal aid to education. Instead of clearing up the matter, however, the meeting further illustrated the dilemma of many evangelical colleges. According to a joint review presented by the EAC and the Education Commission, conservative Protestants were torn between two extremes demarcated by those who "feel that massive assistance must come from the participation of the Federal government if the colleges are to match the demand both inside and outside the country for the upgrading of our national human resources" and "those who eschew all forms of Federal aid."[24]

At the same time, the conference showed that the advocates of subsidiarity were gradually winning the argument. The lack of financial support for higher education from within the movement seriously increased the allure of federal funding. Although they deplored federal aid, evangelicals themselves rarely offered to support the rising costs of church-related higher education. Judged by their budgetary commitment, the NAE's James Forrester grumbled, evangelicals "do not believe that higher education is important to them." Crucially, he regarded foundation money and corporate giving as only very limited alternatives, since "these sources are often not committed to a specifically Christian perspective any more than is the Federal government." Although he suggested that evangelical colleges should realize the potential of beneficial tax laws to build up endowments and provide scholarships, Forrester's somber conclusion was that "in the absence of aid from private sources and church groups, many boards of small church-related colleges see the loan programs as the only available option to mediocrity or extinction."[25] In light of the availability of federal funding while church support was drying up, many evangelical colleges had few alternatives if they were to heed the evangelical theologian Carl Henry's admonition that "Christianity must not withdraw from the sphere of education, but must infuse it with new spirit and life."[26]

The indirectness of higher education funding streams and the absence of intrusive government control further encouraged this "subsidiarist turn." As Forrester emphasized, government loans carried "no danger of control" since "the government functions as a fiduciary agent only." He also regarded federal funds to higher education as more acceptable to evangelicals because they were available via tuition waivers, rather than via direct grants and contracts.[27] In short, there was an increasing recognition on the part of many evangelicals that certain types of federal support posed little threat to the content of Christian education.

Nonetheless, during the 1960s evangelicals increasingly denounced the "syndromes of socialism" and "the penetration of naturalistic humanism" in the field of publicly funded education.[28] By the end of the decade, the NAE regularly expressed concern that "both public and private institutions of higher learning are feeling the effect of public influence from the level of the federal government." The 1969 NAE General Convention, for example, cited incidences where campus buildings constructed by churches with federal money were not allowed to be used to hold religious classes, to pray, or to teach the Bible.

Obviously, these warnings contrasted sharply with the growing evangelical sense that federal aid came with few strings attached. It was exactly this combination of being suspicious of an intrusive secular state and being increasingly aware of the benefits of public aid that formed the core of the new evangelical attitude to public aid. When the NAE resolutions during the convention condemned government for blocking the use of federally funded campus buildings for religious purposes, delegates used this not to reject federal aid but to call for types of funding that allowed private colleges to "receive the support they need if they are to survive and provide a truly Christian education."[29]

The main issue for evangelical colleges "in a world threatened by militant, scientific, and atheistic communism" was thus no longer "whether they will accept some form of Federal aid, but how they can preserve their spiritual integrity, autonomy, and goals in doing so."[30] This shift in emphasis from insisting on the separation of church and state to protecting the evangelical mission under public funding arrangements paved the way for a major policy revision. "Our office has written and presented to key people on the hill a suggested plan for direct taxpayer aid to our schools of higher education in the form of a Tax Credit Plan," Clyde Taylor reported to the EAC in April 1969. According to this proposal, "taxpayers would be permitted to give a percentage of their Federal tax contributions to the college of their choice."[31] The NAE convention delegates duly concurred. "A possible solution lies in some plan designed to provide tax relief to all citizens supporting education, whether private or public, and without discrimination," the 1969 resolutions read.[32] By the early 1970s the NAE had firmed up this embrace of federal aid to higher education along the lines of tax credits, underscoring the shift from traditional resistance to public aid to the embrace of state funding.[33]

Primary and Secondary Education

While public funding for higher education was highly controversial among evangelicals, aid to sectarian primary and secondary schools was an even more difficult pill for them to swallow, mainly because of their historically strong investment in the campaign to fight it. Fiercely supported by evangelicals, anti-aid legislation, dating back to the "Blaine Amendment" campaign in the nineteenth century, continued to be a potent impediment to federal funding in the post–World War II period. Motivated by anti-Catholic sentiment, James G. Blaine had led a crusade to add a constitutional amendment forbidding direct government aid to religious educational institutions. Though the campaign failed on the federal level, it succeeded in putting exclusions on religious funding into enabling legislation for new territories applying for statehood and into commensurate state legislation. These restrictions remain effective in more than two-thirds of the states to this date. Moreover, Supreme Court rulings put severe restrictions on federal funding of primary and secondary education but at the same time left a vast array of government subsidies to church-based hospitals, colleges, welfare organizations, and foreign aid agencies largely unchallenged (for further details see also chap. 7 by Emma Long in this volume).[34]

Even in this controversial arena, however, church-state ties continued to get stronger in the postwar period. Tax money subsidized bus transportation, textbooks, and auxiliary educational services. Aid to "federally impacted areas" (i.e. districts that had experienced severe overcrowding and stress on services due to new defense installations) was gradually expanded and survived into the 1980s as a version of federal aid. Moreover, the Great Society's landmark Elementary and Secondary Education Act (1965) established a precedent for the controversial funding for parochial schools by providing indirect federal funds to students.[35]

Once again evangelicals struggled with the question of how to respond. Until well into the 1960s, the NAE ran a vitriolic anti-Catholic campaign against public funding for parochial schools. However, even this cause célèbre of evangelical separationism eventually led down the path of accommodation. Crucially, the Supreme Court's decision prohibiting Bible reading and compulsory prayer in public schools left evangelicals fearful that "extremists in the field of civil rights, plus the usual assortment of agnostics and atheists try to use the decision to remove all mention of religion and God from public life" if "God-fearing people abandon government and society to the godless."[36] Calling for a "Christian Amendment to the Constitution," the general convention of the NAE declared in 1964 that "while Church and State must be separate, the State . . . has an obligation to inculcate in rising generations the belief that religion, morality and knowledge are essential to good government and the happiness of its citizens."[37]

Ironically, help in this crusade came from quarters that evangelicals normally regarded as antagonistic to their aspirations. The Elementary and Secondary Education Act laid the foundation for the use of vouchers as a means of providing federal aid to religious schools. Administered by the quintessential Great Society agency, the OEO, this provision of indirect federal funds to students offered evangelicals a way out of getting caught between traditional separationism and fears of secularist control. It ushered in the conversion of conservative Protestants, including Southern Baptists, to public funding for private schools.[38] Although the NAE did not offer overt support for the act, it adopted a motion in 1966 that declared some contractual arrangements with the government "acceptable and beneficial."[39] In the ensuing decade it first grappled with and then largely embraced the proposal to provide parents with tuition vouchers to be used in public, private, or parochial schools. Discussions during a 1971 consultation session of the Evangelical Social Action Commission concluded that "the plan can contribute much to the basic reform of American education" because it permitted "experimentation with various philosophical and pedagogical approaches."[40] Once again, this indicated that the evangelical focus had shifted from separationist orthodoxy to efforts to shape the features of aid legislation.

Health Care and Social Services

Finally, the Great Society's large-scale expansion of federal aid to church-related institutions in the health and social-service arena facilitated a new evangelical relationship with the subsidiarist state. In the health-care field, the creation of Medicare and Medicaid provided large-scale funding for evangelical hospitals, mental health institutions, nursing homes, and other agencies. This came on top of federal funds that had been made available for the construction, replacement, and remodeling of hospitals and other medical facilities under the Hill–Burton Act and its various extensions. Southern Baptist hospitals in particular had been beneficiaries of this postwar expansion of the publicly funded nonprofit health-care infrastructure. Moreover, evangelical hospitals had become prime recipients of surplus government property and equipment donated for welfare and educational uses. In this way they obtained valuable land, buildings, and other resources at a heavy discount. According to a 1964 report of the Department of Housing, Education, and Welfare, for example, the Assemblies of God, an NAE member denomination, trailed only the Catholics in federal acreage donation.[41]

The most dramatic change in the 1960s, however, came in the area of social-service funding, where the federal government had not previously played a prominent role. Although the EOA barred direct subsidies of churches and stipulated that federally funded facilities should be devoid of sectarian or religious symbols and decorations, it left plenty of room for aid to religious entities. Head Start, as one of the keystones of the Great Society edifice, established numerous funding relationships with congregation-based child care providers. Funds provided through the OEO helped finance church-based antipoverty efforts, job creation plans, migrant worker programs, and construction projects. Money given to Community Action agencies and mental health centers as alternatives to the state social-service bureaucracies and public state hospitals funneled additional funds into religious agencies.[42]

It was another piece of landmark legislation, however, that truly proved a watershed in the expansion of the federal role in social-service funding and the involvement of evangelical providers. The 1967 Social Security amendments transferred social-service costs from the states to the federal government, vastly expanded the client population, and added new areas of service provision. They institutionalized the two cornerstones of the Great Society credo, namely, the reliance upon direct federal funding of social services and the use of non-profit providers. The legislation allowed states to finance social services with three-quarters of the expenditure provided by federal funds and only one-quarter from either private or state sources. Crucially, it dropped prohibitions against federal funding for voluntary agencies and specifically encouraged states to enter into purchase-of-service agreements with private providers.[43]

Most remarkably, the amendments allocated almost unlimited amounts of money to states for contracting out of social services, and attempts in the mid-1970s to reign in spiraling costs via caps, more rigid oversight, and shifting expenditures back to the states remained largely symbolic. Although Title XX of the Social Security Act (1974) introduced some restrictions, it retained or expanded the types of funding that had benefited religiously based services. This included support for child care and family services, counseling, protective services, health care, family planning, legal services, and provision for the disabled. Under Title XX the system of federal funds remained a crucial incentive for states to buy services from nongovernmental agencies.[44] "Today government regards the church as simply another agency to be used in the furtherance of its social programs," C. Stanley Lowell, associate director of Protestants and Other Americans United for the Separation of Church and State (POAU), bemoaned in the early 1970s, "Government hires churches just as it hires many other kinds of private agencies."[45]

By the 1970s, evangelical hospitals, mental health institutions, and nursing homes were avid participants in funding streams implemented by the Great Society. A study of a midwestern agency of the conservative LCMS, for example, revealed that it received 38 percent of its total budget from public funds in 1950, largely on the basis of purchase-of-service contracting. By 1980, this figure had increased to 59 percent, mainly due to Title XX funds. Overall, the study found few differences between evangelical and mainline agencies in the percentage of government funding received. Most striking was the case of the NAE-affiliated Salvation Army. Prior to the availability of OEO funds, public aid had played only a limited role in overall agency income, except for some purchase-of-service contracting. In the 1970s, however, government funding increased rapidly from 4 percent of the overall budget in 1974–75 to 17 percent by fiscal year 1979–80. The budgets for social services, including community centers, services for ex-offenders, temporary shelters, counseling agencies, and residences for alcoholics, showed a particularly pronounced reliance upon public funds. In these areas 45 percent of income originated in government sources.[46]

This expansion of public aid to sectarian social-service providers in the 1960s ushered in the crucial breakthrough in evangelical support for subsidiarity. Initially, the federalization of aid had awakened fears of government control and Catholic dominance. As the War on Poverty loosened restrictions on federal funding of religious social services and effectively limited the role of the federal government to that of bill payer, it gradually broke down the last vestiges of traditional evangelical separationism. Noting in 1963 that a number of evangelical social-service organizations had applied for and received federal support, the NAE's R. L. Decker acknowledged that "there seems to be little if any disposition on the part of the government . . . to supervise the program in these institutions, after taking precautions to see that the elderly people are physically provided for in the best possible manner."[47]

Moreover, in contrast to the other areas of public funding for church-based provision, evangelicals tended to condone the practice in the welfare realm, since funding ties, particularly for foster care, had had a long tradition on the state and local levels. While the NAE recommended that "separation must be maintained by clear working relationships," its 1964 resolution on "The Church and Welfare" concluded after much soul-searching that "the church may as an agent administer government assistance without compromise of the principle of separation of church and state if the church's policies are not controlled or influenced thereby or vice versa."[48]

In light of both regulatory leniency and growing public aid dependency, NAE lobbying no longer centered on principled opposition to subsidiarity but on ensuring that religious providers receiving public funds would retain their independence regarding staff and content. In an indication that pragmatic considerations and fears of secularism had by the 1980s won the day, the NAE counsel Forest Montgomery rejected "absolutist concepts of the separation of church and state" embedded in legislative proposals through which "child care would be dichotomized," with "secular child care receiving government financial assistance, while private religious child care would have had to compete against government-supported and regulated secularized care." His admission that not allowing religiously affiliated child-care centers to participate "will tend to drive those centers out of business" revealed the level of dependence of many conservative Protestant facilities on public funding.[49] Especially in a nation whose motto was In God We Trust, Montgomery argued in front of the Senate Committee on Finance, it made "little sense, if there is a child-care crisis, to fail to help them on the same basis as their secular counterparts." Likewise, his stance showed that the use of religious liberty arguments had won out over separationist dogma. Excluding religiously oriented child care from federal benefits, Montgomery declared, "cannot be squared with our first liberty" and "subordinates religion to irreligion."[50]

Similarly, the SBC, the largest evangelical organizations that had remained outside of the NAE, came around to openly supporting public aid but only after divisive internal battles and the takeover of its agencies by conservatives in the late 1970s and 1980s.[51] Although public funding remained controversial within the SBC, Richard D. Land, executive director of its Christian Life Commission, supported child-care block grants whereby federal funds were given but regulation was left to state and local government.[52] In short, by making the preservation of autonomy within a system of state subsidies the linchpin of their church-state attitude, Southern Baptists and other evangelicals invoked the rhetoric of the separation of church and state no longer to limit the expansion of government but to maintain a faith-based approach within the context of a growing administrative state.

Subsidiarity and the Rise of the Christian Right

Among the political ironies of subsidiarist welfare-state building in the 1960s is that liberal policies primarily benefited the Right within the evangelical fold. Indeed, the Great Society programs ushered in the conversion of evangelical conservatives to public funding. In many ways the Right completed the subsidiarist turn of evangelicalism begun during the Great Society and used this to strengthen its position within the movement. Conservatives utilized the issue of subsidiarity as part of an "internal backlash" against the moderate and left-leaning evangelicals in the drawn-out political and doctrinal battles within the movement in the 1970s and 1980s. At the same time, they used the public funding issue to forge even closer ties between the religious Right and the Republican party.

Benefiting from the broader political crisis of liberalism, conservatives within the evangelical movement had by the mid-1970s begun to rally successfully in reaction to moderate and left-wing evangelicals who had gained strength in the wake of the progressive social and political activism of the 1960s. On the surface, the message from the Right was blunt and uncompromising: Outright opposition to the welfare state informed its main social and economic agenda and sat alongside its relentless moralism, ferocious anticommunism, and flag-waving patriotism. Discarding traditional evangelical misgivings about the "materialistic" theory of laissez faire, conservatives depicted market capitalism as a biblically endorsed system. Viewing America as engaged in a moral and spiritual war between capitalism and socialism, they called for biblically mandated limits on the power of the state.[53]

Superficially, the Right's position thus suggested a return to traditional antistatist positions. A closer look, however, shows that a much closer relationship to the state was at the heart of the right-wing stance. What characterized the Right was the embrace of state building embedded in an antistatist message; calibrating between institutional integration into the subsidiarist regime and cultural alienation from the liberal state gave conservatives a competitive edge in the post-sixties climate of opinion. By fusing antistatist rhetoric with the affirmation of postwar state building, they kept alive the countercultural rejection of managerial liberalism while thriving on public funds. In contrast, many liberal and left-leaning evangelical groups, such as Sojourners, preserved the separationist legacy in their disillusionment with the pitfalls of the Great Society, Vietnam, and corruption in high places.

The effort to engineer a right-wing political mobilization of evangelicals was most apparent in the thriving parachurch agencies. By the 1970s the NAE, the paragon of mainstream evangelicalism, was fragmented and weakened in part because it had failed to organize an effective national coordinating body for social action comparable to Catholic Charities USA or the SBC's Christian Life Commission. At the same time, the organization had been immensely successful in spawning powerful affiliates and single-issue movements, such as World Relief, National Religious Broadcasters (NRB), and the Evangelical Foreign Missions Association (EFMA). Frequently dominated by conservatives, many of these parachurch organizations participated actively in public funding arrangements, especially for religious schools, child-care providers, foreign aid agencies, and the military chaplaincy. Prison Fellowship Ministries (PFM), for example, founded by Watergate villain Charles Colson, combined a softened stance toward public funding and a political drift to the right (see also chap. 6 by Kendrick Oliver in this volume).[54]

As conservatives picked up the cause of tuition tax credits, child-care vouchers, and similar programs, they turned the evangelical movement farther away from its traditional close cooperation with separationist groups. By the late 1970s, as the Right began to emerge victorious, attacks on public aid had largely dropped out of sight, and the NAE had severed its ties with Americans United for the Separation of Church and State (AU), the successor organization of POAU that had previously been a loyal ally of the NAE in the campaign against government funding for religious agencies. In the aftermath, the NAE initially concentrated its energies on pushing for tax credits. When it became apparent that the tax credit proposal would not be successful, however, the NAE, rather than reverting to a traditional separationist position, pushed instead for vouchers. Dismissing previous concerns that the voucher scheme would mean state regulatory control, the NAE's director Robert P. Dugan Jr. argued that vouchers, unlike federal grants and contracts, constituted aid to *parents*, not to the recipient institution. Instead of rejecting the scheme, he simply demanded "explicit language permitting these vouchers to be used in facilities providing religious instruction, and inclusion of moral tenets protection."[55] In his view, vouchers were now acceptable as long as regulations did not limit religious instruction and restrictive hiring.[56]

By the early 1980s any lingering reservations about either tuition vouchers or tax credits within the NAE had disappeared almost completely as the organization endorsed the plan with a 91 percent majority. "This is an historical reversal," Dugan proudly declared, "Ten years ago, probably more than 91 percent would have opposed tuition tax credits, ascribing it to a Roman Catholic conspiracy to get parochiaid. Even four years ago, a resolution on the subject was considered too controversial to bring to the floor of the convention."[57] A 2007 survey confirmed that evangelical Protestants had indeed come around to supporting the basic ideas behind subsidiarity. According to its findings, only one-quarter to one-third of congregations felt that government should have little or no role in care for the needy and that the religious community should not work directly with government in providing these services. In contrast, more than eight out of ten (82 percent) agreed with the statement that "meeting the needs of the poor demands collaboration between government, the religious community, and the secular community."[58]

The Right's embrace of subsidiarity also helped strengthen its ties with secular conservatism and nonevangelical religious groups. Unencumbered by the traditional separationist wing of the evangelical movement, a new generation of partisan NAE leaders who had close ties with the Republican party in the 1980s and 1990s, such as Dugan, emerged as forceful promoters of public-funding policies for religious agencies. In conjunction with the "politics of morality," centered on fighting secularization and moral permissiveness, this push for tuition vouchers, child-care grants, and similar proposals shifted the evangelical discourse away from the insistence on church-state separation toward a conservative vision of utilizing the subsidarist state.

Dugan's support for Paul Weyrich's "cultural conservatism" in particular showed that the right-wing political mobilization of evangelicals was not rooted in the rejection of government. Weyrich, one of key architects of New Christian Right, maintained that solutions to poverty involved the federal government, not just markets. He called for government contracting with churches and community groups. Likewise, neo- and theo-conservative advocates of the devolution of social provision to charities, such as Nathan Glazer, Peter L. Berger, and Richard John Neuhaus, called for state subsidies for nongovern-mental social-service providers, but packaged this in the rhetoric of an independent sector as an alternative to government-run services and the need to limit intrusive government regulation. As Berger and Neuhaus put it, "the mediating structure proposal is not antigovernment. We are favorably disposed toward government. We strongly support the form of government which has marked the American experiment at its best, namely, self-government."[59]

As the New Christian Right appropriated liberal policies and simultaneously presented them as alternatives to the alleged iniquities of the liberal welfare state, evangelical agencies increasingly benefited from a variety of direct and indirect public aid programs. By the 1990s, conservative Protestant colleges and universities were outstripping Roman Catholic and mainline Protestant entities in the receipt of public funds. While 35 percent of conservative Protes-tant institutions received more than 20 percent of their income—the highest category—from public funds, only 23 percent of Catholic and 25 percent of mainline Protestant institutions did. Among colleges and universities that received between 10 and 19 percent of their income from public sources, conservative Protestant institutions were also in the lead; 42 percent were in the latter category, as opposed to 33 percent of Catholic and 37 percent of mainline Protestant entities. Despite being leaders in discriminatory hiring and admissions policies and mandatory religious exercises, 78 percent of conservative Protestant colleges and universities receiving public funds reported no problems whatsoever with government pressures to limit their sectarian practices.[60] Recalling the impact of federal support ranging from student aid to construction grants, a professor at Azusa Pacific University, a leading evangelical college in California, concluded in 2005 that "without federal aid, the institution would not have flourished. With federal aid, the university took flight and grew into a significant institution that produces thousands of graduates. This is an example of how the government aided a religious organization without intruding on its autonomy or its faith-based mission."[61]

Likewise, in the past few decades, significant amounts of public funds have gone to evangelical social-service providers. As Stephen Monsma found in the early 1990s, 39 percent of conservative Protestant child-service agencies reported receiving more than 60 percent of their income from public funds, and a further 18 percent reported receiving 20–60 percent. Once again, traditional concerns about government intrusiveness were largely unfounded. Although conservative Protestant child-service agencies headed the field in exclusive hiring, compulsory religious activities, and religious commitment, the percentage reporting problems with government was only marginally higher (34 percent) than the average for all religiously based agencies (30 percent). While 22 percent felt forced to curtail practices, the highly religious agencies reported the most positive effects of public funding, with 89 percent viewing public funds as a means of expanding services.[62]

Recent Faith-Based Legislation

In light of the large-scale expansion of federal aid to church-related institutions pioneered by the Great Society and the "subsidiarist turn" of conservative Protestantism, the two recent pieces of aid-to-religion legislation that many critics regard as having opened the floodgates for taxpayer money draining toward religious entities turn out to be simply two additional holes in the already porous dike separating church and state. The Clinton administration's little-noticed Charitable Choice provision of the landmark 1996 Personal Responsibility and Work Opportunity Reconciliation Act (PRWORA) and the George W. Bush administration's 2001 Faith-Based Initiative mainly put the finishing touches on the long-term process by which evangelical groups were institutionally and ideologically integrated into the structures of the subsidiarist state.

Charitable Choice, sponsored by Senator John Ashcroft (R-MO), a conservative Christian who later became attorney general in the George W. Bush administration, not only prohibited discrimination against religious nonprofits in the contracting process, it "specifically required state and local governments to open the door to faith-based organizations when buying services from nongovernmental sources."[63] In so doing, the provision allowed states to use federal funds to enter into service contracts with charitable and faith-based organizations while removing elements of federal oversight. It permitted restrictive hiring of employees in religious agencies contracting with government, and abandoned requirements for religious social-service agencies to be separately incorporated and tax exempt under IRS codes as a prerequisite for receiving public funds. It also allowed the display of religious icons and other symbols where government services were provided. Similarly, the Faith-Based Initiative allowed for federal funds to be given directly to churches, rather than just denominational charities, and further limited the ability of the state to interfere with the religious content.[64]

The two programs thus addressed the remaining concerns evangelicals had in regard to public funding. First, they broadened the definition of eligible recipients of aid and loosened restrictions on religious agencies while, at the same time, limiting the potential for government intrusion. Second, they strengthened the legislative basis for the overt embrace of religious content in social policy, which had previously been tolerated via a policy of benign neglect but had not been written into the statutes. Under the new laws, religious providers retained autonomy from all levels of government and control over the definition, development, practice, and expression of religious beliefs. They were able to assert their spiritual dimension, strengthening the influence of religious imagery, narrative styles, and moral concepts in the welfare debates.[65]

Charitable Choice and the Faith-Based Initiative, rather than constituting a dramatic change in established practice, thus marked the final step in a long-term process of turning a religious group, which had traditionally adhered to a strict separation of church and state, into a champion of public funding. According to a nine-state study, twenty of the eighty-four contracts engaged conservative and evangelical faith-based organizations in Charitable Choice contracting.[66] Thus, by the 1990s the odd man out in the subsidiarist state was no longer evangelicalism but "that assortment of strict separationists, leftist critics, and theological liberationists who from their various perspectives find government funding of religiously grounded activities abhorrent to the best interests of American democracy."[67]

Conclusion

In arguing that evangelicals mobilized politically primarily via the "backlash," most research has focused on how a pietistic and largely apolitical religious group hostile to the liberal state was jolted back into the political realm in the process of reacting against the expanding power of government. In contrast, this chapter suggests that evangelicalism's involvement *with*, rather than just its reaction *against* the Great Society's main public policy initiatives, was a key factor in the movement's organizational and political resurgence. Liberal social policies in the 1960s created a legal and political climate that encouraged closer ties between evangelical entities and the federal government. In providing lavish funds with few strings attached, 1960s social policies supported the institutional growth of religious agencies while safeguarding their independence and spiritual mission. As a result, evangelicals, while continuing to denounce the "moral failure" of the welfare state, increasingly participated in and benefited from expanded public aid provision for their educational, health care, and social-service institutions.

By the 1970s the main evangelical debate on public aid had shifted from ubiquitous warnings about the dangers of a church-state combine to efforts to ensure the equal access, autonomy, and spiritual mission of religious agencies under public funding arrangements. Although evangelicals continued to conjure up the specter of secular intrusion, their main concern was no longer the size of government but the specifics of the funding arrangement. They rejected state subsidies when they threatened to infringe upon religious providers but demanded them when it came to making sure religious agencies were not excluded from public aid. Removed from the realm of unquestioned dogma, church-state separationism thus became largely a matter of pragmatic policy, which covered up the growing closeness to the structures of the subsidiarist state. Indeed, evangelical antistatism was less indicative of the rejection of government than of the desire to retain organizational autonomy at a time when public funding for religious agencies was rapidly becoming the norm.

These findings are relevant for understanding the dynamics of religious mobilization that has seen the loosely organized evangelical movement become the largest single religious faction in the United States and conservative Protestants form one of the most strongly Republican groups in the religious spectrum.[68] In the late 1970s and 1980s, the embrace of subsidiarity became a key platform of the resurgent New Christian Right within the evangelical movement. By combining vociferous antistatism and proprietary individualism with staunch support for the national security state, liberal capitalism, and public aid for nongovernmental agencies, resurgent conservatism appealed to an electorate that was both viscerally opposed to federal intrusion and had benefited from Cold War government spending. The Christian Right's ability to combine aversion to the state with embracing the instrumentalities of government funding helped bridge the ideological gap within conservatism between calls for restoring the free market and the broad-based acceptance of Social Security, Medicare, deficit spending, military contracting, and corporate subsidies.[69]

In summation, these findings complicate established conceptions of both liberal state building and resurgent evangelicalism. First, they suggest that the liberals who had pioneered the War on Poverty essentially advocated the devolution to third-sector actors that is usually associated with the conservative rhetoric of "retrenchment," "privatization," and "empowerment of mediating structures." Though commonly vilified by conservatives as advocates of government intrusiveness, they anticipated both the Clinton administration's Charitable Choice legislation and the Bush administration's Faith-Based Initiative popular with conservative Protestants. Second, this chapter indicates that the right-wing political mobilization of evangelicals can be understood as part of a "statist turn" of resurgent conservatism. While the political basis of Cold War liberalism collapsed, the Right developed an ideology that, while advocating a reduction in the size of government, helped perpetuate the established patterns of state building. The main difference is that conservatives shifted the focus to facilitating the flow of monies to religious organizations and to limiting the potential for government interference.

NOTES

1. Richard D. White, *"It's Your Misfortune and None of My Own": A New History of the American West* (Norman: University of Oklahoma Press, 1989).

2. Matthew D. Lassiter, "Political History beyond the Red-Blue Divide," *Journal of American History* 98 (2011): 764. For an illustrative example of this, see also chap. 2 by Darren Dochuk in this volume.

3. Brian Balough, *A Government Out of Sight: The Mystery of National Authority in Nineteenth Century America* (New York: Cambridge University Press, 2009).

4. Russell Baker, "The Awful Truth," *New York Review of Books*, November 6, 2003, 12.

5. See Lester H. Salamon, *Partners in Public Service: Government-Nonprofit Relations in the Modern Welfare State* (Baltimore: Johns Hopkins University Press, 1995), 19; Peter Dobkin Hall, "Philanthropy, the Welfare State, and the Transformation of American Public and Private Institutions, 1945–2000" (working paper no. 5, The Hauser Center for Nonprofit Organizations, Harvard University, 2000), 17, http://www.hks.harvard.edu/hauser/PDF_XLS/workingpapers/workingpaper_5.pdf; Donald T. Critchlow, "Implementing Family Planning Policy: Philanthropic Foundations and the Modern Welfare State," in *With Us Always: A History of Private Charity and Public Welfare*, ed. Donald T. Critchlow and Charles H. Parker (Lanham, MD: Rowman & Littlefield, 1998), 212.

6. Bruce Nichols uses the term subsidiarity to describe public-nonprofit relations in the foreign aid field. See Nichols, *The Uneasy Alliance: Religion, Refugee Work, and U.S. Foreign Policy* (New York: Oxford University Press, 1988), 206.

7. Hall, "Philanthropy," 1. On postwar public funding of nongovernmental organizations, see also Steven Rathgeb Smith and Michael Lipsky, *Nonprofits for Hire: The Welfare State in the Age of Contracting* (Cambridge, MA: Harvard University Press, 1993), 5, 15–16, 46, 70–71, 179–180; Peter Dobkin Hall, "The Welfare State and the Careers of

Public and Private Institutions Since 1945," in *Charity, Philanthropy and Civility in American History*, ed. Lawrence J. Friedman and Mark D. McGarvie (New York: Cambridge University Press, 2003), 363–383; Ralph M. Kramer, *Voluntary Agencies in the Welfare State* (Berkeley: University of California Press, 1981), 67–69; Helen Laville and Hugh Wilford, eds., *The US Government, Citizen Groups and the Cold War* (London: Routledge, 2006), 175–193.

8. Peter Dobkin Hall and Colin B. Burke, "Historical Statistics of the United States Chapter on Voluntary, Nonprofit, and Religious Entities and Activities: Underlying Concepts, Concerns, and Opportunities,"(working paper no. 14, The Hauser Center for Nonprofit Organizations, Harvard University, 2002), 9, http://www.hks.harvard.edu/hauser/PDF_XLS/workingpapers/workingpaper_14.pdf. See also Dorothy M. Brown and Elizabeth McKeown, *The Poor Belong to Us: Charities and American Welfare* (Cambridge, MA: Harvard University Press, 1997), ch. 5; David C. Hammack, "Failure and Resilience: Pushing the Limits in Depression and Wartime," in Friedman and McGarvie, *Charity, Philanthropy*, 263–280.

9. Stephen V. Monsma, *When Sacred and Secular Mix: Religious Nonprofit Organizations and Public Money* (Lanham, MD: Rowman & Littlefield, 1996), 1, 9. On postwar public funding for religious nonprofits, see also Theda Skocpol, "Religion, Civil Society, and Social Provision in the U.S.," in *Who Will Provide? The Changing Role of Religion in American Social Welfare*, ed. Mary Jo Bane (Boulder, CO: Westview, 2000), 21–50; Charles L. Glenn, *The Ambiguous Embrace: Government and Faith-Based Schools and Social Agencies* (Princeton: Princeton University Press, 2000); Robert J. Wineburg, *A Limited Partnership: The Politics of Religion, Welfare, and Social Service* (New York: Columbia University Press, 2000); Paul J. Weber and Dennis A. Gilbert, *Private Churches and Public Money: Church-Government Fiscal Relations* (Westport, CT: Greenwood, 1981); Lew Daly, *God and the Welfare State* (Cambridge, MA: MIT Press, 2006); Robert Wuthnow, *Saving America? Faith-Based Services and the Future of Civil Society* (Princeton: Princeton University Press, 2004).

10. Smith and Lipsky, *Nonprofits for Hire*, 54, 71; Michael O'Neill, *The Third America: The Emergence of the Nonprofit Sector in the United States* (San Francisco: Jossey-Bass, 1989), 96–97. On the Community Mental Health Centers Act, see Stephen Rathgeb Smith and Deborah A. Stone, "The Unexpected Consequences of Privatization," in *Remaking the Welfare State: Retrenchment and Social Policy in America and Europe*, ed. Michael K. Brown (Philadelphia: Temple University Press, 1988), 236; Hall and Burke, "Historical Statistics," 12, 19. On the Community Action component of the Economic Opportunity Act, see Smith and Stone, "Unexpected Consequences," 235. On subsidies to private nursing homes and other agencies provided via Medicare and Medicaid, see Smith and Lipsky, *Nonprofits for Hire*, 65–66, 68; and Kenneth A. Wedel, Arthur J. Katz, and Ann Weick, eds., *Social Service by Government Contract: A Policy Analysis* (New York: Praeger, 1979), vi.

11. *Catholic Standard*, February 17, 1966.

12. Quoted in C. Stanley Lowell, *The Great Church-State Fraud* (Washington, DC: Robert B. Luce, 1973), 178.

13. I have explored this in more detail in Axel R. Schäfer, *Piety and Public Funding: Evangelicals and the State in Modern America* (Philadelphia: University of Pennsylvania Press, 2012).

14. Bernard Coughlin, *Church and State in Social Welfare* (New York: Columbia University Press, 1965), 55, 64, 84, 104, 108, 130–131. See also Ellen F. Netting, "Secular and Religious Funding of Church-Related Agencies," *Social Service Review* 56 (1982): 603.

15. Minutes, Conference on Church-State Relations, February 6–7, 1961, 2, 5, National Association of Evangelicals Records, Wheaton College Archives and Special Collections, Wheaton College, Illinois (hereafter cited as NAE Records). See also Clyde W. Taylor, "Report of the Office of Public Affairs to the NAE Executive Committee," September 14, 1961, 5, NAE Records.

16. For excellent recent books on the NAE and the rise of postwar neo-evangelicalism, see Larry Eskridge and Mark A. Noll, eds. *More Money, More Ministry: Money and Evangelicals in Recent North American History* (Grand Rapids, MI: William B. Eerdmans, 2000); John G. Turner, *Bill Bright and Campus Crusade for Christ: The Renewal of Evangelicalism in Postwar America* (Chapel Hill: University of North Carolina Press, 2008); Steven P. Miller, *Billy Graham and the Rise of the Republican South* (Philadelphia: University of Pennsylvania Press, 2009); Daniel K. Williams, *God's Own Party: The Making of the Christian Right* (New York: Oxford University Press, 2010); and Darren T. Dochuk, *From Bible Belt to Sun Belt: Plain Folk Religion, Grassroots Politics, and the Rise of Evangelical Conservatism* (New York: Norton, 2011).

17. This applied in particular to attitudes toward the teaching of religion in public schools. Supporting "release-time" programs in the 1940s for students to participate in religious education during school, for example, United Evangelical Action pointed out that "Our side has insisted that the phrase 'separation of church and state' is a shibboleth. It's a doctrine and belief which must not be appealed to in argument." *United Evangelical Action*, October 15, 1945, 4. I would like to thank the anonymous reviewer of this volume for this reference.

18. R. L. Decker, "Government Grants and Loans to Charitable Institutions," National Conference on Church-State Relations, NAE, Winona Lake, Indiana, March 6–8, 1963, 5, NAE Records. See also Nolan B. Harmon, "Church and State—A Relation in Equity," *Christianity Today*, February 4, 1972, 4–7.

19. James DeForest Murch, "The Protestant Position Today," National Conference on Church-State Relations, NAE, Winona Lake, Indiana, March 6–8, 1963, NAE Records; Lowell, *Church-State Fraud*, 54, 154–161. See also Hall and Burke, "Historical Statistics," 12, 16–17, 29–30; Skocpol, "Religion," 26.

20. John Lee Eighmy, *Churches in Cultural Captivity: A History of the Social Attitudes of Southern Baptists* (Knoxville: University of Tennessee Press, 1972), 164–165; Lowell, *Church-State Fraud*, 188.

21. Clyde W. Taylor, "Report of the Office of Public Affairs to the NAE Board of Administration," October 7, 1963, 2, NAE Records.

22. James DeForest Murch, "Report of the Evangelical Action Commission to the Board of Administration," October 8–9, 1962, 1, NAE Records.

23. James DeForest Murch, "Report of the Commission on Evangelical Action to the Board of Administration," April 10–12, 1962, 1, NAE Records.

24. James Forrester, "Federal Aid to Higher Education and the Church Related College," National Conference on Church-State Relations, Winona Lake, Indiana, March 6–8, 1963, 1–2, 6, NAE Records.

25. Ibid., 5–6. On the funding crisis of evangelical colleges, see also James W. Pruyne, "The Church and Higher Education," typescript for Great Rivers Presbytery, November 17, 1987, *Christianity Today* International Records, Billy Graham Center Archives, Wheaton, Illinois.

26. Carl F. H. Henry, "Dare We Renew the Controversy? The Evangelical Responsibility," *Christianity Today*, July 22, 1957, 24.

27. Forrester, "Federal Aid to Higher Education," 6, NAE Records. See also James Forrester, "New Paths in Christian Higher Education," *Christianity Today*, August 28, 1964, 810.

28. Forrester, "Federal Aid to Higher Education," 1, NAE Records.

29. Minutes, NAE National General Convention, April 17, 1969, 10, NAE Records.

30. Forrester, "Federal Aid to Higher Education," 1, 6, NAE Records.

31. Clyde W. Taylor, "Report of the Evangelical Action Commission and the NAE Office of Public Affairs to the Board of Administration," April 14, 1969, 2, NAE Records.

32. Minutes, NAE National General Convention, April 17, 1969, 10, NAE Records.

33. "Resolution on Higher Education," NAE General Convention, Third Session, April 20, 1972, NAE Records.

34. Joseph P. Viteritti, *The Last Freedom: Religion from the Public School to the Public Square* (Princeton: Princeton University Press, 2007), 82; N. J. Demerath III and Rhys H. Williams, "A Mythical Past and Uncertain Future," in *Church-State Relations: Tensions and Transitions*, ed. Thomas Robbins and Roland Robertson (New Brunswick, NJ: Transition, 1987), 77–90; Phillip E. Hammond, "American Church/State Jurisprudence from the Warren Court to the Rehnquist Court," *Journal for the Scientific Study of Religion* 40 (2001): 455–464.

35. Diane Ravitch, *The Troubled Crusade: American Education, 1945–1980* (New York: Basic Books, 1983), 27–42; Eighmy, *Churches in Captivity*, 160, 164; Lowell, *Church-State Fraud*, 11, 188. See also Taylor, "Report of the Office of Public Affairs," September 14, 1961, NAE Records.

36. Clyde W. Taylor, "Church and State-1963, A Year of Re-examination," typescript for article in *Eternity Magazine*, November 13, 1963, NAE Records; [Clyde W. Taylor], "Confrontation—a Sharp Look at the Issues Facing Evangelicals in 1966," NAE Circular, NAE Records. On the anti-Catholic campaign, see Clyde W. Taylor, "Memo to Show Dr. Decker," March 28, 1947, NAE Records; "Committee on Christian Liberty of the National Association of Evangelicals," October 19, 1948, in Minutes

of the Meeting of the Executive Committee, November 19, 1948, NAE Records; Murch, "Report of the Commission on Evangelical Action," April 10–12, 1962, NAE Records.

37. Minutes, Twenty-second Annual Convention, April 8, 1964, 6–7, NAE Records. See also "Resolutions," Twenty-first Annual Convention, April 25, 1963, NAE Records.

38. Eighmy, *Churches in Captivity*, 160, 164; Lowell, *Church-State Fraud*, 11, 188.

39. "Federal Aid to Education," Resolutions Committee Report, Twenty-fourth Annual Convention, Second Session, April 20, 1966, 5, NAE Records.

40. "Educational Voucher System," Findings of the Evangelical Action Consultation, January 15–16, 1971, NAE Records.

41. Salamon, *Partners in Public Service*, 88–91; Coughlin, *Church and State*, 47, 69–73, 109–110, 160; Eighmy, *Churches in Captivity*, 160, 164–165; Hall, "Welfare State and Careers," 365; Lowell, *Church-State Fraud*, 148–149, 163. On Hill–Burton and subsequent expansions of public funding for nongovernmental health care, see U.S. Department of Health and Human Resources, "Hill–Burton," http://www.hrsa.gov/hillburton /compliance-recovery.htm.

42. Mary M. Bogle, "A Survey of Congregation-Based Child Care in the United States," in *Sacred Places, Civic Purposes: Should Government Help Faith-Based Charity*, ed. E. J. Dionne Jr. and Ming Hsu Chen (Washington, DC: Brookings Institution, 2001), 226; Robin Garr, *Reinvesting in America: The Grassroots Movements That Are Feeding the Hungry, Housing the Homeless, and Putting Americans Back to Work* (Reading, MA: Addison-Wesley Publishing Co., 1995), 7; Smith and Lipsky, *Nonprofits for Hire*, 60–61, 71; Lowell, *Church-State Fraud*, 147, 173–174, 176–182.

43. On the 1967 changes, see Smith and Lipsky, *Nonprofits for Hire*, 55–56; Smith and Stone, "Unexpected Consequences," 236; Marguerite G. Rosenthal, "Public or Private Children's Services? Privatization in Retrospect," 34–36, http://archive.epinet.org /real_media/010111/materials/rosenthal.pdf.

44. Smith and Stone, "Unexpected Consequences," 239. For details on Title XX, see 238–239; Wedel, Katz, and Weick, *Social Services*, 3. On lobbying by nongovernmental groups for Title XX, see O'Neill, *Third America*, 96–97.

45. Lowell, *Church-State Fraud*, 13; see also 170–171, 179–180.

46. Netting, "Secular and Religious Funding," 589–591, 602. See also Salamon, *Partners in Public Service*, 94; Anna Greenberg, "Doing Whose Work? Faith-Based Organizations and Government Partnerships," in Bane, *Who Will Provide*, 180.

47. Decker, "Government Grants and Loans to Charitable Institutions," March 6–8, 1963, 4, NAE Records.

48. "Church-State Separation Policy Statements," in General Convention Business Session Minutes, April 8, 1964. NAE Records.

49. Forest D. Montgomery to Robert P. Dugan Jr., "Memorandum Re: Child Care," [1988], 2, 5, NAE Records. See also Robert P. Dugan Jr., "Statement of Robert P. Dugan Jr., Director, Office of Public Affairs, National Association of Evangelicals on

Child Care Welfare Programs and Tax Credit Proposals before the Committee on Finance, United States Senate," April 19, 1989, 1–7, NAE Records.

50. Forest D. Montgomery, "Statement of Forest D. Montgomery, Counsel, Office of Public Affairs, National Association of Evangelicals on the Federal Role in Child Care before the Committee on Finance, United States Senate," September 22, 1988. NAE Records.

51. See Nancy Ammermann, *Baptist Battles: Social Change and Religious Conflict in the Southern Baptist Convention* (New Brunswick, NJ: Rutgers University Press, 1990); Barry Hankins, *Uneasy in Babylon: Southern Baptist Conservatives and American Culture* (Tuscaloosa: University of Alabama Press, 2002).

52. Richard D. Land, Executive Director, Christian Life Commission, Southern Baptist Convention, "Child Care Legislation," House Republican Study Committee, April 12, 1989, NAE Records; "Resolution on Institutional Childcare," Southern Baptist Convention, San Antonio, Texas, June 14–16, 1988, NAE Records; Oliver S. Thomas, "Statement of the Baptist Joint Committee on Public Affairs on Child Care Welfare Programs and Tax Credit Proposals," Committee on Finance, United States Senate, April 17, 1989, 2–3, NAE Records.

53. Craig Gay, *With Liberty and Justice for Whom? The Recent Evangelical Debate over Capitalism* (Grand Rapids, MI: William B. Eerdmans, 1991), 3, 17–18, 73–97; Robert Booth Fowler, *A New Engagement: Evangelical Political Thought, 1966–1976* (Grand Rapids, MI: William B. Eerdmans, 1987), 26–27, 154, 185; David H. Watt, *A Transforming Faith: Explorations of Twentieth-Century American Evangelicalism* (New Brunswick, NJ: Rutgers University Press, 1991), 49–71; Millard J. Erickson, *The Evangelical Left: Encountering Post-conservative Evangelical Theology* (Grand Rapids, MI: Baker Books, 1997). See also the contributions by David R. Swartz (chap. 10) and Eileen Luhr (chap. 3) in this volume. I have explored these issues in Axel R. Schäfer, *Countercultural Conservatives: American Evangelicalism from the Postwar Revival to the New Christian Right* (Madison: University of Wisconsin Press, 2011).

54. On PFM see, for example, Tanya Erzen, "Testimonial Politics: The Christian Right's Faith-Based Approach to Marriage and Imprisonment," *American Quarterly* 59 (2007): 991–1015.

55. Robert P. Dugan Jr. to George Bush, July 8, 1988, NAE Records; "Will President Bush Sell Out Evangelicals?" NAE press release, January 29, 1990, NAE Records.

56. Robert P. Dugan Jr. to John H. Sununu, May 1, 1991, NAE Records. See also Robert P. Dugan Jr., "NAE Office of Public Affairs Semi-Annual Report to the Board of Administration," October 9, 1991, NAE Records. As Mary Bogle has noted, whereas grants or contracts prohibit religious instruction, employment, and/or admission discrimination on the basis of belief, the key appeal of vouchers was that they prohibited none of these and allowed for faith-based provision in child care. Bogle, "Survey of Congregation-Based Child Care," 226–227.

57. Robert P. Dugan Jr. to Morton C. Blackwell, Special Assistant to the President for Public Liaison, March 22, 1983, NAE Records. See also Robert P. Dugan Jr. to

James A Baker III, Chief of Staff and Assistant to the President, March 22, 1983, NAE Records.

58. John C. Green, "American Congregations and Social Service Programs: Results of a Survey," The Roundtable on Religion and Social Welfare, 2007, 47–49, quote on 49. http://www.religionandsocialpolicy.org/docs/public_resources/American CongregationsReport.pdf.

59. Peter L. Berger and Richard John Neuhaus. *To Empower People: From State to Civil Society*, ed. Michael Novak, 2nd ed. (Washington, DC: American Enterprise Institute for Public Policy Research, 1996), 152.

60. Monsma, *Sacred and Secular*, 9–10, 68–70, 72–74, 84.

61. David Weeks, personal communication with the author, July 23, 2005.

62. Monsma, *Sacred and Secular*, 68–69, 72–78, 84–86, 90–91, 93; Bogle, "Survey of Congregation-Based Child Care," 228. The NAE Records contain numerous letters from ministers in member churches requesting information on voucher money.

63. Stanley Carlson-Thiess, "Charitable Choice: Bringing Religion Back into American Welfare," *Journal of Policy History* 13 (2001): 118.

64. On statutory and procedural changes relating to church-state relations under Charitable Choice and the Faith-Based Initiative, see Hall, "Philanthropy," 35–36; Carlson-Thiess, "Charitable Choice," 114–115, 117–118; Greenberg, "Doing Whose Work?," 183; Derek Davis and Barry Hankins, eds., *Welfare Reform and Faith-Based Organizations* (Waco, TX: J. M. Dawson Institute of Church-State Studies, 1999); Sheila Suess Kennedy and Wolfgang Bielefeld, *Charitable Choice at Work: Evaluating Faith-based Job Programs in the States* (Washington, DC: Georgetown University Press, 2006).

65. Greenberg, "Doing Whose Work?" 180–181, 183; Carlson-Thiess, "Charitable Choice," 116–118; Ram A. Cnaan with Robert J. Wineburg and Stephanie C. Boddie, *The Newer Deal: Social Work and Religion in Partnership* (New York: Columbia University Press, 1999), 280–283. See also Amy L. Sherman, "Testimony," U.S. House of Representatives, Committee on the Judiciary, Hearing before the Subcommittee on the Constitution, "State and Local Implementation of Existing Charitable Choice Programs," 107th Cong., 1st sess., April 24, 2001, http://commdocs.house.gov/committees/judiciary/hju 72145.000/hju72145_0.HTM.

66. Sherman, "Testimony," 27. For data on public funding for religious social-service agencies under Charitable Choice and the Faith-Based Initiative, see Green, "Congregations and Social Service Programs"; Mark Chaves, "Religious Congregations and Welfare Reform: Who Will Take Advantage of 'Charitable Choice?'" *American Sociological Review* 64 (1999): 836–846; and Lisa M. Montiel with Jason D. Scott, Joyce Keyes-Williams, and Jun Seop Han, "The Use of Public Funds For Delivery of Faith-Based Human Services: A review of the research literature focusing on the public funding of faith-based organizations in the delivery of social services," 2nd ed., The Roundtable on Religion and Social Welfare Policy, 2003, http://www.religion andsocialpolicy.org/docs/bibliographies/9-24-2002_use_of_public_funds.pdf.

67. Nichols, *Uneasy Alliance*, 206.

68. Geoffrey Layman, *The Great Divide: Religious and Cultural Conflict in American Party Politics* (New York: Columbia University Press, 2001), 199, 171; Williams, *God's Own Party*.

69. George Gallup Jr. and Jim Castelli. *The People's Religion: American Faith in the 90s* (New York: Macmillan, 1989), 217, 249; Matthew Lassiter, *The Silent Majority: Suburban Politics in the Sunbelt South* (Princeton: Princeton University Press, 2006); Schäfer, *Piety and Public Funding*.

9

Tempered by the Fires of War

*Vietnam and the Transformation
of the Evangelical Worldview*

ANDREW PRESTON

Few conflicts in American history have been as divisive as the Vietnam War. Even the most consensual and easily comprehensible foreign conflicts, such as World War II, have provoked dissent and opened up divisions.[1] But Americans argued more bitterly, and with more rancor, over Vietnam than they had over any other war before or since. The antiwar movement remains fixed in the collective consciousness as the main feature of domestic opinion on Vietnam. But opposition to the war was something of a minority movement, at least according to national polls, until the Tet Offensive of January and February 1968 shattered any illusions of eventual American victory; even after Tet, though most Americans told pollsters that they wanted the war to end, they still did not necessarily sympathize with the radical antiwar activists who continue to dominate the memory of the Vietnam War homefront.[2] In the national argument over the war, it appears that conservatives outnumbered radicals, and that they provided a key source of support for the beleaguered president Lyndon Johnson.

Within the historiography of domestic opinion on Vietnam, scholars have only hinted at the presence of a more conservative body of opinion that supported the presidency in a time of national emergency, fiercely criticized the antiwar movement (radical and liberal alike), and even endorsed the war's controversial objectives and methods.[3] Most overviews of the rise of the conservative movement treat Vietnam in passing, if at all.[4] Otherwise comprehensive accounts of the rise of the religious Right give the war an only cursory examination.[5] Even the Republican party, itself internally divided on the war but mostly supportive of upholding containment in Southeast Asia, has been placed at the margins of the historiography.[6] Instead, the dominant narrative of "the war within" portrays American citizens who opposed the war in conflict with the Johnson and Nixon administrations. In other words, the war within was supposedly between U.S. citizens and their government rather than between two opposing sets of American citizens who disagreed about the war specifically, and about U.S. foreign policy more generally.[7]

When their views on Vietnam are considered at all, evangelicals are automatically lumped together with the war's most ardent supporters and not given much further thought. Considering their cultural conservatism and nascent political activism, many historians assume that evangelicals reflexively supported America's mission in Southeast Asia. And so they did, in large numbers and with great conviction. But many evangelicals also expressed reservations about the war, on both strategic and moral grounds, and were often uncertain about the war's purpose, tactics, and impact on American society and politics. As Rebecca Klatch has demonstrated, within the conservative movement traditionalists and libertarians argued over Vietnam, with traditionalists, including evangelicals, reflexively supporting the Johnson and Nixon administrations, and libertarians opposing them largely on the grounds of the draft and the expansion of executive war powers.[8] But tensions and divisions existed even among the traditionalists. Instead of standing together as a unified bloc of patriotic support for the Johnson administration and its war in Indochina, evangelicals were often deeply ambivalent, especially as the war became more difficult and, after 1968, appeared unwinnable. They did not sympathize with antiwar radicals or even antiwar liberals, but nor did they always unquestioningly assume the virtue, wisdom, or necessity of Washington's policies in Indochina.

In the post-1960s rise of conservatism, the antiwar movement provided much of the momentum behind a backlash against the perceived excesses of liberalism. Organized labor, for example, had been a bedrock constituency of the New Deal coalition, but the relationship between labor and liberalism, and more specifically between labor and the Democratic Party, became fraught with tension over the antiwar direction of many liberals and many Democrats. Groups such as the "hardhats," union members who worked blue-collar jobs in factories and construction, were at times violently critical of antiwar activists. The working class was by no means monolithic, of course, and antiwar activists could be found within labor's ranks. But for many working class Americans, the antiwar movement tarred liberalism's previously good name with an un-patriotic and elitist brush.[9]

With the growth of conservative Protestant churches and the corresponding decline of their liberal mainline counterparts, it is natural to include evangelical-ism within this anti-antiwar backlash, which in turn helped fuel the surging conservative movement. Yet it is also a mistake. Evangelicals were indeed anti-antiwar and, in large part, also staunchly pro-war. But their views on the war, and on the antiwar movement, were not the product of a backlash. Rather, evangelical views on matters of war and peace were much older and much more consistent than the backlash paradigm suggests. Moreover, and more interestingly, evangelicals used the decade of the 1960s, and the social, cultural, and geopolitical tumult caused by the war, as a spur to pioneer a new conserva-tive internationalist worldview, which wedded an intense and undiminished belief in American exceptionalism with traditionally liberal ideas about the promotion of international development and global human rights.

The Evangelical Pro-war Movement

By 1966, widespread opposition to the war was already forming in America's colleges, churches, civil rights organizations, and newsrooms. Antiwar activism was growing both in degree and in kind: mass protest began in the spring, while the tenor and tactics of student direct action became increasingly radical through the summer and into the fall. Even more striking was the outright dissent by members of Congress—especially among President Lyndon Johnson's fellow Democrats—who openly criticized the Vietnam War in a manner un-precedented since the Philippine War more than sixty years earlier. Polls continued to show that Johnson held the support of a majority of Americans, yet polling data also reflected a growing unease with his handling of the conflict. In the midst of this growing unrest of 1966, the National Association of Evangelicals (NAE) offered the White House a lifeline of support. "Since it is apparent that the people and government of the U.S.A. are confused as to the basic issues of the war in Viet Nam, and the course of action to be followed by our government," stated an NAE resolution on the war, "we as evangelicals declare":

1. That we would decry any action by our government that would favor communism under the leadership of Red China.
2. That we would object to any action by our government that would weaken the security of the non-Communist nations of the world.
3. That we as evangelicals declare our loyalty to the established Constitutional government of our country and the accompanying requirements of civil obedience.[10]

Such unwavering support for the application of global containment stemmed not simply from traditional Christian anticommunism, but also from Christian conservatives' anger at the activities of the mainline Protestant churches. By 1966, the NAE's main rival, the much more liberal National Council of Churches (NCC), had become a pillar of the antiwar movement; in addition, the NCC was by then the main sponsor of Clergy and Laymen Concerned About Vietnam (CALCAV), an increasingly radical antiwar organization that counted John Coleman Bennett, Martin Luther King, and Richard John Neuhaus, the future Catholic neoconservative, among its members.[11] Christian conservatives viewed liberal dissent as not only wrongheaded but potentially treasonous. Several biblical passages, particularly within the gospels of Matthew (chap. 22), Mark (chap. 12), and Luke (chap. 20), and Paul's epistle to the Romans (chaps. 8 and 13), stipulate that Christians have a duty to obey civil authority so long as it is properly constituted and not in violation of God's law. Evangelicals, of course, had long been much more closely tied to the commands of the Bible than their liberal mainline counterparts, for whom the Bible was allegorical and metaphorical, perhaps even mythical, but certainly not the literal word of God.

Vietnam was not the first issue to test the moral boundaries of evangelical devotion to proper governing authority. Race relations presented a much more vexing issue because the questions it raised seemed less categorical than those surrounding the war in Vietnam. To many evangelicals, racism was a sin; but also to most evangelicals, whose instincts were strongly patriotic but also inherently antistatist, the solution was not to dictate a change in race relations through protest or legislation.[12] Instead, Christians needed to change themselves, from within, without state sanction. Yet among white institutions, religious or otherwise, the NCC took an early lead in overtly protesting Jim Crow segregation in the South, and they did so in the name of a Christian witness that demanded immediate change.[13] To evangelicals, this was counterproductive, perhaps even unchristian; it was certainly un-American. "Unquestionably, the whole philosophy of the National Council of Churches is socially oriented and, as a result, they take positions which, as a Presbyterian, I feel are contrary to those which a church should take," evangelical columnist L. Nelson Bell told one of his readers. "It is also a fact that many of their objectives coincide with the recommendations of the Communist Party. This may be incidental, but it is also suggestive."[14] Or as Edmund P. Clowney, president of Westminster Theological Seminary, put it in a detailed biblical exegesis of religion and politics, "The Church cannot redeem society by political action; when evangelism becomes politics, it is no longer the Gospel of Christ's Kingdom."[15] To be sure, this apolitical worldview enabled some racist Christian conservatives, such as George Wallace, Jerry Falwell, and Jesse Helms, to defend Jim Crow ostensibly in the name of local autonomy and thus avoid defending segregation by name.[16] But even those evangelicals who were sympathetic with the goals of the civil rights movement, such as Billy Graham and Carl Henry, were dismayed and unsettled by the liberal clergy's political activism.[17]

Civil rights was one thing, Vietnam completely another. Evangelicals were incensed that the liberal clergy, particularly their fellow Protestants, would deign to criticize the president in a time of war. And they resisted all attempts, such as Martin Luther King Jr.'s, to link the causes of racial oppression at home to the prosecution of the war Vietnam. When King proposed a boycott of all activities that helped the war, directly or indirectly, evangelicals reacted with dismay. "If this is the most viable alternative," intoned the editors of *Christianity Today*, "it may indicate the wisdom of the present American course in Viet Nam, painful as that may be." In contrast to King's passionate protests, the magazine hoped that Americans would "not determine U.S. foreign policy on the basis of emotion."[18]

To evangelicals, there was little reason to be emotional at all. The Johnson administration's conduct of the war in Vietnam, designed as it was to resist the expansion of godless and totalitarian communism, was perfectly consistent with biblical injunctions to respect civil authority, so there was every reason to support the government and no reason to resist it. "I have no sympathy for those clergymen who [urge] the U.S. to get out of Vietnam," Billy Graham explained on one of his crusades in Denver. The issue was in fact simple, the controversy unnecessary: "Communism has to be stopped somewhere, whether it is in Hawaii or on the West Coast. The President believes it should be stopped in Vietnam."[19] The president's judgment was good enough for Graham, just as it was for most evangelicals. This evangelical perspective on domestic dissent was crucial, because it helps explain why evangelicals remained supportive of a war even after they began to doubt some of the premises of the war itself.[20]

Yet evangelicals were not simply anti-antiwar; they were also steadfastly pro-war. Many if not most evangelicals agreed with the Johnson administration's diagnosis of the problem in Southeast Asia: that North Vietnam was trying to conquer South Vietnam; that it was attempting to do so both with outright force and through internal subversion by sponsoring an insurgency in South Vietnam; that the United States had a moral obligation to aid the South Vietnamese in resisting communism; and that not doing so would put U.S. national security at grave risk. They were, in short, about as steady a source of support as Lyndon Johnson could hope for.

As always, Billy Graham led the way. Despite his relationships with Dwight Eisenhower and Richard Nixon, he and Johnson grew personally close after LBJ became president in 1963. Johnson was a religious man who had been raised by an intensely evangelical Southern Baptist mother and converted to the evangelical but progressive Disciples of Christ as a teen. He and his own family—his wife Lady Bird and their daughters—later experimented with other religions, especially the Episcopal and Catholic faiths, even after LBJ became president.[21] His religiosity intensified as the crises of his presidency mounted, not least the war in Vietnam. "Over time," recalled Joseph Califano, one of Johnson's closest advisers, "the President talked more often about seeking guidance from the Almighty and praying. I had a sense that he found comfort in his relationship with God, particularly during his final year in office."[22] The stalemated war in Vietnam took a heavy emotional toll, and soon Graham found himself acting as Johnson's "spiritual counselor."[23] At the moment of decision to Americanize the war, when Johnson felt torn between a range of unappealing options, Graham offered him a private word of solace. "I want to reassure you of my support, friendship, and personal affection," he wrote LBJ. "The Communists are moving fast toward their goal of world revolution. Perhaps God brought you to the kingdom for such an hour as this—to stop them. In doing so, you could be the man that helped save Christian civilization."[24]

Graham, moreover, offered LBJ political support, at least as much public support as the assiduously apolitical evangelist felt he could provide. In the 1940s and 1950s, Graham had been one of the Cold War's most passionate holy warriors. With its materialism, aggressive atheism, and totalitarianism, communism represented the very antithesis of everything Billy Graham stood for. Anticommunism featured heavily in the 1948 Los Angeles crusade that cemented his evangelical stardom and launched him to national fame, and he reiterated the message consistently in the following decade. And although his anti-communist ardor and holy warrior mentality had matured somewhat by the time Johnson entered office, Graham still reflexively believed that an American anticommunist war was inherently also a just war. "War is sinful, yes," he declared in words rooted in his belief in humankind's original sin. "But as long as you have human nature so wild as it is, you're going to have to use force."[25] "Pacifism will fail," he argued elsewhere, probably with radical religious leaders like A. J. Muste and Dorothy Day in mind, "for the pacifist acts as if all men are regenerate and can be appealed to through persuasion and goodwill. The pacifist also refuses to recognize the role of power in the preservation of justice, along-side the role of love."[26]

On the whole, the evangelical establishment followed suit and threw its considerable, and considerably growing, political and moral weight behind the Johnson administration's foreign policy. This was true from the very onset of war, in the spring and summer of 1965, when Johnson significantly escalated the conflict in March—by beginning the Operation Rolling Thunder bombing campaign and deploying the first U.S. ground troops—and then Americanized the war in July—by committing another 50,000 troops to bring the total to 125,000, thus taking over the fighting from the beleaguered and ineffectual South Vietnamese army. These military measures, which clearly meant that the powerful and wealthy United States was at war with impoverished North Vietnam, brought the antiwar movement to life. But they also stirred the pro-war camp to the defense of a wartime president, and evangelicals were at the fore.

In March, after only a few weeks of sustained U.S. bombing of North Vietnam, Graham's father-in-law, *Christianity Today* columnist L. Nelson Bell, received a letter from Edwin T. Dahlberg of the Clergymen's Emergency Committee for Vietnam. Dahlberg was not only a renowned mainline churchman—he had once been president of the Northern Baptist Convention—he was also a leading pacifist, and the Clergymen's Emergency Committee for Vietnam was itself a subgroup of the staunchly pacifist Fellowship of Recon-ciliation. Dahlberg's form letter urged the nation's clergy to speak out against the escalating war: "It is especially important that the President should know how the leaders in our nation's religious life feel about this country's involve-ment in Vietnam." But nothing could have been designed to incense Bell more. Not only did he agree with Johnson's foreign policy, including on Indochina, but he resented the mainline clergy's assumption that it spoke for all the nation's churches. He did, however, agree with Dahlberg that religious leaders should make their views known to Johnson, and he wrote LBJ several missives of support. He was concerned, he wrote, that Johnson would "be misled by the noise of a minority which does not represent true Christianity in this country."[27] Instead, Bell wrote in another letter a month later, LBJ's "courageous actions," not only in Vietnam but also in the Dominican Republic, which the United States had recently invaded with twenty thousand Marines in the name of containing communism, "are appreciated by a great many of us." In contrast to the defeatism of the antiwar clergy, Bell exulted that "the flag flies just a little jauntier because our nation is trying to stand firmly in a world so dominated by evil."[28]

Bell was thoroughly conservative on almost all issues of the day, but evangelicals who were more sympathetic to the liberalism of LBJ's Great Society reforms were also staunchly pro-war. Sherwood Wirt was one of Graham's closest associates. He traveled on several of Graham's global crusades, and he edited Graham's own in-house mass-circulation magazine, *Decision*. He favored Johnson's stance on civil rights, and especially the Great Society's War on Poverty, which most if not all mainline clergy did as well. Where Wirt and other evangelicals differed from their liberal counterparts, however, was the war. "Vietnam becomes rather the same basic issue that free men have faced in two World Wars and Korea," he wrote in 1968: "*Will a man fight for his freedom? Because if he won't, in a sinful planet he will not have it long.*"[29]

Many evangelical leaders maintained their staunch pro-war support even after the Vietcong's Tet Offensive of 1968. Tet came as a tremendous shock to all Americans: to those in the military, including personnel in positions of command and in the field in South Vietnam; to the Johnson administration; to the media; and to the public. Coming after a year of official optimistic predictions and reports of progress, the communist attack, which was coordinated across virtually all of South Vietnam, seemed to demonstrate that a U.S. victory and communist collapse were not imminent, and that it would take significantly more time, money, and U.S. troops to win the war. American and South Vietnamese forces eventually reversed all of the Vietcong's gains, but for a war-weary American public, feeling betrayed by Johnson's portrayal of the war, this was not enough. Post-Tet polling data showed a decisive turn against the war, even among those Americans who had little sympathy for antiwar protesters.[30] Yet Christian conservatives bucked this national trend and felt that if Johnson needed to change his policies it should be to escalate further rather than retreat. For example, a poll of religious opinion in the summer of 1968—after Johnson had halted Rolling Thunder, placed a ceiling on U.S. deployments to

Indochina, and entered into peace talks with the North Vietnamese in Paris—recorded that 70 percent of Missouri Synod Lutherans and a staggering 97 percent of Southern Baptists supported an increase in U.S. bombing.[31] Another poll revealed that Moody Bible Institute students were more than twice as likely to support an increase in bombing as students at secular colleges.[32]

Among evangelicals, nobody epitomized the post-Tet pro-war movement more than Rev. Harold John Ockenga, a conservative Congregationalist from Park Street Church in Boston. A driving force behind the National Association of Evangelicals, and one of its founding members, Ockenga's voice carried far among Christian conservatives, including on foreign policy issues. By coincidence, he was touring Vietnam when the Vietcong launched the Tet Offensive, and he was in Saigon to witness much of the fallout. But rather than be dismayed or deterred, Ockenga's pro-war views hardened in the aftermath of Tet. "The great concern expressed here is that the U.S. government will work out a compromise with the VC, bringing them into a coalition government," he wrote in February from Saigon. "Then everything for which this people has fought and suffered will be lost." He noted with disgust that American liberals, the very same people who had escalated the war, were calling for withdrawal. These antiwar voices "weaken our cause by their calls for negotiation." Vietnam was not an easy war, Ockenga conceded, but that made a non-communist American-led victory even more imperative. As he saw it, the United States had three options. The first, outright withdrawal, was unthinkable. The second, negotiations over a coalition government that would include the communists, was unpalatable because, "As in China, so here this would ultimately mean a Communist takeover." This left Americans with only Ockenga's third option, an all-out effort for all-out victory. Johnson must remove all the constraints he had placed on the military: Haiphong, North Vietnam's main port, should be blockaded and mined; North Vietnam must be invaded with U.S. troops; Laos and Cambodia should be bombed and, if necessary, invaded too, in order to sever the Ho Chi Minh Trail. Johnson had resisted such measures, since they risked significantly widening the conflict. Ockenga fully recognized that his plan "means chancing a bigger war and an encounter with Russia and China," but he thought the risk was worth running. If the United States was at war, a just war against communism no less, it should commit itself to victory. Anything less was simply selfish, immoral, and unchristian, no matter what the consequences: "Why should 200,000,000 Americans continue to live as usual while 15,000 Americans die and 100,000 are wounded in Viet Nam? These men have as much right to live as you and I. If we must hazard their lives, we must hazard our security, too. Let us ask the ultimate questions and give courageous answers.

Then let us act upon our conclusions." The Johnson administration's experiment in limited war had yielded nothing good. It was, Ockenga declared, now time to choose between victory and defeat.[33]

Ockenga's report was published in *Christianity Today*, whose American readers were immersed in the domestic divisions caused by the war. While he was in Vietnam, however, Ockenga found himself surrounded by like-minded Christian anticommunists. In the postwar decades, conservative Protestants proselytized to the U.S. armed forces. They were so successful that by the 1960s, military personnel, especially the officer corps, had become increasingly evangelical. General William Westmoreland, the overall theater commander in South Vietnam, invited religious luminaries like Catholic archbishop Francis Cardinal Spellman to visit the troops. Westmoreland also invited Billy Graham, who made two trips to South Vietnam, in 1966 and 1968. The military's other prominent Christian warriors included Army Chief of Staff Gen. Harold K. Johnson, who seconded Westmoreland's efforts to bolster the war effort with Christian fervor. Evangelicals began their missionary efforts to the armed services in World War II, and though they found some success, it was not until the Vietnam era that they made a major breakthrough. In evangelical leaders such as Graham, Wirt, and Ockenga, and in the thousands of enlisted men and officers who identified themselves as born-again Christians, a grateful U.S. military found its most solid base of support. In return, military leaders facilitated the evangelization of the armed forces.[34]

A common ground of upright moral conduct also facilitated cooperation between evangelicals and the military. In an era marked by profound and rapid social and cultural change, from civil rights and second-wave feminism to the sexual revolution and the gay rights movement, the armed forces offered Christian conservatives both a model and a safe haven. Not coincidentally, evangelicals and enlisted men found that patriotism flowed easily from this shared cultural conservatism. This was in contrast to many of the other institutions, such as universities and mainline Protestant churches, that had traditionally set the nation's political and cultural standards but were now enthralled by secularism, moral relativism, and social justice. Antiwar protestors had been corrupted by their loss of true and traditional faith, Col. Theodore V. Koepke, an evangelical chaplain on Westmoreland's staff, argued in a speech to the National Religious Broadcasters' annual convention in 1967. As a result, they had lost their moral bearings. "Some people in our land seem to forget that the blessings of liberty must be purchased again and again at great cost." Instead of showing moral courage, antiwar activists believed "that the best way to combat aggression is for all of us to turn our backs upon indiscriminate torture and murder of women, children and civilian officials." The army, by contrast, was different, and to Col. Koepke the reason for this was simple: "We have no beatniks, no long-hairs, no odd balls. Our men are mature, moral, capable, imaginative, patriotic and deeply spiritual."[35]

Evangelical missionaries in South Vietnam offered a similar foundation of support for America's mission and Johnson's war. American Protestant missionaries first went to Vietnam in 1911, when the Christian and Missionary Alliance (CMA) established a station in Cochinchina. They met with limited success until the 1950s, when the departure of the French and the arrival of the Americans facilitated evangelical evangelism. By the time Lyndon Johnson Americanized the war in 1965, there were conservative mission stations flourishing across South Vietnam, including those from the Southern Baptist Convention, the Worldwide Evangelization Crusade, the Seventh-Day Adventists, United World Missions, and the ubiquitous CMA. All had stations in Saigon, but most also had outposts in and around Danang and other regional centers like Hue and Vinh Long. Evangelical missionaries felt bullish about their future in South Vietnam, even in a time of conflict. As CMA's foreign secretary Louis L. King commented as late as 1968, "Far from sounding the death knell to evangelism, the war has opened new doors of remarkable opportunity, and people are generally more responsive than they were" before the Americanization of the war three years earlier.[36] Similarly, Protestant faith-based nongovernmental organizations, such as World Vision, had a significant presence in South Vietnam, and they concentrated predominantly on the massive and constantly growing problem of refugee assistance.

True to their faith and culture, conservative Protestant missionaries had little hesitation in supporting America's purposes in Vietnam. They were careful not to work too closely with military personnel—although both groups battled communism, their methods were simply too discordant to allow for close cooperation—yet missionaries saw themselves as anticommunist foot soldiers for both God and country. In Hue, for example, the NAE's World Relief Commission teamed up with the CMA and the indigenous National Evangelical Church of Viet Nam to train both local lay preachers and local entrepreneurs.[37] Mission leaders did much the same by arguing that the only real antidote to Vietnamese communism was Vietnamese anticommunism, which in turn needed direction from American evangelicals and protection from the U.S. military. Missionaries claimed to find eagerness for the gospel among the South Vietnamese who were accustomed to the apathy of Buddhism and false promises of Roman Catholicism. The Vietcong, said the missionary magazine *Jungle Frontiers*, were trying to impose their doctrine of communist atheism by force, but the Vietnamese "have a different plan: they want to win their village to Christ."[38] It was simply a matter of creating the right conditions for this to happen.

Even so, missionaries often needed protection themselves. Unsurprisingly, the Vietcong viewed these American Protestant anticommunists as a threat, or at least a nuisance, and evangelical missionaries were often targeted for assassination. Several died as a result, including six CMA missionaries stationed in Ban Me Thuot in one attack during the Tet Offensive. Yet such violence did little to deter evangelical missionaries. The "martyrdom of six faithful soldiers of the cross will result in [the] multiplication of the gospel effort," predicted the missionary periodical, the *Alliance Witness*. "Our God never makes a mistake, and His work in Viet Nam will advance in spite of the grave loss."[39]

Indeed, few Americans, particularly those living in South Vietnam, remained as hopeful as evangelical missionaries. Typical was one woman affiliated with the CMA and stationed in Quang Tri province, scene to some of the most bitter fighting in the entire war. In 1971, she wrote to the NAE's Evangelical Foreign Missions Association to complain about the pessimism of U.S. military officials and the American public at large; for this reason, and because her criticisms were so caustic, she wished to remain anonymous. This was no time for defeatism, she charged, but forward advance. The partisan antiwar American media had completely—and, she charged, deliberately—misrepresented what she claimed were the true facts on the ground. "It seems that the communists must control about 99 percent of our mass communication media," she wrote; "either that or we have no newsmen of integrity." This was not mere supposition: "I know this," she admonished her readers, "from my own personal knowledge." The Vietcong and North Vietnamese were guilty of the very worst crimes against humanity, including "torturing and massacring of incredible cruelty," and yet Americans were now turning a blind eye. She pleaded for more patience from officials in Washington, and from Americans in general, for there was still hope in South Vietnam—but only if U.S. forces stayed. There was "little doubt in the mind of any South Vietnamese citizen" about what would happen after a total U.S. withdrawal: "a communist takeover." And after South Vietnam, the communists would be "well on their way to taking over Southeast Asia—and after that the rest of the world."[40] It was an extreme form of the domino theory, which Dwight Eisenhower had first used to justify U.S. intervention in 1954 but which even the most hawkish officials had discarded years before. But for evangelicals, 1971 was little different than 1954: the cause was still just, and the stakes were still high.

A Profound Ambivalence

The Vietnam War was an incredibly confusing conflict, tough to comprehend and difficult to support, and it demanded from the American people, even its most ardent supporters, almost superhuman levels of perseverance. This helps explain why the Johnson and Nixon administrations had such an arduous time explaining their purposes, and it helps explain why the habitual national backing for a wartime president evaporated so easily. Yet it also helps explain the ambivalence that began to settle uneasily in the consciences of many evangelicals. For them as for other Americans, Vietnam provoked questions, doubts, and uncertainty. If there was an evangelical backlash against the antiwar movement, there was also an evangelical backlash against the logical absurdities and anticommunist excesses of the Vietnam War.

Billy Graham had, of course, offered Lyndon Johnson not only friendship and spiritual counsel but also pro-war support. Yet the war did not always sit well even with Graham. He found Vietnam "complicated, confusing, and frustrating." He also worried that the war was tearing apart the fabric of American society. As he recalled years later, "the seemingly endless war in Vietnam contributed to an atmosphere of fear, uncertainty, confusion, and even mindless escapism." Graham did not advocate withdrawal, at least not in the 1960s, but he saw little prospect for victory short of a total war effort that could trigger a third world war. Ockenga arrived at the same conclusion during his 1968 tour of South Vietnam, but Graham, by contrast, was unwilling to run such risks. "How can we have peace?" he asked. "I don't know. I don't have any answers." As he put it to an audience during a crusade to Hawaii, "We either face an all-out war with Red China, or a retreat that will cause us to lose face throughout Asia. Make no mistake about it. We are in a mess." Thus began Graham's conversion from hawk to dove, from the committed Christian anticommunist of the 1940s and 1950s to the antinuclear campaigner for détente in the 1980s. Before the travails of Vietnam, he vowed never to compromise with communist tyranny; in the 1970s, however, he began to soften his tone; and in the early 1980s, well before Mikhail Gorbachev came to power, he found himself traveling to Moscow, in dialogue with the very communist leaders he had once denounced as evil.[41]

Christianity Today, the mainstream publication for evangelicalism that was quickly supplanting the liberal *Christian Century* as the nation's most popular Protestant magazine, had long been one of the most important sources of pro-war opinion. But the war sat uneasily in the minds of the editors of *Christianity*

Today, too. Doubts were often expressed within otherwise vitriolic pro-war articles, as evangelical intellectuals such as Carl Henry, *Christianity Today*'s widely respected editor-in-chief, wrestled with the perplexing quandary of Indochina. The "predicament" of Vietnam, the magazine editorialized as early as January 1966, was "enough to make every God-fearing man cry, God help us." The antiwar protestors did their country a disservice, but they might be right in saying that the war could not end well for a prideful United States. Instead of victory, the editors drew on the same doctrine of original sin that had led many evangelicals initially to support the war to warn against hubris. "It may be that we shall now be compelled to learn that the consequences of human greed, of lust of glory, and of the will to power can so beset men that there is no way of escape, except that God himself intervene in ways we cannot now even dimly conceive."[42] This was an astonishing admission from *Christianity Today*. Even more astonishingly, it was not all that far off the philosophy that underpinned the antiwar stance of mainline liberal Christian realists such as Reinhold Niebuhr and John Coleman Bennett, or of one of one of *Christianity Today*'s competitors and political and theological rivals, *Christianity and Crisis*.

Such heretical thinking was not unique. In other editorials, including those before the watershed of Tet, *Christianity Today* queried the very bases of Johnson's containment policies in Southeast Asia. Even while castigating the antiwar movement, especially the activist mainline clergy in the NCC and CALCAV, and even while denying any moral equivalence between American and communist military tactics, the editors wondered in 1967 whether the war's evangelical supporters had properly thought through the moral issues at stake. "The Bible nowhere encourages the notion that the United States is the crux of God's purpose in history," they admonished their readers in a strikingly Niebuhrian tone. "The course of world history is downward, and for all its glorious heritage, the United States is not exempt from that decline." War, moreover, was not always the answer, especially if it appeared to be unjust. "Most evangelical Christians reject the pacifist doctrine that war is always unjust. But do they unconsciously accept the notion that war is always just?"[43] Questions and doubts turned to despair following Tet. "Big as America is and powerful as its nuclear armaments are, the Viet Nam imbroglio seems beyond its ability to terminate." Maybe, *Christianity Today* speculated in 1969, American officials should emulate Jehoshaphat and cry, "We are powerless" and "do not know what to do."[44]

Even missionaries, Christ's foot soldiers in the holy war against communism, could be ambivalent about the actual war in Vietnam. They did not always perceive the war in terms of American power versus communist power; more often, in fact, they envisioned it as a struggle between Christ and communism, with the United States playing at most an incidental role in an even greater cosmic drama. Consider Homer E. Dowdy's *The Bamboo Cross*, a nonfiction account of Vietnamese Protestantism first published in 1964. The hero is Sau, a Vietnamese Protestant convert who leads his village against the depredations and brutality of Vietcong insurgents and the authoritarianism of traditional Catholicism. In Dowdy's telling, Sau's Christian gospel succeeded where bullets and village defenses failed. Noticeably absent in *The Bamboo Cross* are American missionaries, who simply stand back to allow indigenous Vietnamese evangelicalism to survive and thrive.[45] Other Vietnamese converts, such as Rev. Doan Van Mieng, president of South Vietnam's National Evangelical Church, spread a similar message in the cities.[46] Evangelical missionaries may have believed in American exceptionalism, but they believed in Christian exceptionalism even more. Missionaries in Vietnam, lamented *Christianity Today*, were often "stigmatized" as "agents of 'American imperialism.' Nothing could be further from the truth, if only because the Gospel sets men free—really free—from all imperialism and brings them to the loyalty of Jesus Christ."[47] Evangelical NGOs, such as World Vision, also perceived their efforts as both unavoidably connected to, but mostly independent from, American military and diplomatic efforts in South Vietnam.[48]

In 1971, the same year the anonymous CMA missionary complained about American defeatism, missionaries were also recognizing that the struggle in Vietnam transcended American concerns and Americans' efforts. They also realized, as did much of the rest of the country, that the war would soon come to an end, and that the United States would depart South Vietnam without a final victory or even stability intact. But they did not lose hope, for Vietnam's salvation was not in America's hands. "Viet Nam will not all be tragedy," one missionary reflected upon departing Vietnam. "Where war has lost, Christ can save! As troops flow out, tools flow in! Weapons have killed. Tools will give life! This must be the right way—no longer to 'search and destroy,' but to 'search and save.'" America's task was finished. "The job of evangelizing war-struck Viet Nam must devolve upon the native Christians."[49]

After its 1966 pro-war interjection into the national debate on Vietnam, the National Association of Evangelicals did not issue another resolution about the war until 1971. Much had changed in five years: militarily, in both tactical and strategic terms, the war had been disastrous for the United States; socially and culturally, the war had torn apart American society and undermined national self-confidence; politically, the conflict had severely eroded Americans' trust in their elected officials and destabilized the government's ability to function effectively. Just as important, a new president, Richard Nixon, was in the midst of completely reorienting U.S. foreign policy away from its implacable hostility to the Soviet Union and the People's Republic of China and into a new era of détente and peaceful coexistence. For evangelicals, as for most conservatives, the war in Vietnam had been first and foremost an effort to contain Chinese communist expansionism, and so Nixon's opening to Beijing removed one of the main bases of the pro-war position. Perhaps most importantly, it was difficult for Christians of all political and doctrinal persuasions to justify the destruction wrought upon the peoples of Indochina. In its 1971 resolution, then, the NAE revisited its pro-war stance of five years before without explicitly repudiating it:

> America is being torn apart by dissenting voices concerning its involvement in Viet Nam. We note with approval the promise of President Nixon to disengage us from a war that has lasted too long and brought sorrow and suffering to many homes. We wish that it were possible to end our involvement overnight but we take notice of the fact that the consequences of such a precipitate action might worsen an already difficult situation. Therefore the National Association of Evangelicals assures our President of our approval of our intention to end our involvement in the war as soon as possible and of our prayers to hasten this objective. We further call for massive help and rehabilitation of the lands that have been devastated and the people who have suffered so greatly.[50]

Evangelical visions of the Vietnam War, then, were neither monolithic nor unified, and they did not remain static throughout the war. The antiwar movement was never popular among evangelicals, who remained strongly anti-antiwar throughout the 1960s and into the next decade. But evangelicals often reflected thoughtfully about the problems raised by Vietnam, including the problem of American power in a globalizing world, and they did not always reflexively and unthinkingly support the application of containment to Indochina. Instead, following Graham's model, they used the trauma of Vietnam to transform their own worldview, from one fixated on the communist menace to one that recognized global complexity and interconnectivity.[51] They retained their belief in America's virtue, and they remained more nationalistic than the average American, particularly about America's mission in the world. But following Vietnam, they grafted onto it an internationalist awareness of worldwide humanitarian crises, such as civil war, famine, and poverty. This was not so much a result of backlash as it was a process of transformation in which the evangelical worldview was tempered by the fires of war in Vietnam.

NOTES

1. On internal division and dissent in World War II, see Michael C. C. Adams, *The Best War Ever: America and World War II* (Baltimore: Johns Hopkins University Press, 1994); Steven Casey, *Cautious Crusade: Franklin D. Roosevelt, American Public Opinion, and the War against Nazi Germany* (New York: Oxford University Press, 2001); Luis Alvarez, *The Power of the Zoot: Youth Culture and Resistance During World War II* (Berkeley: University of California Press, 2008); Glenda Elizabeth Gilmore, *Defying Dixie: The Radical Roots of Civil Rights, 1919–1950* (New York: W. W. Norton, 2008), 297–399; and Kevin M. Kruse and Stephen Tuck, eds., *Fog of War: The Second World War and the Civil Rights Movement* (New York: Oxford University Press, 2012). Division and dissent were common even— indeed, perhaps especially—among American Christians. See Gerald L. Sittser, *A Cautious Patriotism: The American Churches and the Second World War* (Chapel Hill: University of North Carolina Press, 1997); and Andrew Preston, *Sword of the Spirit, Shield of Faith: Religion in American War and Diplomacy* (New York: Alfred A. Knopf, 2012), 365–383.

2. David W. Levy, *The Debate Over Vietnam*, 2nd ed. (Baltimore: Johns Hopkins University Press, 1995), 140–143, 161.

3. The pro-war movement has received scant attention, but hints of it can be found in overviews such as Tom Wells, *The War Within: America's Battle Over Vietnam* (Berkeley: University of California Press, 1994), 56–57, 63, 134, 144, 374–375; and James T. Patterson, *Grand Expectations: The United States, 1945–1974* (New York: Oxford University Press, 1996), 629, 770.

4. See, for example, Lisa McGirr, *Suburban Warriors: The Origins of the New American Right* (Princeton: Princeton University Press, 2001); Jonathan M. Schoenwald, *A Time for Choosing: The Rise of Modern American Conservatism* (New York: Oxford University Press, 2001); John Micklethwait and Adrian Wooldridge, *The Right Nation: Conservative Power in America* (New York: Penguin Press, 2004); Kevin M. Kruse, *White Flight: Atlanta and the Making of Modern Conservatism* (Princeton: Princeton University Press, 2005); Matthew D. Lassiter, *The Silent Majority: Suburban Politics in the Sunbelt South* (Princeton: Princeton University Press, 2006); Bruce J. Schulman and Julian E. Zelizer, eds., *Rightward Bound: Making America Conservative in the 1970s* (Cambridge, MA: Harvard University Press, 2008); and David Farber, *The Rise and Fall of Modern American Conservatism: A Short History* (Princeton: Princeton University Press, 2010).

5. See, for example, Robert Wuthnow, *The Restructuring of American Religion: Society and Faith since World War II* (Princeton: Princeton University Press, 1988); Mark Silk, *Spiritual Politics: Religion and America since World War II* (New York: Simon and Schuster, 1988); William Martin, *With God On Our Side: The Rise of the Religious Right in America* (New York: Broadway Books, 1996); Frank Lambert, *Religion in American Politics: A Short History* (Princeton: Princeton University Press, 2008); and Daniel K. Williams, *God's Own Party: The Making of the Christian Right* (New York: Oxford University Press, 2010). However, for recent exceptions, see Patrick Allitt, *Religion in America since 1945: A History* (New York:

Columbia University Press, 2003), 100–107; David E. Settje, *Faith and War: How Christians Debated the Cold and Vietnam Wars* (New York: New York University Press, 2011), 65–71; and Preston, *Sword of the Spirit*, 532–538.

6. For the exceptions, see Terry Dietz, *Republicans and Vietnam, 1961–1968* (New York: Greenwood Press, 1986); and Andrew L. Johns, *Vietnam's Second Front: Domestic Politics, the Republican Party, and the War* (Lexington: University Press of Kentucky, 2010).

7. Wells, *War Within*, is not only emblematic of the standard narrative, it is also the best and most comprehensive one-volume account of the antiwar movement.

8. Rebecca E. Klatch, *A Generation Divided: The New Left, the New Right, and the 1960s* (Berkeley: University of California Press, 1999), 211–213.

9. Rhodri Jeffreys-Jones, *Peace Now! American Society and the Ending of the Vietnam War* (New Haven: Yale University Press, 1999), 178–221; David Maraniss, *They Marched Into Sunlight: War and Peace, Vietnam and America, October 1967* (New York: Simon and Schuster, 2003); Jefferson Cowie, *Stayin' Alive: The 1970s and the Last Days of the Working Class* (New York: New Press, 2010), 135–138. On labor's own antiwar movement, see Christian G. Appy, *Working-Class War: American Combat Soldiers and Vietnam* (Chapel Hill: University of North Carolina Press, 1993).

10. Quoted in James H. Smylie, "Ethics in the Revival Tent: Something Happened to Conservatives on the Way to Vietnam," *Worldview*, November 1973, 30–35.

11. On CALCAV, see Mitchell K. Hall, *Because of Their Faith: CALCAV and Religious Opposition to the Vietnam War* (New York: Columbia University Press, 1990); and Jill K. Gill, *Embattled Ecumenism: The National Council of Churches, the Vietnam War, and the Trials of the Protestant Left* (DeKalb, IL: Northern Illinois University Press, 2011).

12. Historically and ideologically, the antistatism of Christian conservatives stems from the fear that the government would regulate religion. But for a sophisticated and nuanced explanation of how evangelicals came to terms with the statism of the post–New Deal order, see Axel R. Schäfer, *Piety and Public Funding: Evangelicals and the State in Modern America* (Philadelphia: University of Pennsylvania Press, 2012).

13. James F. Findlay Jr., *Church People in the Struggle: The National Council of Churches and the Black Freedom Movement, 1950–1970* (New York: Oxford University Press, 1993); Michael B. Friedland, *Lift Up Your Voice Like a Trumpet: White Clergy and the Civil Rights and Antiwar Movements, 1954–1973* (Chapel Hill: University of North Carolina Press, 1998); Gill, *Embattled Ecumenism*.

14. L. Nelson Bell to J. C. Pierce, July 1, 1968, Box 39, Folder 3, L. Nelson Bell Papers, Billy Graham Center Archives, Wheaton College, Wheaton, Illinois (hereafter cited as LNBP).

15. Edmund P. Clowney, "A Critique of the 'Political Gospel,'" *Christianity Today*, April 28, 1967, 11.

16. See, respectively, Dan T. Carter, *The Politics of Rage: George Wallace, the Origins of the New Conservatism, and the Transformation of American Politics* (New York: Simon and Schuster, 1995), 235, 298–299, 459–460; Susan Friend Harding, *The Book of Jerry Falwell: Fundamentalist Language and Politics* (Princeton: Princeton University Press, 2000), 21–28,

112–113, 180–181; and William A. Link, *Righteous Warrior: Jesse Helms and the Rise of Modern Conservatism* (New York: St. Martin's, 2008), 56–57, 125–127, 177–178.

17. On Billy Graham and civil rights, see especially Steven P. Miller, *Billy Graham and the Rise of the Republican South* (Philadelphia: University of Pennsylvania Press, 2009).

18. "Peace Through Boycott?" *Christianity Today*, April 28, 1967, 27.

19. Quoted in William Martin, *A Prophet with Honor: The Billy Graham Story* (New York: William Morrow, 1991), 312.

20. This dynamic is treated well in Darren Dochuk, *From Bible Belt to Sunbelt: Plain-Folk Religion, Grassroots Politics, and the Rise of Evangelical Conservatism* (New York: W. W. Norton, 2010), 296–299.

21. Preston, *Sword of the Spirit*, 504–505.

22. Joseph A. Califano Jr., *The Triumph and Tragedy of Lyndon Johnson: The White House Years* (New York: Simon and Schuster, 1991), 335.

23. Billy Graham, *Just As I Am: The Autobiography of Billy Graham* (San Francisco: HarperSanFrancisco, 1997), 414. On the Johnson–Graham friendship, see Nancy Gibbs and Michael Duffy, *The Preacher and the Presidents: Billy Graham in the White House* (New York: Center Street, 2007), 113–156.

24. Quoted in Williams, *God's Own Party*, 79.

25. Quoted in Marshall Frady, *Billy Graham: A Parable of American Righteousness* (New York: Simon and Schuster, 1979), 424. Ironically, Graham's use of the doctrine of original sin to defend the war in Vietnam contrasted sharply with that of the doctrine's other mainstream practitioner, Reinhold Niebuhr, who opposed the war. On Graham, Niebuhr, and original sin, see Andrew S. Finstuen, *Original Sin and Everyday Protestants: The Theology of Reinhold Niebuhr, Billy Graham, and Paul Tillich in an Age of Anxiety* (Chapel Hill: University of North Carolina Press, 2009). On Niebuhr's opposition to Vietnam, which Finstuen does not discuss, see Richard Wightman Fox, *Reinhold Niebuhr: A Biography* (New York: Pantheon, 1985), 284–288; and Mark Hulsether, *Building a Protestant Left: Christianity and Crisis Magazine, 1941–1993* (Knoxville: University of Tennessee Press, 1999), 125–134.

26. Billy Graham, *World Aflame* (Garden City, NY: Doubleday, 1965), 209.

27. Edwin T. Dahlberg to Bell, March 20, 1965, and Bell to Lyndon Johnson, April 2, 1965, both in Box 30, Folder 22, LNBP.

28. Bell to Johnson, May 13, 1965, ibid.

29. Sherwood Eliot Wirt, *The Social Conscience of the Evangelical* (New York: Harper & Row, 1968), 125. Emphasis in the original.

30. On Tet as the war's turning point, see Mark Atwood Lawrence, *The Vietnam War: A Concise International History* (New York: Oxford University Press, 2008), 115–136.

31. Levy, *Debate Over Vietnam*, 94.

32. Williams, *God's Own Party*, 78–79.

33. Harold John Ockenga, "Report from Viet Nam," *Christianity Today*, March 15, 1968, 35. On the evangelical preference for victory over compromises in Vietnam, see also Michael Lienesch, *Redeeming America: Piety and Politics in the New Christian Right* (Chapel Hill: University of North Carolina Press, 1993), 61.

34. Anne C. Loveland, *American Evangelicals and the U.S. Military, 1942–1993* (Baton Rouge: Louisiana State University Press, 1996), esp. 118–164.

35. Theodore V. Koepke speech to the annual convention of the National Religious Broadcasters, 1967, Box 9, Folder 12, Eugene R. Bertermann Papers, Billy Graham Center Archives, Wheaton College, Wheaton, Illinois.

36. David E. Kucharsky, "Viet Nam: The Vulnerable Ones," *Christianity Today*, March 1, 1968, 17.

37. "Compassion Gap in Viet Nam," *Christianity Today*, April 14, 1967, 40.

38. "Steadfast Under Threat," *Jungle Frontiers* 23 (Summer 1966): 10.

39. "They Wear the Martyr's Crown," *Alliance Witness*, March 13, 1968.

40. Anonymous letter from CMA missionary in South Vietnam, April 4, 1971, Box 108, Folder 4, Records of the Evangelical Fellowship of Mission Agencies, Billy Graham Center Archives, Wheaton College, Wheaton, Illinois.

41. Graham, *Just As I Am*, 421; Preston, *Sword of the Spirit*, 534–535, 597–598 (Graham quoted on 534).

42. "Viet Nam: Where Do We Go from Here?" *Christianity Today*, January 7, 1966, 31.

43. "Viet Nam: A Moral Dilemma," *Christianity Today*, January 20, 1967, 28.

44. "Decision Time on Viet Nam," *Christianity Today*, March 28, 1969, 27.

45. Homer E. Dowdy, *The Bamboo Cross: Christian Witness in the Jungles of Viet Nam* (New York: Harper & Row, 1964).

46. Doan Van Mieng, "Vietnam Pastor," *Decision*, June 1967, 6.

47. "Spotlight on Asia," *Christianity Today*, July 30, 1965, 3.

48. For a more comprehensive expression of this view, see Bob Pierce, with Nguyen Van Duc and Larry Ward, *Big Day at Da Me* (Waco, TX: Word Books, 1968). Pierce was World Vision's founder.

49. "Viet Nam Tragedy Now . . . the *Right* Way," *Faith Digest*, June 1971.

50. Quoted in Smylie, "Ethics in the Revival Tent."

51. See my essays "Universal Nationalism: Christian America's Response to the Years of Upheaval," in *The Shock of the Global: The 1970s in Perspective*, ed. Niall Ferguson, Charles S. Maier, Erez Manela, and Daniel J. Sargent (Cambridge, MA: Harvard University Press, 2010), 306–318; and "Evangelical Internationalism: A Conservative Worldview for the Age of Globalization," in *The Right Side of the Sixties: Reexamining Conservatism's Decade of Transformation*, ed. Laura Jane Gifford and Daniel K. Williams (New York: Palgrave Macmillan, 2012), 221–240.

TAKING IT TO THE STREETS?
NEW PERSPECTIVES
ON EVANGELICAL MOBILIZATION

10

The Evangelical Left and the Move from Personal to Social Responsibility

DAVID R. SWARTZ

In 1947 the theologian Carl F. H. Henry published *The Uneasy Conscience of Modern Fundamentalism*. This seminal tract of the "new evangelicalism" decried the obscurantism of his fundamentalist religious heritage. Modernity, Henry began, was replete with social evils, among them "aggressive warfare, racial hatred and intolerance, liquor traffic, and exploitation of labor or management, whichever it may be." But fundamentalist evangelicals, motivated by an animus against religious modernism, had given up on worthy humanitarian efforts. Henry and his new evangelical colleagues intended to fully apply the gospel.[1]

Henry's clarion call, however, had limits. As a graduate of Wheaton College in Illinois, and editor of *Christianity Today*, Henry embodied a passive conservatism that characterized much of Billy Graham–style evangelicalism. In *Uneasy Conscience*, for example, Henry's clearest suggestion for social change ironically had less to do with party politics and social activism than with individual effort. Authentic social transformation could be sparked only by personal spiritual transformation, he declared. Henry's conception of social engagement consisted

212 TAKING IT TO THE STREETS?

largely of placing redeemed individuals into positions of social importance more than specifying particular programs to oversee society. Notwithstanding fundamentalist mobilization in California in the 1960s, this individualist approach represented a significant strain within the diverse, fluid reality of Cold War evangelical politics. The historian John Turner, who charted the political activism of Campus Crusade, states that "many evangelicals remained wary of the messy nature of political activism and wanted to concentrate on preaching the gospel."[2]

By the 1980s, evangelical politics looked very different. Many evangelicals, going well beyond Henry's vision of individualistic social transformation, were participating in unembarrassed political advocacy. The Moral Majority offered very specific policy prescriptions on issues as diverse as abortion regulation, prayer in school, economics, and diplomacy. Millions of evangelicals lifted Jimmy Carter to victory in 1976. Over fifty million Americans claimed to be born-again Christians. Major news magazines ran cover stories on the recent surge in evangelical political and cultural power. *Newsweek* even dubbed 1976 the "year of the evangelical." Evangelicals, many clearly in a post-pietist context, no longer had to legitimize participation in debates over the public good.

What factors led to this evangelical surge? And why the sudden burden to extend evangelical responsibility from the personal to the corporate and social realms? Clues to this remarkable shift can be seen in the urban- and northern-centered evangelical Left of the 1960s and 1970s. Groups such as the Post-American community in Chicago, the Christian World Liberation Front (CWLF) in Berkeley, California, and progressive faculty and students at evangelical liberal arts colleges helped articulate this new shift toward corporate responsibility. Profoundly shaped by the civil rights movement, Vietnam protests, the initiatives of the War on Poverty, and key elements of the counterculture, the evangelical Left amplified a postwar willingness to engage social and political systems.

Civil Rights

No issue better reflected the individualist orientation of midcentury evangelicalism than race. Viewing racism primarily in terms of willful oppression by one individual toward another individual, most condemned personal racism. "My parents," remembered one young evangelical, "rebuked the 'colored jokes' we kids brought home from our friends and their parents." But their response to institutional racism was very different. Participation in the civil rights movement, they maintained, leaned toward the Social Gospel, which inevitably led away from the more important mission of evangelism. In fact, evangelism itself would promote racial equity and peace more effectively than the forced integration proposed by the civil rights movement. An individualistic conception of racism typified the majority evangelical response to that movement.[3]

The story of young John Alexander, however, reflects a shift among some white evangelicals away from soul-winning as the singular fix for racism. Alexander, with a Southern Baptist background and a graduate education in philosophy from Northwestern University, taught philosophy at the flagship evangelical liberal arts college Wheaton and edited a civil rights magazine called *Freedom Now*. In the early 1960s Alexander stressed the importance of individual behavior. He eyed Martin Luther King Jr.'s connections with socialists and communists with suspicion. He worried that King's protests might provoke white backlash. Black contributors also articulated these concerns. Reporting on bus boycotts in the South, Bill Pannell editorialized that it "ill-behooved a minister to meddle in civic affairs." William Banks of Moody Bible Institute in Chicago repeatedly urged readers to practice patience and moderation. Banks wrote, "The social gospeler who thinks that changing the environment and raising the standards of living is the answer is badly mistaken. . . . He must not prostitute his calling by dabbling in politics and stressing the physical aspects of life." Through 1965, the same year that the Voting Rights Act finally passed Congress, *Freedom Now* echoed the midcentury evangelical mantra that changing hearts, not laws, could best transform society.[4]

As the 1960s wore on, however, Alexander began to doubt the efficacy of evangelism to spark social change. After all, many of the converted evangelicals that *Freedom Now*'s contributors knew best—Baptists in the South, people in their congregations, even their own parents—remained flagrantly racist. How, asked a disparate but growing group of younger evangelicals, could their parents' generation sing about blacks being precious in God's sight, yet fail to condemn segregation? How could they decry the march on Washington as a "mob spectacle"? How could they condemn interracial marriage? Meanwhile, Alexander and like-minded evangelicals saw progress in the flurry of activism and civil rights legislation in the mid-1960s. Though many states remained recalcitrant in integrating public schools, others integrated quickly and peacefully. At Wheaton, students in 1962 integrated the city's barbershops by lobbying the local chamber of commerce and publicizing the injustice in local newspapers. These successes convinced an emerging evangelical Left to bring, however belatedly, political power to bear on racial injustices.[5]

The assassination of King in 1968 accelerated this trajectory. According to Alexander, who lamented that "we had been fiddling while Rome burned," King's death "pressed home a sense of urgency." *Freedom Now*'s tone and method abruptly shifted: "The time for polite discussion is past. . . . It is time for you, for your political party, for your denomination to become involved in a massive action program." In a Wheaton chapel service, Alexander told students to quit "thinking white" and demanded that blacks compose 20 percent of the student body. A *Freedom Now* correspondent reported on his participation in the Poor People's Campaign, a march by a "multiracial army of the poor" from Mississippi to Washington, D.C., over the course of several months in 1968. Sixty Wheaton students, led by Alexander and the college's Social Action Forum, marched in Chicago's western suburbs in solidarity with the campaign. *Freedom Now* also urged the busing of white and black children to ensure integrated schools and complained about the lack of federal funds for Upward Bound, Head Start, the rural South, and the inner city.[6]

Prominent civil rights leaders reinforced Alexander's call to action among a broader set of evangelicals. At a 1965 meeting of the National Conference on Religion and Higher Education, evangelical participants were stunned and impressed by the myriad student projects launched by mainliners. They were rebuilding burned-out black churches in the South and serving poverty-stricken residents of the inner city. One InterVarsity administrator, used to working with evangelical students at state universities, reported that Paul Potter of Students for a Democratic Society (SDS) made "our summer program of camp activities seem rather superficial." Four years later, at the 1969 U.S. Congress on Evangelism organized by Billy Graham in Minneapolis, another prominent civil rights leader spoke to nearly five thousand evangelicals. The Southern Christian Leadership Council's Ralph Abernathy encouraged evangelicals to acknowledge the systemic sources of racial inequality. He quoted the biblical prophets, exhorting the delegates to "let justice roll down like the waters."[7]

A chorus of black evangelicals also urged white evangelicals to extend the focus beyond soul-winning. William Bentley, a black Pentecostal preacher with a degree from Fuller Seminary in Pasadena, criticized government priorities "that privileged the military budget over education, child care and poverty relief." Tom Skinner, a former Harlem Lords gang leader and current evangelist, wrote that black America would not follow a "white Christ," by which he meant a "defender of the American system, president of the New York Stock Exchange, head of the Pentagon, chairman of the National Republican Committee, a flag-waving patriotic American—and against everything else." John

Perkins, whose evangelistic work in the early 1960s in rural Mississippi precluded social-oriented work, began in the late 1960s to link racial justice to economic redistribution. Frustrated with lack of progress since the passage of the Civil Rights Acts—segregation persisted and more than half of black families in Simpson County lived under the poverty line—Perkins issued a document titled "Demands of the Black Community." It insisted on 30 percent black employment in all Mendenhall businesses, the desegregation of public spaces, a minimum-wage campaign for domestic workers, paved streets in black neighborhoods, removal of the police chief and his cohorts, and a thorough overhaul of arrest procedures. Perkins's new focus signaled an important shift in young black evangelical thought: that true reconciliation could come only through cultural equity and the redistribution of economic resources.[8]

A broadening of evangelical vocation affirmed the insistent chorus of black evangelicals. Nearly every contributor to *Freedom Now* held a job in education or the social services. The fields of sociology and social work grew substantially at evangelical colleges in the 1960s and 1970s. At Wheaton, the emerging academic departments of sociology and political science encouraged students to consider structural dimensions of society. Lamberta Voget, a popular professor of sociology, took students on urban immersion trips to Chicago. A founder of the National Association of Christians in Social Work, she sponsored many of the new organization's conferences at Wheaton. Voget drove the growth and vitality of the social science division itself, helping to hire young, aggressive PhDs from respected universities across the country. By the 1970s Wheaton's department of sociology featured diversity that the rest of the college lacked: the African American Ozzie Edwards, Ka Tong Gaw, Voget, and Zondra Lindblade. The department did much to promote the Peace Corps program in the 1960s and the Human Needs and Global Resources (HNGR) program. Students and faculty in the social sciences dominated the Clapham Society, a group of self-proclaimed "liberal" students, who vehemently argued against capital punishment, nuclear proliferation, elements of free enterprise, and invited Democratic Party candidates to speak to their club. A succession of clubs—the National Association for the Advancement of Colored People (NAACP), Social Action Forum, Americans for Democratic Action, the Young Democrats, and the Jonathan Blanchard Association—carried on this progressive tradition through the 1980s.[9]

Evangelicals elsewhere also drew from progressive sources. Seminarians in Chicago, for instance, read dog-eared copies of *Soul on Ice* (1967), the Black Panther Eldridge Cleaver's collection of lyrical essays on racial liberation. They studied *The Other America* (1962), the Catholic socialist Michael Harrington's exposé on poverty in the United States. Of the Kerner Report on the 1967 race riots, Jim Wallis wrote, "I must have read that report at least five times, studying its more than six-hundred pages with a thorough intensity. It completely confirmed my experience of the black community. The causes of urban violence were poverty and its accompanying miseries: bad housing and inadequate education, lack of medical care, high unemployment." Taking social scientific studies seriously inevitably led young evangelicals away from the traditional evangelical notion of evangelism as the primary engine of social change. Instead of understanding racism as a long series of personal white-on-black abuse, they increasingly thought of racism as built into economic, social, and cultural systems. Each suggested the need for corporate, not merely personal, responsibility.[10]

Progressive evangelical rhetoric reflected these new influences. Many used language such as "cultures of poverty," "institutional structures," "the mal-distribution of the nation's wealth and resources," citing the psychological damage of institutional racism, and the inequities of economic structures leading to urban rioting. James O. Buswell III, a Wheaton anthropologist, urged authorities to place blacks in positions of power in order to help fight the Sambo myth. Charles Furness, a social worker in Newark, New Jersey, asserted that race riots were rooted in intolerable economic conditions. The Christian World Liberation Front, an evangelical intentional community in Berkeley, California, virulently criticized white flight, spoke of racism as "embedded" in American society and religion, and composed bibliographies on "race and poverty." The evangelical sociologist David Moberg released a popular book that denounced "social sin." The promotion of racial civil rights in the 1960s led quickly to a consideration of crime, housing, and economic structures.[11]

The encounter with civil rights thus added a structural component to evangelicalism's social theory. From an emphasis on individual actions to help disenfranchised southern blacks emerged a holistic effort to raise the psychological, economic, and political health of a race. In the case of Alexander and *Freedom Now*, these structural considerations about race led to debates over capitalism, peace and war, gender, and simple living. In fact, the magazine was renamed in 1970 from *Freedom Now* to the *Other Side* to reflect this broadened agenda. Articles treating the structural sources of poverty even appeared in the conservative *Christianity Today*. The evangelical engagement of civil rights has often been characterized solely by reactionary white segregation academies. But the movement in fact also sensitized many to corporate responsibility of the sort trumpeted by the liberal mainstream.

Vietnam

The majority evangelical response to Vietnam, as Andrew Preston has chronicled in chapter 9, consisted of steadfast anticommunism and a staunch anti-antiwar posture. But as the war ground to a stalemate, traditionalist neo-evangelical stalwarts expressed ambivalence and younger progressive evangelicals virulently dissented to military intervention in Indochina. Like civil rights, Vietnam initially inspired a visceral reaction to human pain. Progressive evangelicals couched their critique in moral repugnance, decrying the napalm, the defolia-tion of forests, the fragging of officers, the killing of civilians, and the damaged psyches of soldiers. An InterVarsity student mourned the "bloated corpses floating down the river somewhere in Cambodia or Vietnam." By the early 1970s, however, this antiwar instinct hardened the evangelical attention to social structures begun by the civil rights movement. Progressive evangelical angst— rooted in an instinctive sense that segregation and Vietnam were wrong— matured into a more substantial structural critique and a more directly political approach to the nation.[12]

The problem with America, evangelical progressives began to argue, was not that a particular general made a wrong decision to bomb an innocent Vietnamese village or that a southern racist had called someone a nigger. Rather, a society "committed to the rightness of whiteness" and a church complicit in systemic evil was to blame. At InterVarsity's 1970 convention, the evangelist Leighton Ford said, "Maybe once upon a time we could think of the missionary as a superior soul from Canada the good, or America the beautiful, going to set the poor heathen right. But no more. We've seen the burned out ghettoes . . . the rural slums . . . the bodies at Kent State . . . the stupidity and greed that has killed Lake Erie. No longer can we labor under the illusion that God is our great white father and that Jesus Christ wears red, white, and blue." Members of the Christian World Liberation Front criticized the "huge defense contracts" that kept the United States from phasing out its military activity in Vietnam. The United States, rather than a source of justice or even a benign institution, was instead a purveyor of injustice.[13]

These conclusions were in part indebted to the New Left. Critical of the expansionist foreign policy and unlimited economic growth of the postwar liberal consensus, groups like SDS opposed the escalation of the Vietnam War. In the late 1960s Jim Wallis joined Michigan State University's SDS chapter, which protested the university's heavy-handed treatment of protesters, revela-tions of campus ties to defense contractors and the CIA, the May 1970 Kent

State shootings, and the U.S. military incursion into Cambodia. By his senior year Wallis enjoyed a national profile, claiming to be able to activate ten thousand people in a few hours' time for protests. He was a key organizer in the national student strike in the spring of 1970.[14]

When Wallis began his theological studies at Trinity Evangelical Divinity School near Chicago in the fall of 1970, he carried along these same New Left commitments. Evangelicalism "was a church," Wallis insisted, "whose god is American, white, capitalist, and violent; whose silent religion and imagined neutrality goes hand in hand with 'nigger' and 'napalm.'" Captivating dozens of fellow seminarians with his passion and critiques, he formed the Post-Americans, which became an intentional community and then a magazine. The first issue of the *Post-American*, issued in the fall of 1971, featured a cover with Jesus wearing a crown of thorns and cuffed with an American flag that also covered his bruised body. America, the depiction implied, had re-crucified Christ. The application of New Left sociology onto evangelical piety and theology resonated with surprisingly high numbers of young evangelicals. Within two years, twelve hundred people had subscribed to the *Post-American*; within five years, nearly twenty thousand. A similar magazine published by CWLF printed even more copies full of antiwar rhetoric.[15]

Evangelical animus against the Vietnam War also had roots in a less expected and more mainstream source. Mark Hatfield, a Republican senator from Oregon and the most prominent evangelical politician in America, spoke out early and often against the war. His opposition, which culminated in the 1970 Hatfield–McGovern Amendment to end the Vietnam War, reflected broader ambivalence toward the nation. "Our involvement in Indochina was mistaken, got out of hand," explained Hatfield, "and raised questions about our national character." He argued that the war had laid bare American abuses of imperialism for economic gain, infringements on domestic freedoms, and the idolatry of presidential power. According to Hatfield, the war also exposed evangelicalism at its worst: a tradition with a watered-down faith willing to baptize whatever the nation did. To be sure, Hatfield explained as the war ground to a stalemate in the early 1970s, civil religion, rooted in a Constantinian legacy that bound Rome and Jerusalem, was not uniquely evangelical or American. But the melding of the profane and sacred in the Roman Empire in the fourth century had appeared again in an American civic religion that revolved around repudiation of "godless international communism." Vietnam, echoed Bill Lane, a *Post-American* contributor who helped produce a twenty-minute slide show with recorded music and a script that criticized civil religion, "has highlighted the fact that the basic generating principles of citizenship in the secular society and in the citizenship in the kingdom of God are mutually exclusive. . . . Our allegiance to the country is temporal and conditional. There can be no Christian support for what we have done in Vietnam." Evangelicalism, critics declared in mainstream and progressive evangelical magazines alike, had succumbed to devotion of a pernicious civil religion, unwilling to assume a prophetic posture in the face of America's sins.[16]

According to Hatfield, this egregious failure required not only a critical posture toward the nation itself but also repentance. Hatfield's rebuke of President Richard Nixon during the National Prayer Breakfast speech in 1973, in which the senator declared, "Today, our prayers must begin with repentance. . . . We must turn in repentance from the sin that scarred our national soul," was merely the most famous riff in a jeremiad that extended through Hatfield's entire career. A year later in Senate chambers, Hatfield proposed such a process of repentance, formalized by a national day of humiliation. Modeled after Lincoln's "Proclamation of a Day of Humiliation, Fasting, and Prayer" in 1863, Hatfield's proposal called for Americans to "confess our national sins," citing idolatry of national security and a failure to share national prosperity with the world, among other sins. Thomas A. Carruth, an evangelical professor at Asbury Theological Seminary in Kentucky, rented a "wide-area telephone line" to lobby Congress to pass the resolution. Though the bill itself languished in the House after passing the Senate, thousands of congregations observed the day.[17]

As the Watergate scandals emerged in 1973, growing numbers of evangelicals repented of conflating faith and nation. Civil religion, argued the Fuller Seminary professor Jack Rogers, sacralized the status quo. He faulted evangelicals for obsessing about the struggle between communism and democracy when the "real issues" were between "rich and poor, strong and weak, and white and nonwhite." Nixon's policies—baptized by Billy Graham who all but endorsed the incumbent in 1972—perpetuated this preoccupation with communism and exposed "the pernicious nature of this civil religion—the religion of Americanism." Graham's July 4, 1970, sermon at an Honor America Day in Washington, D.C., based on 1 Peter 2:17, a scripture passage which read "Honor all men . . . Fear God. Honor the King," particularly horrified the evangelical Left. Graham preached that evangelicals should honor the nation, bemoaning that "lately our institutions have been under attack: the Supreme Court, the Congress, the Presidency, the flag, the home, the educational system, and even the church!" "On that day," wrote a trio of evangelical antiwar historians—Robert Linder (Kansas State), Richard Pierard (Indiana State), and Robert Clouse (Indiana State)—"honoring America and God was implicitly synonymous with sustaining Nixon's aims in Southeast Asia." Hatfield and others began to confront Graham in the pages of moderate evangelical journals about being "used" by the White House for political gain.[18]

Hatfield's resonance with the New Left, disgust with the Vietnam War, and distaste for civil religion, however, stopped short of his most radical evangelical comrades' pessimism. Hatfield still saw redemptive potential in the nation and sought to engage American political culture more than damn it. The nation, while fallen, humiliated, and in need of repentance, was not irretrievably lost. Unlike the Post-Americans, Hatfield never expressed contempt toward the nation by corrupting patriotic phrases into "Amerika" or "the American Way of Death." Rather, Hatfield sought to repair the nation and to invest it with spiritual resources. From state senator to governor to U.S. senator, he worked his way up political structures seeking justice from within the system. Politics, he contended, was "a legitimate expression of Christian faithfulness" on par with "full-time Christian service." Hatfield thus leavened his revulsion toward an apostatizing nation with a compulsion to reshape it. This constructive impulse made Hatfield representative of growing evangelical trends.[19]

Politics as an Evangelical Vocation

As progressive evangelicals moved from an individual to corporate orientation, they began to follow Hatfield's lead into politics. Dozens of books in the late 1960s and early 1970s justified political involvement theoretically. Then in 1972, animus against the Vietnam War and persistent racial inequalities took electoral form as the Messiah College professor Ron Sider launched Evangelicals for McGovern. The progressive evangelical vision may not have carried the day in the decades that followed, but it did help establish politics as an evangelical vocation.

This political interest was rooted in a growing confidence in technical expertise and the government's ability to correct social ills. Since most felt that spiritual conversion in itself could not rescue the urban poor from poverty and discrimination, they began to rely on social science. *Freedom Now*'s John Alexander wrote, "The best means are found by hard-headed analysis and experimentation, not by appeal to revelation. . . . If a person is a Christian he will know he should be concerned about high unemployment, but he won't automatically know whether unemployment can best be decreased by tax cuts, government construction projects, or unbridled competition in an open market. This is a very complicated, technical question of economics which the Christian as such has no special competence to judge. That is a question which, like it or not, has to be left to experts." Comfortable in the halls of the academy, progressive academicians associated with the *Reformed Journal* held out hope that researchers could solve global hunger, poverty, even militarism. James Daane of Calvin College wrote, "Because of the advance of science and technology, and particularly with the coming of automation, the potential wealth of the world is for all practical purposes infinite. For the first time in history it is technically possible to eliminate poverty on a world scale." In one of the first organized meetings of the evangelical Left, delegates intoned the lyrics of the hymn "From Thee All Skill and Science Flow."[20]

The emerging evangelical Left turned to politics to implement solutions to complex structural problems. Evangelicals needed to work within the system, to practice a "progressive realism," in the words of Stephen Monsma, a political scientist at Calvin College and a Democratic member of the Michigan House of Representatives from 1974 to 1978. Good politicians, argued the Evangelical Free layperson and 1980 presidential candidate John B. Anderson, "are attempting to create public policies and political decisions which are faithful to their own viewpoints insofar as political reality allows. They realize that to abandon the field of politics to those who hold principles other than their own is to abdicate their own moral responsibility." Edward Loucks, a government researcher in California, wrote, "The Christian has certain political responsibilities which he cannot justifiably shirk. . . . He *must* participate meaningfully in the political process because he is scripturally obligated to *care* for his neighbor." By 1973 a book aptly titled *Political Evangelism* by Calvin professor Richard Mouw (now president of Fuller Theological Seminary) had come to typify the approach of a new guard that began to see politics as a legitimate, even divinely appointed office.[21]

Even Jim Wallis, fired by anger toward Nixon, participated in electoral politics as a regional manager for McGovern's campaign. While the liberal candidate "does not yet deal adequately with . . . the need for basic and fundamental change in our economic and political institutions, our consumer patterns, or most importantly, the basic spiritual crisis of values we face as a nation," McGovern did represent "a definite change in direction and can be a first ray of hope in the midst of widespread despair." Voting out of desperation to end the war, Wallis embraced, temporarily at least, the compromising politics of reformist evangelicalism. The Post-Americans, as they developed an evangelical theory of nonviolent direct action, increasingly explained that exhibitions of dissent were appropriate only after attempts to work within existing power structures. In other words, they urged negotiation before the use of contentious tactics. Before protesting at a supermarket chain, they talked with the managers to see if they might agree to carry United Farm Workers' grapes and lettuce. "Meet with the key policymakers," urged the Post-Americans, "and see if they can be persuaded to change."[22]

The emerging reformists, newly tolerant of the ambiguities and compromises of politics, sought to avoid overly pessimistic attitudes toward national politics. Too many evangelicals, wrote Paul Henry, a political scientist at Calvin who launched the annual Calvin Conference on Christianity and Politics and his own political career in the early 1970s, "have shunned politics as a dirty, worldly, and humanistic endeavor alien to the concerns of the gospel." Gary Tuttle, a Fuller Theological Seminary student, told his fellow students in a speech that *everything* is not rotten in America. . . . For example, it is a strength of our democratic system that public dissent is a possibility." He continued, "We must keep in our consciousness those things in America which guarantee and facilitate raising a dissenting voice. If we do, then our dissent will be healthy, constructive, and geared toward life and building up, rather than merely tearing down and destroying." The former Mark Hatfield aide and *Post-American* editor Wes Michaelson advised evangelical voters to be satisfied with less-than-perfect candidates. Another similarly urged attentiveness to "political viability" when selecting candidates. Relying solely on church aid to tackle poverty, these reformist young evangelicals advised, might be ideal, but religious organizations lacked expertise and a central organization to address structural injustices. In a nation of rugged individualism and a harsh capitalism, argued James E. Johnson, the federal government "can and should be used to meet the economic needs of people today." What evangelical conservatives "have failed to see," wrote Paul Henry, "is that the gospel itself is, among other things, a gospel of political redemption." Numerous evangelicals, echoing Henry's conclusion, chastised Harold Hughes for dropping out of the Senate to work for a religious foundation. "Why can't he fully commit himself to God in politics?" asked the *Reformed Journal*'s George DeVries.[23]

Dozens of books—in 1972 alone, evangelical publishers released *Evangelicalism and Social Responsibility*, *The Great Reversal*, *The Cross and the Flag*, *A Christian Political Option*, and *Politics: A Case for Political Action*—fleshed out this new socio-political vision. A set of periodicals—*Post-American* (55,000 at its highest circulation), *Other Side* (13,000), *Eternity* (46,000), *Vanguard* (2,000), *Right On* (65,000), *HIS* (90,000), *Wittenburg Door*, *Inside*, and others—kept up a running commentary on current political developments from a progressive perspective. These publications echoed Henry's point that the gospel could bring about political redemption.

This political impulse took electoral shape in Evangelicals for McGovern (EfM), the first explicitly evangelical organization in postwar American politics formed to support a presidential candidate. Progressive evangelicals found McGovern's political ideology congenial to their own reformist instincts. "We like the way McGovern is getting his feet dirty. He's concerned about hunger, war, poverty and ecology," explained Wheaton professor Robert Webber to a *Newsweek* reporter. Official EfM documents praised McGovern's evangelical background, his religious rhetoric, and his stances on school busing, poverty, and the war. "A rising tide of younger evangelicals," asserted an early news release, "feels that the time has come to dispel the old stereotype that evangelical theology entails unconcern toward the poor, blacks and other minorities, and the needs of the Third World."[24]

As the presidential contest entered its final months, EfM seemed to gather momentum. Strong support came from evangelicals associated with *Other Side*, *Post-American*, Fuller Seminary, and Gordon-Conwell Seminary. In an attempt to win the evangelical middle, EfM engineered a McGovern appearance at Wheaton on October 11, 1972. After being introduced by Tom Skinner, McGovern spoke fluently in evangelical idiom in front of an overflow crowd of more than two thousand during the Tuesday chapel address. He sprinkled his Wheaton address with biblical passages and allusions. He expressed resonance with the rising evangelical impulse to stress moral and spiritual leadership in the public square. Affirming John Winthrop's declaration on the Arbella in 1630 of America as a "city on a hill," McGovern concluded his speech with a statement that could have come from a rising religious Right: "The wish of our forebears," he concluded, "was to see the way of God prevail. We have strayed from their pilgrimage, like lost sheep. But I believe we can begin this ancient journey anew." Citing evangelical figures such as Jonathan Edwards, John Wesley, and William Wilberforce, McGovern contended that his presidency would nurture conditions in which spiritual, moral, and social revival could occur. Faith, he declared in contradistinction to President John F. Kennedy's careful delineation before a gathering of Protestant clergy in Dallas just ten years earlier, would very much shape his presidency.[25]

The results of the campaign, however, disappointed McGovern's evangelical supporters. The candidate suffered a resounding loss on November 7, 1972—a 520–17 minority in the Electoral College and a 23 percent margin in the popular vote, the second largest margin in American history. For its part, EfM contributed only negligible amounts—$5,762 from only 358 people—to the coffers of a presidential campaign in desperate need of more money and votes. Despite the disheartening defeat, many in the evangelical Left remained upbeat. They had experienced the exhilaration of finding like-minded evangelical progressives. Collectively they had challenged the evangelical establishment and earned wide coverage of their political activism in the national press. Their mobilization effort was, in some respects, respectable given its late starting date just two months before the election and its birth within a politically passive tradition. EfM had succeeded in its hope "that evangelicals as a group can be heard."[26]

EfM—and a line-up of progressive politicians—accelerated a new era in which politics was a more accepted option for moderate evangelicals. That roster was surprisingly large. Michael Haynes, a black evangelical who had little patience with "white brothers who pay no attention to social justice," served as a three-time Democratic state legislator in Massachusetts, member of the state parole board, and founder of the Evangelical Committee for Urban Ministries in Boston. Iowa's Democratic senator Harold Hughes, Hatfield's closest confidant in the Senate and an outspoken evangelical Methodist, helped expose the unauthorized bombing of North Vietnam and the secret bombing of Cambodia, authored the Hughes–Ryan Amendment forbidding covert operations by the CIA, and reduced military aid going to South Vietnam. He co-sponsored the McGovern–Hatfield Amendment and shared Hatfield's pro-life position on abortion and other matters like capital punishment and poverty. Paul Henry worked on environmental concerns in the 1970s as staff director for the House Republican Conference, chair of the Kent County (MI) Republican Party in 1974, and member of the Michigan State Board of Education, the Michigan State House of Representatives, the Michigan State Senate, and the U.S. House of Representatives. Don Bonker, an outspoken evangelical from the state of Washington in the U.S. House of Representatives, worked on equitable foreign trade, environmental issues, and human rights. Stephen Monsma, a political scientist at Calvin College and a Democratic member of the Michigan Senate and House of Representatives, chaired a natural resources subcommittee and led passage of the "bottle bill." And the Evangelical Free Church–affiliated John B. Anderson, who as an independent went on to challenge Ronald Reagan and Jimmy Carter for the presidency in 1980, had earlier voted for the Open Housing Act, pushed for the War on Poverty, and opposed the Vietnam War, calling it "a ghastly error." All these politicians—in addition to Mark Hatfield—saw their work on military, poverty, and environmental matters in the 1960s and 1970s as an outgrowth of Christian vocation. Evangelicals on the left thus added to the growing numbers of evangelicals on the right who clearly, insistently, and powerfully articulated that evangelical faith required social and political action.[27]

❖

To be sure, the evangelical Left itself enjoyed relatively little success in politics strictly defined. It nonetheless has significantly shaped the culture of many evangelicals, many of whom now work hard on issues of poverty, women's rights, and inequities in the global economy. This growing social consciousness characterizes the work of megachurch pastors Rick Warren and Bill Hybels, editors at *Christianity Today*, and many other evangelicals, the majority of whom have never closely identified with the politically conservative televangelists Jerry Falwell and Pat Robertson. After attending the 1989 missionary convention Lausanne II in Manila, Philippines, Ron Sider, organizer of EfM, could in good faith, despite the evangelical Left's utter failure in electoral politics, declare, "What especially impressed—and delighted—me was the extent to which . . . holistic concern for both evangelism and social action has now become the prevailing perspective of mainstream evangelicalism worldwide. That was not the case . . . in 1973!" Today's moderate evangelicals, increasingly comfortable with the language of social justice, have roots in yesterday's evangelical Left.[28]

This new sense of corporate obligation extended to nearly all sectors of evangelicalism. Evangelicals on the left and right now agree—in far greater proportion than in the 1950s—that the Gospel calls for holistic, not just personal, transformation. Several threads run through evangelicalism's politicization in the late twentieth century. First, nearly all of the drivers of the move toward corporate responsibility emerged from the educational sector. John Alexander, perhaps the most dynamic white evangelical promoter of civil rights, taught at Wheaton College and wrote for InterVarsity's magazine, whose readers were primarily evangelical students at public universities. Many of the Post-Americans were active in SDS chapters at universities. Like most young Americans in the postwar period, evangelicals flooded the nation's universities. The proportion of evangelicals who had been to college tripled between 1960 and 1972. While the level was still below the national average, it was an impressive leap and an indicator of evangelicalism's rising social status. Second, evangelicals grew more attentive to social structures. The evangelical Left, by engaging issues of institutional racism, poverty, and war, sought to ameliorate the vagaries of the industrial revolution. In its own way, the religious Right sought to address some of the same dislocations through civic participation. Followers of Jesus, evangelicals now say almost in unison, must address social ills.[29]

These two elements of corporate responsibility suggest new avenues of interpretation. The plunge of broader evangelicalism into social and political engagement can be seen as a result of a steady integration into American culture as much as a reaction against it. Decreasingly isolated from cultural norms, evangelicals had less incentive to be prophetic. Increasingly invested in civic organizations, they recognized the efficacy of gradualism within structures. Backlash to the 1960s did not solely—or even primarily—provoke the emergence of a public evangelicalism.

NOTES

1. Carl F. H. Henry, *The Uneasy Conscience of Modern Fundamentalism* (Grand Rapids, MI: Eerdmans, 1947), 4.

2. John G. Turner, *Bill Bright and Campus Crusade for Christ: The Renewal of Evangelicalism in Postwar America* (Chapel Hill: University of North Carolina Press, 2008), 168.

3. Jim Wallis, *Revive Us Again: A Sojourner's Story* (Nashville: Abingdon Press, 1983), 24; Wallis interview with Terri Gross on *Fresh Air*, National Public Radio, January 20, 2005.

4. On *Freedom Now*'s initial suspicion of civil rights activism, see "Books in Review," *Freedom Now*, September-October 1967, 19; William Pannell, "Memorial to Martin Luther King, Jr." *Freedom Now*, May-June 1968, 4–5; "The Social Gospel and the Black Preacher," *Other Side*, March-April 1972, 41.

5. On progress in integration, see Jim Wallis, "America's Original Sin: The Legacy of White Racism," *Sojourners*, November 1987, 14–17. On the integration of Wheaton's barbershops, see "S.C. Civil Rights Committee Views Local Discrimination," *Wheaton Record*, November 1, 1962, 1.

6. On King's assassination, see Alexander, "Communications Conference," 12; Alexander, "Taking Jesus Seriously," 10–15; Alexander, "A Time to Act," 3, all in *Freedom Now*, May-June 1968. On the Poor People's Campaign, see Donald Oden, "On the Bus Back to Akron," *Other Side*, November-December 1968, 21–22. On busing, see Loy, "Busing: The Real Issue," *Other Side*, July-August 1972, 14; Steve Mott, "Busing and Racism in Boston," *Right On*, September-October 1976, 13. On Alexander at Wheaton, see "Alexander Edits Civil Rights Magazine, 'Freedom Now!'" *Wheaton Record*, November 22, 1968, 4.

7. On Potter, see Charles Troutman to John Alexander, May 4, 1965, Box 41, Folder 13 "Association for the Coordination of University Religious Affairs, 1965-1975," InterVarsity Collection, Billy Graham Center Archives, Wheaton College, Wheaton, Illinois (hereafter cited as IVC). On Abernathy, see "Abernathy Urges Brotherhood; Graham Criticized," *Jet*, October 2, 1969, 50.

8. William Bentley, "The Other America," *Other Side*, January-February 1970, 30–33. For "white Christ," see Tom Skinner, *How Black Is the Gospel?* (Philadelphia: Lippincott, 1970), 13, 69, 108–109, 120; Tom Skinner, untitled article, *Other Side*, July-August 1970, 34; Tom Skinner, "Jesus or Barabbas?" *Right On*, February 3, 1971, 1–2. For

Perkins's "Demands," see Charles Marsh, *The Beloved Community: How Faith Shapes Social Justice from the Civil Rights Movement to Today* (New York: Basic Books, 2006), 153–154.

9. For a sample of the vocations of *Freedom Now* contributors, see "The Writers," *Other Side*, May-June 1969, 30. On the growing importance of the social sciences within evangelicalism, see "Sociology Forum Questions Church Role, Pastorate as Highest Christian Vocation," *Wheaton Record*, February 10, 1966, 5; Mark Olson, "Radical Social Activists Blame Chicago Machine," *Wheaton Record*, December 8, 1967, 5; Alan Keith-Lucas, *Integrating Faith and Practice: A History of the North American Association of Christians in Social Work* (St. Davids, PA: North American Association of Christians in Social Work, 1994); David Moberg, *Inasmuch: Christian Social Responsibility in the Twentieth Century* (Grand Rapids, MI: Eerdmans, 1965), 154–157; Richard Cartrell, "Sociology Forum Questions Church Role, Pastorate as Highest Christian Vocation," *Wheaton Record*, February 10, 1966, 5. NACSW grew from 132 members in 1963 to 1,368 in 1979.

10. On the Kerner Report and other examples of social scientific literature, see Wallis, *Revive Us Again*, 49; Post-American bibliography in Box VII7, Folder "People's Christian Coalition, Trinity," Sojourners Collection, Wheaton College Archives & Special Collections, Wheaton, Illinois (hereafter cited as SC); Don and Madelyn Powell, "We Stayed in the Inner City," *HIS*, November 1969, 18–19; William Bentley, "The Other America," *Other Side*, January-February 1970, 30–33.

11. James O. Buswell III, "Sambo and Jim Crow," *Other Side*, January-February 1972, 36–42; Charles Furness, *The Christian and Social Action* (Old Tappan, NJ: Fleming H. Revell Company, 1972), 35–44; David Gill, "More on School Busing," *Right On*, January-February 1977, 16; Ron Mitchell, "Christianity and American Racism," *Right On*, March 1974, 9–10; "Notes from the Catacomb," *Right On*, September-October 1976, 2; "The Church and Economics," *Right On*, September-October 1976, 6–7; David O. Moberg, *The Great Reversal: Evangelism versus Social Concern* (Philadelphia: Lippincott, 1972), 120–149; Ron Sider, "Mischief by Statute: How We Oppress the Poor," *Christianity Today*, July 16, 1976, 14.

12. "Programmed for Murder," *Manna*, October 5, 1970, copy in Box 344, Folder 4, IVC; Wallis, *Revive Us Again*, 62.

13. On deception by government leaders, see Nicholas Wolterstorff, "ITT: Wickedness in High Places," *Reformed Journal*, May-June 1972, 4; Carl T. McIntire, "The American Army on Trial," *Vanguard*, May-June 1971, 4. On "niggers" and "napalm," see Jim Wallis, "The Movemental Church," *Post-American*, Winter 1972, 2–3. For "red, white, and blue," see Robert Lehnhart, "Urbana 70: We Can't Afford to Ignore It," 4, in Folder "Tom Skinner," Archer Weniger Collection, Bob Jones University, Greenville, South Carolina; Jill Shook, "Vietnam Today," *Right On*, July-August 1974, 7.

14. On Wallis at Michigan State University, see Carol Langston, "Campus Rebel Finds New 'Revolt,'" *Tulsa Tribune*, March 26, 1971, 5B; "Crucible of Community," *Sojourners*, January 1977, 14; Student government candidate platform of Jim Wallis, Jim Moore, Bob Sabath, and Tom Morris in Box VII8, Folder 6 "Jim Wallis at Trinity," SC; Jim Wallis, *The Call to Conversion* (New York: HarperCollins, 1981), xv.

15. On the growth of the *Post-American*, see "Crucible of Community," 16; Wallis, *Revive Us Again*, 87–89; "Newsletter No. 4," May 1972, Minutes of the Peoples Christian Coalition, September 26, 1971, and "Newsletter No. 3," in Box VII7, Folder 6 "Peoples Christian Coalition Trinity," SC; John Stott, "Impressions of American Christianity," copy in Box VII8, Folder 6 "Jim Wallis at Trinity," SC; Ed Spivey Jr., interview, June 22, 2005.

16. Mark O. Hatfield, "Civil Religion," *Evangelical Visitor*, August 10, 1973, 4–5, 104; Bill Lane, "Lessons from Vietnam," *Post-American*, March-April 1973, 8–9; "Seeds," *Sojourners*, October 1976, 26; Mark O. Hatfield, *Between a Rock and a Hard Place* (Waco, TX: Word Books, 1976), 75–109; Mark O. Hatfield et al., *Amnesty? The Unsettled Question of Vietnam: Now!* (Lawrence, MA: Sun River Press, 1973), 114, 123; Mark O. Hatfield, "Judgment and Repentance," *Vanguard*, October 1973, 9–11; "Piety and Patriotism," *Post-American*, May-June 1973, 1–2; "Law, Order, and Justice: An Interview with Senator Hatfield," *Freedom Now*, November-December 1968, 23–29.

17. Kenneth Woodward, "The New Evangelicals," *Newsweek*, May 6, 1974, 86; James C. Hefley and Edward E. Plowman, *Washington: Christians in the Corridors of Power* (Carol Stream, IL: Tynedale House Publishers, 1975), 114.

18. For "real issues," see Jack Rogers, "Confessions of a Post-Conservative Evangelical," *Reformed Journal*, February 1971, 11. For "the pernicious nature of this civil religion," see Richard Pierard, "The Golden Image of Nebuchadnezzar," *Post-American*, January-February 1973, 10–11. For criticisms of Graham and Nixon, see Hatfield, *Between a Rock*, 100–102; David Kucharsky, "Billy Graham and 'Civil Religion,'" *Christianity Today*, November 6, 1970, 56–58; "News on Watergate," *Christianity Today*, May 25, 1973, 46; Mark O. Hatfield, *Conflict and Conscience* (Waco, TX: Word Books, 1971), 110, 112, 120. For "honoring America and God," see Robert D. Linder and Richard V. Pierard, *Twilight of the Saints: Biblical Christianity and Civil Religion in America* (Downers Grove, IL: InterVarsity Press, 1978), 170–171. For a small sample of the large evangelical Left oeuvre on civil religion, see Robert G. Clouse, Robert D. Linder, and Richard V. Pierard, *Protest and Politics: Christianity and Contemporary Affairs* (Greenwood, SC: Attic Press, 1968); Richard V. Pierard, *Unequal Yoke: Evangelical Christianity and Political Conservatism* (Philadelphia: Lippincott Co., 1970); Robert G. Clouse, Robert D. Linder, and Richard V. Pierard, eds., *The Cross & the Flag* (Carol Stream, IL: Creation House, 1972); Robert Jewett, *The Captain America Complex: The Dilemma of Zealous Nationalism* (Philadelphia: Westminster Press, 1973); Craig Watts, "Identity and Idolatry?" *Other Side*, July 1984, 10; Perry Cotham, Review of *Politics, Americanism, and Christianity*, *Eternity*, September 1976, 48; John F. Alexander, "Land of the Free?" *Other Side*, August 1978, 12–16; Linder and Pierard, *Twilight of the Saints*, 21; Joe Roos, "American Civil Religion," *Post-American*, Spring 1972, 8–10.

19. On politics as a Christian vocation, see Lon Fendall, *Stand Alone Or Come Home: Mark Hatfield as an Evangelical and a Progressive* (Newberg, OR: Barclay Press, 2008), 44; Hatfield, "Can a Christian be a Politician?" *HIS*, October 1967, 1–5.

20. On the importance of specialization in solving social problems, in reaching target audiences, and addressing theoretical concerns, see Roger L. Dewey, "Editorial," *Inside*, November 1973. For "hard-headed analysis," see John Alexander, "A Politics of Love," *Other Side*, July-August 1972, 3. On eliminating poverty, see James Daane, "The War on Poverty Can be Won," *Reformed Journal*, April 1964, 3. For the hymn, see the worship program titled "A Celebration of Hope," in Folder "1974 Thanksgiving Workshop," Evangelicals for Social Action Collection, Billy Graham Center Archives, Wheaton College, Wheaton, Illinois (hereafter cited as ESAC).

21. Stephen Monsma, *The Unraveling of America* (Downers Grove, IL: InterVarsity Press, 1974); John Anderson, *Vision and Betrayal in America* (Waco, TX: Word Books, 1975), 121; Edward A. Loucks, "Deciding How to Vote," *Other Side*, September-October 1972, 25; "Back to That Old Time Religion: Gaudy and Vital U.S. Evangelicalism Is Booming," *Time*, December 26, 1977, 52; Richard Mouw, *Political Evangelism* (Grand Rapids, MI: Eerdmans, 1973); James M. Dunn, "Lobbying Isn't a Dirty Word," *Eternity*, July 1975, 12–14, 29–30; Wes Michaelson, "Politics and Spirituality," *Post-American*, April 1974.

22. Jim Wallis, "The Issue of 1972," *Post-American*, Fall 1972, 2–3; Richard K. Taylor, "Manual for Nonviolent Direct Action," *Post-American*, November 1974, 25.

23. Paul Henry, *Politics for Evangelicals* (Valley Forge, PA: Judson Press, 1974), 22; Gary Tuttle, "On Dissent," *Opinion*, May 26, 1970, 4; Ronald Michaelson, "Positive Politics," *HIS*, May 1972, 13; Emilio Castro, "Strategies for Confronting Unjust Social Structures," 1, speech delivered at the 1974 Thanksgiving Workshop, Chicago, Ilinois, copy in Folder "1974 Thanksgiving Workshop," ESAC; Johnson, "The Christian and the Emergence of the Welfare State," in *Protest and Politics*, ed. Clouse et al., 95, 116; George DeVries, "Mr. Hughes Leaves Washington," *Reformed Journal*, November 1973, 6–7. Hughes recounted discussions with Billy Graham as well as evangelical Washington insiders Mark Hatfield, Doug Coe, Graham Purcell, and Al Quie on whether to leave the Senate and politics altogether. "To a man they felt that I should stay in the Senate," wrote Hughes. See Harold Hughes, *The Man from Ida Grove: A Senator's Story* (Waco, TX: Word Books, 1979), 317–319.

24. For Webber's quote, see "The Evangelical Vote," *Newsweek*, October 30, 1972, 93. For "a rising tide," see Ron Sider, news release from Evangelicals for McGovern, October 6, 1972, ESAC.

25. Jeri Drum to Walden Howard, October 22, 1972, ESAC; "Religion in Transit," *Christianity Today*, November 24, 1972, 48. Text of McGovern speech at Wheaton, October 11, 1972, copy in Folder "Evangelicals for McGovern," ESAC; Michael McIntyre, "Religionists on the Campaign Trail," *Christian Century*, December 27, 1972, 1319–1322.

26. Walden Howard letter, ca. October 1972, ESAC.

27. On Haynes, see "Back to That Old Time Religion: Gaudy and Vital U.S. Evangelicalism Is Booming," *Time*, December 26, 1977, 52. On Hughes, see Hughes, *Man from Ida Grove*, 214, 234, 256–257, 307; Fendall, *Stand Alone*, 18; Wes Pippert, "Christ

and Crisis in Washington," *HIS*, April 1974, 1–4. On Paul Henry, see Doug Koopman, ed., *Serving the Claims of Justice: The Thoughts of Paul B. Henry* (Grand Rapids, MI: Calvin College, 2001). On Monsma, see "Profile/Senators," *Grand Rapids Accent*, January-February 1980, 38, copy in Box 1, Folder 1, "Bibliographic Data, 1976–1980," Paul Henry Collection, Calvin College Archives, Grand Rapids, MI; Monsma, *Unraveling of America*. On Anderson, see John B. Anderson, *Between Two Worlds: A Congressman's Choice* (Grand Rapids, MI: Zondervan, 1970); John B. Anderson, *Vision and Betrayal in America* (Waco, TX: Word Books, 1975), 90, 121. For more vignettes of evangelical politicians, see "God on Capitol Hill," *Christianity Today*, October 10, 1969, 48–50.

28. On Lausanne II, see Ron Sider fundraising letter, December 5, 1989, in Folder "1989," ESAC.

29. On evangelical rates of college attendance, see John Stephen Hendricks, "Religious and Political Fundamentalism: The Links between Alienation and Ideology" (PhD diss., University of Michigan, 1977).

I I

"The Harvest Is Ripe"

American Evangelicals in European Missions, 1950–1980

HANS KRABBENDAM

In 1974, more than a thousand evangelical Christians met in Lausanne, Switzerland, to talk about their main mission to the world. They came from all the corners of the world with great expectation, stimulated by Billy Graham's opening address confirming this optimism: "The Harvest is Ripe."[1] At the conclusion of the meeting the participants left for home re-energized. They committed themselves to a new missionary élan in the world under the motto Let the Earth Hear His Voice. The Lausanne movement meant to set a new agenda, but it was also a moment of triumph. Evangelicals had succeeded in establishing an international podium and had made themselves visible as a third force to be reckoned with alongside the Roman Catholic Church and the World Council of Churches (WCC). American believers had played a crucial role in mobilizing this force.

The conference was important for a second reason. The delegates carefully drafted a doctrinal statement, which created cohesion and would be the basis for future action. One of the recommendations that did not yet make it into the final statement, however, was a proposal from the so-called radical evangelicals.[2]

This statement summarized the main evangelical concerns with proclaiming the Gospel, submitting to the authority of the Bible, and the commitment to calling people to repent, but, crucially, added the effort "to identify in him [God] with the oppressed and work for the liberation of all men and women in his name" to the catalogue of resolves.[3] This final phrase was not standard evangelical fare. It seemed to have come straight from any mainline WCC document, of which the evangelicals had been and were so critical. Yet, its presence as a matter of discussion revealed that evangelicals were ready to embrace social issues. This article explains the developments leading to this landmark meeting and its consequences for both European-American religious relations and the position of American evangelicals at home.

American Evangelicals' Global Turn

At first sight, the birth of modern American evangelicalism seemed to be a domestic affair. However, from its very beginning it had a strong international orientation that not only spurred American patriotism but also confronted it. The involvement of postwar American evangelicals in foreign missions was part of the formation of a growing subculture and, though it was a response to dominant liberal trends, it advanced their entrance into the mainstream in America. The National Association of Evangelicals (NAE), its partner organizations, and the Billy Graham Evangelistic Association (BGEA) were the key players.[4] These overlapping networks built a number of important stable institutions with a vast and growing international scope. Their concern for Europe added a new area to international missions in the 1950s and remained important throughout. Indeed, missions in Europe confronted evangelicals with the intellectual challenge of coming to terms with the evaporation of their historical spiritual source.

Mission historians have drawn attention to the major change in the scope of religious outreach among American evangelicals in the mid-1970s, but they rarely connected these trends either to resurgent evangelicalism's social and political agenda in the United States or to Europe. The culmination point at the international Lausanne Conference in 1974, however, confirmed the evangelical influence at home and abroad and mapped out the trends for the coming decades. All this had been twenty years in the making. Evangelicals entered the international arena by three interlocking and simultaneous initiatives: (1) the efforts to create a global evangelical association, leading to the World Evangelical Fellowship (WEF); (2) the coordination of evangelical foreign mission associations; and (3) the international reach of Billy Graham's outreach.

The Creation of the World Evangelical Fellowship

The missionary advances of the neo-evangelicals after World War II should come as no surprise. When Harold John Ockenga and other leading evangelicals founded the NAE in 1942, this inaugurated a nationwide revival, with Youth for Christ (YFC) as its main expression and vehicle. Historically, revivals always stimulated international missionary work.[5] Since the early nineteenth century, bringing the gospel to the nations, in evangelical parlance, prepared the world for the approaching millennium. Hence, the winning of souls had a high priority. Evangelicals were also involved in relief work after World War II (such as the humanitarian efforts of World Vision), but preaching the gospel came first. The fledgling Youth for Christ International organization lived up to its full name and immediately went abroad to reach out to Europe in the fall of 1946. The Billy Graham generation thus had an international orientation from the beginning of its ministry.[6]

The summer of 1948 was saturated with religious meetings. Apart from the WCC and the small fundamentalist International Council of Christian Churches in Amsterdam (ICCC), the WEF, YFC, and the student organization InterVarsity Christian Fellowship also met in July and August in Switzerland. Many delegates of smaller conferences chose to be observers at the WCC. R. L. Decker, for example, pastor of the Temple Baptist Church in Kansas City and executive secretary of the NAE, still gave the WCC the benefit of the doubt, since he found that the American modernist element was much weaker than he had anticipated.[7]

The establishment of new global organizations proved contagious. Soon after the war had ended, American evangelicals made efforts to revive the nineteenth-century Evangelical Alliance as a global organization of evangelicals. The NAE actively promoted the WEF to collect like-minded souls in Europe as a solidly evangelical alternative to the ecumenicals. The WEF's goal was to stimulate evangelism, coordinate missionary and literature agencies, and defend persecuted Christians. It was not an international council of churches but of national evangelical fellowships. It took the structure of the NAE as its organizing principle: individual churches and people could join this national organization.

The first effort to found the WEF happened in the summer of 1948 when one hundred delegates from twelve countries met for three days at a college in Clarens, close to Montreux in Switzerland.[8] Clyde Taylor, the NAE's secretary of public affairs, measured the mood among European evangelicals: "None of them seemed at all inclined to bow their knee to the United States or to United States organizations. In fact a number of them showed considerable resentment over the American Council attitude." He advised the organizers to keep the

United States in the background, and leave the podium to the Europeans "because they seem to be oversensitive with a certain type of inferiority complex now which has come upon them as a result of the war. They are keenly aware of their deficiency and their weaknesses as evangelicals in Europe, and on the other hand they can't forget that they were old nations when our people were still out in the woods hunting redskins."[9]

The WEF absorbed remnants of earlier efforts but remained a relatively small organization. Financially, it continued to suffer and was never far from bankruptcy. It had to overcome the resistance to formal arrangements of its constituency, which was suspicious of obligatory global arrangements. Moreover, because Americans provided most of the finances and organizational energy, their non-American partners saw the WEF as an American institution, promoting an American agenda.[10] This caused tensions, but because the NAE representatives were very much aware of these European sensitivities, they were able to stay in the background. This was one of the reasons why the WEF was more attractive to Europeans than the much more patriotic American Council of Christian Churches, founded by the fundamentalist hardliner Carl T. McIntyre, who also sought to establish an international network.

Mission Coordination

International consultation with other evangelicals, however, was needed to respond to new global developments. First, to protect their own interests, and second, to counteract consolidations among ecumenical organizations. The humanitarian and political turn in the mainline denominational mission organizations alienated many people in the pews. The expected incorporation of the International Missionary Council into the WCC (which was formalized in 1961) troubled missionary-minded evangelicals. They saw this merger as yet another blow to the priority of the proclamation of the gospel, the core of missions in their opinion, and a prerequisite for global harmony as well. At the same time, the growth of the WEF was too slow and hesitant to take on this challenge. In turn, the response was drafted at ad hoc conferences organized to coordinate missionary activities and formulate alternative strategies to the liberal challenge.

Evangelical mission agencies were indispensable in this response. One of the first acts of the NAE had been the creation of an umbrella organization for missions, called the Evangelical Fellowship of Missions Agencies (later renamed the Evangelical Foreign Missions Association, EFMA) in the fall of 1945. It was less conservative than the Interdenominational Foreign Mission Association (IFMA), which representatives of faith missions had established in 1917 to coordinate their activities. The IMFA was explicitly nondenominational, while the EFMA sought to include only denominational mission agencies. Though separate, the two organizations shared the goal of counteracting liberalism and became close partners.[11]

As a new organization, the EFMA had to get recognition from the countries where it did mission work—initially from the colonial powers—and to break the monopoly of the liaison of WCC-related organizations, the World Church Service.[12] The NAE president J. Elwin Wright envisioned in 1948: "We are rapidly approaching the time when it may become more difficult for evangelicals to continue their worldwide propagation of the gospel unless they are able to join their hands effectively in defense of their Christian liberties."[13] He feared that the WCC would terminate mission activities to transfer this responsibility to the national Christian churches, which would then be the official negotiating partners for national governments, while the WCC would speak to the United Nations. In this way the evangelicals were excluded on both sides. "It is imperative that this situation be corrected without delay," he concluded. The evangelicals hoped that the WEF would secure the communication with national and international levels of authority.

The WEF adopted NAE's statement of faith and, despite its global spread, depended on American support. The European evangelicals were weak and also suffered from currency restrictions as European governments took a large share out of foreign currency exchanges. This made support from the northern European countries to missionary activities in the southern countries almost impossible. Moreover, the quality of their gospel tracts was poor. Most of them were direct translations of American gospel tracts and were counterproductive as they were often taken as American propaganda.[14]

The NAE, EFMA, and WEF were an explicit response to the ecumenical victory of the 1940s.[15] In the late 1950s they laid the basis for a cohesive, proactive international evangelical movement. After the founding of *Christianity Today* in 1956 and Billy Graham's New York crusade in 1957—involving mainline churches—had marked the break between evangelicals and fundamentalists, the IFMA and EFMA were invited as partners to conferences on missions at Wheaton College in 1966 and on evangelism in Berlin later that same year. Both themes were top priorities for evangelicals and very much formulated to focus their own minds and to confront the WCC.

Initially, American evangelicals were in awe of the WCC's sheer size, which they were suspicious of, although this waned when their own numbers increased in later years.[16] They did not so much object to the aim of the World Council than to its means. Evangelicals saw the WCC as replacing the search for a way to honor the authority and unity of the Bible by efforts to accept different religious traditions as equals, and they believed this to be an insecure foundation for ecumenical cooperation. In addition to criticizing the WCC's direction and procedure, evangelicals felt they could not enter the discussion about ecumenism. They experienced pressure from the WCC leadership to adopt liberal views and were irritated about the theological vagueness of terms that frustrated a fundamental theological discussion.

Feeling locked out, the evangelicals flocked together and defined the WCC as their anti-model.[17] Actually, reaching a strong organizational unity among evangelicals would have been difficult. The consequence of their diversified membership was a wariness, even suspicion, of organization. The historian Joel Carpenter aptly characterized the allergy toward institutions as the main weakness of independent organizations: "The spirit of religious enterprise, which led visionaries to form ministries without consulting anyone but the Almighty, would not be channeled."[18] Here a dual sentiment is apparent: not only opposition to modernist theology and rationalism of the kind advocated by the mainline National Council of Churches (NCC) and the WCC, but also antipathy toward a (man-made) overarching institutional authority. As other contributors to this volume show, this reservation had a parallel in the resistance to the liberal state. At the same time, however, while evangelicals often saw themselves as the ideological counterparts to the ecumenicals, they clearly wanted to avoid further fragmentation. They placed themselves in the historically ecumenical tradition of John R. Mott of the Student Volunteer Movement in the pursuit of a universal missionary agenda to which internal fragmentation was a real threat.

Billy Graham

Parallel to these two official organizational efforts, the evangelism campaigns of Billy Graham also channeled evangelical energy toward unity. He ignored the constant appeals from the fundamentalist side to radically reject modernist ecumenicals. Graham was civil but distant to the professional WCC-picket Carl McIntire, who denounced everything on the left as belonging to the party of the Antichrist. McIntire represented the fundamentalists' ultimate fear of an eventual unification of evangelicals with ecumenicals, but because he succeeded in alienating many kindred souls on the conservative evangelical side, his extreme separatism alienated the evangelical community and drove it more toward the center. His single goal of heaping scorn on communism was too narrow, and the international scope of his organization was necessarily small, since he attracted just one small denomination per country.[19]

Yet, McIntire's arguments hit a sensitive nerve in the evangelical body. James DeForest Murch, the editor of *United Evangelical Action*, the house organ of the NAE, warned American Protestants that the WCC could very likely develop into a Superchurch. Quoting the goal "one church for one world," he cautioned that it resembled the dominance of the Roman Catholic Church in the Middle Ages. The WCC denied the charges and emphasized it was only a council, but the goal of unity, nonetheless, made the evangelicals suspicious.[20] Murch saw too many ominous signs in the WCC to be fully at ease: the potential Superchurch, theological aberrations, leftist social policies, thirst for power, ineffective evangelism and mission, and the threat of exclusion to those who brought an evangelical message. With so little confidence in the ecumenical goal, only a separate organization would be able to rescue the evangelical perspective from the claws of the WCC.[21]

While Billy Graham extended his evangelical network and was critical of the ecumenical agenda that sought unity rather than truth, he did not lock the doors to other ecumenical organizations, though he cannot have felt overly welcome at WCC meetings that accused him of verbosity and dismissed his ministry as old-fashioned. The NAE wanted to reach the many evangelicals who belonged to American member churches affiliated with the WCC with their warnings and to keep the channels of communication open. Moreover, Graham appreciated many ideals and actions of the ecumenical movement.[22] Therefore, he was present at the creation of the World Council in Amsterdam (1948), considered an invitation to Evanston (1954), and attended the general assemblies of the WCC in New Delhi (1961) and Uppsala (1968), and other WCC conferences.[23] As he said in response to questions about his participation of the Uppsala conference, "I am looking forward to this type of dialogue very much, because I consider myself an evangelical and I think that we ought to make our position known as clearly as we can. Especially will I go there to speak on evangelism and to defend the need for evangelism."[24] This he could say, because at this point Graham and the evangelicals had become a religious force to be reckoned with. An astounding 85 percent of Americans polled by Gallup identified Graham correctly. Moreover, behind the scenes, representatives of the evangelicals and the WCC met in private to discuss common concerns.[25] In summation, in the first decade after World War II, American evangelicals had successfully pulled their foreign missionary activities together, had pioneered the formalizing of an international evangelical network, and had cast off fundamentalist marginality. How these initiatives materialized in practice can be seen in Europe.

Evangelicals Discover Europe

British and American missionaries had long built transatlantic revivalist networks, and after the Civil War, American evangelical preachers, such as Dwight Moody and Hannah Whitall Smith, though not beyond criticism, were respectable enough for England.[26] Meanwhile, American denominational missions without a continental European presence, such as the Methodists, Adventists, and other new religious movements, became increasingly active in Europe in the nineteenth century and in the decades between the two world wars. However, these activities were small and limited to southern and eastern Europe, although a number of western European immigrants who had joined churches in the United States returned to their native countries to support the free churches there.[27] Nonetheless, not until after World War II did Europe become the focus of sustained evangelical missionary activism. In 1952, Europe for the first time emerged in periodically published mission statistics as a separate mission field.

While American mainline churches had strong institutional contacts with their European counterparts and brought much relief to war-torn Europe, they kept only a small presence on the ground through a few fraternal workers. In 1958, American WCC-related churches listed only twenty-nine people working in Europe, 0.3 percent of their entire staff.[28] The increasing number of missionaries in postwar Europe was thus overwhelmingly due to evangelical initiatives. In 1958, about 250 American missionaries, or 1 percent of all 25,000 Americans working overseas, worked in Europe. After this year a strong upward tendency set in. In 1972, 5 percent of the 35,000 American missionaries were stationed in Europe, and in 1979, 10 percent (3,436).[29] This increase lifted Europe to the position of the fastest-growing area in evangelical missions (see table 1).

From the very beginning, evangelicals learned that they could not avoid political debates and pressure when engaging in missions in parts of southern Europe. Spain, Italy, and Portugal made headlines in the evangelical and the mainline Protestant press in the late 1940s and early 1950s. Both sets of media complained that Protestants were second-class citizens in Roman Catholic Europe. The beacon of the mainline Protestant press, the *Christian Century*, noted the restoration of the Catholic faith as the sole religion of Italy. It protested against this monopoly as a violation of the principle of freedom of religion,

Table 1: American missionaries active in Western European countries, 1958–1985

	1958	1962	1964[a]	1968[b]	1968	1972	1975	1979	1985
France	57	107	35	267	264	372	416	652	716
Italy	31	68	23	139	79	171	190	248	308
Portugal	24	33	11	31	58	37	53	109	168
Belgium	24	25	13	24	33	83	158	158	175
Spain	23	37	15	102	39	202	228	346	438
Austria	17	18	14	73	23	145	165	220	250
Ireland	11	—	2	32	9	11	55	89	98
Germany	37	117	34	279	275	391	445	616	661
Great Britain	19	3	14	82	40	139	170	504	445
Netherlands	8	22	12	38	59	45	151	124	78
Switzerland	8	20	15	32	41	66	79	70	74
Scandinavia[c]	7	14	11	34	28	52	77	131	127
Europe	—	11	8	27	3	—	—	169	171
Total Europe	**266**	**475**	**207**	**1,160**	**951**	**1,714**	**2,187**	**3,436**	**3,709**
Total world	25,058	21,520	—	32,087	—	35,070	35,458	34,018	37,490
EU as % of total world	1.0	2.2	—	3.6	—	4.9	6.2	10.0	9.9
Roman Catholic[d]	187	288	—	668	—	1,021	1,265	1,732	2,153
RC as % of total EU	70.0	60.6	—	57.6	—	60.0	57.8	50.4	58.1

Sources: *North American Protestant Foreign Mission Agencies*, 5th ed. (New York: Missionary Research Library, 1962); *North American Protestant Foreign Mission Agencies*, 6th ed.(New York: Missionary Research Library, 1964); *North American Protestant Ministries Overseas*, 8th ed. (New York: Missionary Research Library, 1968); Edward R. Dayton, ed., *Mission Handbook: North American Protestant Ministries Overseas*, 11th ed.(Monrovia, CA: Marc, 1976). For 1979 and 1985, see Samuel Wilson, ed., *Mission Handbook: North American Protestant Ministries Overseas*, 13th ed. (Monrovia, CA: Marc, 1986).

[a] Refers to number of agencies active, not individual missionaries.

[b] The first 1968 column lists North American missionaries overseas; the second 1968 column lists the number of nationals cooperating with an American agency.

[c] The Scandinavia figure for 1962 includes only Sweden and Denmark; later years include Norway, Sweden, Denmark, and Finland.

[d] Roman Catholic (RC) countries include France, Italy, Portugal, Belgium, Spain, Austria, and Ireland.

which was anchored in the Atlantic Charter and which Italy had signed with the 1945 peace treaty. Similarly, in Spain the public presence of Protestant activities was seen as criticism of Roman Catholicism and thus an affront to Francisco Franco, the totalitarian leader of the country. When mobs attacked Protestant churches and police disrupted Bible study groups in private homes in Spain, the *Christian Century* judged the situation worse than in the communist East. The journal kept reminding its readers that the public exercise of religion was an issue in bilateral relations between America and Europe.[30] Some of the editorials in *Christian Century* sounded exactly like the evangelical press. A report on a conference of European Protestants in Catholic Countries, held in Italy in the fall of 1950, concluded: "the Latin lands are now closed to all evangelization or, more accurately, missionary effort." It offered moral support, hoping that the authorities in Catholic countries would live up to their human rights obligations.[31] In short, liberals and conservatives alike were concerned with the Protestant minorities in southern Europe and noticed the low level of active Christians in those countries.[32]

The evangelicals, however, went further. In addition to launching official protests and putting pressure on the State Department, they strongly encouraged an offensive, not only in southern Europe but on the entire continent. In 1951, Gabriel Guedj, pastor of the Memorial Baptist Church of Fresno, California, issued an urgent call for more spiritual investment in Europe: "Europe is the strategic continent. If Washington deems it important to spend billions of dollars and send millions of American men to save the body and the physical assets of Europe, and the Church while professing that the soul is worth more than the body, does little to help bring that continent back to Jesus Christ, will we not be weighed in the balances and found wanting, and ultimately lose both our opportunity and our very existence before the onslaught of Communism and Atheism?"[33] Similarly, the evangelist Oswald J. Smith encouraged the readers of *United Evangelical Action* to give liberally to foreign missions: "To get, you must give. God, I say, is no man's debtor."[34]

The *IFMA News Bulletin* reported on visa grants in Spain but also on refusals in Portugal.[35] Secular organizations, such as trade unions, also put pressure on the Spanish authorities, as well as the American Catholic Church, though this impressed neither the Spanish Catholic Church nor the Vatican.[36] News reports from IFMA were quick to notice hopeful signs of change in the regime, and they "understood" that strict visa rules were necessary to control the communists.[37] But this was only small comfort, because the general trend proved devastating to the evangelical cause. In March 1953 the organization reported: "It is estimated that 75 percent of Europe's population is 'pagan.' We should be praying that by means of literature and radio, the Gospel will get out to every section of that needy mission field."[38] Evangelicals learned to monitor closely the political winds in Europe. The July-August 1953 *Bulletin* mentioned the fall of the Christian Democratic De Gaspari administration in Italy as a severe blow for democracy in Europe and a fearsome sign of communist strength. Political concerns were close to religious ones, and a month later the victory of Konrad Adenauer in Germany was celebrated. The increase in attention paid to Europe, however, killed all optimism about its religious state, which reached a dramatic low in January 1954 when the *Bulletin* quoted that less than 1 percent of Europe was Christian. Stories about religious persecution, church closures, and visa problems continued to dominate the prayer lists of evangelical mission boards. Fear competed with hope and seemed to win. The *Bulletin* sighed in July 1954: "One cannot help but think of Communism as almost synonymous with Europe, as this Godless religion seems to grip more and more of the peoples of Europe in an ironclad grasp."[39]

This growing involvement with Europe contributed to the image of the "old continent" as a negative "other." Europe, it appeared, was cold in need of warming up by America, as the highly influential description of Robert P. Evans characterized the situation. Evans was the son of Baptist missionaries in French-speaking Africa, a graduate from Wheaton College, and a friend of Billy Graham, whom he assisted in his early crusades in Europe. In 1952 he founded the European Bible Institute in Paris, and he remained the key evangelical contact in Europe as coordinator of the Greater Europe Mission. His 1963 publication *Let Europe Hear* became the authoritative source for all missionaries on the "lost continent." The purpose of his book was to recruit supporters for evangelism in Europe, which made him paint the situation with contrasting strokes and draw on familiar stereotypes of European weaknesses. Nevertheless, there is no book that better captures the American evangelicals' view of Europe in the 1950s and early 1960s.[40]

Evans characterized Europe as an overcivilized, but not a Christian, continent. With the exception of Britain, which had an active evangelical minority like the United States, Europe was pagan and de-Christianized. Echoing cultural clichés, France was portrayed as indulgent, Germany as bewitched, Denmark as desperate, and Holland as petrified. The desperate search for spiritual answers by Europe's youth fell on deaf ears among the national churches. The Protestant Reformation had failed to bring the full gospel. It had tied churches to territories, lost authority through internal quarrels, was corrupted by nationalism, limited in scope, and, most of all, it had become too rational. The Reformation legacy had led to intellectual change, not a change of heart.[41]

Yet Evans saw an important future for Europe as a power base, a demographically growing area, and a crucial theater for the end-times. The main obstacle of the European church and mind was its intellectualism, which led to dogmatism. In one word, it was indeed "cold" in Europe, and time was running out. In light of many conflicts and two world wars, the present peace could only be a lull in dangerous times. It was not just communism that endangered Europe's freedom, as many evangelicals in America strongly believed. In a biblical echo of the fearful opposition that the twelve spies encountered during their exploration of Canaan, Evans identified five "Giants in the land," which threatened the penetration of true (evangelical) Christianity: Romanism, Communism, Traditional Protestantism, Secular Existentialism, and Militant Cults.

Again, the contrast with the United States was clear. Even potential allies like the established churches were, in fact, on an equal footing with communism as obstacles for Christianity in Europe. Evans chose his metaphors carefully: next to the communist "Iron Curtain," Europe was cut off from real freedom by the Catholic "Purple Curtain," and the traditional "Stained Glass Curtain."[42] In the same vein, similar books from the early 1960s baptized Europe as the mission field number one.[43]

In 1963, Evans was hopeful that American evangelicals could change this situation, but thirty years later his colleague William Wagner concluded that the American missionaries had been unable to save the church in Europe. No American mission agency had had a lasting impact on a national culture. They had merely reproduced American pluralism in Europe. At best, some independent churches had gathered the marginals, eccentrics, and dropouts. The basic problem was exactly the lack of contacts with the existing churches.[44] What one missionary concluded about France was perhaps true for all of Western Europe: It "developed a reputation as a missionary graveyard."[45] This sobering characterization was meant to restore realistic expectations for missionary work in Europe, but indirectly this verdict showed the limited role of Christian Europe in the world.[46] Evans's supervisor at the Greater European Mission, Walter Frank, justified missionary activities in traditionally "Christian countries": when churches were weak and in an "apostatized anemic condition," they needed American reinforcements. The quadrupling of staff in the quarter-century after World War II to more than 1,600 missionaries looked impressive, but these men and women faced the almost impossible task of reaching a quarter of a million towns and cities without an evangelical church.[47]

Europe Discovers the Evangelicals

This daunting perspective was no reason for despair, because the evangelical efforts did not go unnoticed in Europe. In the second half of the 1960s, European journalists discovered the new force in Protestantism and its American sponsors. Graham's initiative to organize a global conference on evangelism in Berlin in 1966 exposed the strength of this "evangelical orthodox" group.[48] Dutch reporters, for instance, noticed that this group was much better organized than the ecumenicals and reached a broad circle of believers outside the United States. They discovered that *Christianity Today* had a large international group of contributors and a much better international distribution than *Christian Century*. Each new issue reached Amsterdam by special arrangement with the airline KLM and was redistributed throughout Europe within days, while its liberal counterpart *Christian Century* took weeks to reach a foreign destination. They recognized the American origins of this movement, not only because of the presence of Billy Graham and American funds allowing a large section of the 1,250 participants to join the Berlin conference, but also due to the efficient use of a great variety of modern communication means. They spotted hundreds of delegates equipped with bags showing the conference logo and that of its corporate sponsor PanAm.[49] Once these evangelicals had raised public attention, journalists continued to be impressed by the technological innovations, such as the TV connection to other cities, which were tested during Billy Graham's Earls Court Crusade in London in 1967, and which offered the prospect of addressing ever larger audiences. Moreover, Graham's campaign headquarters were fully aware of these positive European responses, as numerous clippings showed.[50]

The movement toward the mainstream was most visible in Billy Graham's use of new communication technology and the subsequent endeavor to train evangelists worldwide in the (American) techniques of evangelism. The next step of the BGEA was to simultaneously transmit a rally in Dortmund to thirty-six European cities between April 5 and 12, 1970.[51] Apart from this daring technology, the evangelicals impressed the media with their streamlined organization and their integrated public relations campaign, including showings of the first Billy Graham film *The Restless Ones* (1965) and translations of his books, such as *The Challenge*. A spokesperson from Philips Eindhoven, the producer of these devices, believed that Graham showed the possibility of using technology to touch a European-wide audience's heart.[52]

The organizers themselves realized, however, that reproducing Graham on numerous TV screens was not as good as the "real thing," but there was a reason why they continued to invest in this type of communication. By the late 1960s and early 1970s, Billy Graham had lost his faith in the willingness and ability of the churches to spread the gospel. This conclusion increased the need to find new means of mass mobilization by specialized organizations and the use of communication technology. His 1966 campaign in London put more effort into the care of converts by sending them to informal groups. While Graham did not want to offend the churches, who offered their volunteers, he believed that the gap within the churches was too wide. At the Berlin conference he stated that this conference was necessary because the established churches neglected spreading the gospel.[53]

The second effect of this abandonment of the European churches was that Graham broadened his reach by taking the practical training of an army of new evangelists into his own hands. In the 1970s, BGEA increased its efforts to empower and train new evangelists apart from organizing mass evangelism events. Amsterdam would become the most important venue thanks to its efficient airport connections, conference facilities, and the easy visa policy of the Dutch authorities. At the end of August 1971, Graham spoke to twelve hundred Europeans on evangelism in the Dutch capital, not as a project of the church but as an attitude that all believers had to embrace. Again, he blamed the churches for neglecting this task and reproached the liberal theologians for breaking down religion and replacing it by political action. He concluded that the European church had become a *target* for evangelism instead of a *source*. European decline contrasted sharply with the vitality of religion in the United States, especially compared to the Jesus Revolution happening in California.[54]

The growth of evangelical missionary activities worldwide and the realization that Europe had become a mission field proved Graham's point. The evangelicals turned the balance in the missionary enterprise in numbers of staff and strengthened their position as a serious contender for leadership of American Protestantism. Between 1935 and 1952, evangelicals increased their share in foreign missions from 40 to more than 50 percent, and by the 1980s evangelicals outnumbered the staff of denominational missions by three to one.[55]

Historical Parallels

This post–World War II increase resembled the birth and dramatic rise of independent missionary societies in the last two decades of the nineteenth century. The earlier growth was a result of the premillennial upsurge.[56] The intellectual cause was the growing expectation of the Second Coming of Christ, which could happen only after the entire world had been reached by the gospel. New fundraising techniques and mass communication made it possible to work outside the established denominational organizations and drew in thousands of candidates who could not easily have entered the existing mission boards. They were committed, but often poorly educated, workers: women and students especially valued the faith mission higher than organized missions. This trend necessitated the founding of mission training programs, which developed into Bible schools. Similarly, after World War II, the evangelicals easily crossed borders, making use of the connections of immigrant churches with their mother countries in Europe.[57] Even stronger than these ethnic ties was the sense of urgency in evangelical America that encouraged full-time Christian service, which prodded students especially to become missionaries. Therefore, the combination of high expectations, a willing staff, strategic decisions, financial traditions, and an explicit purpose to reach the wider world led to an increase in diversity.

Even though the growth figures were clear, the evangelical supremacy was not just a sign of vitality but a result of the pattern of succession in missionary work. Evangelical missionaries followed their predecessors from the mainline denominations in passing through the same stages: from pioneering with many staff to gradually transferring the projects to indigenous churches. Most independent evangelical organizations and fundamentalist agencies were relatively new on the missionary scene and needed the staff. In financial terms, WCC-related churches outspent the evangelicals until approximately 1970.[58] The evangelicals entered the phase of "indigenization" in the 1970s, and this forced them to reflect, to be self-critical, and to openly discuss the relationship between testimony and social action. Whereas earlier evangelicals had vocally denounced social work as not good enough to implement the Great Commission, this gradually changed in the process of emphasizing the differences with the WCC. The Wheaton Declaration of 1966, which came out of the broad consultation on missions, devoted four of its five statements to the place of social concern in the missionary effort, preventing its supremacy over preaching. But behind these protective fences it urged evangelicals "to stand openly and firmly for racial equality, human freedom, and all forms of social justice throughout the world."[59] This process of reflection put the evangelicals in a middle position between liberals, who found evangelicals still too exclusivist, and fundamentalists, who withdrew in growing numbers to unaffiliated organizations with conservative leanings and the sole mission to evangelize.

This process of indigenization gave the receiving (European) countries a stronger voice, which they brought to the series of international meetings sponsored by Billy Graham, culminating in the Lausanne Conference in 1974.

That year qualifies as the marker of the internationalization of evangelicalism. Nonetheless, since the strong independence of the evangelicals prevented a strong official center, the initiative was left to the best organizers, that is, the Americans. It was Billy Graham who launched the idea of the Lausanne Conference on evangelization after a series of regional conferences. The conference hosted 2,500 representatives from 150 countries, and 1,300 additional observers and consultants. The conference was widely covered in the international press, which framed it as the symbol of the new evangelical power.[60]

Broadening Horizons

The visibility of Graham in Europe caused some tensions between European and American priorities. While Graham developed his technique of mobilizing others to become evangelists in the 1970s, John Stott developed his biblical ideas, which broadened the evangelical horizon without losing its biblical source. Fortunately for the evangelical family, Graham the preacher and Stott the thinker got along fine. The final statement, the Lausanne Covenant, confirmed the need for proclamation, but it also put social action on the agenda. It apologized for the neglect of fighting for justice, reconciliation, and liberation, which had sometimes been seen as a competitor with evangelism. The document repeated that social action was not identical to evangelism, but affirmed nevertheless "that evangelism and socio-political involvement are both part of our Christian duty. . . . The salvation we claim should be transforming us in the totality of our personal and social responsibilities. Faith without works is dead."[61] In that respect, the radical evangelicals' statement was perhaps a bit provocative but definitely within acceptable bounds.

The radical evangelicals and some Europeans wanted to maintain this momentum, while the American delegation under Graham's leadership resisted efforts for a continuation committee. Graham still wanted to concentrate on his primary task and felt that the social aspects should be left to others. Stott believed that this separation would be a betrayal of the fundamental character of the agreement.[62] This difference in priorities was a result of the different opinion about the church. Graham's side of American evangelicals saw the church organization as the problem and voluntary association as the solution. European evangelicals in the main churches defended an encompassing church with a broad task.[63]

Stott believed that he had successfully saved both the primary task of spreading the gospel and its social consequences, and opened up new fields of activism.[64] The historian David Wells, however, concluded that the Lausanne

Covenant marked not only the climax but also the demise of confessional evangelicalism that Stott represented. Wells's term "confessional" encompassed adherence to a clearly circumscribed body of doctrine along with the thought that cognitive ideas guided the lives of Christians. He saw a change to transconfessionality, a strategy that united different strands within evangelicalism and resulted in a shift in emphasis from doctrine to action and experience, hence the welcoming of charismatics into the evangelical fold.[65]

Conclusion

The international organization of evangelicals was an American response to the ecumenical movement, but not a reactionary one like the fundamentalist International Council of Christian Churches. In fact, the ICCC prevented the evangelicals from withdrawal into a separatist corner and incited them to be more inclusive. The distance between these two groups made the evangelicals less obsessed with Cold War issues than did the fundamentalists. Though most evangelicals were suspicious of bureaucratic organizations such as the WCC, which monopolized activities, they felt that they stood in an older ecumenical tradition. At an early stage they shared the liberal concerns about religious freedom and high hopes for government pressure in Europe. The World and National Council of Churches' increasing neglect of evangelism spurred them into action in order to place mission back on the religious agenda, defend existing interests, and develop new strategies. Until the early sixties, the evangelicals' main concern was to work towards individual salvation. When they had become the dominant force on the mission scene, however, they felt the same need to reflect on the extent and meaning of cross-cultural missions as ecumenicals had experienced a generation earlier.

In the 1960s, the evangelical network became truly international, and the American contingent became increasingly self-confident, especially in its relation to Europe. Evangelicals took over the majority position in the total numbers of American missions and were recognized as a strong factor in the American religious presence in the world. This dominance was in part the result of their domestic resurgence, and in part due to the mobilizing phase in the mission cycle, to which evangelical missions came after the mainline churches.[66] This experience strengthened American evangelicals' sense of the universal applicability and superiority of their approaches.

The 1974 Lausanne Conference marked the broadening of evangelicalism on a global stage. The effects were twofold. On the one hand, Lausanne theologically justified social action as a legitimate cause for evangelicals, which kept the radical wing within the flock. On the other hand, it confirmed the primacy of evangelism. This meant that practicality and action were sanctioned, which legitimized and boosted the methods of American evangelicals. The celebration of diversity opened the gates for ever more cooperation among a broad group of international evangelicals. Lausanne was not the cause but a symbol of change.

Finally, America's evangelical ascent occurred at the cost of Europe, which was effectively relegated from being a partner to being a recipient. Perhaps this negative view of Europe also had a function in the domestic political agenda of the evangelicals. European solutions were no models, but warnings. It might not be a coincidence that in the mid-seventies, leading evangelical intellectual Francis Schaeffer returned from Europe to the United States, and the International Christian Leadership in Europe folded.[67]

This history contributes three elements to the explanation of the timing and shape of the religious Right in America in the 1970s by investigating its international missionary activities. First, the foreign mission story shows that the evangelical resurgence began much earlier than the 1960s. It places the strong international orientation of the evangelicals right at the beginning of their organizational rebirth in the 1940s. The new evangelical leaders emphasized their missionary concerns in opposition to the political agenda of liberal Protestants. While ties to other Christian groups were never cut, evangelicals were convinced that Europe was exhibit A for the bankruptcy of liberal Protestantism. Despite their candid criticism, however, they continued to share significant patterns with their opponents. These historical continuities and aspirations kept them away from separatist fundamentalists. The growing engagement in missions was thus a crucial marker of evangelical identity and linked twentieth-century manifestations with the nineteenth-century evangelical agenda.[68] This tension between the evangelicals' strong oppositional profile on the one hand, and the effort to ensure historical continuity on the other, became apparent in the sequence of the phases of growth and development in mission work: the evangelicals' horizon broadened as they took over the leading position from the mainline churches.

Second, the missionary activities drew evangelicals closer into the religious mainstream, as tens of thousands of mission workers and congregations became involved in international contacts. After the evangelicals had come to occupy the dominant position on the mission field and recovered evangelism, they could broaden their agenda without fearing the loss of their identity. This broadening of perspectives was the result of different international evangelical partners who added social concerns to the agendas of influential international missionary conferences. At the same time, missionaries faced negative responses to American policies evoked by the Vietnam War and the Nixon response, which made them aware of their own cultural sensitivities.[69]

Third, experience with missions in Europe increased the evangelicals' awareness of America's religious superiority. The addition of Europe as a new target area in missions confronted evangelical Americans directly with a kindred culture, which had taken a different turn. This experience strengthened their determination to reach out with the gospel in a wide range of activities, while simultaneously allowing for critical reflections about their methods and aims. During the decades of their involvement in Europe they found that bringing in the harvest was more difficult than they had anticipated, but also that they had friends in Europe.

NOTES

1. Billy Graham, "Why Lausanne?" in *Let the Earth Hear His Voice*, ed. J. D. Douglas (Minneapolis: World Wide Publications, 1975), 35.

2. See chap. 10 by David Swartz, this volume.

3. "Theological Implications of Radical Discipleship," in Douglas, *Let the Earth Hear*, 1296.

4. Another option was Campus Crusade for Christ, but that organization focused more exclusively on youth ministries and was more important in the execution of than in the reflection on mission. See John G. Turner, *Bill Bright and Campus Crusade for Christ: The Renewal of Evangelicalism in Postwar America* (Chapel Hill: University of North Carolina Press, 2008).

5. Joel A. Carpenter, *Revive Us Again: The Reawakening of American Fundamentalism* (New York: Oxford University Press, 1997), 177; Garth M. Rosell, *The Surprising Work of God: Harold John Ockenga, Billy Graham, and the Rebirth of Evangelicalism* (Grand Rapids, MI: Baker Academic, 2008), 213–23; Mel Larson, *Youth for Christ: Twentieth Century Wonder* (Grand Rapids, MI: Zondervan, 1947), 78.

6. Charles E. Van Engen, "A Broadening Vision: Forty Years of Evangelical Theology of Mission, 1946-1986," in *Earthen Vessels: American Evangelicals and Foreign Missions, 1880-1980*, ed. Joel A. Carpenter and Wilbert R. Shenk (Grand Rapids, MI: Eerdmans, 1990), 203–32. The NAE war relief effort also functioned to create goodwill among European evangelicals. See Clyde Taylor, "Memorandum on European War Relief," Box 1, File "Clarens 1948," National Association of Evangelicals Records, Wheaton College Archives and Special Collections, Wheaton, Illinois (hereafter cited as NAE Records).

7. R. L. Decker, "Confidential Report," Box 1, File "Clarens 1948," NAE Records.

8. J. Elwin Wright to delegates, June 19, 1948, and J. Elwin Wright to Arie Kok (European representative of the ACCC in the Netherlands), April 16, 1948, Box 1, File "Clarens 1948," NAE Records. The letters exposed the exaggerated and erroneous

claims of the ACCC. The observers chose the Dutch minister A. H. van Oussoren as temporary chairman. See Minutes of the Clarens Conferences of Evangelicals, August 7–10, 1948, Box 1, File "Clarens 1948," NAE Records.

9. Clyde Taylor, "Confidential NAE Report," 3, Box 1, File "Clarens 1948," NAE Records.

10. D. M. Howard, *The Dream that Would Not Die: The Birth and Growth of the World Evangelical Fellowship 1846–1985* (Exeter, UK: The Paternoster Press, 1986), 54–57. The anti-American sentiments of the Vietnam period prevented Americans from assuming a natural leadership role.

11. Edwin L. Frizen Jr., *75 years of IFMA, 1917–1992: The Nondenominational Missions Movement* (Pasadena, CA: William Carey Library 1992), 193.

12. Report by Clyde Taylor, Box 1, File "Clarens 1948," NAE Records.

13. J. Elwin Wright, Minutes, Box 1, File "Clarens 1948," NAE Records.

14. Letter from the Dutch evangelical leader Dr. R. H. Borkent to NAE, July 23, 1948, and R. L. Decker, "Confidential Resume and Report on Trip to Europe, July 30–August 30, 1948," both in Box 1, File "Clarens 1948," NAE Records.

15. David A. Hollinger, "After Cloven Tongues of Fire: Ecumenical Protestantism and the Modern American Encounter with Diversity," *Journal of American History* 98 (June 2011): 21–48.

16. John Bolten (treasurer of IVCF) to Francis Schaeffer, July 6, 1948, NAE Records.

17. Norvald Yri, *Quest for Authority: An Investigation of the Quest for Authority within the Ecumenical Movement from 1910 to 1974 and the Evangelical Response* (Kisumu, Kenya: Evangel Publishing House, 1978), 243–246. See the opening statements of the 1966 Wheaton Declaration quoted in ibid., 253.

18. Carpenter, *Revive*, 160.

19. Ibid., 154, 158. Associations such as the ICCC offered marginal fundamentalist churches and relatively isolated immigrant churches the opportunity to expand their horizons and their cultural impact. See Farley P. Butler Jr., "Billy Graham and the End of Evangelical Unity" (PhD diss., University of Florida, 1976); Daryl Alan Porter, "*Christianity Today:* Its History and Development, 1956–1978" (master's thesis, Dallas Theological Seminary, 1978), 20–21. See also Clyde Taylor, "Report on Europe," and Taylor, "The Movement for Evangelical Cooperation, part 2: International Developments," which explicitly stated that churches should not interfere in each other's internal affairs. It also stated its distance to the WCC. Box 2, NAE Records.

20. James DeForest Murch, "Amsterdam, 1948. An Evangelical View of the World Council of Churches," *United Evangelical Action*, February 1–May 15, 1949. See also *United Evangelical Action*, February 1, 1953, 16.

21. "The News behind the News from Denver," *United Evangelical Action*, February 1, 1953, 19, 31.

22. Martin Marty, *Modern American Religion. Vol 3: Under God Indivisible, 1941–1960* (Chicago: University of Chicago Press, 1996), 367–368; William Martin, *A Prophet with Honor: The Billy Graham Story* (New York: William Morrow, 1991), 212, 240, 334–335. American ecumenicals in the 1960s drifted into two wings: the more radical anticolonial

supporters of the NCC, and the more traditional constituency of the Church World Service, which had more financial resources, disapproved of the radical NCC political course, and sought to maintain the relationship with the U.S. government. See Jill K. Gill, "The Politics of Ecumenical Disunity: The Troubled Marriage of Church World Service and the National Council of Churches," *Religion and American Culture* 14 (2004): 175–212.

23. Martin, *Prophet with Honor*, 327.

24. Los Angeles Press Conference, May 13, 1968, 20, Box 1, Folder 10, BGEA: Records of News Conferences, Billy Graham Center Archives, Wheaton, Illinois.

25. George H. Gallup, *The Gallup Polls. Public Opinion 1935–1971*, 3 vols., 1490 (June 2, 1957); Interview of Bob Shuster with Arthur F. Glasser, interviews with Arthur Frederick Glasser (Collection 421), Billy Graham Center Archives, Wheaton, Illinois. The partners included Horace Fenton, John Howard Yoder, Lesslie Newbigin, and Eugene Smith. The evangelicals gave up, however, when the WCC assembly in Uppsala approved violence for liberation purposes.

26. Richard Carwardine, *Transatlantic Revivalism: Popular Evangelicalism in Britain and America, 1790–1865* (New York: Greenwood Press, 1978).

27. An early example in 1929 was Oswald J. Smith, the special envoy for Chicago-based preacher Paul Rader and his *World Wide Christian Courier*, who toured in Spain, France, the Russian borderlands in the Baltic, and Poland to meet Russian refugees, covering 20,000 miles in five months. This was an impressive act for a church with sufficient media presence, but three thousand dollars a year to finance missionaries was a modest budget for Europe.

28. R. Pierce Beaver, "Distribution of the American Protestant Foreign Missionary Force in 1952," *Occasional Bulletin from the Missionary Research Library*, July 1953, 1; Frank W. Price and Kenyon E. Meyer, "A Study of American Protestant Foreign Missions in 1956," *Occasional Bulletin from the Missionary Research Library*, November 1956, 27. Wagner argues that the fourth phase between 1975 and 1990 revealed the parachurch explosion, with a flurry of activities in many directions. Evangelical shifted to closer cooperation with evangelical churches in Europe or founded new ones. Wagner counted twenty-seven new agencies in West Germany and twenty-six in the UK. A final phase, beginning in 1990, once again shifted attention to minority (recent immigrant) groups.

29. The Greater Europe Mission took the lead in coordinating the efforts in Europe in 1962, following the 1960 Evangelical Mission conferences. This agency revealed that from now on Europe had a real place on the American missionary map. The GEM's task was coordination and education rather than the development of new strategies.

30. Robert Root, "Twilight of Religious Liberty," *Christian Century*, April 16, 1947. This author feared that the Protestants would suffer more from Catholic domination than from communist rule. See also "Plan Further Restrictions of Spanish Protestants," *Christian Century*, January 7, 1948; "Persecution of Protestants in Spain Spreading," *Christian Century*, September 29, 1948; "Religious Freedom in a Catholic Country," *Christian Century*, October 10, 1951.

31. Howard Schomer, "Europe's Latin Protestants Speak," *Christian Century*, November 8, 1950. See also the series by W. E. Garrison, "Religious Liberty in Spain,"

Christian Century, October 11–November 1, 1950. For an overview of the theological attitude of American Protestants towards Catholics, see William M. Shea, *The Lion and the Lamb: Evangelicals and Catholics in America* (New York: Oxford University Press, 2004), 141–185. See also chap. 12 by Neil Young, this volume.

32. Sidney Correll, "It is time for religious liberty in Spain," *United Evangelical Action*, August 15, 1951, 3–4, 14. See also "New Wave of Persecution Hits Protestants in Spain," *United Evangelical Action*, April 1, 1952; "Will Spain fulfil its promises?" *United Evangelical Action*, May 15, 1952, 11; Sidney Correll "Protestant Purge is Going on in Spain," *United Evangelical Action*, August 1, 1952, 3; Herman A. Parli, "Why Italy Persecutes its Protestants," *United Evangelical Action*, October 15, 1952; and "Religious Freedom in Italy is 'Ideological,'" *United Evangelical Action*, December 1, 1952.

33. *United Evangelical Action*, 1 December 1, 1951, 3.

34. Ibid., 6.

35. *IFMA News Bulletin*, February 1952.

36. Ibid. See also *IFMA News Bulletin* between April and October 1952.

37. *IFMA News Bulletin*, December 1952 (on Portugal). See also the December 1954 issue on news about a new dawn in Spain when anti-Protestant clergy were removed.

38. *IFMA News Bulletin*, March 1953.

39. *IFMA News Bulletin*, July 1954. See also the prayer letters by Samuel Faircloth, American missionary for the Conservative Baptists in Portugal between 1949 and 1985, Papers of Samuel Douglas Faircloth, Billy Graham Center Archives, Wheaton, Illinois.

40. Worldcat lists 111 libraries in the United States that possess copies of the book, including the majority of evangelical colleges and Bible schools.

41. Robert P. Evans, *Let Europe Hear: The Spiritual Plight of Europe* (Chicago: Moody Press, 1963), 47–89. For a secular view of Europe at that time, see David Calleo, *Europe's Future: The Grand Alternatives* (New York: Horizon Press, 1965).

42. Walter Frank, General Director's Report, 1964, Box 21, Folder 10 (GEM 1964–65), Interdenominational Foreign Mission Association Records, Billy Graham Center Archives, Wheaton, Illinois (hereafter cited as IFMA). In 1964, the Greater European Mission had 114 missionaries working in Europe and operated three Bible schools in France, Belgium, and Italy.

43. See also a special issue of *Christianity Today* (Christianity in Free Europe), July 20, 1962; W. Stuart Harris, *Eyes on Europe* (Chicago: Moody Press, 1965); Jack McAlister, *Evangelizing Europe: Heart of the World* (Studio City, CA: World Literature Crusade, 1961).

44. William L. Wagner, *North American Protestant Missionaries in Western Europe: A Critical Appraisal* (Bonn: Verlag für Kultur und Wissenschaft, 1993), 134.

45. Allen V. Koop, *American Evangelical Missionaries in France, 1945–1975* (Lanham, MD: University Press of America, 1986), 94; David E. Bjork, *Unfamiliar Paths: The Challenge of Recognizing the Work of Christ in Strange Clothing: A Case Study from France* (Pasadena, CA: William Carey Library, 1997).

46. See also Richard T. Hughes, ed., *The Primitive Church in the Modern World* (Champaign: University of Illinois Press, 1995).

47. Walter Frank, "IFMA Missions and Church Planting in Areas Where Old Churches are Established," Box 27, Folder 4 (GEM 1970–71), IFMA.

48. *Nieuwe Leidsche Courant,* June 1, 1966.

49. *Algemeen Handelsblad,* November 10, 1966.

50. *Rotterdammer,* February 18, 1967. See Billy Graham Evangelistic Association Clippings File (Collection 360), Billy Graham Center Archives, Wheaton, Illinois.

51. An interview with Bronek Wlochacz on January 28, 2010 confirmed the high expectations attached to new technology, which led to the launch of the Dutch Evangelical Broadcasting Company (Evangelische Omroep); Martin, *Prophet with Honor,* 379–381; John Pollock, *Billy Graham: Evangelist to the World* (New York: Harper and Row, 1979).

52. *Provinciale Zeeuwse Courant,* March 18, 1970; *Friesch Dagblad,* April 1, 1970. *Philips Koerier,* April 18, 1970. The idea that all of Western Europe, including Yugoslavia, was connected to the same event, drew European evangelicals closer together.

53. *Dordts Dagblad,* June 3, 1966, and many other Dutch newspaper clippings in June 8, 1966.

54. *Nieuwsblad van het noorden,* August 30, 1971. *Nieuwe Apeldoornse Courant,* September 4, 1971.

55. Carpenter, *Revive,* 185.

56. Dana L. Robert, "'The Crisis of Missions': Premillennial Mission Theory and the Origins of Independent Evangelical Missions," in Carpenter and Shenk, *Earthen Vessels,* 29–46.

57. Carpenter, *Revive,* 141. In 1970, the general director of the Greater European Mission, Walter Frank, indicated that the incentive for the re-evangelizing of Europe came from European immigrants, especially Scandinavians, who had joined free churches in the United States and compared their newfound allegiance favorably with the situation of religious oppression and persecution in countries with a state church. They had taken up the challenge to reach their native soil "glowing with zeal to preach revival and establish groups of believers." See Walter Frank, "IFMA Missions and Church Planting in Areas Where Old Churches are Established," Box 27, Folder 4 (GEM 1970–71), IFMA.

58. Edward R. Dayton, ed., *Mission Handbook: North American Protestant Ministries Overseas* (Federal Way, WA: World Vision International, 1977). Between 1960 and 1980, the fundamentalists replaced the evangelicals as the group with the largest growth in staff. Meanwhile, ecumenical groups focused more on humanitarian causes and sent fewer staff and more money. See Samuel Wilson, "Current Trends in North American Protestant Ministries Overseas," *International Bulletin of Missionary Research* 5.2 (1981): 74–75; Paul E. Pierson, "Lessons in Mission from the Twentieth Century: Conciliar Missions," in *Between Past and Future: Evangelical Mission Entering the Twenty-first Century,* ed. Jonathan J. Bonk (Pasadena, CA: William Carey Library, 2003), 67–84. Statistics on income in Edward R. Dayton, "Current Trends in North American Protestant Ministries Overseas," *Occasional Bulletin of Missionary Research,* April 1977, 4. Between 1968 and 1976 the percentage of the NCC-related associations dropped from 53 to 22 percent, or from $149.2 million to $137.4 million.

59. Yri, *Quest for Authority*, 269.

60. Timothy Dudley-Smith, *John Stott: A Global Ministry: A Biography of the Later Years* (Downers Grove, IL: InterVarsity Press, 2001), 209–210.

61. Yri, *Quest for Authority*, 313.

62. Dudley-Smith, *John Stott*, 220–221. See chap. 10 by David R. Swartz in this volume.

63. Dudley-Smith, *John Stott*, 222.

64. John Stott, "The Significance of Lausanne," in *The Study of Evangelism: Exploring a Missional Practice of the Church*, ed. Paul Wesley Chilcote and Laceye C. Warner (Grand Rapids, MI: Eerdmans 2008), 305–312; John Stott, *Christian Mission in the Modern World* (Downers Grove, IL: InterVarsity Press, 1975).

65. David Wells, "On Being Evangelical: Some Theological Differences and Similarities," in *Evangelicalism: Comparative Studies of Popular Protestantism in North America, the British Isles and Beyond, 1700–1990*, ed. Mark A. Noll, David W. Bebbington, and George A. Rawlyk (New York: Oxford University Press, 1994), 389–410; Billy Graham, *Just as I Am: The Autobiography of Billy Graham* (New York: HarperCollins/Zondervan, 1997), 567–583. See also Martin Klauber, *The Great Commission: Evangelicals and the History of World Missions* (Nashville: B & H Publishing Group, 2008).

66. More research is needed to assess the effect of the experiences of these tens of thousands missionaries at home. Did they support the political involvement of their co-religionists and if so, in which direction? Charles Van Engen believes that evangelicals in mission areas were more politically aware than if they had stayed at home but offers no evidence. See Engen, "A Broadening Vision," 211.

67. Barry Hankins, *Francis Schaeffer and the Shaping of Evangelical America* (Grand Rapids, MI: Eerdmans, 2008) 160–161; Hans Krabbendam, "A Christian Bilderberg? The International Christian Leadership, 1948–1968," in *Who's the Boss? Leadership and Democratic Culture in America*, ed. Hans Krabbendam and Wil Verhoeven (Amsterdam: VU University Press, 2007), 187–198.

68. Angela Lahr, *Millennial Dreams and Apocalyptic Nightmares: The Cold War Origins of Political Evangelicalism* (New York: Oxford University Press, 2007); Hartmut Lehmann, ed., *Transatlantische Religionsgeschichte: 18. bis 20. Jahrhundert* (Göttingen: Wallstein Verlag, 2006). Billy Graham's crusades in Eastern Europe in the 1970s and later were part of America's demarcation against a godless communist world.

69. N. J. Demerath, "Cultural Victory and Organizational Defeat in the Paradoxical Decline of Liberal Protestantism," *Journal for the Scientific Study of Religion* 34 (1995): 458–469; Robert Wuthnow, *Boundless Faith: The Global Outreach of American Churches* (Berkeley: University of California Press, 2009), ch. 6. The trend toward a global missionary exchange is described by Candy Gunther Brown in *Religion in American History*, ed. Amanda Porterfield and John Corrigan (Chichester: Blackwell Publishing, 2010), 319. See also Daniel H. Bays and Grant Wacker, eds., *The Foreign Missionary Enterprise at Home: Explorations in North American Cultural History* (Tuscaloosa: University of Alabama Press, 2003).

12

"A Saga of Sacrilege"

Evangelicals Respond to the Second Vatican Council

NEIL J. YOUNG

On the morning of October 11, 1962, millions of viewers around the world turned their televisions to the live coverage of the Second Vatican Council's opening assembly. An hour-long procession of twenty-five hundred council fathers, draped in all-white vestments with matching white miters on their heads, snaked across the grand square of the Vatican and into the soaring majesty of St. Peter's Basilica. At the end of the parade, carried aloft in an ornate portable throne by a dozen sturdy attendants dressed in red, came Pope John XXIII, the visionary of this great meeting. While the spectacle and pageantry represented to many Catholics both the seriousness and grandeur of such an occasion, for the church's critics it evidenced again Roman Catholicism's most outrageous excesses and extravagant traditions. Just a few weeks before Vatican II commenced, the evangelical magazine *Christianity Today* had predicted the first day of the council "will doubtless be marked by pomp and ceremony such as only the Roman penchant for spectacle can produce." "To the 550,000,000 on Roman Catholic rolls," *Christianity Today* continued, "the deliberations will be sacred sessions. To other millions they will be a saga of sacrilege."[1]

Evangelicals had long critiqued what they saw as the ostentatious ritualism of the Catholic Church, of course, but their pointed attacks on Vatican II had been shaped by the specific events of the recent presidential election as much as they had by the longer general history of evangelical anti-Catholicism. Two years before Vatican II opened, John F. Kennedy had become the nation's first Catholic president despite concerted opposition from many Protestant leaders. Joined by leaders from across Protestantism's theological spectrum, conservative evangelicals argued that a Catholic president would take orders from the pope and allow the Catholic Church to corrupt the purity of American democracy with its foreign ritualism and its anti-individualistic loyalty to hierarchical authority. A Catholic president, C. Stanley Lowell of the anti-Catholic organization Protestants and Other Americans United for Separation of Church and State (POAU) contended, would showcase his church's excessive rituals and symbols with little regard for Protestant aversions to such things. Lowell imagined a "daily circus of priests and nuns parading in full regalia in and out of the White House," should Kennedy take office.[2] The Catholic pageantry that a Kennedy administration would promote, evangelical leaders argued, would provide a distraction from the true sinister political ambitions of the church to overtake the nation. "Now the Catholic genius for politics is taking a new direction," Lowell continued in his article that soon became a popular pamphlet circulated throughout the country, "It turns from king-maker to king. It would like, perhaps, to achieve in the nation what it has already achieved in New York, Boston, and Chicago."[3]

Coming in such quick succession, the 1960 election of John F. Kennedy and the Second Vatican Council, which took place in ten-week sessions every fall from 1962 to 1965, provided evangelicals with an extended opportunity to revive and remake their arguments against the Catholic Church, but how evangelicals responded to these two events has remained curiously disconnected by historians. Indeed, although historians have given close attention to the evangelical (and larger Protestant) opposition to the Kennedy campaign, scholars of American evangelicals have largely failed to examine evangelical reactions to Vatican II.[4] On the other hand, Vatican II has been widely viewed as the critical moment in which the Catholic Church updated itself for the modern era through its reforms, such as allowing the vernacular to enter the Mass and other changes in the liturgical celebration, and in its declarations, most especially on ecumenism and on religious liberty. The historiography of this transformative event, produced steadily since the council's last session in 1965, has focused on Vatican II as one of the Catholic Church's most important historical moments and viewed the proceedings within Catholic institutional, intellectual, and theological histories.[5]

Yet the church had made history by opening its proceedings to representatives from various branches of Christianity, and the religious media closely watched and commented on the unfolding developments and changes in Rome. From the United States, Protestant publications like the liberal mainline magazine *Christian Century* and evangelical periodicals like *Eternity* and the newcomer *Christianity Today* sent reporters to Rome and covered the proceedings closely throughout. The historical narrative of the Second Vatican Council has largely overlooked its interdenominational aspect, especially curious considering the rich history on midcentury ecumenical efforts within American religion.[6] For scholars of American evangelicals, the Catholic–evangelical post–World War II relationship has largely focused on the affinities and alliances built between the two faiths in the aftermath of the Supreme Court's landmark 1973 *Roe v. Wade* decision legalizing abortion. Yet examining the evangelical response to Vatican II complicates the narrative of an increasingly harmonious Catholic–evangelical partnership in the second half of the twentieth century. By exploring evangelical reactions to Vatican II, especially in light of John F. Kennedy's 1960 presidential campaign, which influenced evangelical interpretations of the council, we can better understand how the roots of the persistent tensions among conservative evangelicals and Catholics trace directly to the events of the council. Evangelical charges during the Kennedy campaign that a Catholic president would take his authority from the pope rather than the Constitution morphed into evangelical arguments throughout Vatican II that contrasted Catholicism's papal authority with evangelicalism's *sola scriptura* biblical authority. Still, the Catholic Church's changing relationship with the Bible, expressed through significant developments during Vatican II, complicated, if not chastened, some of those critiques. In Vatican II's increased emphasis on the Bible, evangelicals saw the opportunity for promising inroads for evangelism of and partnership with individual Catholics while still maintaining their historical reproaches of the institution. Distrustful of the institutional Catholic Church they believed sought dominance over the American nation through the election of a Catholic president and monopolistic control over the Christian faith disguised by Vatican II's broad-minded ecumenism, evangelicals began to view individual Catholics as fellow cultural sympathizers who could ally with them on sociopolitical matters in the public square. And they hoped that some might even become true Christians if they allowed the Bible rather than the Roman Church to take authority over their lives.

For American evangelicals interested in following Vatican II's developments, several publications provided coverage of the events in Rome, but no Protestant media outlet seemed to keep a closer watch on Vatican II than did *Christianity Today*. In its constant articles and editorials dating from 1959 until several years after its closing in 1965, *Christianity Today* shaped and revealed the American evangelical response to the Second Vatican Council. While the council represented a particularly unique religious event, *Christianity Today*'s coverage of it fit within the magazine's larger commitment to closely monitoring the Catholic Church, a priority particularly emphasized throughout the 1960 campaign.

Founded by Billy Graham and other leading evangelical voices in 1956, *Christianity Today* had quickly become the most trusted evangelical publication. With more than 150,000 readers within its first year of publication, the magazine had already equaled the subscription base of its established liberal rival, *Christian Century*, and soon grew to be one of the country's most widely read religious publications.[7] Throughout its brief history, *Christianity Today* had given close critical attention to the Catholic Church. Indeed, providing a consistent evangelical critique of Catholicism had been one of the chief inspirations for Graham and his friends to create their new publication. When the magazine's founders were planning their new venture, they indicated their threefold intention was to attack what they saw as the unscriptural claims of liberal Protestantism, to challenge the negative separatism of Protestant fundamentalism, and to expose the errors and menacing aims of Roman Catholicism. An early document outlining editorial objectives for the magazine explained that *Christianity Today* would tackle the "problem of false sects and how to answer their false teachings" and would "disclose the doctrinal fallacies of Roman Catholicism, its political ambitions and its threat to religious freedom."[8]

Frequent articles through the years outlined the theological differences between Catholic heresy and evangelical truth, attacked the Catholic Church's political ambitions, and even suggested Catholicism's aims for the United States were "no less total and arrogant than are those of Communism."[9] Given the Cold War context, equating Catholicism's objectives with the menace of communism had a powerful resonance, but it also reflected the real fears among evangelicals (not to mention American Protestants, in general) that Catholics would soon dominate and control the nation. Enjoying postwar prosperity and rising cultural visibility, U.S. Catholics took an increasingly public role in American life, bolstered by a vibrant network of parochial schools, Catholic hospitals, universities, and agencies. Thanks to the economic security of the times, Catholic teachings regarding birth control, and the aggressive pronatalism of the Cold War years, Catholic families enthusiastically increased in number, rapidly expanding the membership rolls of their church. By 1960 the Catholic Church counted more than forty million members in America, representing nearly a quarter of the country's population and making Catholicism by far the largest denomination in the country.[10]

Evangelical publications like *Christianity Today* decried this trend and warned what the Catholic Church's growth in the United States would mean for the nation's institutions. "She will infiltrate government, education, and labor," one article bemoaned.[11] Another article, ominously titled "If the U.S. Becomes 51% Catholic," darkly predicted the Catholic Church would overturn laws that barred public funding of religious institutions and pass other laws that would prevent any criticisms of Catholicism. Eventually, the article concluded, "Roman Catholicism would be named the country's official religion."[12] In Catholicism, evangelicals saw not only a theological threat but a challenge to the nation's constitutional principles and political traditions that, they believed, promoted individual conscience thus allowing the gospel to flourish.

When John F. Kennedy captured the Democratic nomination for the presidency in 1960, evangelicals felt certain that their fears of the Catholic hierarchy in Rome seizing authority over the United States were all the closer to becoming dangerously realized. But evangelicals were not alone in this worry. Joining in a pan-Protestant political movement that spanned the theological spectrum, evangelicals linked with moderate and liberal Protestants to oppose the Catholic Kennedy from entering the White House, but this would be the last major moment evangelicals would find themselves so closely aligned with their Protestant counterparts in relation to the question of Catholicism in America. Furthermore, Kennedy's bid for the presidency shaped and increased the evangelical response to Vatican II that soon followed, as it set in motion many of the concerns that re-emerged for evangelicals during the council's tenure. Kennedy's win had realized evangelical fears about Catholicism's political aims in the United States. The developments of Vatican II, especially regarding the topics of ecumenism and religious liberty, seemed to many evangelicals like the next assault the Catholic Church might make on Protestant America. Inside the Kennedy camp, it surprised some that his Catholicism would be treated as a political liability considering the mediocrity of his faith. "I think it's so unfair of people to be against Jack because he's Catholic," Jacqueline Kennedy said of her husband. "He's such a poor Catholic."[13] But, as the *New York Times* pointed out that year, those raising objections to Kennedy's campaign "aren't running against the candidate, but the pope."[14]

From the first hints that Kennedy would run for the presidency, Protestants across the political spectrum began to organize to keep him out of the White

House. The liberal *Christian Century* published several articles and editorials questioning how much the Catholic Church had liberalized on matters of separation of church and state and religious liberty, and to what extent a president would be independent of church dictates. As a liberal publication, the magazine could never bring itself to endorse Nixon, but it still ran frequent pieces, especially throughout the Democratic nomination process, that were highly critical of Kennedy's candidacy.[15] In one article, as the important West Virginia primary approached, *Christian Century*'s editors contended "we are compelled to recognize that religion may be nothing more than a device by which a candidate, often with the help of clergy and laity, marshals church and religious pawns for the chess game of politics."[16] When Kennedy later won the nomination, *Christian Century* described it as the "capture" of the Democratic Party accomplished by the northern party machines "dominated in almost every instance by Roman Catholic politicians."[17]

In the conservative corners of Protestantism, Kennedy's critics launched an even more virulent attack on Catholic political ambitions. The Southern Baptist Convention, the largest evangelical denomination and the dominant majority of the Democratic South, struck a blow at the Kennedy candidacy with a full-fledged assault. At the SBC's annual meeting in 1960, 13,000 delegates in Miami Beach unanimously passed a resolution that expressed grave fears about Kennedy's candidacy. Though the "Resolution on Christian Citizenship" made no direct mention of Kennedy's name or his Catholicism, this was in keeping with a frequent tactic employed by Kennedy's opponents throughout the race, as the historian Shaun Casey has pointed out. The resolution instead affirmed the historic Baptist commitment to the separation of church and state, and warned against members of other faiths seeking political office who were "inescapably bound by the dogma and demands" of their church. "This is especially true," the resolution continued, "when that church maintains a position in open conflict with our established and constituted American pattern on life as specifically related to religious liberty, separation of Church and State . . . and the prohibition against use of public monies for sectarian purposes."[18] Other arms of the SBC supported the message coming from the top. Eight state conventions and every state convention Baptist newspaper in 1960 expressed fears about the election of a Catholic president.[19] The SBC's president, Ramsey Pollard, also encouraged his denomination's pastors to develop sermons on the issue so that all Southern Baptists could appreciate "our concern over the candidacy for the president of the United States of one who indisputably would be under pressure of his church hierarchy to weaken the wall of separation."[20]

Pastors across the SBC embraced the statement's directives, preaching anti-Kennedy sermons throughout 1960. W. A. Criswell, pastor of the SBC's largest church, First Baptist in Dallas, Texas, and the most famous Southern Baptist after Billy Graham, led a spirited charge against JFK that other Southern Baptist pastors would mimic. In a sermon on July 3, Criswell warned that Kennedy's election would spell the end of religious liberty in America. "Kennedy Is Attacked," read the headline in the *New York Times* the next day.[21] Criswell's talk, titled "Religious Freedom, the Church, the State, and Senator Kennedy," acknowledged the American disinclination to criticize other religions, but explained that the habits of the Catholic Church ruptured this truce. "The institution of Roman Catholicism is not only a religion," Criswell preached, "it is a political tyranny . . . we are faced with a political system that, like an octopus, covers the entire world and threatens those basic freedoms and those constitutional rights for which our forefathers died in generations past."[22]

Criswell's sermon outlined several reasons that Kennedy's bid for the presidency should be stopped. First, by adhering to papal authority, a Catholic president would allow his church to have undue influence in governmental affairs, and Catholic "toleration" of other religions, rather than liberty, would mean that non-Catholic faiths would suffer as a result. "Toleration is a gift from man," Criswell preached, "while liberty is a gift from God." Also, Criswell warned that a Catholic president would establish diplomatic ties with the Vatican, something Baptists and most Protestants thoroughly opposed. Finally, Criswell argued the pope would intervene in American politics and imperil religious liberty and national autonomy. Quoting from a Vatican newspaper article, Criswell read to his members a passage, which explained that the Catholic Church had the power and right to direct, guide, and correct all Catholics on any of their actions or ideas, including those of politics. "That was published," Criswell explained, "in order that John Kennedy himself might know that, despite his avowals, he cannot be disassociated from and free from, the directives of the Roman Catholic Church." No matter what Kennedy claimed, Criswell contended, the candidate could not separate himself from the authority the Catholic Church claimed over everything he did, including leading the nation. Criswell described the Catholic Church as a stealth virus, willing to work slowly in order to accomplish its ultimate aims. "The Roman Church wins most of its victories with the weapons of time," Criswell warned. Kennedy's win would be another step forward for Catholic political ambition in the nation. Next would come full diplomatic ties, state-supported church schools, and "finally, recognition of one church above all others in America."[23]

Other evangelicals joined in. In Kennedy's hometown, the influential evangelical pastor Harold Ockenga preached a sermon during the summer of 1960 that repeated many of the arguments Baptist pastors had made about how Kennedy's candidacy threatened the democratic principle of church-state separation.[24] The year before, Ockenga had written to Nixon personally: "If there's anything I can do in the advancement of your candidacy for the President of the United States, I should be glad to do it and I assure you that you will have the loyal support of thousands of people in our own constituency."[25] Ockenga's historic Park Street Church, perched on the edge of Boston Common, occupied an equally privileged place in northern evangelical circles, and Ockenga had been a founding organizer of both *Christianity Today* and the National Association of Evangelicals (NAE). Both of those institutions now joined in the fight against Kennedy's bid for the White House.

In 1959, as *Christianity Today* anticipated Kennedy's possible nomination to the Democratic ticket, an editorial in the magazine asked, "Should Americans Elect a Roman Catholic President?" "If the Roman Catholic church were like most denominations," the magazine answered, "all Americans would welcome a qualified Roman Catholic citizen in the White House. . . . But the nature of the Roman Catholic church and the provisions of its canon law raise problems in considering a Catholic presidential candidate that do not arise in the case of a Protestant or a Jew."[26] The editorial attracted an unusual amount of responses. A few Catholics wrote the magazine, condemning its position. One Catholic from New York City explained he had had no intention of voting for Kennedy, "but on second thought," he and "hundreds and hundreds of other Roman Catholics may accept your challenge" to ensure a Catholic became president.[27] Evangelical readers, however, expressed their appreciation for the magazine's stand. "It is illogical for Protestants to vote themselves into second-class citizenship by voting for a Catholic U.S. President," one man from California wrote.[28] Another agreed and urged Protestant unity: "Protestants and all others who do not give allegiance to the pope must unite as one to see that no Roman Catholic occupies the White House."[29]

The NAE joined in the fight against the senator from Massachusetts. One leader with the NAE wrote Nixon during the summer of 1960 explaining that the group would work quietly but with dedication so that its ten million members understood the severity of the election.[30] To that end, the NAE's magazine, *United Evangelical Action*, published Criswell's anti-Kennedy sermon in full.[31] At its annual convention in 1960, the NAE passed a resolution on "Roman Catholicism and the President of the United States." "Due to the political-religious nature of the Roman Catholic Church," the resolution read, "we doubt that a Roman Catholic president could or would resist fully the pressures of the ecclesiastical hierarchy."[32]

Behind the scenes, the NAE organized to prevent the Catholic takeover of the nation it had been predicting since the group's founding nearly twenty years before. During the 1950s, the NAE regularly published anti-Catholic pamphlets that presented Catholicism as antithetical to basic American values. One tract, "Shall America Bow to the Pope of Rome?" demonized the tyranny of papal authority by including a large cover photograph of the U.S. envoy to the Vatican, Myron Taylor, prostrating before the pope. Inside, the pamphlet's twenty pages decried the "Roman Catholic system" as "fundamentally fascist and opposed to democracy." Unlike American democracy, the Roman Catholic organization "is an Imperium in Imperio—a state within a state." The Catholic Church did not control the United States, of course, but it slowly sought ultimate control through a creeping influence into every corner of the nation, gathering up peoples and institutions that would kowtow to its authority. "Every day brings new evidence," the pamphlet ominously warned, "that this battle for the capture of America is on in real earnest." Ignoring the more than forty million Americans who called themselves Catholics, the pamphlet called on every "true American" to oppose any further Catholic influence on the nation and for evangelicals to band with "the Jews, the Mormons, the Unitarians and the atheists who as American citizens are as gravely endangered as we. Unless such a united front can be presented against the united forces of Catholicism we are defeated before we start."[33]

That united front of non-Catholics would be merely symbolic, rather than organizational or strategic. It was far easier to unite Protestants against the Kennedy campaign than it was to link those Protestants in real partnership with other faiths like Judaism and Mormonism. (Indeed, despite Mormonism's own anti-Catholic history, evangelical arguments about Catholicism's authoritarianism hardly appealed to Mormons who belonged to their own highly institutional and hierarchical faith.) Within the Protestant community, Protestants and Other Americans United for Separation of Church and State served as the umbrella organization linking evangelical, moderate, and liberal Protestants together in a coordinated effort to stop Kennedy. To that end, POAU worked with the NAE, Billy Graham, and the liberal Protestant pastor of New York's Marble Collegiate Church, Norman Vincent Peale, to organize a meeting of 150 Protestant leaders from thirty-seven denominations at Washington, D.C.'s Mayflower Hotel on September 7, 1960. Speakers at the all-day event attended sessions and listened to speeches on how to keep a Roman Catholic out of the White House.[34] "Let the Church be the Church and the State be the

State," Harold Ockenga implored in his address to the group. "Let the wall of separation continue."[35]

Despite the vigorous efforts to link Kennedy's election to a papal plot to undermine constitutional authority, Kennedy eked out a narrow victory that November. Evangelicals had led the religio-political campaign against the Catholic candidate, but they had enjoyed able assistance from across the Protestant spectrum. Indeed, no other moment would again reveal such a united Protestant front. Anti-Catholic arguments regarding the threat of papal authority to the constitutional system and American individualism had powerfully united the incredibly diverse and schismatic American Protestant community. But evangelicals seemed to take Kennedy's win most heavily. After the election, *Christianity Today* lamented that the "American dream and destiny this week seem hazier than for decades." Still, the magazine reminded its readers that though Kennedy had won with the help of a large Catholic populace, "Statistically, evangelical strength almost rivals that of Catholics in the United States. . . . Whether the evangelical movement learns to address Roman Catholics aggressively . . . remains to be seen."[36]

The Second Vatican Council soon gave evangelicals the opportunity for that aggressive engagement with Catholicism that *Christianity Today* desired. That response, most powerfully demonstrated through the rich evidence of *Christianity Today*'s writings alongside other evangelical commentary, showed that American evangelicals reacted to Vatican II by questioning the Catholic Church's ambitions, lamenting the persistence of papal authority, and worrying about the future of sacred American ideals like individualism, pluralism, and religious liberty. In evaluating the council, American evangelicals expanded on many of the arguments they had voiced during the Kennedy campaign. Importantly, they also revealed a conception of themselves not as political and cultural outsiders but rather as passionate and perhaps even solitary defenders of American tradition because mainline and liberal Protestants, in general, did not share their reactions to the council. Through their responses to Vatican II, American evangelicals offered warnings, couched in their reactions to Kennedy's election and their larger Cold War concerns regarding totalitarianism and communalism, about the future of the American nation. Long before any backlash responses to the cultural and political transformations of late-1960s liberalism, American evangelicals used the religious event of the council as an opportunity to advocate for their increased participation in the American political process so as to guard against external threats to the nation and to preserve the American experiment they believed was rooted in Protestant ideas and values. Throughout their close observances of Vatican II, evangelicals emphasized their sole devotion to biblical authority as contrasted to Catholic allegiance to the pope, adherence to tradition alongside scripture, veneration of Mary and the saints, and other Catholic practices and beliefs they deemed extra-biblical. But evangelicals also hoped that Vatican II's reforms regarding the Bible might mean new relationships with Catholic laypersons, if not the Catholic Church itself, and their response to this development of the council shaped the most significant consequence for evangelical-Catholic relations in the years to come.

❖

Just three months after assuming the papacy, Pope John XXIII had stunned the Catholic Church with his announcement on January 25, 1959, calling for a Second Vatican Council. During the First Vatican Council (1869–70), the church had defined papal infallibility as dogma. Because of that pronouncement, many Catholics and others assumed there would never be another council since it had been declared the pope held all the answers to any problems the church faced. But John XXIII had a new vision for his church and he expected the second council would bring about these transformations. John XXIII's announcement of the council outlined two broad goals for the sessions that would open in 1962. First, the council would promote "the enlightenment, edification, and joy of the entire Christian people." Secondly, the council would offer "a renewed cordial invitation to the faithful of the separated communities to participate with us in this quest for unity and grace."[37]

Pope John XXIII's invitation to "separated brethren" to participate in the proceedings marked an important turnabout from the church's historic isolationism. Papal decrees throughout the twentieth century had repeatedly forbidden ecumenical interactions. Pope Pius XI's 1928 encyclical *Mortalium Animos*, for instance, had denounced the ecumenical movement and implored those who called themselves Christians to return to the "one true church." But in his call for the council, the new pope was suggesting a more open relationship between the Catholic Church and other Christians.

Given the ecumenical push that seemed to be coming from Rome, many evangelicals wondered what Vatican II meant for them and their faith. "One thing it means," the evangelical magazine *Eternity* made clear, "is that evangelicals will have to become more aware of their differences with Roman Catholicism."[38] A reader of *Christianity Today* agreed that the occasion of Vatican II marked "*the* time to analyze the differences between Romanism and Protestantism."[39] To that end, *Christianity Today*, *Eternity*, and other evangelical outlets devoted numerous pages to outlining those distinctions, ranging across a broad spectrum of theological, historical, and institutional divergences. Within the catalogue of disagreements, however, "three major areas of conflict," as *Eternity* magazine described, emerged time and again in evangelical evaluations of the Catholic Church on the eve of Vatican II. These three remained the issue of Rome's authority, the role of the "cult of Mary," and the question of the doctrine of salvation. Still, *Eternity* contended, even these three main conflicts boiled down to one basic disagreement regarding the nature of the Bible. For evangelicals, the magazine reminded, the Bible held sole authority; Catholics looked to their church for authority.[40] Adhering to different authorities, evangelicals and Catholics stood at an impasse regarding reconciliation, no matter the aims of the council. "The Catholic Church will certainly not compromise its position on papal and ecclesiastical authority," *Eternity* argued. "And we as evangelicals must never compromise our position on the authority of the Word of God."[41]

While the attack on papal authority represented no new development of evangelicalism's historic critique of Catholicism, some evangelical leaders had come to admire the person of Pope John XXIII even if most of that respect remained unvoiced until his death in the summer of 1963. Still, in expressing a somewhat positive evaluation of John XXIII as distinct from their long-standing unfavorable beliefs about the papacy itself, evangelicals reflected their growing conviction that Catholics as individuals should be regarded differently than the Catholic Church as an institution. *Eternity* remembered John as a "pastor pope who demonstrated a great love for his flock."[42] Unlike lay Catholics, of course, John XXIII could never be totally disentangled from his papal position, so even in eulogizing John's positive attributes, evangelical critics still seized the occasion of his death to inveigh against the teachings of the Catholic Church, presently revealed through the proceedings of Vatican II. *Christianity Today* praised John for his commitment to doctrine while so many other churches seemed willing to compromise dogma for the sake of unity, but the magazine reminded its readers that many of the teachings Protestants regarded as "biblical and basic" had been denounced at the Council of Trent (1545–63). "Rome has since reaffirmed the anathemas" by the decisions of Vatican II, *Christianity Today*'s editors contended. "A pontiff's love and a council's anathemas," the magazine's eulogy concluded, "We hope the former is replaced, but it cannot restore the unity of the Church until the latter are displaced."[43]

But before John's passing and their measured praise of his leadership, evangelical thinkers questioned the pope's invitation to an ecumenical council and his call for a more open relationship with other churches. Writing in *Christianity Today* not long after the pope announced the upcoming council, G. C.

Berkouwer, the Dutch Reformed theologian and frequent contributor to the magazine, argued that the Catholic Church's relationship vis-à-vis Protestantism did not really depend on the particular viewpoint of any given pope, but rather owed itself to the church's very structure itself. Given this, it was "impossible for any pope to speak about unity without the background of the pretentions [*sic*] of Rome as the Catholic the one and only Church." Rather than opening up a dialogue among Christians, the pope truly meant for "the rest of us to *return*. . . . For this reason the coming council ought not to be seen as signifying a change in Rome."[44] *Eternity* magazine agreed that whatever changes the council produced would only be "practical and non-doctrinal aspects — *but not one iota as far as her doctrines or dogmas are concerned*. . . . and many of her dogmas are in flagrant opposition to evangelical truths."[45]

Christianity Today's readers were warned to doubt the pope's pronouncements regarding the council, but they were also encouraged to see his words as a "challenge to us for searching our own hearts." While the Catholic Church advocated reunion in the disguise of dialogue, *Christianity Today* called for evangelicals to think about the "true" nature of Christian unity — one found only through a spiritual unity based on adherence to the message in the Word of God rather than an allegiance to any earthly church.[46] As the council opened, the NAE offered a more pointed definition of Christian unity as "found only in the Holy Scriptures and in the apostolic heritage carried forward by the Reformation."[47] Even as they decried the Catholic Church's insistence on itself as the sole repository of truth and the only locus for Christian unity, evangelicals contended that they were the only heirs of the true Christian tradition and, therefore, truth itself — a truth that had been corrupted, not carried, by the Catholic Church and had been recovered by the defiant acts of a German monk more than four hundred years earlier who challenged the church's authority by insisting on the sole authority of the Bible.

American evangelicals had been thinking hard about the question of Christian unity and ecumenism for more than twenty years by the time the Second Vatican Council began. Neo-evangelicals like Billy Graham, Carl Henry, and Harold Ockenga had self-consciously begun to organize themselves first through the NAE, founded in 1942, and also in the pages of *Christianity Today* that printed its first issue in 1956. In creating these and other institutions, these evangelicals hoped to push back at two trends they worried were dominating American Protestantism. On one hand, evangelicals were resisting the highly separatist and legalistic impulses of fundamentalism that they believed ignored the biblical mandate of civic engagement and too easily devolved into vicious infighting over unimportant theological matters.

Liberal Protestantism, of course, worried evangelicals far more. Among the many critiques evangelicals had of liberal Protestantism, none stood out more than their charge that liberals no longer preached a message of salvation and that they cared more about "Church Unionism" than Christian unity. Church Unionism, characterized most clearly by the liberal Federal Council of Churches, prioritized ecumenism over doctrinal soundness, evangelicals argued. "The ecumenical movement," Carl Henry wrote in one of *Christianity Today*'s first issues, "elevates the doctrine of the unity of the body above every other doctrine. There is a driving emphasis on this unity accompanied by a rather pale and anemic concern for basic Christian doctrine."[48] While liberal ecumenists advocated unity of the body over doctrinal orthodoxy and theological purity, evangelicals countered that true Christian unity depended on "the spiritual unity of believers," as the NAE's "Statement of Faith" had called for.[49] Spiritual unity allowed for—even required—denominational integrity but demanded theological consistency. In essence, evangelicals posited an inverse conception of unity than liberal ecumenists advocated. For evangelicals, one true Christian gospel could spiritually unite believers across hundreds of diverse denominations and organizations. For liberal ecumenists, one great church body, they hoped, would one day institutionally unify the broad range of Christian belief and practices.

The push for institutional unionism among Protestant ecumenists perplexed evangelicals who contended that one of the Reformation's chief purposes had been to break up the Catholic Church's totalitarian hold on the Christian faith. Now the ecumenical movement unwittingly seemed to be pushing Protestantism back into the control of Rome. Protestant ecumenists were foolish, evangelicals argued, if they believed anything but Catholic domination would be the end result of any ecumenical efforts. Ecumenicity's "ultimate form is the pope of Rome," Carl Henry had cautioned in 1956.[50] Three years later when the Catholic Church announced its intentions to hold an "ecumenical council," one headline in *Christianity Today* bleakly warned, "Rome Projects Strategy for a World Church."[51] Vatican II, one writer for *Christianity Today* contended, demonstrated that "we as evangelical Protestants need to be aware that Jesus Christ is challenging us to demonstrate that we as the people of God are the real Body of Christ, the Church invisible, to which both radical Protestant and Roman Catholic are incited to return, not in slavish submission but in believing, apostolic faith."[52] A reader of the magazine agreed. "It would be well," Benjamin Sharp of New York wrote to *Christianity Today*, "if the evangelicals of our time would open their eyes to the prophetic significance of the Bible and recognize that all this breathless hunt for some kind of agreement and understanding . . . is not of God nor of his Christ."[53]

Liberal Protestants, however, heralded Vatican II's ecumenical emphasis, enthused that the Catholic Church appeared to be embracing a movement they felt they had long shouldered alone. If liberal Protestants worried about anything, it was that the Second Vatican Council would not go far enough in embracing true ecumenism—the very opposite of evangelical concerns of the council. In nervous anticipation of the event, the liberal *Christian Century* predicted it would be "an impressive denominational spectacle, but nothing yet said or done indicates that it will be an *ecumenical* council."[54] Where evangelicals envisioned a Catholic Church stealthily using ecumenical talk to increase its global dominance and continue its creeping takeover of America through swallowing up large chunks of a compliant and confused corner of Protestantism, liberal Protestants braced for the disappointment that Vatican II would not go far enough in committing the Catholic Church to true ecumenism.

Vatican II made real for evangelicals the suspicions they had long harbored that the Catholic Church intended to regain monopolistic control of Christianity. In resisting this intention, American evangelicals aimed to defend not only the true Christian gospel of evangelicalism but to also preserve American democracy that allowed for both truth and error to coexist against the autocratic nature of papal authority. "The American religious system is under fire today," a *Christianity Today* article bleakly concluded at the close of the 1964 session, and this meant that the nation's very constitutional principles and its historic values also were under threat. The council's push for ecumenism and the growing support for church unionism in liberal American Protestantism would have disastrous results for the faith and for the nation, the magazine contended. "Where will the dissenter, the nonconformist, the individualist go," *Christianity Today* asked, if the Catholic Church succeeded in re-establishing one universal church.[55] The larger vision that the article sketched of Vatican II's threat to the American system is worth quoting here in full:

> We are afraid of a superchurch, just as we are afraid of a superstate, and not because of a lack of faith in God. What we recognize is the fact that man cannot be trusted without checks and balances upon his power and authority—not even in the church. The various branches of Christendom now act as checks and balances, one upon the other, and they have a purifying effect on each other. Remove this tension, and we could be back to the pre-Reformation struggle between church and state with the individual man caught in the middle.[56]

Evangelical reactions to the ecumenical emphasis of Vatican II easily connected to evangelical fears about the future of American religious liberty. For evangelicals, these two issues were closely related throughout the 1950s and 1960s, and the reality of the Second Vatican Council, close on the heels of the

1960 election, only heightened for evangelicals the urgent need to protect the nation's constitutional principles and traditions.

Throughout the council's proceedings, however, the bishops had been debating a "Declaration on Religious Liberty," and this document more than any other attracted the most attention from outside observers of Vatican II. Evangelicals skeptically questioned whether the Catholic Church would achieve any substantive reforms on religious liberty, knowing that the European bishops were resisting an endorsement of church-state separation. Additionally, evangelicals charged that Catholics meant something entirely different by religious liberty than how most Americans—meaning Protestants—used the term. "When the Roman Catholic Church talks about religious liberty," one *Christianity Today* article explained, "it is talking about the right to preach and practice Catholicism in Communist countries such as Poland." "But when Baptists talk about religious freedom," the article pointed out in contrast, "they are talking about equal rights with Catholics in Spain and Portugal."[57] Liberal Protestants, however, failed to join evangelicals in assuming the Catholic Church could not develop an acceptable document on religious liberty. Instead, they looked to the Vatican's "Declaration on Religious Liberty" with great anticipation, seeing in it, as the *Christian Century* described, the hope that it would "contribute greatly to ecumenical rapprochement."[58]

What the Catholic bishops produced in the declaration surprised most observers, especially American evangelicals. It declared that "the human person has a right to religious freedom," and this right was "to be recognized in the constitutional law whereby society is governed."[59] Heavily influenced by the American bishops who had helped produce it, this *Dignitatis Humanae* had reversed the Catholic Church's historic position on religious freedom and also provided a tacit endorsement of American constitutional principles.

Considering this development, evangelical leaders were forced to acknowledge the important transformation this represented, but they resisted a full endorsement. "On the surface," the declaration appeared revolutionary, *Eternity* admitted. "But as you study the document closer, you begin to have mixed feelings about it. . . . As you read it critically, it seems to favor religious liberty only if the Catholic church [*sic*] is recognized as the one true church."[60] *Christianity Today* also recognized the document's significance, but even in doing so they reminded their readers of the Catholic Church's bad history on the matter and suggested evangelicals retain a healthy skepticism of the church's declaration. "If one wonders why it took the Roman Catholic Church until 1965 to become what the secular press is designating as 'modernized,'" one editorial sneered, "the answer lies in the way the Roman Catholic Church has viewed itself. Believing itself to be the true representative of God on earth . . . and the power to which all other temporal powers are subject, it too often functioned as God and denied the right of error to exist in its presence. Since nothing is a greater terror to freedom than something that thinks itself divine, the history of the Roman church has been muddied by its use of coercion and even persecution to further its aims."[61] After Vatican II's close in late 1965, *Christianity Today* pointed out that many evangelicals, such as Barry Garrett, a Baptist newsman and frequent critic of the Catholic Church, believed that the "Declaration on Religious Liberty" had not gone far enough in defining religious freedom. For instance, while the document had declared that no person should be coerced into religious belief, it still contended that people had to embrace Catholicism as the "one true faith" once they understood its claims, the very point *Eternity* magazine also contended lurked beyond a surface reading of the document.[62] This, *Christianity Today* suggested, meant Catholicism continued to pose a problem for the future of American pluralism, especially if liberal Protestants increasingly entertained ecumenical talks with the Catholic Church. Protestant ecumenists did express regret that the declaration included words regarding the "one truth faith," but unlike evangelicals they saw this language as a regrettable flaw in an otherwise "exceptionally good document," as the *Christian Century* editorialized. "Seen in the context of the great good achieved," the magazine continued, "the harm that was done diminishes in importance."[63] American evangelicals could not agree. Instead, they saw the Catholic Church's inclusion of an exclusive truth claim in a document about religious liberty as proof of Catholicism's inherent inability to be reformed and as a sign of its true domineering intentions when it came to ecumenism.

Though there had been some important changes in the Catholic Church's position on religious liberty, Vatican II reaffirmed other Catholic teachings that evangelicals could not endorse, such as papal infallibility and authority, Mariolatry, and salvation through grace and works—the three issues *Eternity* magazine had identified at the council's start as unbiblical Catholic positions that evangelicals could not countenance. "In light of these statements," one *Christianity Today* article contended as the council began its last session in 1965, "we must conclude that Rome has not fundamentally changed. There are important changes in climate, in approach, in emphases, even in aspects of truth; but the system as such has not changed."[64] Characterizing Catholicism as a "system"—a man-made authority replete with flaws and falsehoods as contrasted to the unquestionable truth of the evangelical gospel rooted in the authority of the Holy Scriptures—had been a frequent aspect of evangelical criticism of the Catholic faith at midcentury, including W. A. Criswell's famous anti-Kennedy sermon at First Baptist Dallas. By calling the Catholic Church a "system," *Christianity Today* also placed Catholicism in the magazine's larger conversation with the other systems of communism and liberalism it had been taking on for the past decade. The Second Vatican Council, with its pomp and formality, its often inflexible bureaucracy, and its rigorous and protracted debates over Catholic teachings and traditions rather than, in the minds of evangelicals at least, the Holy Scriptures themselves, underscored again for evangelicals their conviction that the Catholic Church stood as an institutional monstrosity that strangled the gospel and possibly threatened America's democratic experiment, much like communism threatened to do. Just after the first session of Vatican II had begun, one writer for *Christianity Today* concluded exactly what the outcome of the council would be. "The church will seem less an intransigent institution to non-Catholics after the captains and kings have departed," the writer predicted, "yet . . . it will not have changed its essential nature one iota."[65]

This essential nature, evangelicals argued, owed to the Catholic Church's view of itself as the ultimate authority rather than the Holy Scriptures as sole authority over the life of the believer. Indeed, evangelical beliefs about the Bible—and specifically their beliefs about Catholicism's relationship to the Bible—appeared throughout their reactions to all of the council's decisions. In their critiques of Vatican II's declarations and statements on issues of authority, the papacy, the Virgin Mary, and even religious liberty, evangelicals tied their particular disagreements with each issue to larger claims about the Catholic Church's erroneous interpretations and use of the Bible. But while their own interpretation of the Bible served as the consistent cudgel by which evangelicals attacked Vatican II, they still saw one promising development in the council's emphasis on the Bible, and they highlighted this change throughout the council and in the years that followed.

The decision to use the vernacular in the Mass meant Catholics would hear biblical scriptures in their native tongues, and Vatican II also suggested that priests give more attention to the scriptures in their sermons and encouraged Catholics to read their Bibles more often and to participate in Bible studies. In response, evangelical publications urged their readers to join Bible studies with Catholics.[66] Although they viewed Vatican II's ecumenical aims with suspicion in general, evangelical leaders suddenly celebrated this spirit of the council when they understood it might work to their advantage in regards to the Catholic Church's increasing openness with Bible study. "How thankful we can be for Rome's ecumenical vision," *Eternity* proclaimed during Vatican II's last session without any hint of the consistent skepticism regarding ecumenism evangelicals had shown throughout the council. "This has opened lines of communication," the magazine continued, "that have previously been closed. Rome dialogues out of security, but every orthodox Protestant should welcome this unprecedented opportunity to witness."[67]Although the Catholic Church intended that Vatican II's ecumenical efforts would bring *all* Christians back into its fold, evangelicals argued, the reforms regarding the Bible "might just accomplish under God much more than Rome either expects or hopes," *Christianity Today* editorialized, because the Catholic Church failed to recognize the very power for transformation that the Bible contained.[68] In joint Bible studies, evangelicals imagined, they could point their Catholic friends to the gospel without interference from Catholic authorities. And Catholics who committed to private devotionals would encounter on their own the biblical truth that might bring about changes similar to those that had happened when Martin Luther had buried himself in the Bible. "Something is bound to happen when people begin reading the Bible," *Eternity* magazine declared.[69] "The Word of God does not return void," *Christianity Today* concurred. "It is still the power of God unto salvation, able to divide the thoughts and intents of the heart. Not even the rigidity of Roman Catholic tradition nor her structured monolithic power can in the end resist the movements of the biblical Word and its power to renew and reform. Protestants should remember the Reformation; what the Word wrought once, it can work again."[70]

Throughout Vatican II, the bishops had debated the document on scriptures that was finally promulgated by Pope Paul VI, John's successor, near the close of the council's last session in 1965. The "Dogmatic Constitution on Divine Revelation," or *Dei Verbum*, meaning "Word of God," as it was officially known, had attracted close evangelical attention throughout the proceedings because as a constitution it would redefine Catholic doctrine.[71] Given the other decisions and pronouncements on the Bible issued throughout the council, evangelicals hoped this final document would substantially alter Church doctrine regarding scripture, but it drew mixed reactions. Parts of the text read "like an evangelical document," *Eternity* magazine noted, but "other portions may provoke violent disagreement."[72]

That disagreement centered on the Catholic Church's balance between sacred tradition and sacred scripture. As the "Constitution on Divine Revelation" reaffirmed, tradition and scripture "are closely bound together, and communicate one with the other. . . . Thus it is that the church does not draw its certainty about all revealed truths from the holy scriptures alone. Hence, both scripture and tradition must be accepted and honored with equal devotion and reverence."[73] Claiming that tradition—which one evangelical critic of

Vatican II argued "might better be called sacred interpretation"—stood alongside the Bible proved impossible enough for evangelicals to accept, but that the chapter on sacred tradition came before the one on sacred scripture revealed in clear print that the Catholic Church in reality saw itself "above the Scriptures and not subservient."[74]

In sanctifying tradition, evangelicals argued, Catholic Church leaders had fallen prey to the twin errors of blasphemously regarding themselves as divine agents of truth while also subjecting the scriptures to the "human and sinful limitations" of their own interpretive abilities.[75] For evangelicals, the reaffirmation by Vatican II that tradition and scripture stood on par together, as the "Constitution on Divine Revelation" declared, "as the supreme rule of its faith," meant that the Catholic Church had not lessened in any way its longstanding insistence on its own ultimate authority. To claim that tradition stood alongside scripture, evangelicals argued, was in reality to declare that scripture remained subject to human authority. Scripture either held sole authority over the life of the believer, evangelicals reasoned, or it was always subservient to the authority of flawed human actors. The very act of equating scripture with tradition was, in fact, an assertion of the Church's supremacy over the Bible and the institutional practice by which the Catholic Church justified the teachings and traditions that evangelicals most opposed as unbiblical, including papal infallibility, the veneration of Mary, and the theology of salvation through grace and works.

While many evangelicals had hoped that Vatican II would bring about important reforms in the Catholic Church, as the proceedings drew to a close they recognized that whatever reforms an institution that saw itself as the ultimate authority carried out would never be enough. "What the church of Rome needs is not 'reform,' which amounts to pruning away some of the historical accretions," the influential evangelical theologian and journalist Klaas Runia wrote near the end of Vatican II, "but 'reformation,' that is, new, completely new, understanding of the Gospel itself."[76] That the Catholic Church would undergo a full scale reformation remained unlikely, evangelicals acknowledged, but owing to Vatican II's changes regarding the Bible, evangelicals believed that some individual Catholics, if not the church itself, might undergo their own personal reformations. "It is possible that forces are being let loose in the Roman church that only God can control," *Christianity Today* predicted.[77] In 1972, on the tenth anniversary of the opening of the Second Vatican Council, *Christianity Today* looked back on the historic event and praised the council for unleashing the power of biblical truth within the Catholic Church, but it also stressed the "swelling Catholic interest in the Scriptures offers hope for perplexed souls, if not necessarily for structures."[78]

This idea among evangelicals that the increased attention on the Bible in Catholic circles would reform and renew some individual Catholics, rather than the church itself, would shape evangelical–Catholic relations in the years ahead. As the 1970s opened, conservative Christians worried about the fate of a nation that had undergone the transformations of the 1960s and now faced what they saw as new assaults on tradition through things like the passage of the Equal Rights Amendment in 1972 and the federal legalization of abortion in 1973. In light of these developments, some religious conservatives began to suggest that they band together across denominational and theological divides to preserve the nation's Judeo-Christian heritage and to protect the family. "The feeling may . . . be growing among both Protestants and Roman Catholics," *Christianity Today* commented at the end of 1973, "that the issues separating them are becoming less important than their common perils in an increasingly secular and atheistically dominated world."[79]

That ecumenical aligning for the sake of politics proved to be a complicated, challenging, and often unsuccessful project, but even the discussion of building bridges for political gain between traditionally antagonistic groups, especially Catholics and evangelicals, was historically significant. As evangelical leaders first began to suggest a Catholic–evangelical alliance to oppose abortion and other political and social ills, they imagined a grassroots association of *individual* Catholics and evangelicals, rather than any partnering of religious institutions. In part, this reflected the evangelical conviction that Christians rather than churches should be engaged in civic affairs and political matters, but it also revealed the lingering distrust and discomfort evangelicals felt about the Catholic Church itself. As *Eternity* magazine explained, "if we can not [*sic*] have fellowship with the *institution*, we can sometimes have fellowship with its members."[80] The Second Vatican Council had been instrumental in this new and developing relationship between evangelicals and Catholics even as it allowed evangelicals to reconfirm and recapitulate their critiques of the institutional church in defense of the American constitutional system and the authority of the Bible.

NOTES

1. "Protestant Preview of Second Vatican Council," *Christianity Today*, September 28, 1962, 36.

2. C. Stanley Lowell, "Protestants, Catholics and Politics," *Christianity Today*, July 20, 1959, 8.

3. Ibid., 5. On pamphlet, see John Wicklein, "Anti-Catholic Groups Closely Cooperate in Mail Campaign to Defeat Kennedy," *New York Times*, October 17, 1960.

4. The best account of the "religious question" in the 1960 election is Shaun A. Casey, *The Making of a Catholic President: Kennedy vs. Nixon 1960* (New York: Oxford

University Press, 2009). Casey pays particular attention to how evangelicals reacted to the Kennedy campaign. See also "Protestant Underworld: John F. Kennedy and the 'Religious Issue,'" in Randall Balmer, *God in the White House: A History* (New York: HarperOne, 2008), 7–46.

5. For a thorough account of the Council's proceedings, see John W. O'Malley, *What Happened at Vatican II* (Cambridge, MA: Harvard University Press, 2008). A team of international scholars led by Giuseppe Alberigo, with an English version directed by Joseph Komonchak, produced a five-volume history of the proceedings, which was completed in 2006. See Joseph Alberigo, ed., *History of Vatican II* (Maryknoll: Orbis, 2006, 5 vols.). See also Melissa J. Wilde, *Vatican II: A Sociological Analysis of Religious Change* (Princeton: Princeton University Press, 2007). On the effects of the Second Vatican Council on the lives, beliefs, and practices of American Catholics, see Andrew M. Greeley, *American Catholics Since the Council: An Unauthorized Report* (Chicago: The Thomas More Press, 1985); and Joseph A. Komonchak, "Interpreting the Council: Catholic Attitudes toward Vatican II," in *Being Right: Conservative Catholics in America*, ed. Mary Jo Weaver and R. Scott Appleby (Bloomington: Indiana University Press, 1995), 17–36.

6. On mid-century ecumenicalism, see Patrick Allitt, *Religion in American Since 1945: A History* (New York: Columbia University Press, 2003); Mark Silk, *Spiritual Politics: Religion and American Since World War II* (New York: Simon & Schuster, 1988); and Robert Wuthnow, *The Restructuring of American Religion: Society and Faith Since World War II* (Princeton: Princeton University Press, 1988).

7. See Phyllis Elaine Alsdurf, "Christianity Today Magazine and Late Twentieth-Century Evangelicalism" (PhD diss., University of Minnesota, 2004); J. David Fairbanks, "The Politics of *Christianity Today*: 1956–1986," in *Contemporary Evangelical Political Involvement*, ed. Corwin E. Smidt (Lanham, MD: University Press of America, 1989), 25–43; and Mark G. Toulouse, "*Christianity Today* and American Public Life: A Case Study," *Journal of Church and State* 35 (Spring 1993): 241–284. See also William Martin, *A Prophet With Honor: The Billy Graham Story* (New York: William Morrow, 1991), 211–217 on the founding of *Christianity Today*.

8. Memo, "Editorial Objectives," undated, Box 15, Folder 11, Records of Christianity Today International, Billy Graham Center Archives, Wheaton College, Wheaton, Illinois.

9. Philip Edgcumbe Hughes, "Review of Current Religious Thought," *Christianity Today*, April 1, 1957, 39.

10. Patrick Allitt, *Catholic Intellectuals and Conservative Politics in America, 1950–1985* (Ithaca, NY: Cornell University Press, 1993), 16–48; James Hennesey, S.J., "Roman Catholics and American Politics, 1900–1960: Altered Circumstances, Continuing Patterns," in *Religion and American Politics: From the Colonial Period to the Present*, ed. Mark A. Noll and Luke E. Harlow (New York: Oxford University Press, 2007), 247–265. On Cold War pronatalism, see Elaine Tyler May, *Homeward Bound: American Families in the Cold War Era* (New York: Basic Books, 1988), 129–152.

11. "Billy Graham and the Pope's Legions," *Christianity Today*, July 22, 1957, 21.

12. C. Stanley Lowell, "If the U.S. Becomes 51% Catholic," *Christianity Today*, October 27, 1958, 12.

13. Balmer, *God in the White House*, 12.

14. John Wicklein, "Anti-Catholic View Found Widespread In Parts of South," *New York Times*, September 4, 1960.

15. Casey, *The Making of a Catholic President*, 38–39.

16. "Moratorium on Bigotry," *Christian Century*, April 27, 1960, 499.

17. "Planned Politics Pays Off," *Christian Century*, July 27, 1960, 867.

18. John Wicklein, "Baptists Question Vote for Catholic," *New York Times*, May 21, 1960; Casey, *The Making of a Catholic President*, 103. For full text of "Resolution on Christian Citizenship," see http://www.sbc.net/resolutions/amResolution.asp?ID=339.

19. Wicklein, "Anti-Catholic View Found Widespread In Parts of South."

20. Casey, *The Making of a Catholic President*, 108.

21. "Kennedy Is Attacked," *New York Times*, July 4, 1960.

22. W. A. Criswell, "Religious Freedom, the Church, the State, and Senator Kennedy," http://contentdm.baylor.edu/cdm4/document.php?CISOROOT=/04 wood&CISOPTR=7637&REC.

23. Ibid.

24. William Martin, *A Prophet With Honor: The Billy Graham Story* (New York: William Morrow, 1991), 274.

25. Casey, *The Making of a Catholic President*, 95.

26. "Should Americans Elect a Roman Catholic President?" *Christianity Today*, October 26, 1959, 22.

27. Jack McNulty, Letter to the Editor, "Rome and the Presidency," *Christianity Today*, March 14, 1960, 15.

28. C. Pollard, Letter to the Editor, "Rome and the Presidency," *Christianity Today*, March 14, 1960, 15.

29. Byron O. Waterman, Letter to the Editor, "Rome and the Presidency," *Christianity Today*, March 14, 1960, 15.

30. Casey, *The Making of a Catholic President*, 96.

31. W. A. Criswell, "Religious Freedom and the Presidency," *United Evangelical Action*, September 1960, 8–9.

32. National Association of Evangelicals, "Roman Catholicism and the President of the United States" in "Resolutions Adopted in 1960," in Box 43, Folder 6, Papers of Thomas Fletcher Zimmerman, Billy Graham Center Archives, Wheaton College, Wheaton, Illinois (hereafter cited as TFZ).

33. James DeForest Murch, "Shall America Bow to the Pope of Rome?" 1951, Box 65, Folder 19, National Association of Evangelicals Records, Wheaton College Archives and Special Collections, Wheaton, Illinois (hereafter cited as NAE Records).

34. Casey, *The Making of a Catholic President*, 109–110, 136–143.

35. Ibid., 143.

36. "Another Era Underway in the American Venture," *Christianity Today*, November 21, 1960, 21.

37. O'Malley, *What Happened at Vatican II*, 17.

38. "What Will Happen in Rome?" *Eternity*, November 1962, 34.

39. Francis K. Hornicek, Letter to the Editor, "Durable Dialogue," *Christianity Today*, June 21, 1963, 19. Emphasis in original.

40. Herbert Henry Ehrenstein, "Peter, the Pope, and the Vatican," *Eternity*, November 1962, 18.

41. Ibid., 20.

42. Ralph L. Keiper, "Roman Catholicism," *Eternity*, January 1964, 24.

43. "A Pontiff's Love and a Council's Anathema," *Christianity Today*, June 21, 1963, 27.

44. G. C. Berkouwer, "Review of Current Religious Thought," *Christianity Today*, September 28, 1959, 33. Emphasis in original.

45. Wilton M. Nelson, "Is the Roman Catholic Church Changing?" *Eternity*, October 1963, 22. Emphasis in original.

46. Berkouwer, "Review of Current Religious Thought," 33.

47. National Association of Evangelicals Board of Administration statement quoted in "Evangelicals and Unity," *Christianity Today*, October 26, 1962, 34.

48. "The Perils of Ecumenicity," *Christianity Today*, November 26, 1956, 20.

49. National Association of Evangelicals, "Statement of Faith," 1943, in James DeForest Murch, *Cooperation Without Compromise: A History of the National Association of Evangelicals* (Grand Rapids, MI: Eerdmans, 1956), 66. The NAE gave special attention to the question of Christian unity and ecumenism in the years leading up to and throughout the Second Vatican Council. See, for example, Paul P. Petticord, "True Ecumenicity," 1958, and Clyde W. Taylor, "Evangelicals Examine Ecumenicity," 1964, both pamphlets in Box 65, Folder 11, NAE Records. See also, National Association of Evangelicals, "Memorandum on Christian Unity," 14 July 1961, and related documents in Box 66, Folder 13, NAE Records. See also, National Association of Evangelicals, "Ecumenical Relations of the Church" in "Resolutions Adopted in 1964," Box 43, Folder 6, TFZ.

50. "The Perils of Ecumenicity," 21, 22.

51. Frank Farrell, "Rome Projects Strategy for a World Church," *Christianity Today*, February 16, 1959, 27–28.

52. Leslie R. Keylock, "The Ecumenical Atmosphere: An Evangelical View of Vatican II," *Christianity Today*, April 12, 1963, 32.

53. Benjamin B. Sharp, Letter to the Editor, "Durable Dialogue," *Christianity Today*, June 21, 1963, 19.

54. "Catholic World Council Delayed Two Years," *Christian Century*, February 18, 1959, 189. Emphasis in original.

55. Henry A. Buchanan and Bob W. Brown, "The Ecumenical Movement Threatens Protestantism," *Christianity Today*, November 20, 1964, 21, 22.

56. Ibid., 23.

57. Ibid., 22.

58. "Rome and Saigon," *Christian Century*, September 4, 1963, 1068.

59. "Declaration on Religious Liberty," 12/7/65, in *Vatican Council II: The Basic Sixteen Documents*, ed. Austin Flannery (Northport, NY: Costello Publishing Company, 1996), 552.

60. Ralph L. Keiper, "The Catholic Church and Religious Liberty," *Eternity*, March 1966, 17.

61. "Rome and Religious Liberty," *Christianity Today*, October 8, 1965, 36.

62. "1965: Religion in Review," *Christianity Today*, January 7, 1966, 52.

63. "Imperious Ecumenism," *Christian Century*, December 8, 1965, 1500.

64. Klaas Runia, "The Church of Rome and the Reformation Churches," *Christianity Today*, June 18, 1965, 17.

65. J. D. Douglas, "Plea for 'Unity' Pervades Vatican Council," *Christianity Today*, October 26, 1962, 34.

66. "Study the Bible with Roman Catholics," *Eternity*, November 1963, 6, 8.

67. Edward Palmer, "A is for Aggiornamento," *Eternity*, September 1965, 45.

68. "The Vernacular and the Bible in Rome," *Christianity Today*, November 8, 1963, 31.

69. Nelson, "Is the Roman Catholic Church Changing?" 20.

70. "The Vernacular and the Bible in Rome," 31.

71. "Dogmatic Constitution on Divine Revelation," 11/18/65, in *Vatican Council II*, ed. Flannery, 97–115. On the bishops' debates over *Dei Verbum*, see O'Malley, *What Happened at Vatican II*, 226–229.

72. Ralph L. Keiper, "The Catholic Church and the Bible," *Eternity*, February 1966, 11.

73. "Dogmatic Constitution on Divine Revelation," 102–103.

74. Keiper, "The Catholic Church and the Bible," 12.

75. Ibid., 13.

76. Runia, "The Church of Rome and the Reformation Churches," 17.

77. "The Vernacular and the Bible in Rome," 31.

78. "Tenth Anniversary of Vatican II," *Christianity Today*, October 13, 1972, 35.

79. David Kucharsky and Edward E. Plowman, "An Evangelical Awakening in the Catholic Church?" *Christianity Today*, December 7, 1973, 47.

80. Nelson, "Is the Roman Catholic Church Changing?" 22. Emphasis in original.

Contributors

PAUL BOYER (1935–2012) was Merle Curti Professor of History at the University of Wisconsin–Madison. His many books include *Purity in Print: Book Censorship in America from the Gilded Age to the Computer Age* (University of Wisconsin Press, 2002), *When Time Shall Be No More: Prophecy Belief in Modern American Culture* (Harvard University Press, 1992), and *By the Bomb's Early Light: American Thought and Culture at the Dawn of the Atomic Age* (Pantheon, 1985).

DARREN DOCHUK is associate professor in the humanities at the John C. Danforth Center on Religion and Politics, Washington University in Saint Louis. He is the author of *From Bible Belt to Sunbelt: Plain-folk Religion, Grassroots Politics, and the Rise of Evangelical Conservatism* (Norton, 2010) and coeditor of *Sunbelt Rising: The Politics of Space, Place, and Region* (University of Pennsylvania Press, 2011). He is currently writing a book about the politics of oil and religion in modern America.

HANS KRABBENDAM is assistant director of the Roosevelt Study Center, Middelburg, the Netherlands, and the author of *Freedom on the Horizon: Dutch Immigrants to America, 1840–1920* (Eerdmans, 2009). His work in progress is a history of American evangelicals in Europe, 1945–1985.

EMMA LONG is lecturer in American Studies at the University of East Anglia in the UK. She is the author of *The Church-State Debate: Religion, Education and the Establishment Clause in Post-War America* (Continuum, 2012).

EILEEN LUHR is associate professor of history at California State University, Long Beach. Her monograph, *Witnessing Suburbia* (University of California Press, 2009), explores the intersection of conservatism, religion, and suburbanization Her current project, *Pilgrims' Progress*, explores the American religious imagination in the late twentieth century.

STEVEN P. MILLER is the author of *Billy Graham and the Rise of the Republican South* (University of Pennsylvania Press, 2009). His second book, tentatively titled *The Age of Evangelicalism: The Meaning of Born-Again Culture and Politics in Recent American History*, will be published by Oxford University Press in 2014. Miller resides in Saint Louis, where he teaches at Webster University and Washington University.

KENDRICK OLIVER is a reader in American history at the University of Southampton. He is the author of three books: *Kennedy, Macmillan and the Nuclear Test-Ban Debate, 1961–1963* (Palgrave Macmillan, 1998), *The My Lai Massacre in American History and Memory* (Manchester University Press, 2006), and *To Touch the Face of God: The Sacred, the Profane and the American Space Program, 1957–1975* (Johns Hopkins University Press, 2013).

ANDREW PRESTON is senior lecturer in American history and a fellow of Clare College at Cambridge University, where he also serves as editor of the *Historical Journal*. He is the author of *The War Council: McGeorge Bundy, the NSC, and Vietnam* (Harvard University Press, 2006) and coeditor, with Fredrik Logevall, of *Nixon in the World: American Foreign Relations, 1969–1977* (Oxford University Press, 2008). His most recent book is *Sword of the Spirit, Shield of Faith: Religion in American War and Diplomacy* (Knopf, 2012).

AXEL R. SCHÄFER is professor of modern U.S. history and director of the David Bruce Centre for American Studies at Keele University, UK. His most recent books are *Countercultural Conservatives: American Evangelicalism from the Postwar Revival to the New Christian Right* (University of Wisconsin Press, 2011) and *Piety and Public Funding: Evangelicals and the State in Modern America* (University of Pennsylvania Press, 2012). He is also the author of *American Progressives and German Social Reform, 1875–1920: Social Ethics, Moral Control, and the Regulatory State in a Transatlantic Context* (Franz Steiner Verlag, 2000).

DAVID R. SWARTZ teaches at Asbury University and is the author of *Moral Minority: The Evangelical Left in an Age of Conservatism* (University of Pennsylvania Press, 2012).

DANIEL K. WILLIAMS is an associate professor of history at the University of West Georgia and the author of *God's Own Party: The Making of the Christian Right* (Oxford University Press, 2010).

NEIL J. YOUNG earned his PhD in U.S. history from Columbia University. He is author of *We Gather Together: Conservative Ecumenism in the Age of the Religious Right* (Oxford University Press, forthcoming). He teaches at Princeton University.

Index

STUDIES IN AMERICAN THOUGHT
AND CULTURE